C000178053

STR[...]

North Hampshire

First published in 1994 by

Philip's, a division of
Octopus Publishing Group Ltd
2–4 Heron Quays, London E14 4JP

Second colour edition 2002
Second impression 2003

ISBN 0-540-08104-3

© Philip's 2002

Ordnance Survey

This product includes mapping data licensed
from Ordnance Survey® with the permission
of the Controller of Her Majesty's Stationery
Office. © Crown copyright 2002. All rights
reserved. Licence number 100011710

No part of this publication may be
reproduced, stored in a retrieval system or
transmitted in any form or by any means,
electronic, mechanical, photocopying,
recording or otherwise, without the
permission of the Publishers and the
copyright owner.

To the best of the Publishers' knowledge, the
information in this atlas was correct at the
time of going to press. No responsibility can
be accepted for any errors or their
consequences.

The representation in this atlas of a road,
track or path is no evidence of the existence
of a right of way.

Ordnance Survey and the OS Symbol are
registered trademarks of Ordnance Survey,
the national mapping agency of Great Britain

Printed and bound in Spain
by Cayfosa-Quebecor

Contents

III **Key to map symbols**

IV **Key to map pages**

VI **Route planning**

VIII **Administrative and Postcode boundaries**

1 **Street maps** at 2½ inches to 1 mile

209 **Town maps** of Winchester, Portsmouth and Southampton

212 **Index** of towns and villages

213 **Index** of streets, hospitals, industrial estates, railway stations, schools, shopping centres, universities and places of interest

Digital Data

The exceptionally high-quality mapping found in this atlas is available as digital data in TIFF format, which is easily convertible to other bitmapped (raster) image formats.

The index is also available in digital form as a standard database table. It contains all the details found in the printed index together with the National Grid reference for the map square in which each entry is named.

For further information and to discuss your requirements, please contact Philip's on 020 7531 8439 or ruth.king@philips-maps.co.uk

Key to map symbols

Symbol	Description	Symbol	Description
(22a)	Motorway with junction number	Walsall	Railway station
	Primary route – dual/single carriageway		Private railway station
	A road – dual/single carriageway		Bus, coach station
	B road – dual/single carriageway		Ambulance station
	Minor road – dual/single carriageway		Coastguard station
	Other minor road – dual/single carriageway		Fire station
	Road under construction		Police station
	Pedestrianised area	+	Accident and Emergency entrance to hospital
DY7	Postcode boundaries	H	Hospital
	County and unitary authority boundaries	+	Place of worship
	Railway	i	Information Centre (open all year)
	Railway under construction	P	Parking
	Tramway, miniature railway	P&R	Park and Ride
	Rural track, private road or narrow road in urban area	PO	Post Office
	Gate or obstruction to traffic (restrictions may not apply at all times or to all vehicles)	Å	Camping site
	Path, bridleway, byway open to all traffic, road used as a public path		Caravan site
	The representation in this atlas of a road, track or path is no evidence of the existence of a right of way		Golf course
			Picnic site
174 94	Adjoining page indicators	Prim Sch	Important buildings, schools, colleges, universities and hospitals
		River Medway	Water name

Acad	Academy	Mkt	Market
Allot Gdns	Allotments	Meml	Memorial
Cemy	Cemetery	Mon	Monument
C Ctr	Civic Centre	Mus	Museum
CH	Club House	Obsy	Observatory
Coll	College	Pal	Royal Palace
Crem	Crematorium	PH	Public House
Ent	Enterprise	Recn Gd	Recreation Ground
Ex H	Exhibition Hall	Resr	Reservoir
Ind Est	Industrial Estate	Ret Pk	Retail Park
IRB Sta	Inshore Rescue	Sch	School
	Boat Station	Sh Ctr	Shopping Centre
Inst	Institute	TH	Town Hall/House
Ct	Law Court	Trad Est	Trading Estate
L Ctr	Leisure Centre	Univ	University
LC	Level Crossing	Wks	Works
Liby	Library	YH	Youth Hostel

- Railway, stream
- Lock, weir
- Water
- Tidal water
- Woods
- Houses
- Church — Non-Roman antiquity
- ROMAN FORT — Roman antiquity

■ The dark grey border on the inside edge of some pages indicates that the mapping does not continue onto the adjacent page

■ The small numbers around the edges of the maps identify the 1 kilometre National Grid lines

The scale of the maps on the pages numbered in blue is 3.92 cm to 1 km • 2½ inches to 1 mile • 1: 25344

0	¼	½	¾	1 mile
0	250 m	500 m	750 m	1 kilometre

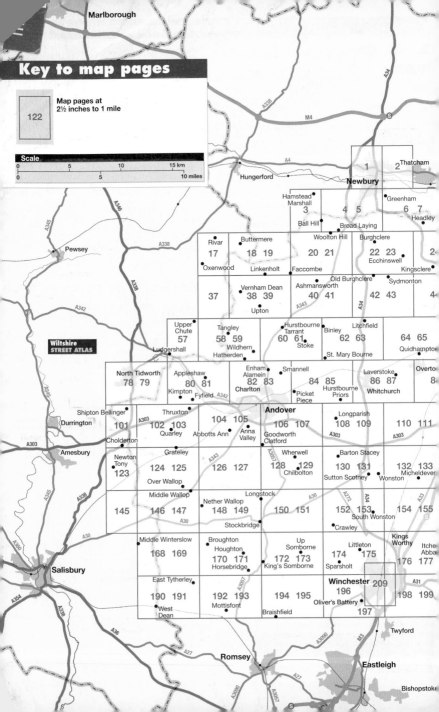

Key to map pages

Map pages at
2½ inches to 1 mile

122

Scale

0 — 5 — 10 — 15 km
0 — 5 — 10 miles

Marlborough

Hungerford

Newbury

Thatcham

Hamstead
Marshall

Greenham

3

4 5

6 7

Headley

Pewsey

Rivar

Ball Hill

Broad Laying

Woolton Hill

Burghclere

17

18 19

20 21

22 23

2

Oxenwood

Buttermere

Linkenholt

Faccombe

Ecchinswell

Kingsclere

37

Vernham Dean

Ashmansworth

Old Burghclere

Sydmonton

38 39

40 41

42 43

4

Upton

Upper
Chute

Tangley

Hurstbourne
Tarrant

Binley

Litchfield

57

58 59

60 61

62 63

64 65

Ludgershall

Wildhern

Stoke

Quidhampton

Hatherden

St. Mary Bourne

North Tidworth

Appleshaw

Enham
Alamein

Smannell

Laverstoke

Overto

78 79

80 81

82 83

84 85

86 87

8

Kimpton

Charlton

Hurstbourne
Priors

Whitchurch

Fyfield

Picket
Piece

Shipton Bellinger

Thruxton

Andover

Longparish

Durrington

101

102 103

104 105

106 107

108 109

110 111

Quarley

Abbotts Ann

Goodworth
Clatford

Cholderton

Anna
Valley

Amesbury

Newton
Tony

Grateley

Wherwell

Barton Stacey

123

124 125

126 127

128 129

130 131

132 133

Over Wallop

Chilbolton

Sutton Scotney

Wonston

Micheldever

Middle Wallop

Longstock

145

146 147

148 149

150 151

152 153

154 155

Nether Wallop

South Winston

Stockbridge

Crawley

Salisbury

Middle Winterslow

Broughton

Up
Somborne

Littleton

Kings
Worthy

Itche
Abba

168 169

Houghton

170 171

172 173

174 175

176 177

Horsebridge

King's Somborne

Sparsholt

East Tytherley

Winchester

190 191

192 193

194 195

196

209

198 199

West
Dean

Mottisfont

Braishfield

Oliver's Battery

197

Twyford

Romsey

Eastleigh

Bishopstoke

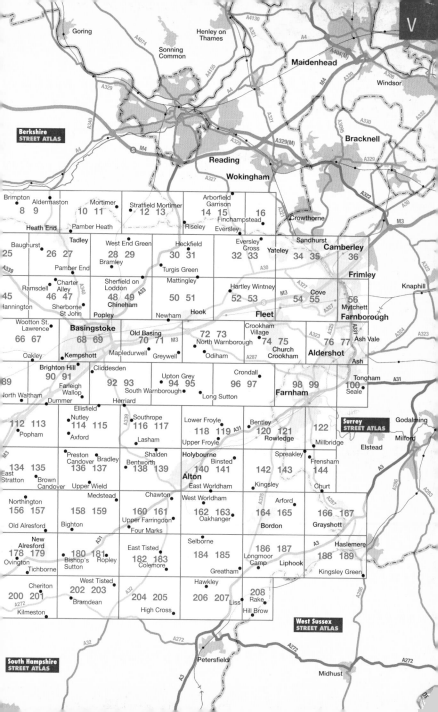

V

Goring

Henley on Thames

Sonning Common

Maidenhead

Windsor

Berkshire STREET ATLAS

Bracknell

Reading

Wokingham

Brimpton
8 9

Aldermaston

Mortimer
10 11

Stratfield Mortimer
12 13

Arborfield Garrison
14 15

16

Crowthorne

Heath End

Finchampstead

Riseley

Eversley

Baughurst
25

Tadley
26 27

West End Green
28 29

Heckfield
30 31

Eversley Cross
32 33

Yateley

Sandhurst
Camberley

34 35

36

Pamber Heath

Bramley

Turgis Green

Frimley

Ramsdell
Charter Alley
46 47

Sherfield on Loddon
48 49

Mattingley
50 51

Hartley Wintney
52 53

Cove
54 55

56

Knaphill

45

Pamber End

Chineham

Mytchett

Hannington

Sherborne St John

Popley

Newnham

Hook

Fleet

Farnborough

Wootton St. Lawrence
66 67

Basingstoke
68 69

Old Basing
70 71 M3

72 73
North Warnborough

Crookham Village
74 75

76 77

Ash Vale

Oakley

Kempshott

Mapledurwell

Greywell

Odiham

Church Crookham

Aldershot

Ash

Brighton Hill
90 91

Cliddesden

Upton Grey
94 95

Crondall
96 97

98 99

Farnham

Tongham
100

89

Farleigh Wallop
92 93

South Warnborough

Long Sutton

Seale

North Waltham

Dummer

Herriard

Ellisfield

Lower Froyle
118 119

Bentley
120 121

122

Godalming

Surrey STREET ATLAS

112 113

Nutley
114 115

Southrope
116 117

Rowledge

Millbridge

Elstead

Milford

Popham

Axford

Lasham

Upper Froyle

Preston Candover Bradley
136 137

Shalden
Bentworth
138 139

Holybourne
140 141

Binsted

Spreakley

Frensham
144

134 135

Spreakley
142 143

East Stratton

Brown Candover

Upper Wield

Alton

East Worldham

Kingsley

Churt

Northington
156 157

Medstead
158 159

Chawton
160 161

West Worldham
162 163

Arford
164 165

166 167

Grayshott

Old Alresford

Bighton

Upper Farringdon

Oakhanger

Bordon

New Alresford
178 179

Ropley
180 181

East Tisted
182 183

Selborne
184 185

Longmoor Camp
186 187

Haslemere
188 189

Ovington

Bishop's Sutton

Colemore

Greatham

Liphook

Kingsley Green

Tichborne

Cheriton
200 201

West Tisted
202 203

204 205

Hawkley
206 207

Rake
208

Kilmeston

Bramdean

High Cross

Liss

Hill Brow

West Sussex STREET ATLAS

South Hampshire STREET ATLAS

Petersfield

Midhurst

Major administrative and Postcode boundaries

- County and unitary authority boundaries
- District boundaries
- Postcode boundaries
- Area covered by this atlas

Scale

0 5 10 15 km
0 5 10 miles

Counties / Unitary Authorities

Bracknell Forest
Wokingham
West Berkshire
Surrey
West Sussex
Hampshire
Basingstoke and Deane
Hart
East Hampshire
Test Valley
Winchester
City of Portsmouth
Havant
City of Fareham
Gosport
City of Southampton
Eastleigh
New Forest
Bournemouth
Poole
Isle of Wight
Wiltshire
Dorset

Grid references

ST SU
SY SZ
SU SZ
ST SU
SY SZ

Place names and postcodes

Camberley GU15
Frimley GU16
Farnborough GU14
Aldershot GU11
Yateley GU46
Wokingham RG40
Mortimer RG7
Newbury RG14
Tadley RG26
Bramley RG26
Kingsclere RG20
Burghclere
Vernham Green RG17
Tangley SP11
Andover SP10
Thruxton
Over Wallop
West Wellow SO51
Mottisfont
Romsey SO51
Broughton
West Dean SP5
Wick
Fordingbridge SP6
Ringwood BH24
Burley
Ibsley
Martin
Croucheston
Wimborne Minster BH21
Verwood BH31
Ferndown BH22
Poole BH15
Bournemouth BH8
Christchurch BH23
Lymington SO41
Barton on Sea BH25
Sway
Brockenhurst
Beaulieu
Lyndhurst
Cadnam SO40
Totton SO40
Southampton SO15
Hythe SO45
Fawley SO45
Netley
Eastleigh SO50
Winchester SO22
Twyford SO21
Itchen Abbas SO24
New Alresford SO24
Micheldever
South Wonston SO21
Whitchurch
North Waltham
Oakley RG25
Basingstoke RG21
Chineham RG24
Hook RG27
Odiham RG29
Fleet GU51
Bentley GU10
Farnham GU9
Alton GU34
Medstead
Bentworth
Bishop's Waltham SO32
Meonstoke
West Meon
East Tisted
Petersfield GU32
Liss GU33
Liphook GU30
Bordon GU35
Grayshott GU26
Haslemere GU27
Wickham PO17
Fareham PO14
Gosport PO12
Portsmouth PO1
Havant PO9
Hayling Island PO11
Thorney Island PO10
Hambledon
Horndean PO8
West End SO18
St Mary Bourne
SN8
RG19

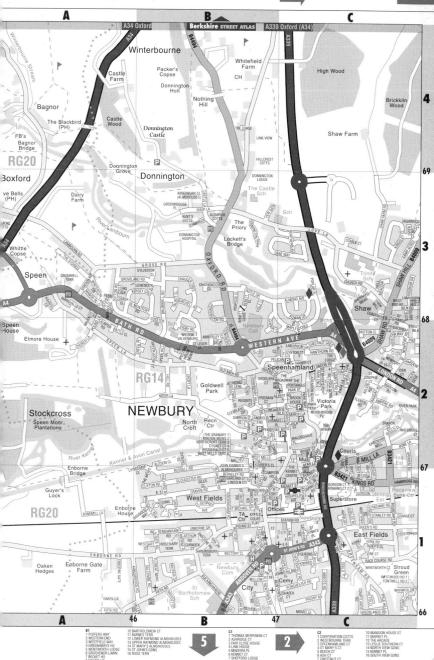

B1
1 PUFFERS WAY
2 WESTERN END
3 WESTFIELD WAY
4 GREENAWAYS HO
5 WENTWORTH COURT
6 GROSVENOR LAWN
7 BECKET HO
8 FISHER HO
9 IMPERIAL CT
10 BARTHOLOMEW CT
11 BARNES TERR
12 LOWER RAYMOND ALMSHOUSES
13 UPPER RAYMOND ALMSHOUSES
14 ST MARY'S ALMSHOUSES
15 ST JOHN'S GDNS
16 ROSS TERR

C1
1 THOMAS MERRIMAN CT
2 ASHRIDGE CT
3 FAIR CLOSE HOUSE
4 LINK HOUSE
5 MADEIRA PL
6 KENNET CT
7 SHERFORD LODGE
8 ILCHESTON CT
9 HILARY HOUSE

C2
1 CORPORATION COTTS
2 WESTBOURNE TERR
3 SPEENHAMLAND CT
4 ST MARY'S CT
5 BEECH CT
6 ASH CT
7 CHESTNUT CT
8 CONISTON CT
9 BRIDGE ST
10 MANSION HOUSE ST
11 MARKET PL
12 THE ARCADE
13 LESLIE SOUTHERN CT
14 NORTH VIEW GDNS
15 KENNET PL
16 SOUTH VIEW GDNS

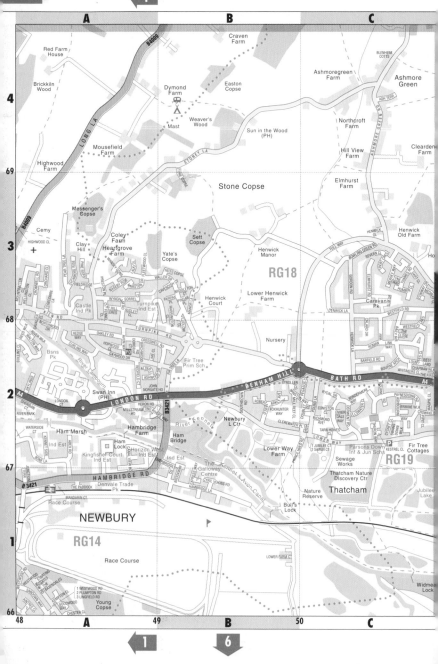

Berkshire STREET ATLAS

Horn
Copse

Kintbury Holt
Farm

Queenhills
Copse

Hankin's La

Mason's
Farm

Barr's
Farm

White Hill
Farm

Hightree
Copse

TINKER'S
CNR

Old
Hat

The
Oaks

FORBURY LA

Hamstead
Marshall

White Hart Inn
(PH)

PARK LA

4

Kintbury

Elm
Farm

MEADOWBANK

Curr Copse

Little Holt
Copse

Great Holt
Copse

Plumb's
Farm

ASH TREE GR

RG17

65

Holt
Lodge

Skew-whiff

Milkhouse
Copse

Briff's
Copse

The
Alders

BURGESS LA

Waterman's
Farm

Waterman's
Copse

Mayhouse
Gullies

HOLTWOOD RD

3

Holt Manor
Farm

Little
Farm

Burgess
Farm

Holtwood
Farm

Holtwood

WATERY LA

Smith's
Bridge

64

Holly La

RG20

River Enborne

Gore End
Bridge

Malt
House

Holly
Copse

Weir

Hazelby
House

Gore End

Studland
Ind Est

Green Farm
Copse

Malthouse
Farm

Smart's
Copse

Hillier's
Farm

NEW
VILLAS

GORE END RD

COTTS LA

2

Fishponds
Farm

Ansell's
Copse

GRAIL'S LA

West
Woodhay

Green
Plantation

Hatch House
Farm

North End

Burlyns
Farm

WELLINGTON COTTS

63

Wilmot's
Farm

Old
Rectory

Hatch House
Plantations

Northenby
House

Burlyns

Oakhurst

1

Woodcut
Copse

Berries
Copse

Hayes

North End
Farm

Berries
Farm

Heath
End

Farm
Copse

62

Berkshire STREET ATLAS

A   B   C

Enborne Copse

Hamstead Park

Enborne

Skinner
Green
Farm

Skinners
Green

Church
Farm

4

Ashtree
Plantation

Wise's
Border

SKINNERS GREEN

COPSE HA

Spicer's
Copse

PARK LA
ASHTREE CNR

Oaken
Copse

Avery's Pightle
(Nature Reserve)

CRUVEN LA

Foxgrove

65

Long
Copse

RG14

Crockhamheath
Farm

CHURCH CO

The Craven Arms
(PH)

Crockham
Heath

WHEATLANDS LA

Redhill Wood

Enborne
CE Prim Sch

Wheatlands
Farm

Enborne Lod
Sch

3

Red Hill

Vanner's Farm

VANNERS LA

Round
Copse

Braylands
Copse

Boame's
Farm

Redding's
Copse

Redhill
Plantation

ENBORNE

Hill Farm

The Cedars

64

RG20

Enborne Street
Farm

Bigg's Hill

ENBORNE ST

BELL HILL

Bunker's Hill

Enborne
Row

Hatt Common

Bigg's Hill
Cotts

ANDOVER RD

2

Knight's
Farm

Ball Hill
Farm

Bourne Farm

Lane End
Farm

Yew
Tree
Farm

River Enborne

Bourne House

WASH WATER

Common
Farm

KNIGHTS LA

Ball Hill

PH

East Woodhay
House

63

Hatt Farm

P

STATION RD

The Chase
(National Trust)

Burley
Moor
Farm

Slade Hill

Woolton House
Stud

HOBBY LA

SLADE HILL
GDNS

1

Harwood
Farm

HARWOOD RISE

ELM COTTS

Woolton
House

Woolton
House

PH

Great Pen Wood

ANDOVER RD

Harwood
Lodge

Broad
Laying

A34

62

FULLERS LA

GRENADIERS

FULTON CLOSE GDNS

MASONS CT

42   A   43   B   44   C

Berkshire STREET ATLAS

| A | B | C |

CHAMBERHOUSE MILL RD

Crookham Manor

Prior's Moor Ditch

River Kennet

Chamberhouse Farm

Avenell's Cottages

Highfield Copse

4

Conduit Copse

Waterside Copse

Hanging Lands Gully

Ashen Copse

Longlane Gully

New Gully

65

BURY'S BANK RD

The Round House

Thornford Hights

Crookham House

Limberlost Farm

Highfield Farm

White Lodge

Cvn Pk

The Travellers' Friend (PH)

3

Crookham Common

George's Farm

Crookham

RG19

Boar's Gully

Foxhold Farm

THORNFORD RD

64

Foxhold House

Ford

South Lands

Long Copse

Kenton's Wood

George's Wood

2

The Oven

Folly Farm

River Enborne

Flaggy Copse

THORNFIELD

Stonylands Copse

Park Lane

63

Forge Farm

Holly Bush Farm

Mill Green

Goose Hill

ASHFORD HILL RD

Stark House Farm

MILLFIELDS

HILLHOUSE LA

Cherry Tree Farm

ST PETER'S CL

Pitts Farm

Hill View Farm

THE GROVE

1

Longcross Farm

Headley

Nursery

COMMON RD

Huntsmoor Hill

The Harrow (PH)

Fuces Farm

Headley Stud

Headley House

A339

VALLEY CL

Old Farm

HILLHOUSE

62

| A | 52 | B | 53 | C |

A   B   C

Berkshire STREET ATLAS | A340 Reading (A4)

Bottle Cottage

River Enborne

Fisherman's Cottage

Malthouse Cottages

Aldermaston CE Prim Sch

Hind's Head (PH)

Aldermaston

Church Farm

The Cedars Sch

4

Landing Strip

Wasing Lower Farm

Wasing Lodge

Forsters Farm

FORSTER FARM CT

Portland House

65

Shalford Farm

The Manor House

Wasing Park

Breaches Gully

Wr Twr

Garden Piece

RG7

Harbourhill Copse

3

Wasing

Paices Wood

Wasing Farm

HOME FARM LA

PAICES HILL

64

Howell's Wood

Broom Close

Young's Ind Est

Paice's Gully

Wasing Wood

2

Old Stock Farm

Larkwhistle Farm

Burnham's Copse

63

Lodge

Wr Twr Mast

APOLLO HO

MERCURY HO

Burnham's Plantation

RG26

The Falcon (PH)

FALCON FIELDS

Borson Cottages

B3051

PLANTATION

FURZE RD

ALMSWOOD RD

PRIORS RD

P

SILCHESTER RD

1

HIGHWORTH COTTS 1
HEATHROW COPSE 2
DOURO CL 3

FOREST CL

CONIFER

BIRCH RD

BURNHAM RD

HANGER

SARUM CL

BOND CL

MEON CL

Liby

Baughurst Common

The Hurst Com Sch L Ctr

Inhurst House Sch

Heath End

BISHOPSWOOD RD

BAYS CT

FRANKLIN AVE

BRACKENWOOD

SILVEDALE RD

S STANFIELD

A340

Haughurst Hill

INHURST WAY

WIGMORE RD

HARTSHILL RD

NEWCHURCH RD

BISHOPSWOOD LA

62

A   58   B   59   C

26 | **10**

B1	B1	C1
1 FORTUNA CT	10 MARS HO	1 BEAVERS CL
2 ORPHEUS HO	11 ZEPHYR HO	2 HUNTSMOOR RD
3 VULCAN HO	12 ZODIAC HO	3 SOUTHDOWN RD
4 JUPITER HO	13 FIR TREE CNR	4 BISHOPS CL
5 MINERVA HO	14 HEATHLANDS	5 WOODCOTT HO
6 TITAN HO	15 HEPPLEWHITE CL	6 OAK TREE CL
7 BACCHUS HO	16 CHIPPENDALE CL	7 TURBARY GDNS
8 MIDAS HO	17 MINTER CT	8 THE PARADE
9 SATURN HO	18 HEATHER DR	9 BLAKE'S LA

| A | B | C |

Berkshire STREET ATLAS

Aqua Vitae
Copse

Ufton Park

Brent's Gully

Upper Lodge
Farm

Padworth

Upper Church
Farm

The Old
Rectory

4

Padworth
Gully

Springhill
Farm

The
Croft

Wrays
Farm

RECTORY RD

MAY'S LA

Hatch Farm
House

65

SPRING LA

CHURCH RD

The
Round Oak
(PH)

The Birches

BLOCK
COTTS

Court
Farm

Padworth
Common

RAGHILL

RAMPTONS LA

Raghill
Farm

Burnt Common

Budd's Firs

3

Black
Pightle

Old Warren

+

WELSHMAN'S RD

Aldermaston
Park

RG7

CHAIN LA

64

Little Heath

Valentine
Wood
Ind Est

Fox Hill

2

Decoy
Pond

Aldermaston
Soke

Alders Slade

Benyon's Inclosure

SOKE RD

Hungry Hill

Pond Farm

Upper Moor's
Gully

63

Catthaw Lands
Copse

WINDMILL LA

SECOND AVE

FIRST AVE

Soke
Pig Farm

Catthawlands
Farm

White House
Farm

PELICAN RD

WAKEFORD CL

SILCHESTER RD

1

KINGS RD

+

Silchester
CE Prim
Sch

SPENCER CL

WAKEFORD CL

KNOLLYS RD

MAPSTONE RD

SCHOOL RD

TADLEY COMMON RD

BROADHALF PENNY LA

Tadley
Court

RG26

CHURCH RD

STROUD
CL

VALLEY WAY

+

THE GLEN

ALEX CL

Pamber
Heath

Silchester Common

Silchester

Calleva
Arms
(PH)

Mu

Tadley Common

CHURCH RD

WESTLYN
RD

HEATH RD

ROMAN FIELDS 1
LITTLE LONDON RD 2

COPSE SIDE

WHISTLERS LA

PETTLE CRN

COPSELANDS

ARNEWOOD AVE

BUDNEY BIT

62

| 60 | A | 61 | B | 62 | C |

Berkshire STREET ATLAS

Oval Pond

Cowpond Piece

Water
Tower

Mast

Warennes
Wood

oundoak
Piece

FOUR HOUSES
CNR

Five
Oaken

Starvale Woods

Gibbet
Piece

FOUR HOUSES
CNR
CVN SITE

CAMP RD

PATSWORTH RD

ISLAND FARM RD

READING RD

Mowbray's
Piece

Holden's Firs

LONGMOOR LA

Bridge's
Farm

Lukin's
Wood

SOUTHVIEW LA

4

Fifty Acre
Piece

COLLEGE PIECE

STEPHENS END

Liby

WINDMILL CNR

WINDMILL RD

65

Hundred Acre Piece

Pickling Yard
Plantation

SWEETBRIAR
CL

PINE RD

KINGS RD

WINDMILL
CT

THE CRESCENT

ST JOHN'S

BRIARLEA RD

VICTORIA RD

HEATHLANDS RD

Mortimer Hill
Farm

ockwell's Piece

Chaplin's Copse

BIRCHLAND CL

QUEENS RD

FAIRFIELD
PK

STEPHENS CL

CROFT RD

GLENAPP
GRANGE

CHURCH RD

WELLS RD

P

PH

Mortimer
St John's
CE Sch

ORCHARD RD

CAMPBELL'S
GREEN

THE STREET

THE AVENUE

LAMBWOOD

WEST END RD

STANMORE
GDNS

GARTH HILL

PH

LAMBS LA

Mortimer

WELSHMAN'S RD

Turner's
Arms
(PH)

LOVE'S
WOOD

WEST END RD

Summerlug

DRURY LA

CHAPEL LA

CHURCH RD

ROWLAND'S
CL

THE BRIDGES

Mortimer West End

RG7

64

West End
Farm

Lovegrove's
Farm

Simms's Copse

SIMMS LA

EDGE LA

Windaboul
Copse

SOTHEROL LA

BACK LA

Mortimer
West End

Simms
Stud
Farm

Red Lion
(PH)

West End Brook

Tanhouse
Bridge

2

Stone Hill

Nine Acre
Copse

Simms's Plantation

Brocas Land
Farm

63

Kiln Yard
Copse

Sheepgrove
Farm

Silchester Brook

P

WILL LA

AMPHITHEATRE

The Drove

PARK LA

1

CALLEVA
ROMAN TOWN
(remains of)

Manor
Farm

Silchester
Hall

P

CHURCH LA

CLAPPERS FARM RD

62

Berkshire STREET ATLAS

A

B

C

Lockram Brook

Bloomfield
Hatch

Conference &
Training Ctr

CROSS LA

Wokefield Park

Great Park
Copse

4

Headlands
Farm

Pond Wood

Mann's
Farm

Mortimer House

65

NIGHTINGALE LA

Little
Copse

Wheat's
Farm

Sewage
Works

Great Park
Farm

3

Monkton
Copse

GORDON PALMER
CL

The Railway
Inn (PH)

THE STREET

Foudry Brook

RG7

Mortimer
St Marys
CE Jun Sch

Tun
Bridge

MORTIMER HALL

Stratfield
Mortimer

RAILWAY
TERR

Mortimer

STATION RD

64

Admiral's
Copse

PITFIELD LA

Perrins
Farm

2

Furze
Ground

THE FOREHEAD

Home Wood

Little Park
Farm

63

Ticklecorner Lane

Butlers
Lands
Farm

Hogs Plat

Park Lane

PARK LA

1

PARK LA

Butlers Land
Copse

NIGHTMERE LA

Wigmore
Farm

Garden Copse

Forelands

NEW ST

62

66

A

67

B

68

C

A33 Reading **Berkshire** STREET ATLAS

A

B

C

4

65

3

64

2

63

1

62

A

B

C

70

71

Clappers Farm

Missels Bridge

Brook Farm

Reid's Bridge

Foudry Brook

Crosslane Farm

Beech Hill Coverts

Wood Lane

Woodcock Lane

A33

BEECH HILL RD

White House Farm

May's Hill

Shinfield

BACK LA

Lamb's Lane Prim Sch

Lamb's Farm Bsns Pk

BASINGSTOKE RD

B3349

Loddon Court Farm

Loddon Court

King's Bridge

Priory Copse

Moat

Home Farm

Beech Hill House

Priory Farm

The Priory

BASINGSTOKE HILL

Y SHIRES

BARGE LA

Handpost Farm

B3349

BASINGSTOKE RD

Trunkwell Farm

WOOD LA

+

Trunkwell House

MILL'S RD

PARK VIEW

Beech Hill

Old Elm Tree (PH)

PRIORY COTTS

River Loddon

RG7

Goddard's Farm

Taylor's Lane

Cannon Bridge

Stanford End Farm

Highgrove Copse

Y SHIRES

Collins Copse

Great Hills Farm

Stanford End

Newbarn House

BULL LA

St Leger's Copse

TROWE LA

DEVIL'S DEN

Chequers

New Barn Farm

BULL LA

SUN LA

B3349

BASINGSTOKE RD

CHEQUER LA

Stanfordend Bridge

WELSH LA

Fair Cross

Lake Pond

Park Corner Farm

Home Farm

Stratfield Saye Park

RG27

Stone Bridge

Top Hill Copse

Lower Tumbling Bay

BASINGSTOKE RD

A33

A B C

Great Wood

RG2

Butler's La

Tanner's Farm

Wokingham Rd

Sheepbridge Court Farm

River Loddon

New Plantation

Great Copse

Swallowfield Park

Swallowfield Rd

4

Sheep Bridge

Kilnclose Pond

Kiln Hill

Wr Twr

Holly Cnr

B3349

65

Wyvols Court

Basingstoke Rd

Cuckoo Pen

Swallowfield Rd

PH

P

+

George & Dragon (PH)

The Naylors

Brookside Bsns Ctr

Salter's Bridge (FB)

Rowe's Farm

Bunglers Hill

3

Swallowfield

Charlton La

Trowe's La

Blackwater River

Cemy

Rutley's La

Fir Grove

Raggett's La

Clarkes Farm

Chill Hill

Daughtry La

Dac... Farr...

B3349

64

The Broadwater

RG7

Wheelers Farm

Sandpit Farm

Springalls Farm

Yew Tree Farm

Part La

Riseley Farm

Wheeler's Copse

2

Glasspool Farm

Riseley Gorse Farm

School Rd

Bottom Fa... House

Basingstoke Rd

Cotts

Riseley

Walnut Tree Farm

School La

Thatcher's or Little Frd

Halpin Rd

Bengall La

Well House La

63

B3349

Kent Cotts

River Whitewater

Cordery's Farm

Ford La

B3349

Shortway

RG27

Odiham Rd

Ham's Wood

P

RG27

1

Pound Copse

Birchen Copse

Bramshill Plantation

Wellington Country Park

Mill Wood

Riseley Mill

Hall's Farm

62

B3349

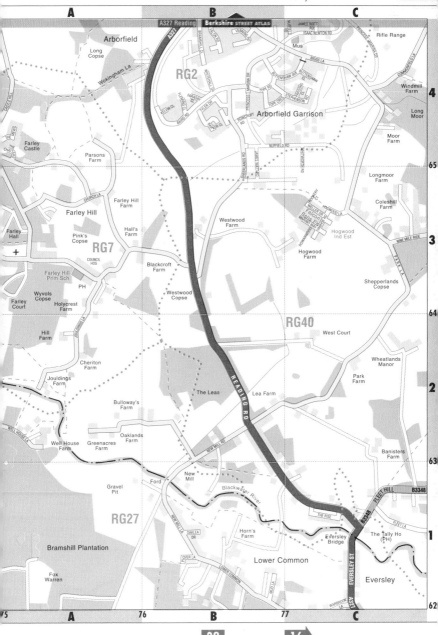

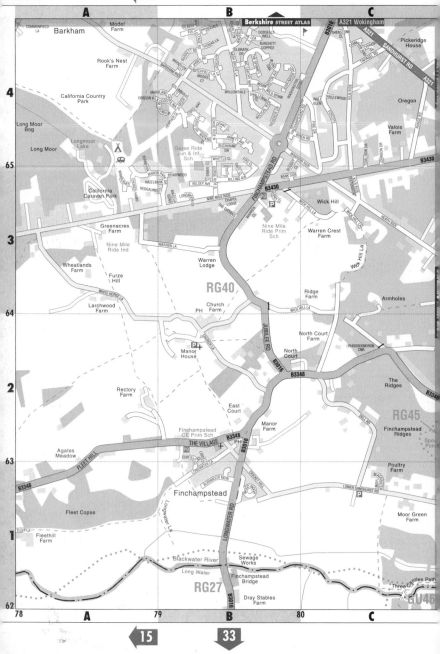

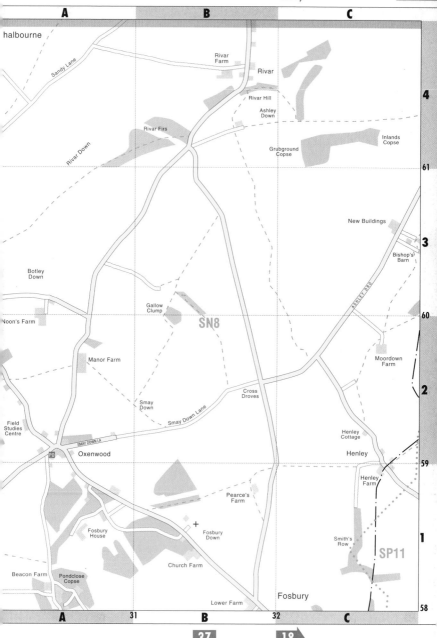

A   B   C

halbourne

Sandy Lane

Rivar Farm

Rivar

4

Rivar Hill

Ashley Down

Rivar Firs

Inlands Copse

Rivar Down

Grubground Copse

61

New Buildings

3

Bishop's Barn

Botley Down

Noon's Farm

Gallow Clump

SN8

60

Manor Farm

Moordown Farm

ASHLEY DRO

Smay Down

Cross Droves

2

Smay Down Lane

Field Studies Centre

Henley Cottage

SMAY DOWN LA

PO

Oxenwood

Henley

59

Henley Farm

Pearce's Farm

Fosbury House

Fosbury Down

Smith's Row

SP11

1

Beacon Farm

Pondclose Copse

Church Farm

Lower Farm

Fosbury

58

A   31   B   32   C

Inkpen Hill

Wigmoreash Drove

Ham Hill

Green Drove

Town Farm

WOODCOTE RD

4

Buttermere

Grange Farm

RG17

61

CHURCH LA

Nut Covert

Buttermere Bottom

SN8

3

Manor Farm

WHITE WAY

HUNGERFORD RD

ASHLEY DRO

Test Way

Sheepless Hill

Wadsmere Down

Buttermere Wood

Bushel's Copse

NEAR LA

Ballyack House

60

Kent's Copse

Rockmoor Down

2

Wind Pump

Combe Wood

Upper Horns Farm

Test Way

Heath Plantation

59

SP11

Rockmoor Pond

ROCKMOOR LANE

Linkenholt Hanging

1

Upper Row Farm

Winterside Farm

Littledown

58

The Boot Inn (PH)

20

A   B   C

Wright's Lane

Walbury Hill

West Woodhay Down

RG20

4

Wright's Farm

mmer Hill

Sandpits Down

Waylarer's Walk

Combe

61

Lower Farm

Park Wood

Manor Farm

CHURCH LA

Sugglestone Down

Combe Hill

3

RG17

Mast

Eastwick

Summerton's Down

60

Hogs Hole

Combe Bottom

Ruffian's Copse

Combe Wood

2

Limber Copse

Birch Copse

Highdown

59

Ken's Wood

art Hill Down

Test Way

Down Copse

SP11

1

Cleve Hill Down

Manor House

Iron's Hill

Pump House

Faccombe

Linkenholt

58

A   37   B   38   C

39   20

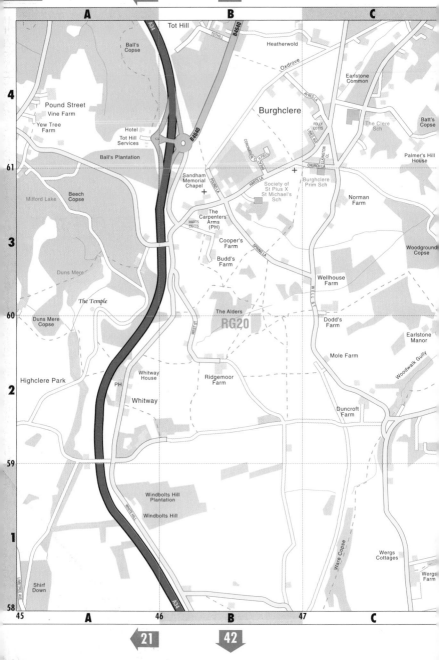

A   B   C

Tot Hill

Heatherwold

Oxdrove

Ball's
Copse

Earlstone
Common

4

Pound Street
Vine Farm

Burghclere

The Clere
Sch

Batt's
Copse

Yew Tree
Farm

Hotel
Tot Hill
Services

Palmer's Hill
House

61

Ball's Plantation

Sandham
Memorial Chapel

Society of
St Pius X
St Michael's
Sch

Burghclere
Prim Sch

Milford Lake

Beech
Copse

The
Carpenters'
Arms
(PH)

Norman
Farm

3

Cooper's
Farm

Woodground
Copse

Duns Mere

Budd's
Farm

The Temple

Wellhouse
Farm

60

Duns Mere
Copse

The Alders

RG20

Dodd's
Farm

Earlstone
Manor

Mole Farm

Woodwalk Gully

Highclere Park

Whitway
House

PH

Ridgemoor
Farm

2

Whitway

Duncroft
Farm

59

Windbolts Hill
Plantation

Windbolts Hill

1

Ware Copse

Wergs
Cottages

Wergs
Farm

Shirf
Down

58

45   A   46   B   47   C

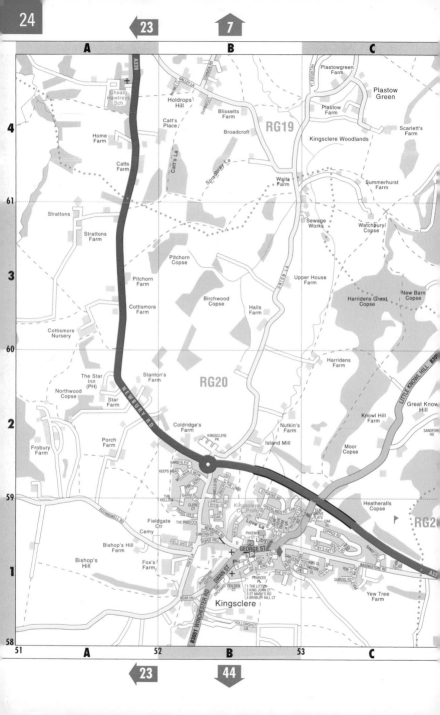

Mount Pleasant

Pamber Heath

Heath Copse

Upper Inhams Copse

THE BUTTS Hotel

Silchester

Tadley Bottom

Bowmont's Bridge

String La

Silchester Brook

Silchester Farm

HYDES PLATT

4

Tadley

Beggar's Bridge Copse

String Lane Copse

Sewage Works

61

RG7

Frame Green Copse

BYES LA

Pamber Forest (Nature Reserve)

Tadley Hill

Gravelpit Copse

Early Bridge Copse

Tadley Com Prim Sch

Bentley Green Copse

3

1 CHRISTY CT
2 WINCHFIELD GDNS
3 TITCHFIELD CL
4 ROTHERWICK RD
5 FARRINGDON WAY

Bridle's Copse

The Fighting Cocks (PH)

SILCHESTER RD

FROG LA

Honey Mill Bridge

Mariner's Copse

King's Hogsty Copse

Froglane Farm

Skates Farm

RG26

60

SKATES LA

RAMSDELL LA

Ravenscot Farm

The Plough (PH)

Kinghern Copse

Lee Copse

Long Copse

Pamber Green

Hill House

Little London

2

Walkner's Firs

ALDERMASTON RD

Cottage Farm

NEW RD

BEACH'S DRIVE

College Farm

Prince's Grove

Wakeford Farm

Court Corner

Berry Court Farm

BOAR'S BRIDGE

59

Wyeford Farm

Simms Corner

Clapperhill

Pamber Place

Pamber End

Pamber Farm

Bell's Water Copse

Elm Park Farm

BRAMLEY RD

1

Fish Weir Copse

RAMSDELL RD

Church Gully

Queen's College Atms (PH)

Holly Bush Copse

Newlands Copse

Ford

The Priory Prim Sch

Priory Farm

A340

Blackwater Copse

58

27
11

A **B** **C**

Greenlands Farm

Dicker's Copse

Dicker's Farm

North Copse

Great Scrub Copse

Ford

Haskers Farm

4

Church Lane Farm

Clapper's Farm

Brickledo Farm

Brook Farm

Pound Farm

Lower Farm

Three Ashes

Park Copse

BRAMLEY RD

BYES LA

CHURCH LA

CLAPPER'S FARM RD

Silchester Brook

61

RG7

Halls Farm

3

Haines Farm

Davnage Copse

Withy Copse

Barefoot House

Latchmere Green

Latchmere Green Farm

FROG LA

El Sub Sta

Holly Cross Farm

60

Latchmore Farm

Bramley Frith Wood

MINCHENS LA

MOAT CL

Bramley CE Prim

Bramle CE Prim

Bramley

2

RG26

Stock's Farm

PH

LC

P

Bramley

Bramley Corner

Bramley Corner Farm

Park Gate Farm

SILCHESTER RD

Middle Farm

Church Farm

POUND RD

RINGSHALL GDNS

JIBBS MOW

Boar's Bridge

CHURCH LANE

59

Tudor House

TUDOR LA

THE MALTINGS

THE STABLES

Middle Lodge

Honey Farm

Street House

King's Copse

1

Park Copse

Beaurepaire Park

Beaurepaire Mill Bridge

Lock's Bridge

RG24

VYNE LA

Bow Brook

Watford Copse

Beaurepaire House

58

63 **A** 64 **B** 65 **C**

27
48

35

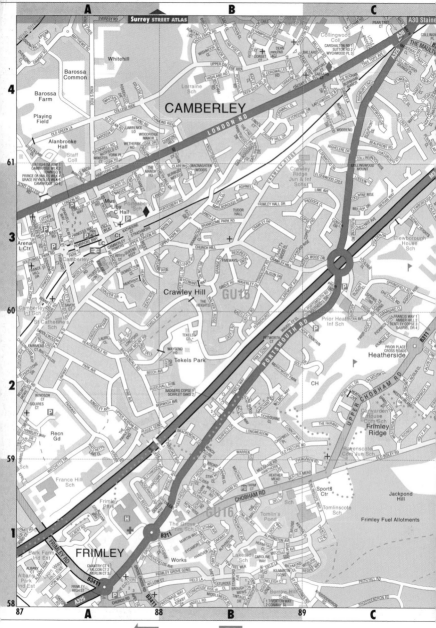

CAMBERLEY

FRIMLEY

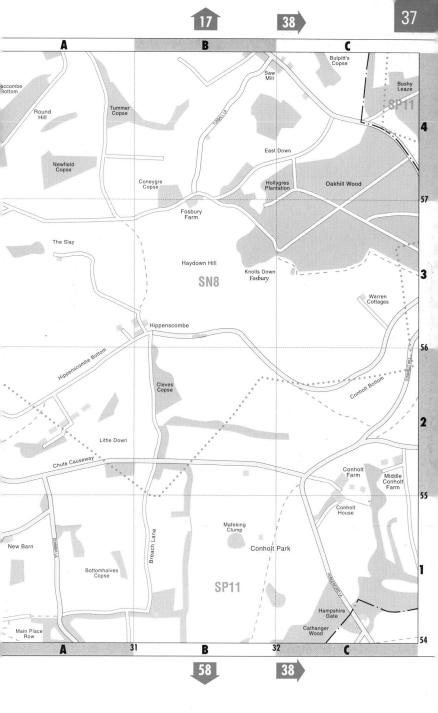

A   B   C

accombe
Bottom

Round
Hill

Tummer
Copse

Saw
Mill

Bulpitt's
Copse

Bushy
Leaze

SP11

4

Newfield
Copse

Coneygre
Copse

East Down

Hollygres
Plantation

Oakhill Wood

57

Fosbury
Farm

The Slay

Haydown Hill

SN8

Knolls Down
Fosbury

3

Warren
Cottages

Hippenscombe

56

Hippenscombe Bottom

Cleves
Copse

Conholt Bottom

Little Down

2

Chute Causeway

Conholt
Farm

Middle
Conholt
Farm

55

New Barn

Breach Lane

Mafeking
Clump

Conholt
House

Bottomhalves
Copse

Conholt Park

SP11

DUNMER LA

NURSEHILL LA

THE TONNING

TIDNELL LA

1

Hampshire
Gate

Cathanger
Wood

Main Place
Row

54

A B C

Manor Farm

Netherton

Netherton House

Heaven Hill

Test Way

Rymer's Barn

4

Green Lane

57

Wilster Copse

Sawyers Wood

Netherton Bottom

Netherton Hanging Copse

Faccombe Wood

3

SP11

56

Day's Copse

Clinchorn Farm

Test Way

Cockley's Copse

2

Parsonage Farm

Upton

River Swift

55

Soper's Farm

Ambley Farm

The Warren

1

Ambley Wood

Ford

Upton Valley

DUNSTAN'S DRO

Fairway

Spring Row

Ppg Sta

Test Way

A343

54

A 37 B 38 C

A   B   C

Ox Drove

CROSS LA

A343

Keepers
Cottage

Three Legs
House

Charters
Farm

Old
Lodge
Ray
Piece

Sidown Hill

Sidown Glades

4

Highclere
Stud

RED HILL

Redhill
Plantation

Field
House

57

RG20

Crux Easton
Farm

Bigg's
Copse

Rabbit
Warren

Wayfarer's Wlk

Sidown
Range

3

Manor
House

Mopper's
Barn

Crux Easton

The
Kennels

Upper
Woodcott
Down

Crux Easton
House

56

Beech
Hanger
Copse

Hook Copse

2

Charlie's
Wood

RG28

Hook
Farm

55

aston Park
Wood

Hall
Cottage

Lower
Woodcott
Farm

Woodcott

SP11

Upper
Woodcott
Farm

Danegrove
Copse

1

Stubb's
Copse

Woodcott
House

ghfield
House

Paul's
Copse

Suggeaston
Copse

54

A   43   B   44   C

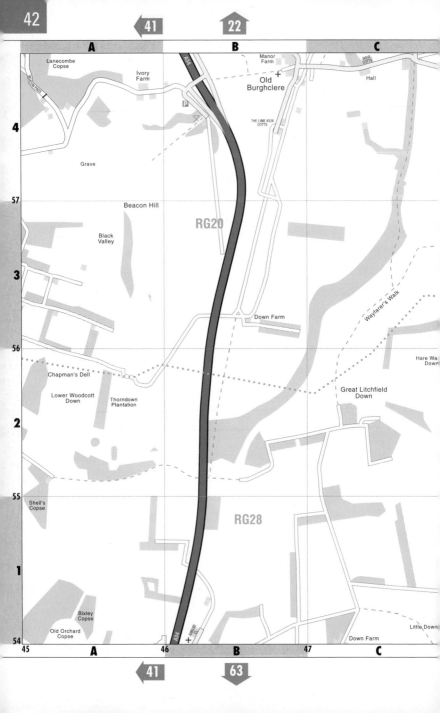

41
22

A   **B**   **C**

Lanecombe Copse

BEACON PASS

Ivory Farm

Manor Farm

Old Burghclere

WGR COTTS

Hall

P

THE LIME KILN COTTS

4

Grave

57

Beacon Hill

RG20

Black Valley

3

Down Farm

Wayfarer's Walk

56

Chapman's Dell

Hare Wa Down

Lower Woodcott Down

Thorndown Plantation

Great Litchfield Down

2

55

Shell's Copse

RG28

1

Bixley Copse

Old Orchard Copse

Little Down

Down Farm

54

45   **A**   46   **B**   47   **C**

41
63

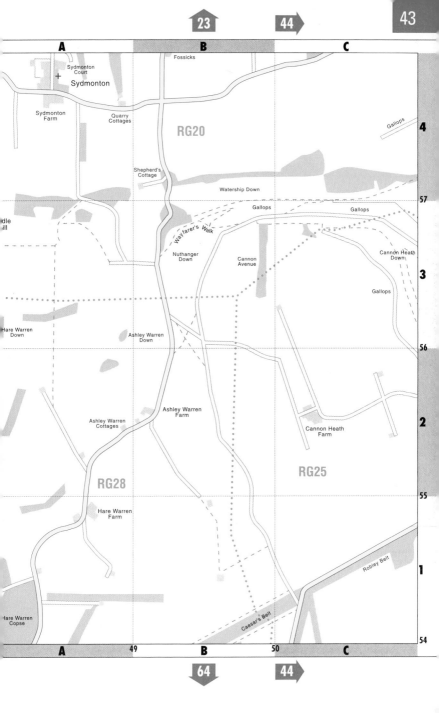

23

44

A   B   C

Fossicks

Sydmonton
Court

Sydmonton

Sydmonton
Farm

Quarry
Cottages

RG20

Gallops

4

Shepherd's
Cottage

Watership Down

57

idle
ill

Gallops

Gallops

Wayfarer's Walk

Nuthanger
Down

Cannon
Avenue

Cannon Heath
Down

3

Gallops

Hare Warren
Down

Ashley Warren
Down

56

Ashley Warren
Farm

2

Ashley Warren
Cottages

Cannon Heath
Farm

RG25

RG28

55

Hare Warren
Farm

Robley Belt

1

Hare Warren
Copse

Caesar's Belt

54

A   49   B   50   C

64

44

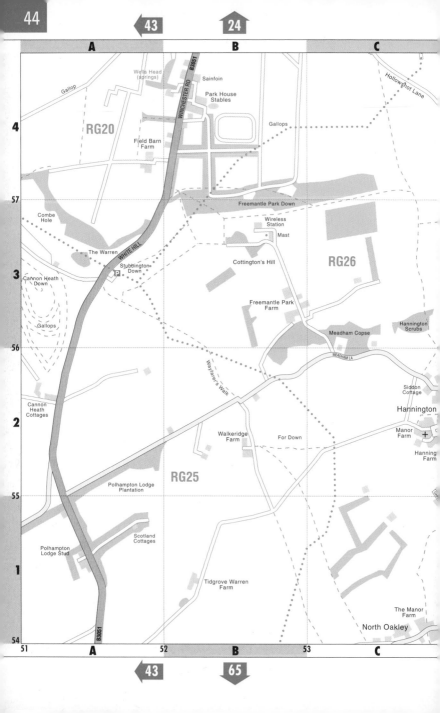

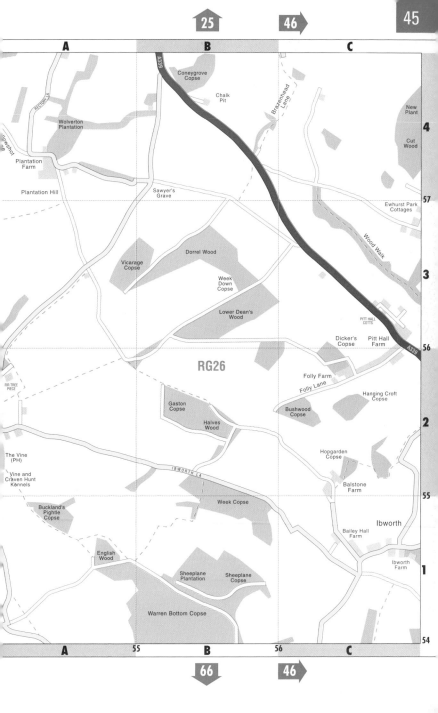

A
B
C

A339

Coneygrove
Copse

Chalk
Pit

Brazenhead Lane

New
Plant

4

Wolverton
Plantation

Cut
Wood

owshot

Plantation
Farm

Plantation Hill

Sawyer's
Grave

57

Ewhurst Park
Cottages

Wood Walk

Dorrel Wood

3

Vicarage
Copse

Week
Down
Copse

Lower Dean's
Wood

Pitt Hall
Cotts

Dicker's
Copse

Pitt Hall
Farm

56

RG26

A339

FIR TREE
PIECE

Folly Farm

Folly Lane

Hanging Croft
Copse

Gaston
Copse

Bushwood
Copse

Haives
Wood

2

The Vine
(PH)

Hopgarden
Copse

Vine and
Craven Hunt
Kennels

IBWORTH LA

Balstone
Farm

55

Buckland's
Pightle
Copse

Week Copse

Ibworth

Bailey Hall
Farm

English
Wood

Ibworth
Farm

1

Sheeplane
Plantation

Sheeplane
Copse

Warren Bottom Copse

54

A
55
B
56
C

A B C

Bushy Copse
Sandpits Copse
Lily Lake
Hollybush Farm
Little Wyford Farm
The White Hart (PH)
Fir Tree Farm
Round Copse
BAUGHURST RD
MONK SHERBORNE RD
Charter Alley

4

Dogkennel Wood
Lloyd's Copse
Ramsdell
THE OLD BRICK KILN TRAD EST
Wither's Copse
Brocas Bridge

Park Copse
Skyer's Farm
Six Acre Copse

57

Home Farm
Ewhurst Park
Ewhurst Pond
EWHURST RD
SKEEWASH LA
May's Cottage

Ewhurst House
Skyer's Wood
Privett Copse

3

May's Copse
Lower Farm

Wood Walk
Lodge
RG26
BASINGSTOKE RD

Spilman's Copse

56

A339

2

Pierce's Copse
Pithall
Piccadilly Hill
Field Barn Farm

Woodgarston Farm

55

KINGSCLERE RD

Upper Wootton

1

HOME LA
Manor Farm
A339

Woodgarston La
Ebenezer Cottage
RG23

Whitedown

54

57 A **58** B **59** C

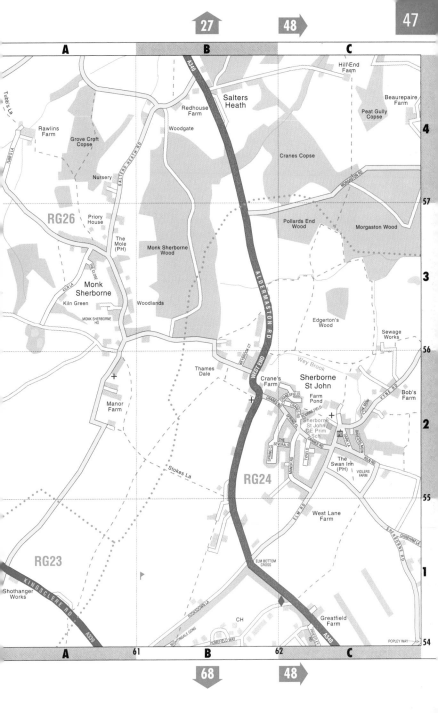

A

B3011

Hazeley
Bottom
Works

Hazeley
House

Hazeley
Heath

Sewage
Works

HULFORDS
LA

The Hartford
Bridge
(PH)

A30

Hartfordbrid

BEECHHILL RD

CALTHORPE
HOS
Hartford
Bridge

River Hart

Hares
Farm

Inholmes
Court

4

The Old
Manor House

BRACKNELL A

James's
Farm

HARTFORD GDNS 1
WALPOLE GDNS 2
DAIRY WLK 3
BELGRAVE MEWS 4
OAKLEY PL 5

HAYWARDEN
PL

CH

HARTLEY
MEWS

CAMPION
WAY

HEATHER GR
SPRINGFIELD AVE

HAWKS CT

57

The
Dutch House

WEST GREEN RD

BRACKLEY AVE

CHURCH LA
CHURCH

ALDERSHOT
MINLEY RD

HAZELEY
HARTLEY
HAZELL

MEADOW LA

B3011

P

Causeway
Farm

MONDAY
PO

HIGH ST

A323

HARTLEY
MEWS

WEST ST

Hartley
Wintney

CRICKET
GREEN
LA

CHURCH
WALBURTON
HO

LONDON RD

HOLMWOOD
TERR

Oakwood
Inf Sch

MILL DAM

MILL LA

3

Grange
Farm

GRANGE LA

ORANGE
GROVE

Greenfields
Jun Sch

COLTHURST

OAKLANDS

PADDOCK CT

CLAYTON
RD

A323

OLD SCHOOL

The Grey
House Sch

FLEET RD

West
Lodge

Fouracre
House

Phoenix
Green

CEDAR
TERR

GREEN FIELD

ST MARY'S CT

WEAVER

WARREN

COTTAGE

CHURCHILL

Church House
Farm

56

THACKHAM'S LA

The Croft
Lodge

PRIEST'S CL

LANE

POTTERY CT

PH

HIGH ST

MABS CL

LARKFIELD

MOUNT

BRAMPTON
GDNS

Three Castles Path

The
Shepherds Cottage

Wintney
Court

Phoenix
Green

B3016

FOTHAM CL

Sergeants
Copse

River Hart

2

A30

Ashley

Taplin's
Farm

Wintney
Farm

Walb
Cop

Nursery

Mabs
Copse

NAB'S LANE PARK A

Winchfield
House

55

Winchfield
Lodge

OLD POTBRIDGE RD

Shapley Heath
Copse

SHAPLEY HEATH

SHAPLEY
HILL

Winchfield

Winchfield

Woody's
(PH)

STATION RD

P

CR MOLE CLERK GN

Cranford's
Farm

Vale
Farm

Winchfie
Hurst

1

Beggar's
Corner

M3

ODIHAM RD

Tossell
Wood

B3016

Furzy Moor

Hurst
Farm

RG29

Bottom
Copse

BAGWELL LA

WINCHFIE
HURST

54

RG27

A B C

4

57

3

56

2

55

1

54

79 80

GU17

Yateley Heath Wood

Three Corner Plantation

Ivyhole Hill Wood

Great Butt

Blackbushes Farm

Elvetham Farm

Muddy Grove Hill

Pont Hill

Mount Zion

BLACKBUSHES RD

Bakers Bridge

The Lake

New Park

RG27

Word Hill Farm

Lichett Plain

River Hart

Elvetham Old Rectory

Turner's Green Farm

Doghouse Bridge

Broomhurst Kennels & Cattery

Sewage Works

Elvetham Hall

Elvetham Park

Elvetham

Rotten Green

Gilldown Farm

M3

Lodge Farm

STREET END

Brickyard Plantation

Spreadburys Heath

Fleet Service Area

Nature Reserve

Turner's Wood

Bushy Hill

Parkfield Copse

FLEET RD

Palelane Farm

The Mounts

KINGS WORTHY RD

Elvetham Heath Prim Sch

GU51

Elvetham Heath

PALE LA

Bentley Lodge

Railroad Copse

FLEET

Fleet Com

Stockton House Sch

WAVERLEY AVE

Culver Copse

GLENDALE PK

READING RD N

Greenwood Manor

The Manor

Hitches Farm

A323

A323

FLEET RD A3013

A3013

Liby

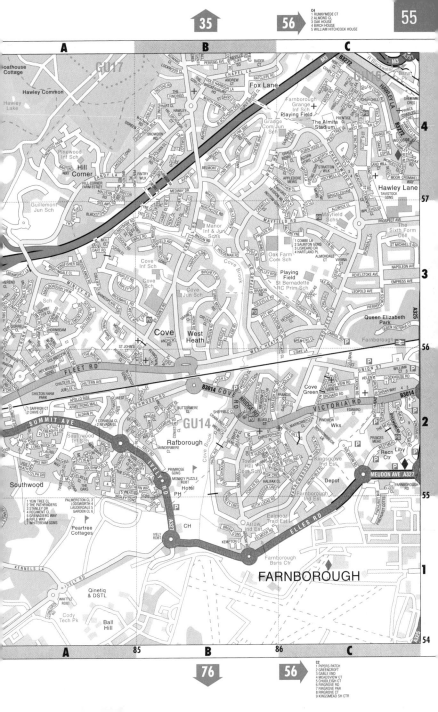

A   B   C

Standen
House

CHURCH LA

BEACH LA

Cathanger
Wood

Chute
Standen

Standen
Farm

Chute
Cadley

Young's
Copse

MALTHOUSE LA

4

Collis
Farm

Home
Farm

NEW
BLDGS

Chessams
Copse

Clarke's Lane

Home F.
Dairy

HOCKWOOD LA

The Hatchet
(PH)

Lower
Chute

53

FORESTLA

Jolly's
Farm

Tangley
Bottom

The
Cricketers Arms
(PH)

Tangle

CLARKES LA

Forest
House

Great Lodge
Copse

Cadley Bottom

Little
Pill

Home
Farm

Mano
Farm

3

Tangley
House

Coldridge Ride

Little Lodge
Copse

Tangley
Park

+

SP11

52

Long Bottom

Poultry
Houses

LODGE LA

COACH HILL

Chute Lodge
Farm

ORCHARD
COTTS

Chute
Forest

Big
Wood

Sexton's
Heath

2

Cooper's
Acre

Longbottom
Farm

Chute
Lodge

Pollards
Farm

51

REDROW LA

Roundaway
Farm

Redhouse
Farm

Mankhorn
Round

Appleshaw
Round

1

Mankhorn
Cottage

South
Lodge

Soper's Bottom

Soper's
Barn

Poultry
Houses

BEDENHAM RISE

NEWHOUSE LA

50

30   A   31   B   32   C

A

B

C

Highfield Farm

Mayfield

Stubb's Copse

Sowleaze Copse

Buckets Down Farm

Long Copse

4

The White House

Great Eastwards

Binley

The Hurdler's Arms (PH)

Park Copse

Wardwick House

Broadclose Copse

Bradley Hill

53

BULL BOTTOM

Long Hedge Drove

Lower Wadwick House

Wadwick

Hollycroft Copse

3

WADWICK BOTTOM

Rolf's Copse

Little Downhams Copse

Egbury Farm

Egbury

SP11

RG28

52

Downhams Farm

Downhams

Downhams Copse

Egbury Castle Farm

2

Cold Harbour Farm

Cold Harbour House

Cooper's in the Wood Farm

51

Breach Farm

SPRING HILL LA

WEST STREET

EGBURY RD

B3048

Newbarn Down Plantation

Hogdigging Copse

1

B3048

PO

PH

Test Way

Jamaica Farm

+ St Mary Bourne

Bourne Rivulet

Pp Ho

50

42

Bourne Court

A

43

B

44

C

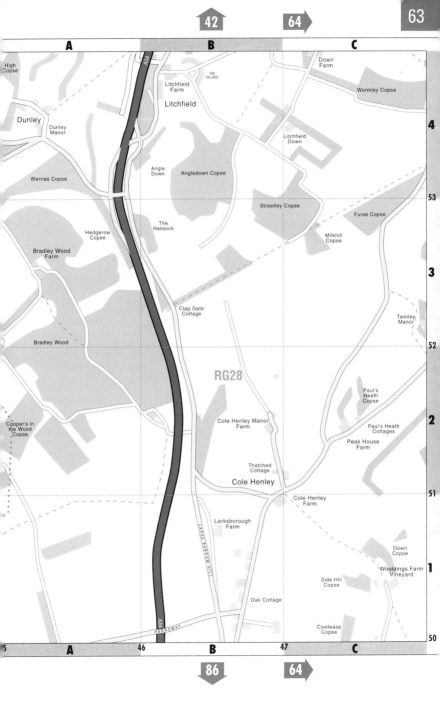

A
B
C

High Copse

Down Farm

Litchfield Farm

THE VILLAGE

Wormley Copse

Litchfield

4

Dunley

Dunley Manor

Litchfield Down

Werries Copse

Angle Down

Angledown Copse

53

Streetley Copse

Furse Copse

The Hassock

Hedgerow Copse

Milkhill Copse

Bradley Wood Farm

3

Clap Gate Cottage

Twinley Manor

Bradley Wood

52

RG28

Paul's Heath Copse

Cooper's in the Wood Copse

Cole Henley Manor Farm

Paul's Heath Cottages

2

Peak House Farm

Thatched Cottage

Cole Henley

51

Cole Henley Farm

Larksborough Farm

LAKES BARROW HILL

Down Copse

Wooldings Farm Vineyard

1

Side Hill Copse

Oak Cottage

Cowlease Copse

A34 HARROWAY

50

5
A
46
B
47
C

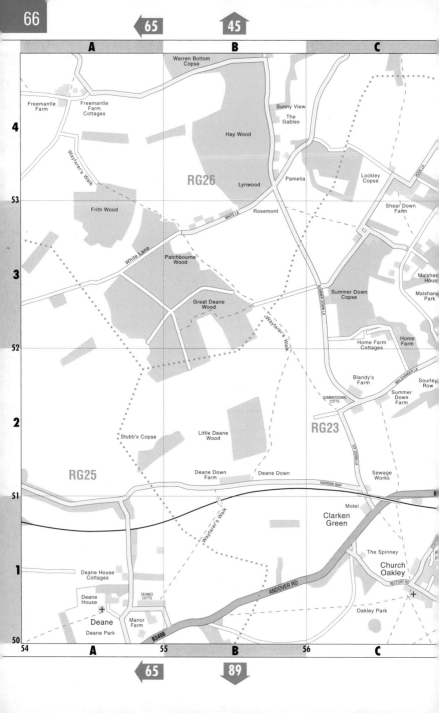

65 45

A B C

Warren Bottom
Copse

Freemantle
Farm

Freemantle
Farm
Cottages

Sunny View
The Gables

4

Hay Wood

Wayfarer's Walk

RG26

Lynwood

Pamelia

Lockley
Copse

53

Frith Wood

Rosemont

Shear Down
Farm

WHITE LA

White Lane

Patchbourne
Wood

SUMMER DOWN LA

Summer Down
Copse

Malshar
Hous

3

Malshan
Park

Great Deane
Wood

Wayfarer's Walk

Home Farm
Cottages

Home
Farm

52

MALSHANGER LA

Blandy's
Farm

Sourley
Row

Summer
Down Farm

SUMMERDOWN
COTTS

2

Stubb's Copse

Little Deane
Wood

RG23

IVY DOWN LA

RG25

Deane Down
Farm

Deane Down

Sewage
Works

HARROW WAY

51

Motel

B

Clarken
Green

Wayfarer's Walk

The Spinney

1

Deane House
Cottages

Church
Oakley

RECTORY RD

Deane
House

DEANES
COTTS

ANDOVER RD

50

Deane

Deane Park

Manor
Farm

B3400

Oakley Park

54 A 55 B 56 C

65 89

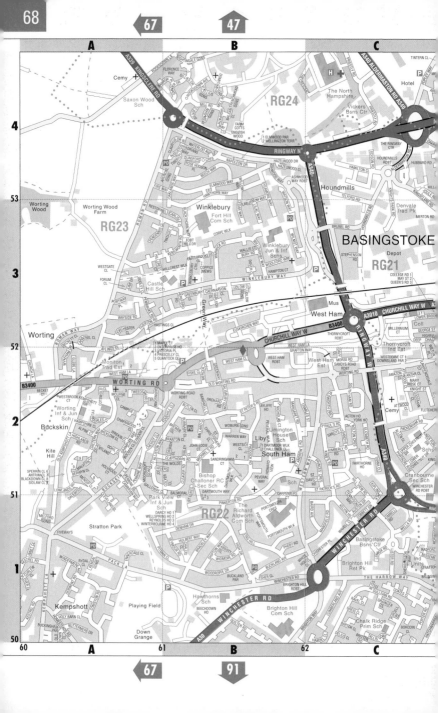

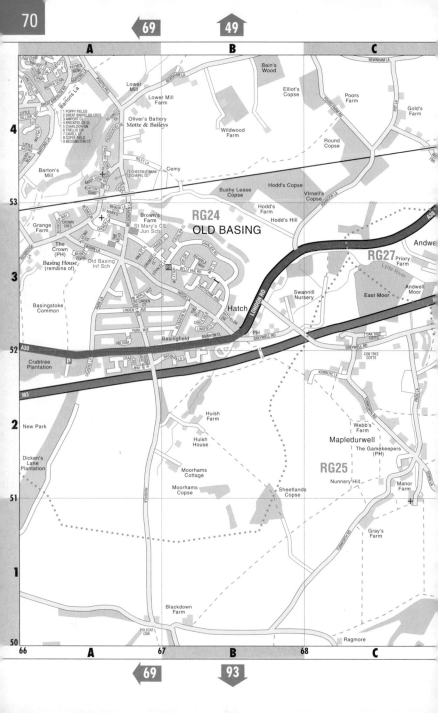

A **B** **C**

4

53

RG24
OLD BASING

RG27

Andwe

3

Basingstoke
Common

Hatch

RG25

2

Mapledurwell

51

1

50

66 67 68

A **B** **C**

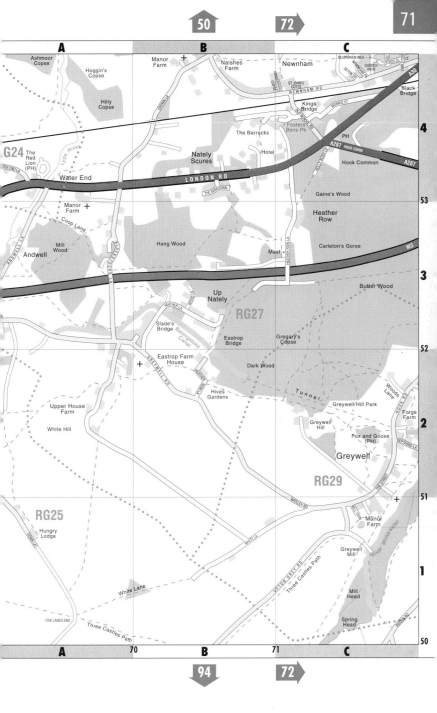

A   B   C

London Rd   A30

Hook P

SOUTH
VIEW
COTTS

CHANTRY
CL

RECTORY RD

B3349

BARTLEY WAY

BARTLEY RD

Hook

Bartley Wood
Bsns Pk

Potbridge

RAWLINGS RD

The
Rose Est

OSBORN WAY

BERRY
CT

GRIFFIN WAY S

4

Bull's Bushes

Monymusk
Farm

Scotland
Farm

Potbridge
Farm

Hook
Common

Bartley
Heath

Airstrip

Poland
Mill

RG27

HOOK RD

Bartley
Heath

B3349

53

6

Whitehall

M3

A287

A287

River Whitemoor

Poland
Farm

POLAND LA

LONDON RD

Butter
Wood

Bartley
Heath

Lodge
Farm

3

Northouse
Copse

HOOK RD

West La

Mill
Corner

B3349

Basingstoke Canal

B3016

The Jolly Miller
(PH)

HOOK RD

52

Odiham
Castle

Ford

Warnborough
Green

Water Witch
(PH)

THE WHARF

Colt
Hill

MILL LA

Three Castles Path

CASTLE
BRIDGE
COTTS

SWAN MEWS

RG29

LINCOLN AVE

DORCHESTER WAY

Swing
Bridge

TUNNEL LA

ALEXANDER TERR 1
THE WILLOWS 2
NURSERY TERR 3

PRIORY
ROW

CANAL

CLEVEDGE
WAY

Valentine
Farm

Hatchwood
Farm

2

Ppg
Sta

DEPTFORD LA

ANDREW LA

MALTHOUSE
COTTS

LAUREL CL

DUNLEYS HILL

B3349

COLT HILL

CHERRY POND DR

MANLEY JAMES CT

FARNHAM RD

TINLEY
GDNS

Hatchwe
House

Deptford
/ Bridge

Adams
Farm

Hockleys
Farm

TERRYS
COTTS

Crumlins
Bsns Est

BALACE GATES
FARM

DEER PARK VW

Hotel

HIGH ST

51

BIDDEN RD

Robert May's
Sch

WESTERN LA

WESTERN
CROSS

LibY

P

BARTON'S
CT

HIGH ST

SOUTH RIDGE

Mayhill
Jun Sch

Cemy

Odiham

ST DAVIDS CL

WEST ST

CROMPTON CL

The Close

ST
CT

Odiham
Cottage

SALISBURY

BUFFINS RD

BLAKES COTTS 1
OLD CT 2
BENFORD CT 3
GURNEY CL 4

Buryfields
Inf Sch

Redbri

1

Mast

Odiham
Firs

ALTON RD

FIR LA

HILLSIDE RD

Chosley
Farm

Mast

Clump
House

B3349

WYKEHAM
CT

LOVE LA

**RG
25**

50

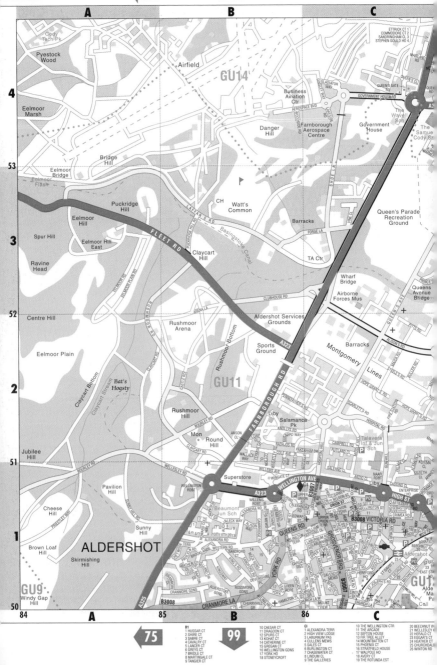

Map labels

GU14

GU11

GU9

GU1

Cody Tech Pk
Pyestock Wood
Airfield
Eelmoor Marsh
Business Aviation Ctr
Danger Hill
Farnborough Aerospace Centre
Government House
The Wavell Sch
The Samuel Cody Sch
Bridge Hill
Eelmoor Bridge
Eelmoor Flash
Puckridge Hill
CH
Watt's Common
Barracks
Queen's Parade Recreation Ground
Spur Hill
Eelmoor Hill
Eelmoor Hill East
Ravine Head
FLEET RD
Claycart Hill
TA Ctr
FORGE LA
Wharf Bridge
Queens Avenue Bridge
Centre Hill
Rushmoor Arena
CLUBHOUSE RD
Aldershot Services Grounds
Airborne Forces Mus
Queens Avenue Bridge
Eelmoor Plain
Claycart Bottom
Bat's Hogsty
Rushmoor Hill
Sports Ground
Barracks
Montgomery Lines
Jubilee Hill
Round Hill
Mon
CLAYCART RD
Liby
Salamanca Pk
Talavera Inf & Jun Sch
Liby
Pavilion Hill
WELLESLEY RD
Superstore
WINGATE RD
WELLINGTON AVE
A323
HIGH ST
Cheese Hill
Sunny Hill
WELLINGTON RD
Beaumont Jun Sch
UNION ST
VICTORIA RD
B3008
Aldershot
Brown Loaf Hill
ALDERSHOT
QUEENS RD
GROSVENOR RD
Skirmishing Hill
YORK RD
B3007
Windy Gap Hill
B3008
CRANMORE LA
CHURCH LA

Index

B1
1 HUSSAR CT
2 SHIRE CT
3 SABRE CT
4 CAVALRY CT
5 LANCER CT
6 GREYS CT
7 BRIDLE CT
8 MARTINGALE CT
9 TANGIER CT
10 CAESAR CT
11 DRAGOON CT
12 SPURS CT
13 KOHAT CT
14 CATHERINE CT
15 GREGAN CT
16 WELLINGTON GDNS
17 YORK HO
18 STONEYCROFT

C1
1 ALEXANDRA TERR
2 HIGH VIEW LODGE
3 LABURNUM PAS
4 CULLENS MEWS
5 SALES CT
6 BURLINGTON CT
7 CHASEWATER CT
8 LINDUM CL
9 THE GALLERIES
10 THE WELLINGTON CTR
11 THE ARCADE
12 SEFTON HOUSE
13 FIR TREE ALLEY
14 MOUNTBATTEN CT
15 PHOENIX CT
16 STRATFIELD HOUSE
17 WALPOLE CT
18 AVERY CT
19 THE ROTUNDA EST
20 BEECHNUT CT
21 WELLESLEY
22 HERALD CT
23 EGGAR'S CT
24 HEATHER CT
25 CHURCHDALE
26 WINTON RD

A1
1 REDAN GDNS
2 AMBER CT
3 POUND RD
4 WINDMILL CT
5 SUNNY VIEW CL
6 BEMBRIDGE CT
7 RYDE CT

C3
1 MELKSHAM HO
2 SAVERNAKE HO
3 CALNE HO
4 PEWSEY HO
5 WESTBURY HO

C4
1 COLLINS CT
2 VOCKINS CL
3 AUCHINLECK HO
4 CUNNINGHAM HO
5 MONTGOMERY HO
6 ALEXANDER HO

7 CHESTNUT AVE
8 ROWAN CT
9 SWINDON HO
10 DEVIZES HO
11 WARMINSTER HO
12 SALISBURY HO
13 TROWBRIDGE HO

14 WILSON HO
15 PRINCES CT

Wiltshire STREET ATLAS The Pennings

A338 Marlborough

A   B   C

4

Sewage
Works

Willis
Wood

South
Park

Andover
Lane
Farm

A342

Freeth
Copse

Cunney's Down
Copse

THE STUD
OFFICES

Home
Farm

The Belt

Redenham
House

West
Lodge

Redenham
Park

49

Great
Shoddesden

Little
Shoddesden

ANDOVER RD

Chapel Copse

Privet
Down

Meadow
Copse

Shoddesden
Grange

East
Lodge

Hill
Cops

3

Little
Eastley

Woodway

Littleton
Copse

KALIS CORNER

48

SP11

The Beeches

DEACON RD

High View

PRIVET LA

LITTLETON
COTTS

FOYLE RD

2

CON LA

Kimpton

Ridgeway
Farm

DOWN RD

47

Fyfield

FIVE
FYFIEL

PH

THE
GREEN

Kimpton
Manor

Littleton
Manor

THE
RANK

Fyfield
House

DUNCAN CL

WALNUT TREE
BRAMLEY CL

The Wayne

Kimpton
House

Kimpton
Lodge

Manor
Farm

1

Kimpton, Thruxton
& Fyfield
CE Prim Sch

Highland
Wedding
(PH)

ELMCROFT RD

46

SNODDINGTON RD

Thruxton Aerodrome

27   A   28   B   29   C

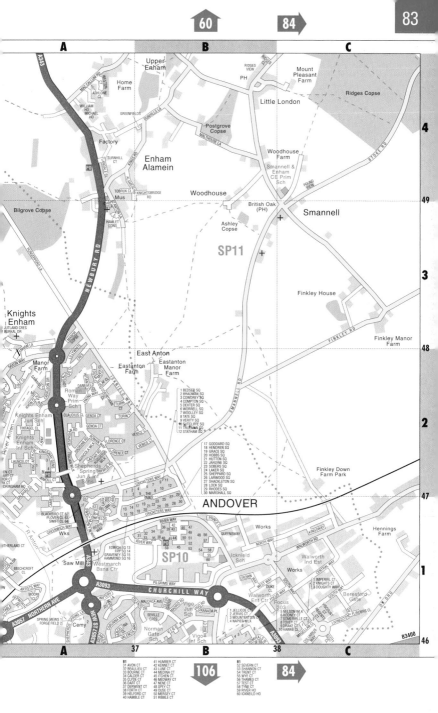

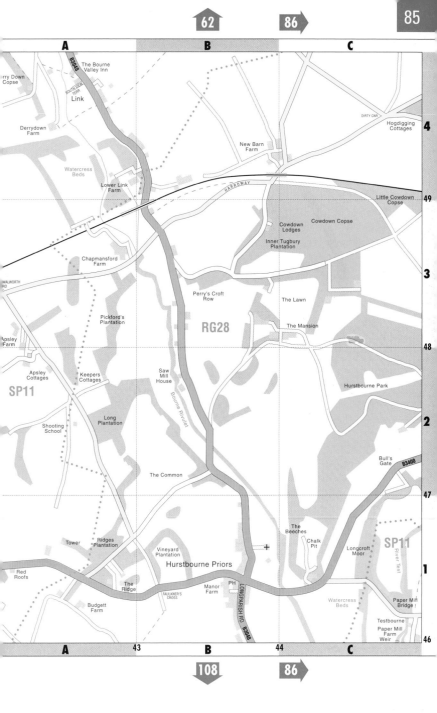

A B C

The Bourne Valley Inn

rry Down Copse

SOUTHVIEW TERR

B3048

Link

Derrydown Farm

4

DIRTY CNR

Hogdigging Cottages

Watercress Beds

New Barn Farm

HARROWAY

Lower Link Farm

Little Cowdown Copse

49

WALWORTH RD

Chapmansford Farm

Cowdown Copse

Cowdown Lodges

Inner Tugbury Plantation

3

Perry's Croft Row

The Lawn

Apsley Farm

Pickford's Plantation

RG28

The Mansion

48

Apsley Cottages

Keepers Cottages

Saw Mill House

Hurstbourne Park

SP11

Shooting School

Long Plantation

Bourne Rivulet

2

Bull's Gate

B3400

The Common

47

The Beeches

Tower

Ridges Plantation

Chalk Pit

Longcroft Moor

SP11

River Test

Vineyard Plantation

Hurstbourne Priors

+

Red Roofs

The Ridge

FAULKNER'S CROSS

Manor Farm

PH

LONGPARISH RD

B3048

Watercress Beds

Paper Mill Bridge

1

Budgett Farm

Testbourne Paper Mill Farm Weir

46

A 43 B 44 C

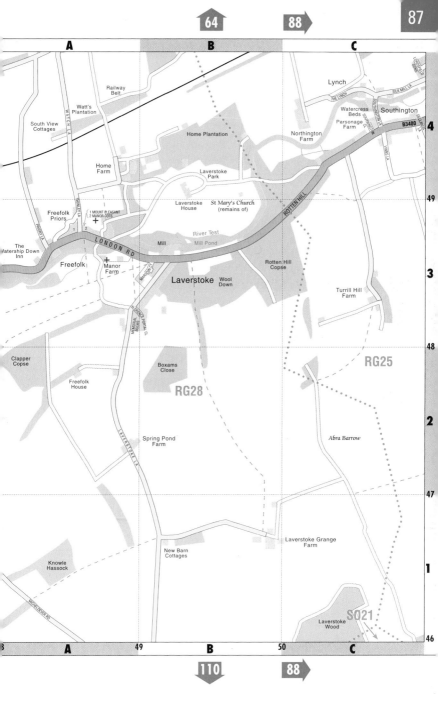

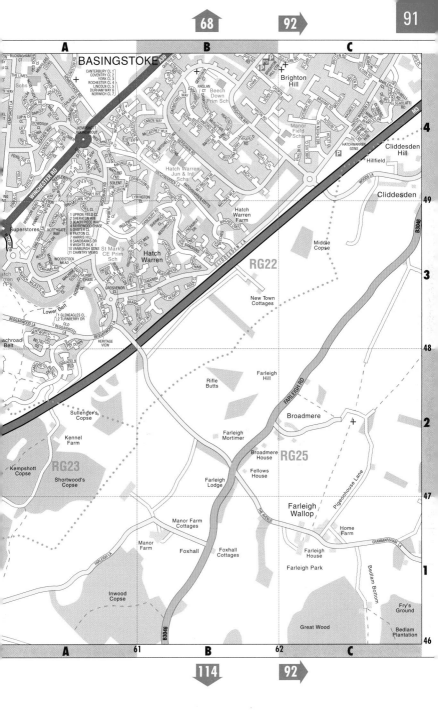

A B C

68 92

BASINGSTOKE

CANTERBURY CL 1
COVENTRY CL 2
YORK CL 3
ROCHESTER CL 4
LINCOLN CL 5
DURHAM WAY 6
NORWICH CL 7.

Brighton
Hill

Beech
Down
Prim Sch

RAGLAN
CT

Manor
Field
Schs

Cliddesden
Hill

Hillfield

HATCHWARREN
GDNS

Cliddesden

4

Hatch Warren
Jun & Inf
Schs

Hatch
Warren
Farm

49

1 UPRON FIELD CL
2 SHERATON AVE
3 BEACH PIECE WAY
4 FAYREWOOD CHASE
5 OYSTER CL
6 PAXTON CL
7 HARRIS HILL
8 SANDBANKS DR
9 WIGHTS WLK
10 VANBURGH GDNS
11 CHANTRY MEWS

Superstores

Northgate
Way

St Mark's
CE Prim
Sch

Hatch
Warren

Middle
Copse

RG22

3

New Town
Cottages

Lower Belt

1 GLENEAGLES CL
2 TURNBERRY DR
OLD
BEGGARWOOD LA

HERITAGE
VIEW

48

Farleigh
Hill

Rifle
Butts

Sullenger's
Copse

Farleigh
Mortimer

Broadmere

2

Kennel
Farm

Broadmere
House

RG25

Kempshott
Copse

RG23

Shortwood's
Copse

Farleigh
Lodge

Fellows
House

47

Farleigh
Wallop

Manor Farm
Cottages

Home
Farm

Manor
Farm

Foxhall

Foxhall
Cottages

Farleigh
House

1

Farleigh Park

Inwood
Copse

Bedlam
Bottom

Fry's
Ground

Bedlam
Plantation

Great Wood

46

A 61 B 62 C

114 92

A **B** **C**

RG22

JAYS CL

M3

B3046

Pensdell
Farm

Audleys
Wood

The
Basin

A339

Spring
Wood

Broad Walk

Hackwood
House

Hackwood
Park

FARLEIGH RD

BOUNDA LA

4

PH

The
Cubs

Cliddesden

CHURCH LA

HACKWOOD LANE

CENTURY CL

STATION RD

RECTORY
ROW

B3046

49

Manor
Farm

Cliddesden
Nurseries

Poultry
Farm

Swallick
Wood

3

Cliddesden
Prim Sch

Lodge
Plantation

Winslade
Farm

Pidden Hill

Winslade

Swallick
Cottages

48

White
Hill

Swallick
Farm

RG25

Buckshorn
Copse

Little Hen
Wood

Eight Acre
Dell

West Field Beeches

Poor Hill

2

Kingsmore
Copse

Whinkney's
Copse

Round
Copse

The Avenue

Doper's
Copse

White Hill
Dell

Fryingdown
Copse

Forfield
Plantation

Three Castles Path

Winslade La

Quidliz
Round

47

Allwood Copse

Little Bushywarren
Copse

Herria
Park

GRAMMARSHAM LA

NORTHGATE LA

Northgate
Farm

1

Webb's
Copse

Great Bushywarren
Copse

Alley La

Hallowed
Litten

GREEN LA

CHURCH LA

BUSHYWARREN LA

OVERTON LA

46

63 **A** **64** **B** **65** **C**

A
B
C

Hackwood Farm

Down Platation

Sturts Copse

4

Roundtown

Tunworth Down House

Down Farm

Knights Wood

Brick Kiln Copse

Priest Wood

Longrodan La

Pudding Copse

Fulham's Copse

Hatwood's Copse

Tunworth Down

49

Picked Craft Copse

Gaston Copse

Tunworth

Tunworth Hill Cottages

3

Tunworth Lodge

Three Castles Path

Copse Close Beeches

Prior's Hill

Manor Farm

The Old Rectory

Dower Farm

The Dower House

48

Tytherlands

Hummock Clump

RG25

Green's Copse

Tidbury Ring

Reeds Farm House

Middle Copse

Hay Down

2

Hen Wood

Coombe Wood

The Board

Weston Corbett

Guy's Copse

Haydown Belt

Manor Farm

47

Herriard Park

Honeyleaze Copse

Eastfield Belt

White La

1

Case is Altered

Case Green

Park Farm

erriard

Home Farm

Herriard House

Great Lipmore

46

A
67
B
68
C

93
71

A   **B**   **C**

Three Castles Path

Three Castles Path

Four Lanes End

Bidden Water

Ford Farm

4

Bidden Grange Farm

Lower Bidden Farm

Bidden

Dean Plantation

49

RG25

Cleves Farm

Gaston Copse

Upton Grey House

Manor Farm

WOODMANFIELD

Little Dean Farm

3

Upton Grey

Little Hoddington

The Hoddington Arms (PH)

PO

48

The Village Farm

Tile Barn Farm

Weston Mark

Hoddington Park

Hoddington House

HODDINGTON COTTS

THE OLD ORCHARD 1
NASH MEADOWS 2

Lee's Farm

2

Hoddington Farm

Dean Farm House

RG29

Weston Patrick House

CHURCH VIEW

47

Manor Farm

Dean Copse

Weston Patrick

Hoddington

1

Wood Lane End

Privett Copse

Little Park Copse

Long La

Westers Lane

46

69   **A**   70   **B**   71   **C**

93
117

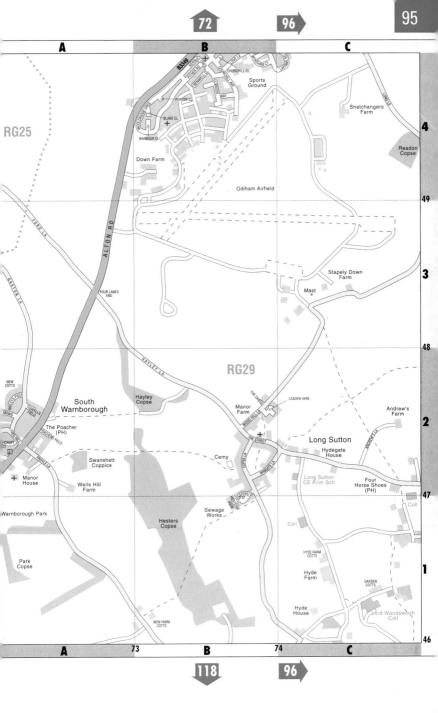

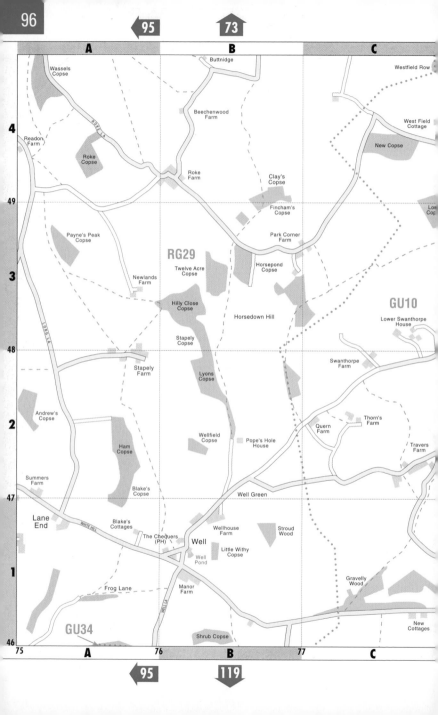

A B C

4

49

3

48

2

47

1

46

Ewshot

Combe
Wood

The
Queens
Arms (PH)

EWSHOT
HILL
CROSS

Redlands
Farm

Warren
Corner

The Warren

Ewshot
Hall

Ewshot
Farm

Dora's Green
Farm

Dora's
Green

GU10

Pond Wood

Pond
Copse

Middle
Old Park

Lower Old
Park

Lower Old
Park Farm

HALF WAY
COTTS

FACTORY
COTTS

Works

BURLES BRIDGE
COTTS

CRONDALL LA

DIPPENHALL RD

Dippenhall

Dippenhall
House

Coxbridge
Farm

Alderley
Farm

Bricksbury
Hill

Chesar's
Camp

Long Bottom

Reservoir

Mast

Water
Tower

Mast

ODIHAM RD

UPPER HALE RD

Hale
Sch

Cemy

Hog Hatch

Folly Hill
Inf Sch

PO

Upper
Old
Park

UPPER OLD PARK LA

GU9

FOLLY HILL

Knowle
Farm

Park Farm

Farnham
Castle
Stables

Claypit
Wood

MIDDLE OLD PK

CH

The
Grange

Farnham
Castle

CASTLE HILL

FARNHAM

The Surrey Inst
of Art & Design

CASTLE FIELD

FRIAR
FIELD

Potters Gate
CE Prim
Sch

WEST ST

Mus

Liby

Millennium
Ctr

Cemy

FARNHAM BY-PASS

Farnham
Bsns Pk

River Wey

1 AMBLESIDE CRES
2 ULLSWATER CL
3 DUKES WLK
4 FOLLY LANE S
5 CHATSWORTH GR
6 WINGS CL

PERRY WAY 1
ST MARKS PL 2
QUEENS CT 3
QUEENS LA 4

A   B   C

A323 A S H R D A323

GU12

Bin
Wood

ASH GREEN LA

ASH
LODGE
DR
BATEMAN GR

Ash Manor
Sch

COMMERCIAL WOODCOTT TERR

KINGS CT

KINGS AVE

St
Michael's
CE Jun
Sch

The Beck
Ind Est

OAK
TREE
CL

OXENDEN
CT

FAIRFAX
EXT

ASH GREEN LA W

Tongham
Mews

THE ELMS

Poyle
Farm

The Connaught
Sch

HAWTHORNE
CL

FIELD WAY
THE
GARDENS

BLENHEIM
CL

GRIEVE
CL

THE CARDINALS

NORTH SIDE

EAST RING

POYLE RD

Tongham

Park
Prim Sch

The Avenue

Aldershot Park

SOUTH SIDE

ST PAUL
CL

Poyle
Farm

49

GU11

Crematorium

ST PAUL
CL

PO

1 ORCHARD RD
2 BRIDGE MEWS
3 GARBETTS WAY

NEW RD

Tongham

Poyle Park

GU9

3

Grange
Farm

MANOR HOUSE
FLATS

Manor
Farm

Manor Farm
Bsns Ctr

Hog's Back
Hotel

A31

West Farm

Hog's
Back

IPSLEY
LODGE

48

A31

The Packhouse

Runfold
Manor

GU10

SANDY
CROSS

SEALE LA

Sand
Pits

MANOR
FIELDS

Seale
Lodge

PUTTENHAM RD

Runfold

WHITEWAYS
END

WOODLANDS

THUNDERY RD

Seale

2

Jolly Farmer
(PH)

GUILDFORD RD

The Park

North Downs Way

Pay
Fi

47

N Downs Way

BINTON LA

Binton
Cottage

Furze Hill

Binton
Farm

Binton
Wood

The Roughs

SANDS RD

CH

Owls Hatch

1

Sandy
Farm

The Sands

LITTLEWORTH RD

Botany
Hill

PO

Barley Mow
(PH)

THE GREEN

The Ridge

BOTANY HILL

46

Soldiers
Ring

Crooksbury
Hill

Surrey STREET ATLAS

Coach
Bottom

87   A   88   B   89   C

101
79

A B C

Shipton Plantation

OLD COACH RD

SNODDINGTON RD

Shipton Wood

4

SP9

Snoddington Down Farm

45

Racedown Farm

RACEDOWN COTTS

3

Snoddington Hill

A3

Thruxton Down House

SP11

44

A303

Thimble Hall

Middlecot House

Thruxton Farm

Thruxton Hill

2

B3084

SP4

Hugh's Settlement

Fairhaven

Cholderton Hill

CHOLDERTON RD

43

Victoria Copse

Windy Dido

Horseshoe Meadow Farm

Curlews

Cholderton Park

1

Coronation Belt

Lodge

Quarley Hill

42

B3084

BRATELEY DRO

24 A 25 B 26 C

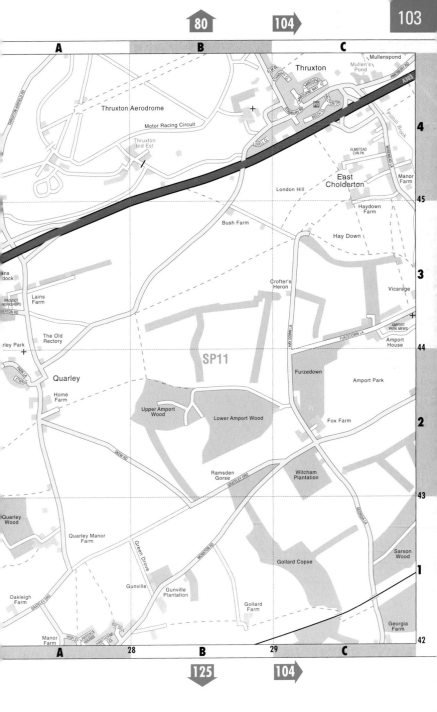

A4
1 WOODPECKERS
2 SPINDLE HO
3 MULBERRY HO
4 THREADNEEDLE HO
5 SWAN CT
6 BLACK SWAN YD

7 ACRE ALMSHOUSES
8 HATHERDEN CL
9 EASTFIELD LODGE
10 GARDEN CT
11 LONGPARISH CT
12 COLD HARBOUR CT
13 LONGSTOCK CT

A4
14 HANOVER HO
15 WESTBROOKE CL
16 WINCHESTER ST
17 PRINCE ALBERT GDNS
18 THE CLOISTERS

105

83

ANDOVER

SP10

Bere Hill

Bere Hill Farm

Iron Bridge

The Grange

Picket Twenty Farm

Lower Farm

Renthall Farm

Cow Down

COWDOWN FARM COTTS

Cowdown Farm Buildings

The Mile House

WINCHESTER RD

Cowdown Farmhouse

COWDOWN LA

Furzy Croft Copse

SP11

Augurs Hill Copse

Clatford Mills

Fourways

BRIEN MEADOWS LA

Manor Farm

CHURCH RD

River Anton

Clatford CE Prim Sch

PH

BARROW HILL

ST ANNES CL

Keepers Cottage

Upping Copse

Harewood Forest

Whitehouse

B3420

B3420

A3057

105

128

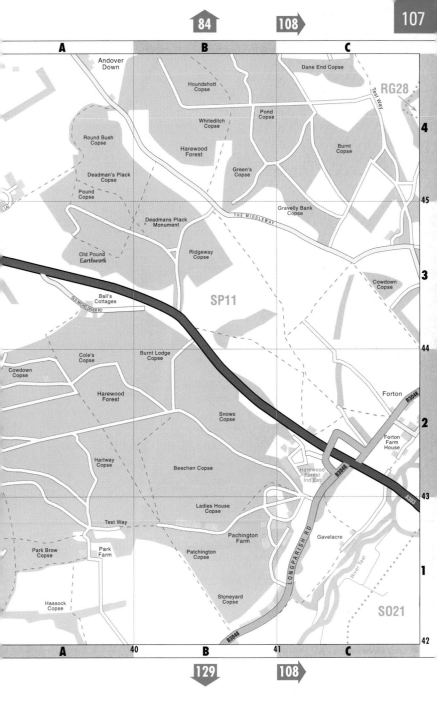

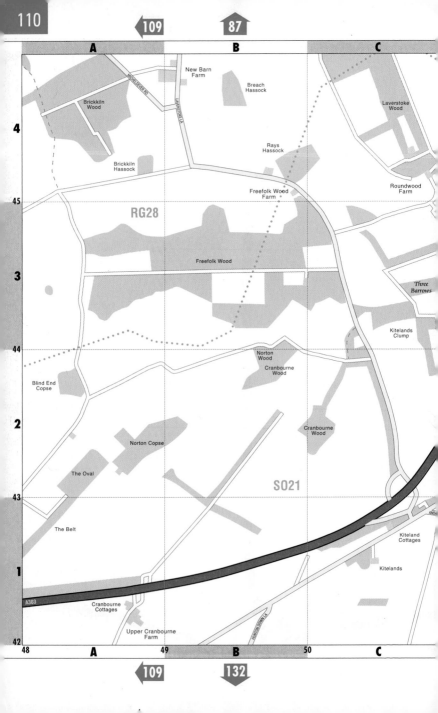

A   B   C

New Barn
Farm

Breach
Hassock

Laverstoke
Wood

Brickkiln
Wood

WINCHESTER RD

LAVERSTOKE LA

4

Rays
Hassock

Brickkiln
Hassock

Roundwood
Farm

Freefolk Wood
Farm

45

RG28

Freefolk Wood

3

Three
Barrows

Kitelands
Clump

44

Norton
Wood

Cranbourne
Wood

Blind End
Copse

Norton Copse

2

Cranbourne
Wood

SO21

The Oval

43

The Belt

ANDO

Kiteland
Cottages

1

Kitelands

A303

Cranbourne
Cottages

HUNTON DOWN LA

Upper Cranbourne
Farm

42

48   A   49   B   50   C

A
B
C

4

45

Village Farm
UP ST
Tower Hill Farm
Manor Farm
Dummer House

Dummer Down Farm

DUMMER DOWN LA

BIBLE FIELDS

Tidley Hill

RG25

Dummer Grange
Grange Copse

Bottom Copse

3

Walker's Copse

Dummer Grange Farm

Wayfarer's Walk

Hogsdown Copse

Hill Copse

44

Popham Down Copse

The Holt

BREACH FARM COTTS

Ewedown Copse
Flockmoor Cottage

Upper Down Copse

Lower Down Copse

Poasley Row

Breach Farm

Poasley Farm

2

Furzedown

Upper Barn Wood

43

SO21

1

Woodmancott Down

Becket's Down

Rucksters

Lilley's Copse

SO24

42

A
58
B
59
C

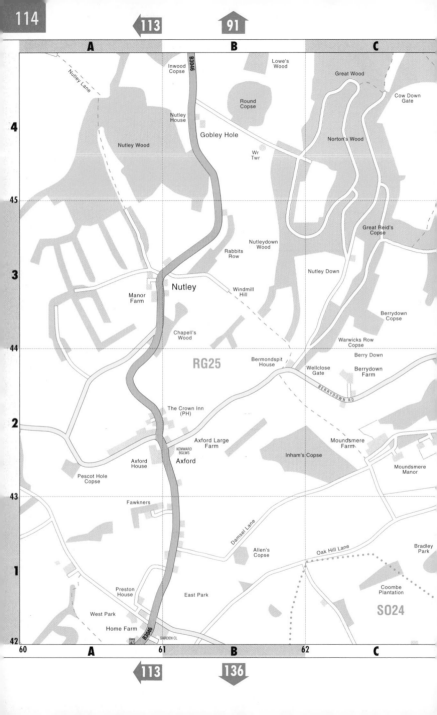

A B C

Nutley Lane

B3046

Inwood Copse

Lowe's Wood

Great Wood

Cow Down Gate

Nutley House

Round Copse

Norton's Wood

4

Nutley Wood

Gobley Hole

Wr Twr

45

Great Reid's Copse

Nutleydown Wood

3

Rabbits Row

Nutley Down

Nutley

Manor Farm

Windmill Hill

Berrydown Copse

Chapell's Wood

Warwicks Row Copse

44

RG25

Bermondspit House

Berry Down

Wellclose Gate

Berrydown Farm

BERRYDOWN RD

The Crown Inn (PH)

2

Axford Large Farm

Moundsmere Farm

KENWARD BGLWS

Axford House

Axford

Inham's Copse

Moundsmere Manor

Pescot Hole Copse

43

Fawkners

Damsel Lane

Allen's Copse

Oak Hill Lane

Bradley Park

1

Preston House

East Park

Coombe Plantation

SO24

West Park

Home Farm

B3046

GARDEN CL

PO

42

60 A 61 B 62 C

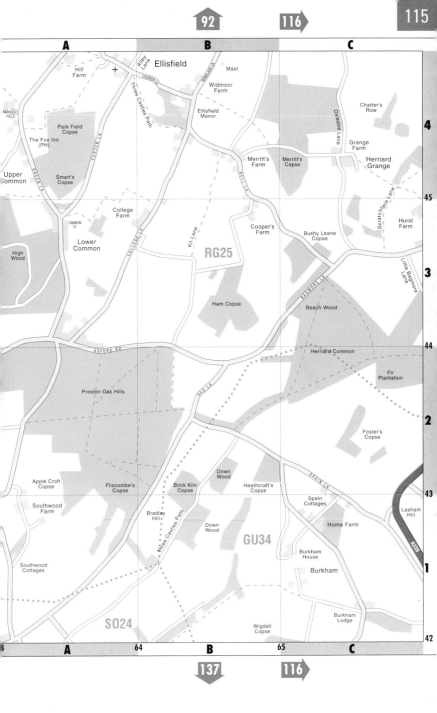

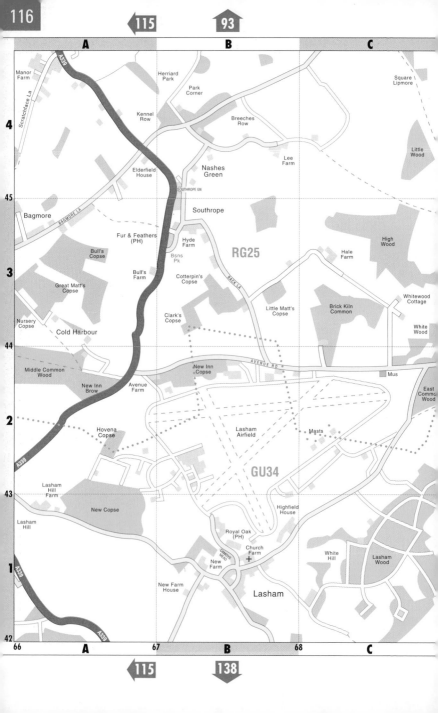

115
93

A **B** **C**

Manor Farm

Scratchface La

A339

Herriard Park

Park Corner

Kennel Row

Breeches Row

4

Square Lipmore

Little Wood

Lee Farm

Elderfield House

Nashes Green

SOUTHROPE GN

45

Bagmore

BAGMORE LA

Southrope

Fur & Feathers (PH)

Hyde Farm

RG25

High Wood

Bull's Copse

Bsns Pk

Hale Farm

3

Great Matt's Copse

Bull's Farm

Cotterpin's Copse

BACK LA

Whitewood Cottage

Nursery Copse

Clark's Copse

Little Matt's Copse

Brick Kiln Common

White Wood

44

Cold Harbour

Middle Common Wood

New Inn Copse

AVENUE RD

Mus

East Common Wood

New Inn Brow

Avenue Farm

2

A339

Hovena Copse

Lasham Airfield

Masts

Lasham Hill Farm

GU34

43

Lasham Hill

New Copse

Highfield House

A339

Royal Oak (PH)

GRANGE MEAD

Church Farm

White Hill

Lasham Wood

1

New Farm

New Farm House

Lasham

42

66 **A** 67 **B** 68 **C**

115
138

117
95

A   **B**   **C**

New Farm

Vinney
Copse

Sheephouse
Copse

4

Pickaxe
Copse

White House
Farm

Highnam
Copse

Sutton
Common

45

RG29

Great
Wood

Gaston
Copse

West
View

Broadlan
Copse

3

Little
Wood

ESSCROFT LA

Hawkins
Wood

Yarnhams
Farm

44

Beech Hangers Lane

Mast

Liddenfield
Copse

Stowell
Copse

Mast

Dicket's
Plantation

Yarnhams
Cottages

Stowell
Cottage

2

Fielders
Copse

Shrub Croft
Copse

Ham Wood

GU34

Masts

43

Spollycombe
Copse

Peakham
Copse

Holybourne
Down

BROCKHAM HILL LA

Brockham Hill
Farm Cottages

Brockham Hill
Barn

1

New Lane

Round
Wood

Howard's
Lane

42

72   **A**   73   **B**   74   **C**

117
140

Cheek's Farm

Grov Far

Willey Copse

Locks Grove

Gasson's Coppice

Highcombes Farm

4

BURY COURT COTTS

Bury Court

Wallfield Copse

Hill Farm

Northbrook Farm

Northbro

45

Perryland

IDLEFIELD COTTS

East Green

╬

Irelands

The Bull Inn (PH)

3

Jenkyn Place

Broadhatch House

Marsh House

GU10

HOLE LA

Welche's House

Bentley

Bentley CE Prim Sch

Turk's Mill

Cotton's Copse

44

THE POLLARDS

SOUTH VIEW COTTS

Bentley Bsns Pk

The Star (PH)

Bentley Ind Ctr

White Bridge

Holt Pound Inclosure

Marelands

South Green Farm

A31

Sewage Works

River Wey

2

Bentley Green Farm

Alice Holt Forest

Forest Wlks

P

Anstey Bridge

P

Bentley

Alice Holt Farm

ALICE HOLT COTTS

43

Isington Close

Alice Holt Lodge

THROWMEAD

GU34

Aldix Copse Farm

Westminster House

Lodge Inclosure

Plain Piece

1

Catham Copse

Broadview Farm

Redcap Copse

Blacknest Ind Pk

A325

42

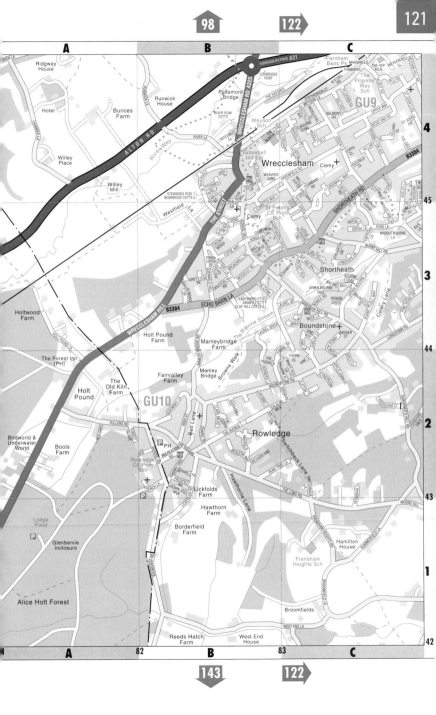

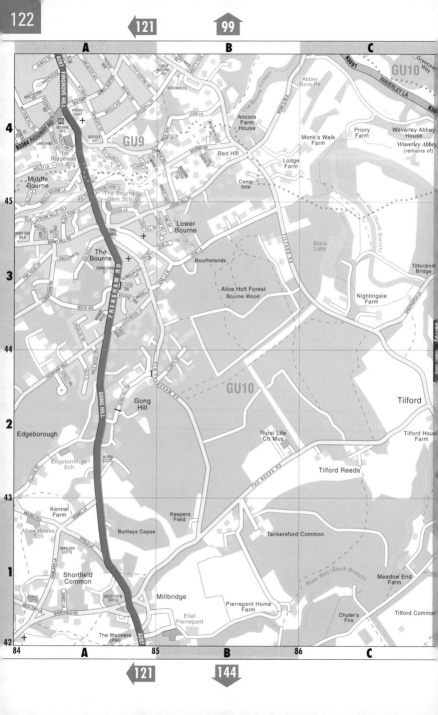

A   B   C

SEARLE RD
GREENHOLS
SHEPHERDS
MOORE DR
FRIGROVE HILL
RIDGWAY RD
A287
OLD PARK
LITTLE AUSTINS RD
GREAT AUSTINS
AUSTEN RD
BOVE AUSTINS

GU10
Greensand Way
B3001
WAVERLEY LA
B3001

GREAT AUSTINS RD
GREENHILLS
LEIGH LA

Abbey
Bsns Pk
The Bourne Stream

PRIORY
CROFT
BOURNE
HTS
AUDLEY
HO

GU9

Ancora
Farm
House

Monk's Walk
Farm

Priory
Farm

Waverley Abbey
House
Waverley Abbey
(remains of)

4

B3384 RIDGWAY RD
LANGHAM
CT
The
Ridgeway
Com Sch
ALDERS RD
VICARY

BOURNE GR

Red Hill

Lodge
Farm

River Wey (North Branch)

Middle
Bourne

POST STREAM FARM CL
The Bourne Com Sch
SCHOOL LA

Camp
Site

45

KILN
ATREAM VALLEY RD
WINSTON
WLK
BURNT HILL RD
LODGE HILL RD

Lower
Bourne

Black
Lake

Tilfordmill
Bridge

The
Bourne

FERNDOWN
DENE CL
DEAN LA

Bournelands

TILFORD RD

3

PINE RIDGE DR
BEECH AVE
FRENSHAM RD
MANOR RD
LADYWOOD RD
DELLAN
THE MINSTEAD
DR
PANSELLS

Alice Holt Forest
Bourne Wood

Nightingale
Farm

GREENHILL LA

44

FRENSHAM VALE
VALE LA
GONG HILL
MANOR RD
FRENSHAM RD

GU10

Tilford

2

Edgeborough

Gong
Hill

Rural Life
Ctr Mus

Tilford House
Farm

Edgeborough
Sch
HEATH
COTTS

Tilford Reeds

43

MOUNE HILL
KENNEL LA
FIELD LA

Kennel
Farm

THE REEDS RD

Keepers
Field

Tankersford Common

More House
Sch
HAMLASH
COTTS
HAMLASH LA

Burtleys Copse

1

GORSE COTTS
SANDY LA
WEST END LA
SHORTFIELD RD

Shortfield
Common

SOUTHVIEW
COTTS

Millbridge

Ellel
Pierrepont

Pierrepont Home
Farm

River Wey (South Branch)

Meadow End
Farm

Chuter's
Firs

Tilford Common

42

84

A

The Mariners
(PH)

A287

85

B

86

C

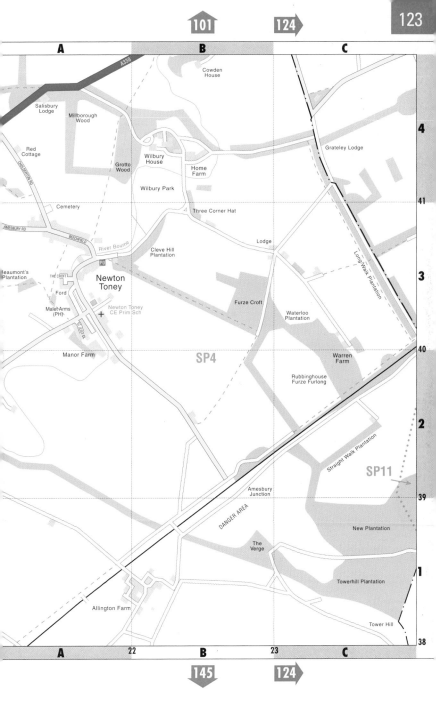

A B C

Cemy
Grateley
Grateley
Prim Sch
Grateley
House Sch
HIGH ST
MORE RD
CHAPEL LA
STATION RD

Georgia
Farm

Great Vinels
Copse

Hurst
Copse

Georgia
Down

Georgia Lane

SP11

Lower Grateley
Wood

Home
Farm

WALLOP RD

Upper Grateley
Wood

Georgia Lane

4

41

OLD STOCKBRIDGE RD

Oklahoma
Farm

3

A1044

Red Lodge
Farm

MT CARMEL RD

ckbarn
Farm

WALLOP RD

40

SO20

Sunnyside
Farm

Poultry
Farm

Park
Farm

KING LA

PARK RD

The Sheiling

2

Craydown

DOWNS RD

CRAYDOWN LA

Works

Mus

39

Poultry
Houses

Tunlands
Farm

A343

tery Drove

KEYHAVEN
COTTS

SYDANE CL

POUND RD

Wallop Brook

APPLETON
CL

Pottery
Farm

KING LANE
COTTS.

GRANGE LA

Northern
Farm

Croft
Farm

PH

Townsend
Farm

STATION RD

Over Wallop

SALISBURY LA

Rosehill
Farm

B3084

A343

Middle Wallop
Airfield

1

38

A 28 B 29 C

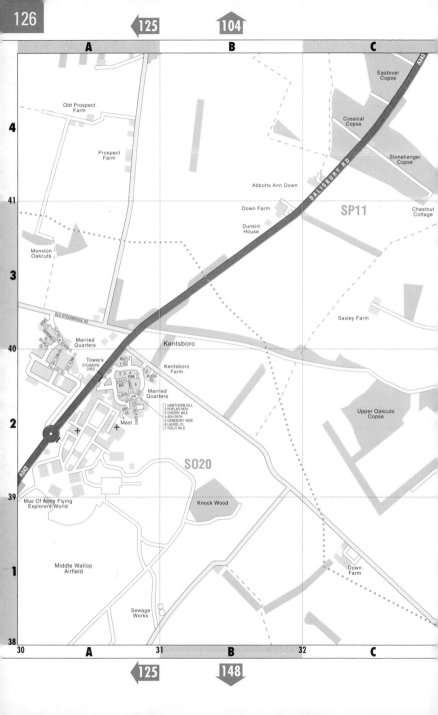

125
104

A   B   C

A343

Eastover
Copse

Old Prospect
Farm

Cossical
Copse

4

Prospect
Farm

Stonehanger
Copse

SALISBURY RD

Abbotts Ann Down

41

Down Farm

SP11

Chestnut
Cottage

Dunkirt
House

Monxton
Oakcuts

3

Saxley Farm

OLD STOCKBRIDGE RD

Married
Quarters

40

Kentsboro

Towers
SYCAMORE
CRES

MAPLE
CL

Kentsboro
Farm

PINE CL

BEECH
CL

BIRCH
AVE

LARCH
RD

Married
Quarters

ELM CL

OAK

1 HAWTHORN HILL
2 POPLAR PATH
3 CHERRY WLK
4 ASH PATH
5 DANEBURY VIEW
6 LAUREL PL
7 HOLLY WLK

Upper Oakcuts
Copse

2

Mast

SO20

A343

39

Mus Of Army Flying
Explorers World

Knock Wood

Down
Farm

1

Middle Wallop
Airfield

Sewage
Works

38

30   A   31   B   32   C

125
148

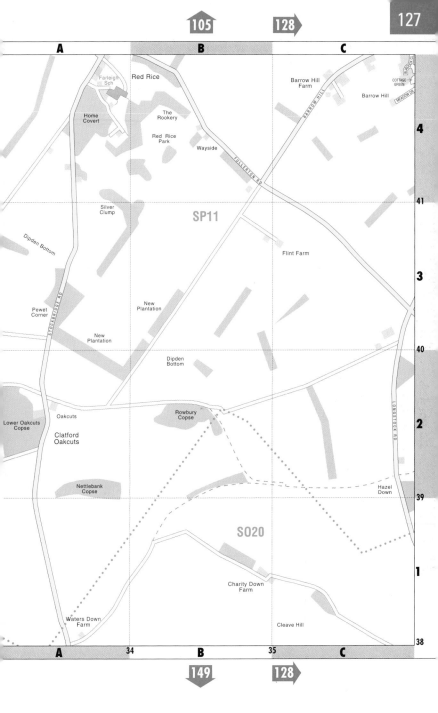

SO21

SP11

Bransbury
Common

LONGPARISH RD

B3048

River Dever

Dublin
Farm

B3420

Wherwell
Prim Sch

River Test

4

41

Lodge

WINCHESTER RD

Priory

Manor
House

Newton
Stacey

3

Manor
House

Manor
Farm

WINCHESTER RD

GRAVELHILL
COTTS

Gravelhill
Farm

Gravel
Hill

40

WINCHESTER RD

ROOM
COTTS

PADDOCK FIELD

Abbots
Mitre
(PH)

PO

Chilbolton

SO20

2

EASTMANS FIELD

DROVE RD

MARTINS LN

39

B3420

BIRCH DR

Aerial
Farm

Radio
Telescope

Radio & Space
Field Station

Middlebarn
Farm

Drift Road

1

Water
Tower

THIRT WAY

Camp
(disused)

38

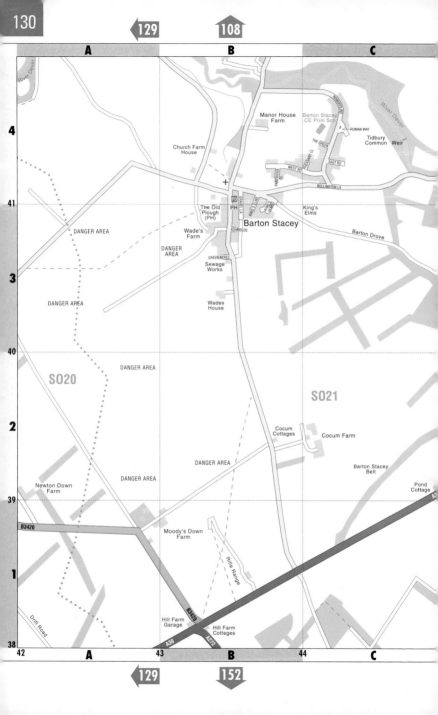

A B C

4

River Dever

Manor House Farm

Barton Stacey CE Prim Sch

NURSERY RD

Roman Way

Tidbury Common Weir

River Dever

Church Farm House

THE GREEN

WEST RD PLEASANT CL

EAST RD

PARTRIDGE CL

41

BULLINGTON LA

The Old Plough (PH)

PH

DANIEL LA

GREAT ELMS

ORCHARD CL

SCHOOL RD

Barton Stacey

King's Elms

ASHFIELDS

Barton Drove

DANGER AREA

Wade's Farm

DANGER AREA

GREEN ACRES

Sewage Works

3

DANGER AREA

Wades House

40

DANGER AREA

SO20

SO21

2

Cocum Cottages

Cocum Farm

DANGER AREA

Barton Stacey Belt

DANGER AREA

Pond Cottage

Newton Down Farm

39

B3420

Moody's Down Farm

1

Rifle Range

Drift Road

B3420

Hill Farm Garage

A30

A272

Hill Farm Cottages

38

42 A 43 B 44 C

A303
A34
A30

Upper Bullington

4

Manor
Farm

Bullington
Manor

Bullington
Bridge

Church
Farm

Watercress
Beds

Lower
Bullington

NORTON
COTTS

41

Norton
Farm

Strouds

Manor
Farm

Church Hill Trees

Watercress
Beds

Norton Manor

BULLINGTON LA

Norton
Lake

Cranbourne
Grange

Hill Barn

Grove Hill

3

Barton
acey Belt

Holly Tree
Farm

SO21

Egypt

Barton Drove

Bogmoor

MANOR

Service
Area

Service
Area

Brightlands

40

Wonston
Grange

Cranbourne
Lodge

PIGEONHOUSE
COTTS

River Dever

BY PASS RD

HOLLY TREE PK
SUTTON PK

BACK STREET

THE
BEECHES

MILLERS YD

1
2

HUNTON LA

STOCKBRIDGE RD

PO

3
4

GRATTON

Wonston
Farm

PH

Wonston

2

Naomi
Ho

Sutton
Manor

5
6

Manor Farm
House

WONSTON LA

HUNTON LA

MARKET LA

MOORCROFT
CL

BOOK SQUARE

WINCHESTER RD

NEW COTTS 1
WHEELERS YARD 2
THE SQUARE 3
WHITE SWAN CT 4
GARDEN CT 5
NEW CT 6

Sutton Scotney

Wonston
House

Upton
House

Sutton Manor
Farm

39

MANOR FARM
COTTS

Pipers
Hill

Manor
Cottage

1

WONSTON LA

Wonston
Manor
Farm

A34

38

A **B** **C**

4

Hunton Down Farm

Victoria Cottages

Counsellor's Walk

41

Hunton Grange Farm

Weston Down Cottages

New Cottages

Chestnut Villas

3

Northbrook House

Norsebury Ring

Hunton Manor Farm

40

SO21

Hunton

Hunton Manor

Norsebury Farm

Lower Norsebury

Norsebury House

Northbrook

NORTHBROOK

HUNTON LA

Norsebury Cottages

Weston Colley

2

Weston Colley

River Dever

Weston Farm

Michaels

Stoke Charity

PO

39

Borough Farm

OLD STOKE RD

WESTON DOWN RD

HUNTON DOWN LA

1

38

48 49 50

A **B** **C**

A
B
C

Black Wood

Works

LUNWAY ST FARM RD

A33

4

Parkhill
Farm

M3

41

Middle
Lodge

Shepherd's
Close

West
Stratton

Stratton
Park

The Bothy

3

Northbrook House
Lodge

West Stratton
Farm

Stratton
End

Northbrook
Dairy

Winchester
Lodge

CHURCH BANK RD

40

SO21

Chapel Ave

Highways
Cottages

Northbrook

Cowdown
Wood

Micheldever

2

Cowdown
Farm

Highways

New
Farm

RYE LANE RD

SOUTHBROOK

DEVER CL

1 LANE END BARNS
2 MEADOW VIEW
3 SOUTHBROOK COTTS

Manor
Farm

Micheldever
CE Prim Sch

P

Highways
Nursery

South Down La

39

DUKE ST

1 2 3

CHURCH LA

Half Moon &
Spread Eagle
(PH)

South
Down

LADYCROFT CL

Cole's
Barn

WINCHESTER RD

Dodsley
Wood

1

SO24

Micheldever
Wood

Folly
Wood

A33

M3

38

A
52
B
53
C

Butcher's
Copse

133
112

A B C

Biddles Wood

Black Wood

A33

M3

Embley Wood

4

Lone Farm

Stratton Park

41

Whiteway Farm

The Cowleys

Stratton House

Norn's Copse

SO21

Well House Copse

3

Cross

Candover Copse

PO

CHURCH BANK

East Stratton

CHURCH BARNS

40

Hazely Copse

Foxhill

East Stratton Farm

The Plough Inn

NEW FARM RD

STREET RD

BARING DL

SO24

2

Thorny Down Wood

Burnt House Copse

Black Hut Copse

OXDELLA

Duke's Copse

STRATTON LA

NORTHINGTON CNR

39

Totford Copse

South Down Lane

South Down

Burcot Farm

1

Dodsley Wood

Wayfarer's W

38

54 A 55 B 56 C

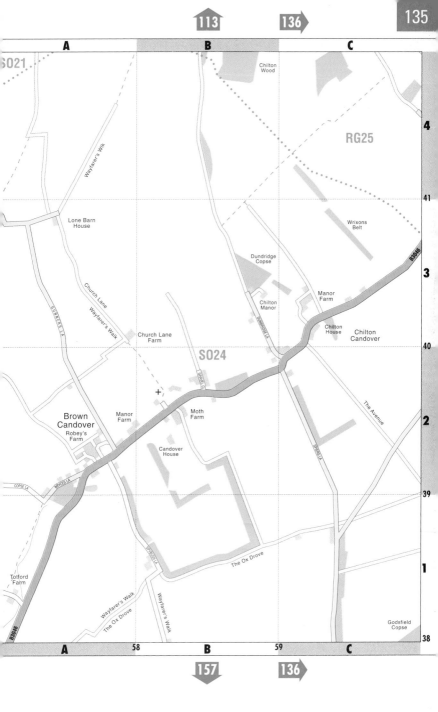

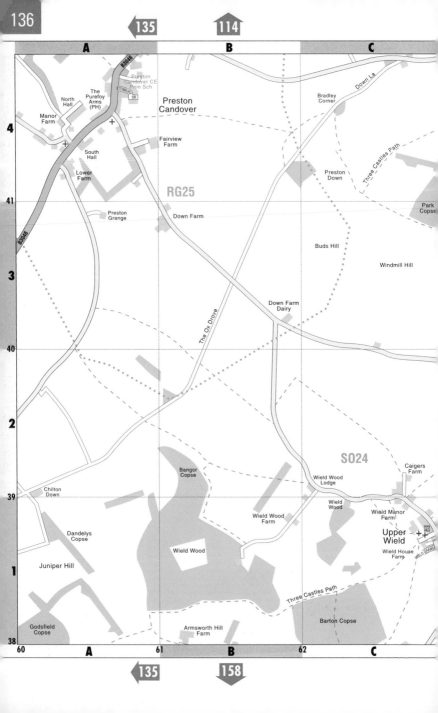

135
114

A **B** **C**

B3046

Preston Candover CE Prim Sch

STENBAC DR

North Hall

The Purefoy Arms (PH)

Manor Farm

South Hall

Lower Farm

Preston Candover

Fairview Farm

Bradley Corner

Down La

4

Three Castles Path

Preston Down

RG25

Preston Grange

Down Farm

Park Copse

41

B3046

Buds Hill

Windmill Hill

3

Down Farm Dairy

40

The Ox Drove

2

Bangor Copse

SO24

Wield Wood Lodge

Caigers Farm

Chilton Down

39

Wield Wood

Wield Manor Farm

Dandelys Copse

Wield Wood Farm

Upper Wield

Juniper Hill

Wield Wood

Wield House Farm

WIELD GRANGE

1

Godsfield Copse

Three Castles Path

Armsworth Hill Farm

Barton Copse

38

60 **A** 61 **B** 62 **C**

135
158

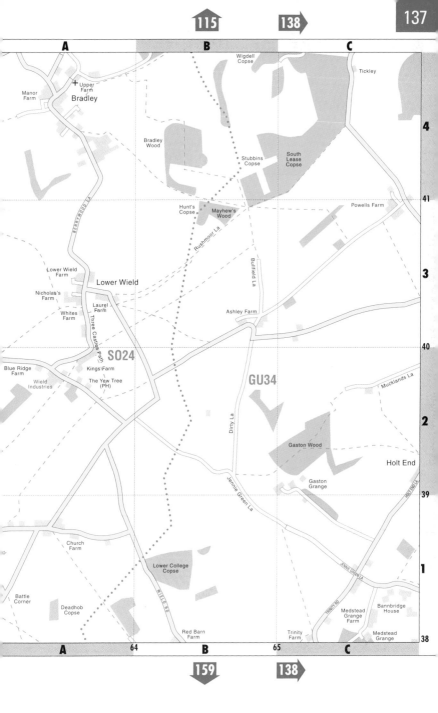

A   **B**   **C**

Wigdell Copse

Tickley

Manor Farm

Upper Farm

Bradley

4

Bradley Wood

Stubbins Copse

South Lease Copse

41

Hunt's Copse

Mayhew's Wood

Powells Farm

Rushmoor La

Bullfield La

Lower Wield Farm

Lower Wield

3

Nicholas's Farm

Laurel Farm

Ashley Farm

Whites Farm

Three Castles Path

40

SO24

Blue Ridge Farm

Kings Farm

Wield Industries

The Yew Tree (PH)

GU34

Mucklands La

Dirty La

2

Gaston Wood

Holt End

Jennie Green La

Gaston Grange

39

Church Farm

Lower College Copse

1

Battle Corner

Deadhob Copse

Medstead Grange Farm

Bannbridge House

Trinity Farm

Medstead Grange

Red Barn Farm

38

A   64   **B**   65   **C**

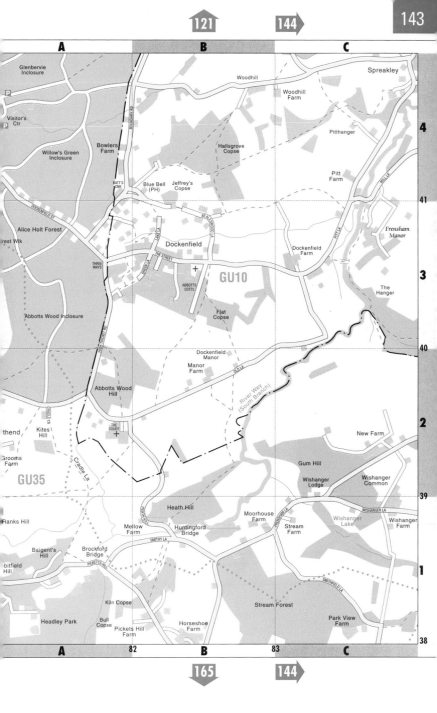

143
122

A **B** **C**

Millbridge

Spreakley

Lane
End

River Wey

PRIORY LA

A287

P

Chuter's
Cottage

River Wey (South Branch)

4

St Mary's
COTTS

MILL LA

THE STREET

COTTS LA

FRASER

THE
GRANGE

St Mary's
CE Inf Sch

Frensham
Little Pond

GRANGE RD

W BELLSHOUSE

Frensham

41

Frensham Common
(National Trust)

CARLING

WELLESLEY RD

LOWICKS RD

3

P

P

Frensham
Country Park

Mon

Lowicks

Gray Walls

Lowicks
House

SANDY LA

Frensham
Great
Pond

GU10

The Flashes

40

Hotel

POND LA

Crosswater
Farm

St
Ju

FRENSHAM LA

BACON LA

2

Hales
Copse

Furze
Hill

Churt
House

CROSSWATER LA

Crosswater

Churt
Common

The
Devil's Jumps

JUMPS RD

Churt Lea

39

WISHANGER LA

Symondstone
Farm

SYMONDSTONE LA

Buttermilk Hill

WAYSIDE
COTTS

TILFORD HILL

STAR HILL

Silverbeck
Farm

JUMPS RD

Old Kiln
Farm

CROFTANGE LA

CARLING CT

1

GU35

Park La

CAMPDOWN LA

OLD KILN RD

+

St Johns
CE Inf Sch

OLD KILN RD

PO

PH

Crossways

HALE HOUSE
FIELDS

Hale House

THE MEADOW

CHURT RD
A287

EDDYSTONE
CT

HALE HOUSE LA

Green Cross
Farm

Avalon

HIGH PARK RD

SANDY LANE

GREEN CROSS
CTS

DRIFT LANE

GREEN LA

Green Cross

CROSSWAYS

CHURT RD
A287

JOBS LANE

CROSSWAYS

38

84 **A** **85** **B** **86** **C**

143
166

A   B   C

Tower

Tower Hill

4

Boscombe Down
East

No Man's
Land

DANGER
AREA

37

Sports
Gd

SP4

Forty Acre
Plantation

Idmiston

3

Idmiston
Down

Blake's Firs

36

Moll Harris's
Clump

Easton Down

Porton
Down

2

SP5

Easton Down
Farm

A30

Winterslow
Firs

35

The
Pheasant
Hotel

1

Refuse
Tip

Lower Barn

A30 Salisbury   Midwinter

34

A   22   B   23   C

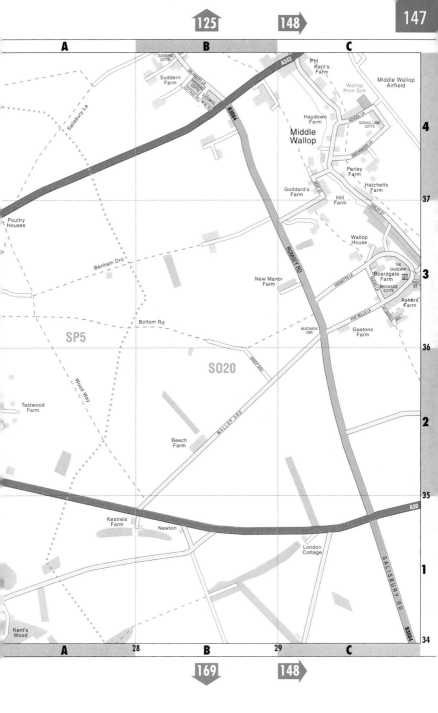

A B C

4

The Turret

Blackstake
Hill

CHURCH RD

VERLYNCH
COTTS

New
Buildings

Cemy

37

Longstock

Brocks
Farm

3

Saddler's
Plantation

Lower Manor
Farm

36

Houghton Down

SOUTHSIDE
COTTS

River Test

SO20

Mill

2

Windyridge

Meon Hill

Stockbridge

Meon Hill
Farm

Windover
Farm

Stockbridge
Prim Sch

Houghton Down
Farm

ROMAN RD

HIGH ST

PO TH

35

WESSEX
MEWS

TRAFALGAR

THE
MILSONS

Test Valley
Sch

Manor
Farm

1

North Houghton

Saxon Farm

Test Way

Common
Marsh

Sewage
Works

Homestead
Farm

North Houghton
Farm

Marshcourt River

34

A 34 B 35 C

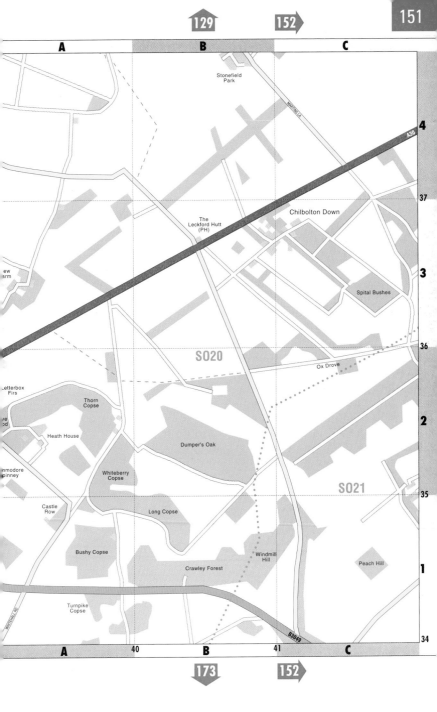

129
152

A   B   C

Stonefield
Park

MARTINS LA

A30

4

37

The
Leckford Hutt
(PH)

Chilbolton Down

ew
arm

3

Spital Bushes

SO20

36

Ox Drove

Letterbox
Firs

Thorn
Copse

ve
od

2

Heath House

Dumper's Oak

nmodore
pinney

Whiteberry
Copse

SO21

35

Castle
Row

Long Copse

Bushy Copse

Windmill
Hill

Peach Hill

1

Crawley Forest

Turnpike
Copse

WHITEHALL RD

B3049

34

A   40   B   41   C

173
152

A B C

4 A30

Brockley
Cottages

Hill Farm

Dead Marrs Belt

A30

Barton Stacey Belt

A272

Barton Stacey Belt

SO20

37

Barton
Ashes

Crawley Down

3

Brockley Warren

Ox Drove

Crawley
Clump

36

SO21

Warren
Wood

2

Warren
Cottages

35

VESTA

CRICKET CL

New
Barn

NEW BARN
COTTS

Crawley
Court

CRAWLEY
COTTS

Crawley

1

Cemy

Fox & Hounds
(PH)

Rack
Belt

Morns
Field

Beeches
Farm

34

42 A 43 B 44 C

ton Down
Farm

Sutton Down
Cottages

Wonston New
Buildings

WINSTON LA

A34

4

West Stoke
Farm

37

Larkwhistle
Farm

South Wonston
Farm

Stainers Lane

3

Sanctuary
Farm

ALRESFORD DRO

Bayley's
Clump

SO21 South Wonston

CHRISTMAS HILL

MANSON
STAVEDOWN RD

GROVE
GROVE CL

ORCHARD RD
ORCHARD
ICU

DOWNLANDS WAY

WALNUT
TREE CL

LOWER RD

DOWNS RD

WRIGHTS CL
WRIGHTS WAY

South Wonston
Prim Sch

DOWN CHERRY CL

CHURCH CL

ST STEPHENS
CL

GOLDFINCH WAY

NORTHDOWN CL
NORTHBROOK CL

WEST HILL RD S

DUNCAN CL

DORMAN
WAY

ANDERS RD

ARMSTRONG
CL

1 PADDOCK CL
2 HORNBEAM CL
3 SPRUCE CL

36

OX DRO

Wr Twr

Little
Grove

Worthy
Grove

Worthy
Down

Race Course
Cottages

2

RILEY RD

35

Worthy Down Camp

BLACKBERRY

TREES RD

MAL PASS

COATE DR

BURNE

COOPERS
CL

OXHAM CL

COWLEY
DR

CONNAUGHT RD

PO

Gallop

1

SO22

SO23

34

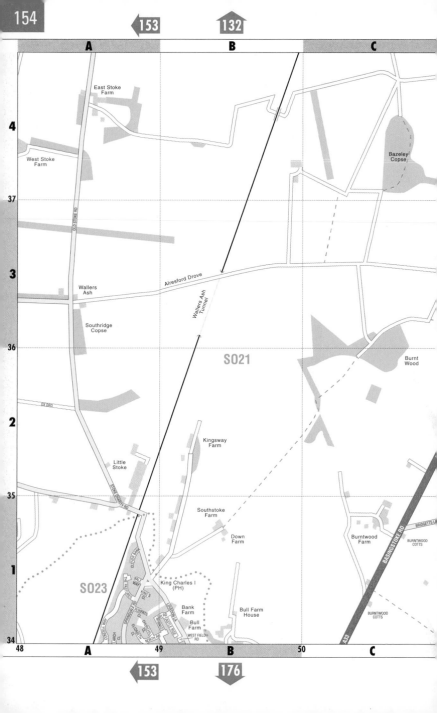

153
132

A
B
C

4

East Stoke
Farm

West Stoke
Farm

Bazeley
Copse

37

OLD STOKE RD

3

Wallers
Ash

Alresford Drove

Wallers Ash Tunnel

Southridge
Copse

Burnt
Wood

36

SO21

OX DRO

2

Kingsway
Farm

Little
Stoke

35

STOKE CHARITY RD

Southstoke
Farm

Down
Farm

Burntwood
Farm

BRIDGETTS LA

BASINGSTOKE RD

BURNTWOOD
COTTS

1

SO23

THE PADDOCK

CLOSE

VAL WAY

KING'S RD

King Charles I
(PH)

Bank
Farm

Bull Farm
House

Bull
Farm

Bull
Farm

SPRINGVALE TERRENTS

CASTLE RD

A33

BURNTWOOD
COTTS

34

LARCH CL

KENNEL LA

NORTH RD

WEST FIELD
RD

48
A
49
B
50
C

153
176

A   B   C

4

37

3

2

36

35

1

34

WINCHESTER RD

A33

M3

BASINGSTOKE RD

Newdown Farm

Alresford Dro

Micheldever Wood

Long Wlk

Mill Lane Copse

SO24

Archaeological Trail

Hassock Copse

SO21

CHILLANDHAM LA

Winchester Services (North)

Itchen Wood

Shroner Wood

Shroner Wood House

Shroner Hill Farm

Winchester Services (South)

Courtney's Copse

The Scrubbs

Rutherley Copse

Chillandham Farm

CHILLANDHAM LA

BRIDGETS LA

Bridget's Farm

Lone Farm

M3

A   52   B   53   C

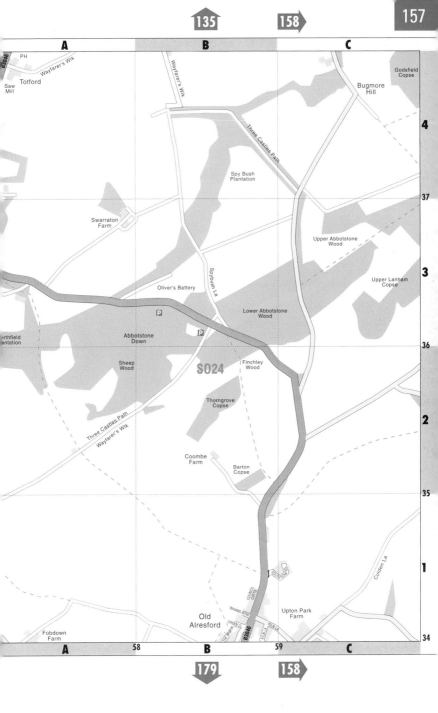

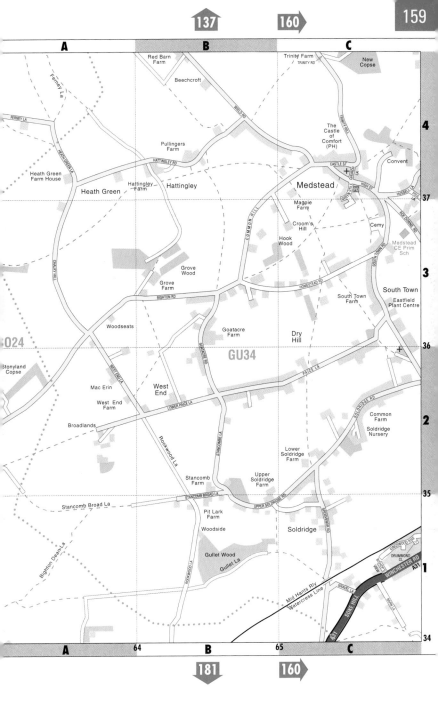

159
138

A   **B**   **C**

Meadow View Farm

Redwood Farm

Jennie Green La

Wheelers Rd

Kings La

The Abbey

Bushy Leaze Wood

Cemy

Redwood

Mast

Brickups La

Abbey Rd

Old Park Farm

4

Redwood Poultry Farm

Russell La

Spruce Copse

The Hassock

Lodge Hill

37

Foul La

Down Copse

Chawton Park Wood

Chawton Park Bungalow

Brickiln La

Roe Downs Farm

High Wood

Bricklin Farm

3

Roe Downs Rd

Roedowns Cottage

Redhill Copse

Gibbet Copse

GU34

Red Hill Farm

Red Hill

P Wr Twr · Mast

Boyneswood Cl

Firtree Copse

36

Five Ash Rd

Beechlands Rd

Eighteen Acre Plantation

Fourteen Acre Plantation

Mid Hants Rly Watercress Line

The Dene

Beverley Farm

Estevan Farm

Boyneswood La

Houghton's Piece

New Copse

2

Lymington Bottom Rd

Woodlea Farm

Works

Medstead & Four Marks

Chawton Park Cl

Weathermore Copse

Weathermore La

Dell Piece

Works

PH

Winchester Rd

Lymington Barn Ind Est.

Station App

Station Rd

Oakgreen Par

Mulberry Cl

Blackberry Cl

Weathermore La

35

Lymington Cl

Pingle Rd

Thirlmere Cl

Semaphore Farm

Pie Far

A31

Penwick Way

Gloucester Cl

St Faith Cl

Red Field

Boxmoor Cl

St Albans Cl

Blackberry Cl

Battles Copse

1

Greenways Farm

Lymington Bottom

Four Marks

Alton La

Garden Ctr

Brightstone La

Thornham La

Kitcombe La

Deachers La

Budgetts Farm

Willis Farmhouse

Willis La

Crofters Farm

CH

34

159
182

161
140

A   **B**   **C**

East
Worldham

Westbrook
Grange

Trencheaunts

Drove
Cottages

Man
Far

B3006

Hamble Pits
Copse

Water La

4

Whitehouse
Farm

Wild Duck
Copse

Caker Stream

West
Worldham

Derby's
Dell

Manor
Farm

West Worldham
Farm

37

Copse
Close

Little Wood
Copse

Hartley
Mauditt

3

Barleywood
Farm

Round
House

Old
Elm

Hartley Park

Hartley Mauditt
Village

Hartley
Pond

SELBORNE RD

GU34

36

Hartley Park
Farm

2

Windmill
Cottages

Wick Hill
Cottages

Milking
Hanger

Frenchmare
Copse

Norton Farm

Long Copse

35

HALL LA

Fielder's
Farm

Hangers Way

1

Noar
Copse

Bush Down

Long
Lythe

Noar
Plantation

Nine
Acres

Oakhanger Stream

Dorton

B3006

GOSLINGS
CROFT

34

72   **A**   73   **B**   74   **C**

161
184

Smiths Farm

Oaklands Farm

B3004   GREEN ST

Lode Farm

B3004   FORGE RD

King John's Hill

Park Farm Cottage

Baker's Farm

Kingsley Stream

Willow Plantation

Ash Plantation

4

Woodland Farm

Binswood

Rookery Farm

Warner's Wood

37

Binswood Cottage

Pheasant Wood

P

Shortheath Pond

New Buildings

Binswood Farm

Sherwood House

Shortheath Common

3

Park Hanger

Waterside Cottage

+

Shortheath

+

GU35

Binswood View Bsns Ctr

GU34

Hangers Way

Hartley Wood

Hartleywood Farm

The Red Lion (PH)

Oakhanger

Binsbrook

36

Candovers

LONG FIELD

Oakhanger Stream

Wick Hill Hanger

2

Wick Hill Farm

Oakhanger Farm

Slab

Chapel Farm

Wick Wood

35

Latchford Copse

Pond Cottages

Priory Farm

Southlands

Coombe Wood

1

Blackland Plantation

Rhode Farm

Rhode Copse

HONEY LA

Works

GU33

Albury Farm

34

◄ 163   ▲ 142

A   B   C

4

37

3

GU35

36

2

BORDON

35

1

34

78   **A**   79   **B**   80   **C**

◄ 163   ▼ 186

B1
1 WISTERIA DR
2 OAK LODGE
3 SHAFTESBURY CT
4 ASHLEY HO
5 COOPER HO
6 JOHN POUNDS HO
7 CONNAUGHT CL
8 BLUE TIMBERS CL
9 BEDFORD CL
10 NORTHUMBERLAND RD
11 OVERDALE PL
12 TWOWAYS CT
13 WITTCOMBE TERR
14 PELHAM CL

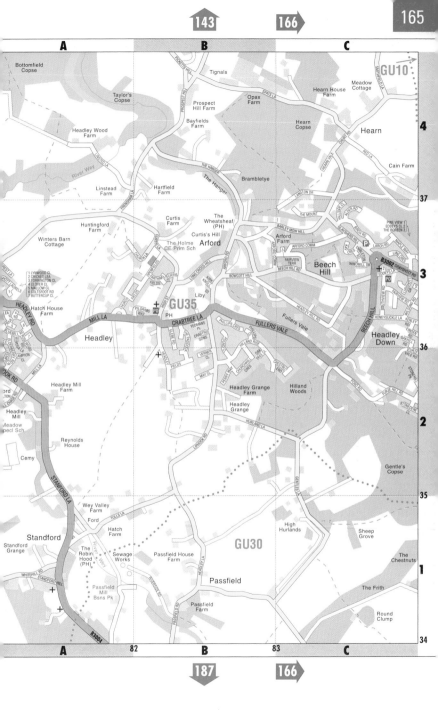

A3 Guildford

GREEN LA

Valley Farm

Hyde Hill

GU10

Gravel Hanger

Marchants Hill

4

Beacon Hill

Marchants Hill Activity Ctr

Highcomb Copse

GU8

Greensand Way

Highcomb Bottom

LIGHT ACRES

37

BONALLACK DR

DRUCE LN

HELYNDE

CRICKET DE

GLEN COURT

HEATH COTTS

LIMESIDE S

PH

Twizzletwig

Meml

YH

Highcombe Farm

Beacon Hill Cem Sch

PALLISER CT

PH

Hotel

HIGHCROFT

WOOD RD

TRIMMERS WOOD

The Beacon

Hindhead Common

3

CHURT RD

HAMPTON TERR

WILLIAMS RD

RIDGEWAY CL

Devil's Punch Bowl

PORTSMOUTH RD

GU26

THIRLSTONE CT

Hindhead

MEAD RD

Golden Valley

Hindhead Commons Nature Trail

36

HIGHFIELD GDNS

ROYAL PAR

PO

P

Meml

P

Whitmore Vale Farm

1 THE KINGS PEACE
2 BEACON VIEW HO
3 THE SQUARE
4 OAKLEA HO
5 ROCKDALE HO
6 THE GABLES
7 SUMMERHOUSE CT
8 WOOLMER VIEW
9 OAK HO
10 HURSTMERE HO

LONDON RD

Hotel

P

Hind Head

P

WHITMORE VALE WOOD LA

GLEN RD

HAZELMERE CT

10

TAHN AV

RUSSELL CT 1
HEATHER CT 2
BROOM SQUIRES 3
HINDMEAD HO 4

TYNDALLS EST

GU27

CHURCH LA

PH

HEADLEY RD

Border Mews

Liby

B3002

Tyndalls Wood

2

ST AUSTINS

CROSTHWAY

St Edmunds Sch

FORESTDALE RD

THE MOORINGS

STONEY BOTTOM

PORTSMOUTH RD

MOWATT RD

THE ROMANS

Nutcombe Down

35

KINGSWOOD FIRS

Kingswood Firs

KINGSWOOD LA

KINGSWOOD FIRS

KINGSWOOD

Nutcombe Valley

HINDHEAD RD

HAZEL GN

Greensand Way

Royal Sch

Mount Ivernia

The Royal Jun Sch

Nutcombe

1

Chasemoor

HIGH PITFOLD

R287

Craig's Wood

Amesbury Sch

SANDY L

Coombswell Copse

STORTLEY HOLLOW

Haslemere

A3

High Pitfold Farm

34

146

190

SP5

East Winterslow

Red La

Hill Farm

Cooper's Farm

Middle Winterslow

THE CAUSEWAY

MILL LA

STONE CL

WEAVERS CL

PADDOCK

COUNCIL RD

SCARLET

THE PLANTERY

GUNVILLE RD

QUEENS CL

PO

COMMON VALE

WESTON LA

PH

THE COMMON

Robin Hill Farm

EASTON COMMON HILL

The Common

WITT RD

TYTHERLEY RD

Yarmley Farm

BENTLEY WAY

Witt's End

Howe Copse

Ramshill House

Ramshill Dro

Noad's Copse

Burretts Grove

Earthpits Wood

Warren Farm

Birchen Copse

The Monarch's Way

Clarendon Way

Upper Noad's Copse

Lower Noad's Copse

Little Buckholt Farm

Elevage Breton

Richwellsted Copse

Picked Copse

Smokeway Copse

Three Sisters Copse

Hedgemoor Copse

Tanglewood

Gravel Shoot Copse

Home Farm

Chickard Wood

Hooping Oak Copse

Bentley Wood

Park La

Prior's Copse

Northaw Sch

Coalpits Copse

Beechways Copse

Redman's Gore

Park Copse

Wiltshire STREET ATLAS

147
170

A   B   C

Khyber Pass
Plantation

Broughton Down
Farm

SALISBURY
RD

B3084

Nutley
Farm

4

Horseshoe
Hill

Horseshoe
Wood

Broughton Down

Bullock's
Hole

Whiteshoot Road

Long Row

Whiteshoot
Hill

Whiteshoot
Plantation

SO20

33

Round
Hat

Nature Reserve

Smith's
Plantation

shen
opse

The Turret

3

Hassock

Clarendon Way

The Monarch's Way

Buckholt
Farm

Vithy
opse

32

SP5

YEW TREE LA

Woodlease
Copse

2

Newmans Barn
Farm

Tails

Ppg Sta

31

NORTH LA

Stride's
Rows

Stanfield
Copse

1

West
Tytherley

Stud
Farm

RECTORY HILL

PRAGNELLS
COTTS

BEALE'S CT

PH

Village
Farm

THE WITHIES

Gray's
Copse

Grays

Redhills
Copse

30

A   28   B   29   C

191
170

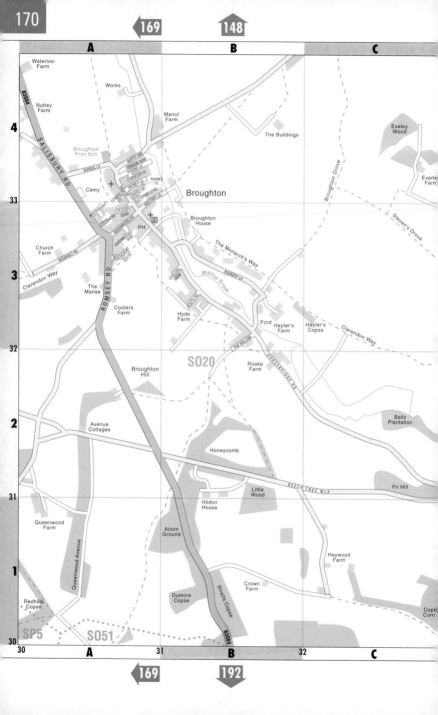

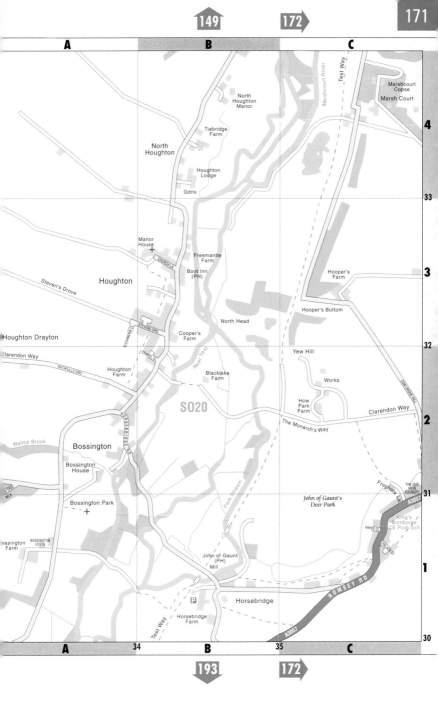

A   B   C

Whitehall

North Park
Farm

Windovers

4

Marshcourt
Farm

North Park
Wood

Winter Down
Copse

33

Somborne
Park

Little
Somborne

3

Park
Farm

New Lease
Farm

32

SO20

CHALK HILL

Chalkvale
Cottage

CHALK VALE

New
Farm

NEW LA

2

Cemy

OLD FROMANS
FARM

Recn
Gd

Manor
Farm

STOCKBRIDGE RD

A3057

Ashley
Manor
Farm

Ashley

OLD VICARAGE LA

WINCHESTER RD

Ashley
Glebe
Farm

31

PO

Ashley
Manor

OLD PALMERS

King's
Somborne

Allot
Gdns

1

THE GORRINGE

HUMBERS VIEW

LUDLOW CL

SOPWITH
CL

Clarendon Way

Ashley
New
Buildings

Bricklin
Drove

LUDLOW RD

LUCKSBRIDGE RD

30

36   37   38

A   B   C

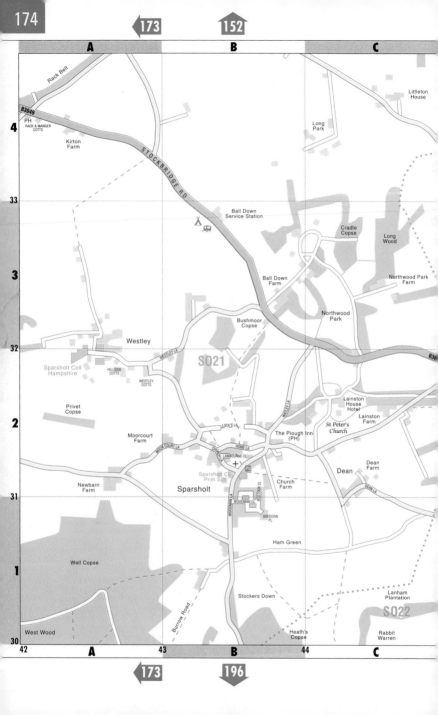

A   B   C

4

Meadow
Farm

Springvale

Cemy
1 GILLINGHAM CL
2 CEDARWOOD

33

Woodhams
Farm

A34

Kings Worthy
Prim Sch

Prince's Mead
Sch

B30

Kings
Worthy

Worthy
Park

B3047

3

Headbourne
Worthy

Abbots
Worthy

Worthy Park
Home Farm

Upper
Farm

Lower
Farm

32

Foresters
Pk

Pudding
House
Farm

Easton
Down

SO21

SO23

Three Castles Path
Itchen Way

Dairy
Farm

Lone
Barn

2

SO22

Abbots
Barton
House

Kings Way
Nuns Wk

River Itchen

Winnall
Cottage Farm

31

Abbotts
Barton

Abbots Barton
Farm House

Shoulder of Mutton
Farm

1

WINCHESTER

North Walls
Recn
Gd

The
Wykeham
Ind Est

SPITFIRE LINK

Hyde
River Park
L Ctr

Chaucer
Ind Est

Dykes
Farm

Superstore

Winnall
Trad Est

Winnall Down
Copse

30

48 A 49 B 50 C

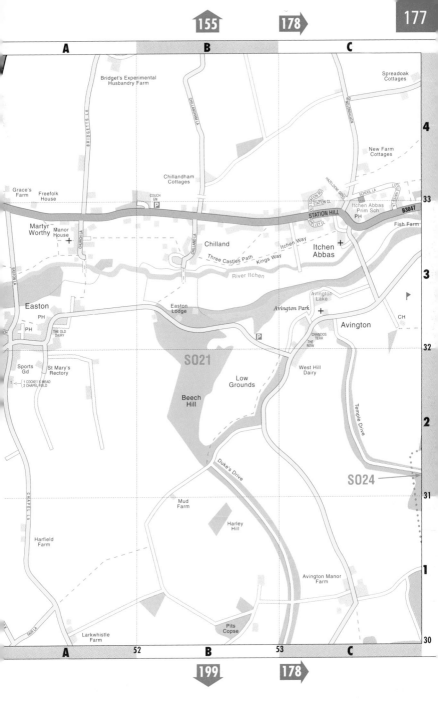

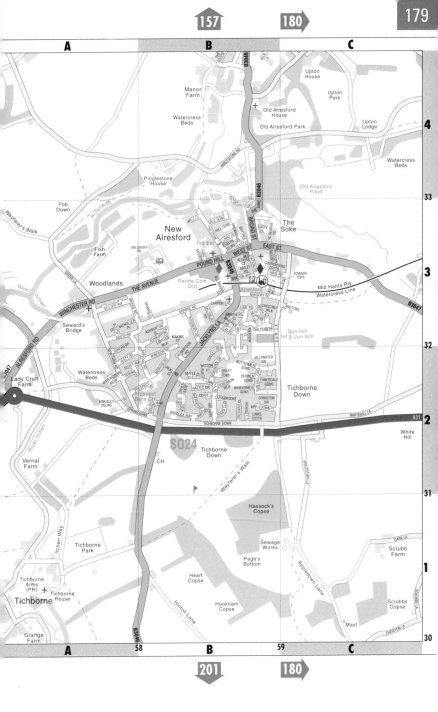

Hunt's
Plantation

Common Barn
Farm

MARY LA

Marylane
Plantation

Marylane
Copse

Pelham
Place

Lodge
Farm

A32

Inadown
Farm

INADOWN
BGLWS

Newton
House

NEWTON LA

Ten Acre
Plantation

Ina Down
Copse

The
Knapp

SHOTTERS LA

Shotters
Farm

Plash
Wood

Grove
Copse

East Tisted

RAILWAY
COTTS

BRIDLE

STATION RD

Old Place
Farm

Rotherfield Park

ALMHOUSES

Home
Farm

HOMEFIELD
COTTS

APPLETON
VIEW

GU34

Monk's
Lodge

Keepers
Cottage

BOXLEY RD

Goleigh Wood

Anchor
Cottage

SHELL LA

Colemore
House

Lye
Farm

The
Knapp

Manor Farm

Colemore

Slade
Farm

Becksteddle
Farm

Keepers
Cottage

Penny Hill
House

Hedge
Corner
Farm

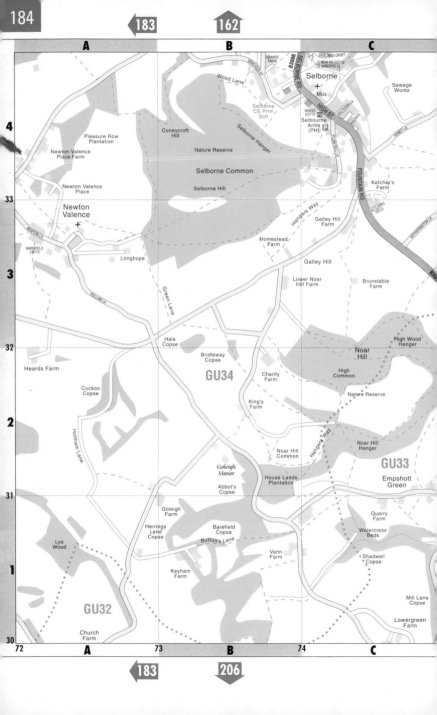

183
162

A   **B**   **C**

GRANGE FARM

GOSLINGS CROFT
1 NEW RD COTTS
2 GANDERS CL

Wood Lane

Selborne
+ Mus

SELBORNE CE Prim Sch

Selborne Arms (PH)

Sewage Works

4

Pleasure Row Plantation

Newton Valence Place Farm

Coneycroft Hill

Nature Reserve

Selborne Hanger

Ketcher's Farm

33

Newton Valence Place

Newton Valence +

Selborne Common

Selborne Hill

Hangers Way

Galley Hill Farm

BARNFIELD COTTS

Longhope

Homestead Farm

Galley Hill

3

Green Lane

Lower Noar Hill Farm

Brunstable Farm

Heards Farm

Hale Copse

32

Bridleway Copse

Noar Hill

High Wood Hanger

Cuckoo Copse

GU34

Charity Farm

High Common

Nature Reserve

King's Farm

2

Holtham Lane

Hangers Way

Noar Hill Hanger

Noar Hill Common

GU33

Empshott Green

Goleigh Manor

House Lands Plantation

Abbot's Copse

31

Goleigh Farm

Quarry Farm

Herrings Land Copse

Barefield Copse

Button's Lane

Watercress Beds

Lye Wood

Vann Farm

Shadwell Copse

1

Keyham Farm

Mill Lane Copse

GU32

Lowergreen Farm

Church Farm

30

72   **A**   73   **B**   74   **C**

183
206

163
186

A   **B**   **C**

ew Barn Farm

HONEY LA

Rhode Hill

Shrubs Copse

Ironpaddock Copse

Albury Farm

Blackmoor Nurseries

Blackmoor Grange

CHURCH COTTS

4

Sotherington Farm

Temple Manor

Temple Wood

Blackmoor

Eveley Farm

GU34

FOTHERINGTON LA

The Withy

33

Burhunt Cottages

Snap Wood

BLACKMOOR HO

Burhunt Farm

Bradshott Wood

Bushy Copse

Blackmoor Wood

Adderhood Hanger

Outshott Hanger

Bradshott Hall

Brock Bridge

Brockbridge Farm

3

Lower Hanger

Hazel Copse

Squiresfield Hanger

32

Le Court Hanger

Sheepcrafts Copse

BENHAMS LA

GU33

Lawrence's Copse

Benhams Farm

Knightsfield Copse

Grange Farm

Stairs Hill House

Le Court

Firsplat Copse

2

Empshott

Reeds Farm

Cott's Shaw

Great Wood

Lowergroves Copse

KINGSHOTT COTTS

The Grange

CHURCH LA

The Queen (PH)

Greatham

31

Deal Farm

LONGMOOR RD

BAKERS FIELD

Lythanger

MILL LA

Little Wood

Rook's Farm

Greatham Prim Sch

1

Lane Copse

Hawkley Hurst

Mill Farm

River Rother

STANDFAST LA

Crabtree Copse

Hatchmoor Farm

SHALDEN LA

Golds Farm

FORGET END

Manor House

B3006

A3

30

A   76   **B**   77   **C**

207
186

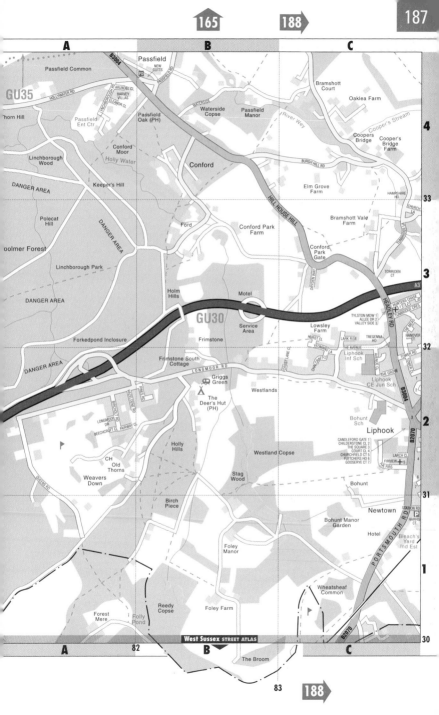

4

33

3

32

2

31

1

30

A　　　**B**　　　**C**

GU35

Passfield Common

NEW COTTS
Passfield

PO

Waterside Copse

Passfield Manor

River Way

Bramshott Court

Oaklea Farm

Cooper's Stream

Coopers Bridge

Cooper's Bridge Farm

HAMPSHIRE HO

HOLLYWATER RD

ARUNDEL CL
HARVEY VILLAS
ELEANOR CL

Passfield Ent Ctr

Passfield Oak (PH)

Thorn Hill

Conford Moor

Holly Water

Linchborough Wood

Keeper's Hill

DANGER AREA

Polecat Hill

DANGER AREA

Conford

Ford

Conford Park Farm

BURGH HILL RD

Elm Grove Farm

Bramshott Vale Farm

HILL HOUSE HILL

Conford Park Gate

CHURCH LA
TUNBRIDGE LA

TORRIDEN CT

oolmer Forest

Linchborough Park

DANGER AREA

Holm Hills

Motel

GU30

Service Area

DRIVER AVE

A3

HEADLEY RD

HUNTS CHASE
TUNBRIDGE CRES

TYLSTON MDW 1
ALLEE DR 2
VALLEY SIDE 3

HANOVER

Forkedpond Inclosure

DANGER AREA

Frimstone

Frimstone South Cottage

LONGMOOR RD

Griggs Green

The Deer's Hut (PH)

Westlands

Lowsley Farm

HURST CL

YEOMANS CL

FOREST LANE CL

OAKCROFT CL

LARK RISE

THE AVENUE

Liphook Inf Sch

TREGAREN HO

THE GROVE

Liphook CE Jun Sch

ARTHUR CL

TOWER RD

TOWER CL

B3004

THE MEWS

HAZELWOOD RD

SPARKES RD

LONGMOOR DR

BEECHCROFT CL FAIRWAY CL

Holly Hills

Weavers Down

CH
Old Thorns

Westland Copse

Stag Wood

Bohunt Sch

Liphook

Bohunt

CANDLEFORD GATE 1
CHILDERSTONE CL 2
THE SQUARE 3
COURT CL 4
CHURCHFIELD CT 5
FLETCHERS HO 6
GOOSERYE CT 7

THE FIRS

FIRVIEW

LARCH CL

B2070

DEELINE RD

Birch Piece

Foley Manor

Newtown

STATION RD

P HARRIS CL

Bohunt Manor Garden

Hotel

Bleach's Yard Ind Est

PORTSMOUTH RD

Forest Mere

Folly Pond

Reedy Copse

Foley Farm

Wheatsheaf Common

B2070

A　82　**B**　　**C**　30

The Broom

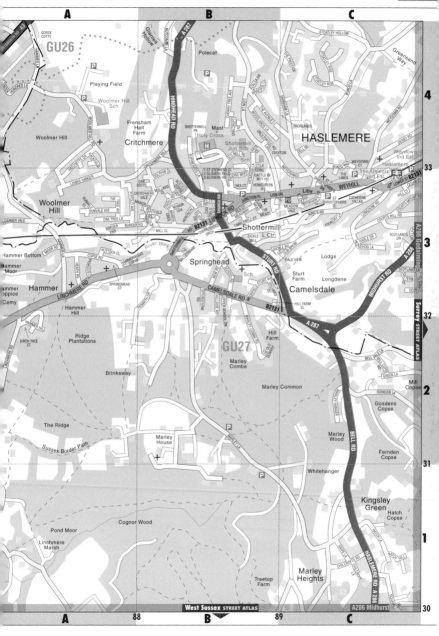

A
B
C

West Tytherley
CE Prim Sch

Church
Farm

Stony
Batter

Stride's
Farm

Manor
Farm

East
Tytherley

Poplar
Farm

Lye
Farm

THE COACH RD

Sopp's
Farm

MANOR
RD

4

DEAN RD

RED LA

The Green

White House

BONNER
COTTS

Oaklands
Farm

29

Drove

SP5

Frenchmoor

Upper Frenchmoor Copse

Lower
Frenchmoor
Copse

Bulls Drove

Lockerley Hall
Park

Lain
Copse

3

Lockerley
Hall

Pug's Hole

HOME FARM
BSNS CTR

28

Holbury Wood

The Star Inn
(PH)

Holbury
Farm

MARK WAY

SO51

2

HOLBURY LA

PARK
VIEW

Holbury Mill

Lockerley Water
Farm

27

Mill Farm

River Dun

nor
rm

LC

East Dean

EAST DEAN RD

PO

1

Lockerley

Dean Hill Barn
Farm

Deangate
Farm

Top
Green

Butt's
Green

PENDLE
GREEN

Dean Hill

Curlew's
Farm

Critchell's
Green

COOK'S LA

26

A
28
B
29
C

A   B   C

4

SP5

29

3

Redhills
Copse

Hackpits
Copse

Deborah
Copse

Pittleworth
Manor

Pittleworth
Farm

Little Bentley
Farm

Great Bentley
Farm

Holm Moor
Copse

SO20

Bentley
Firs

The
Bungalow

Blackpits Wood

Great
Copse

Lain Copse

Clapgate
Copse

Newlyns
Farm

BACK LA

Snook's
Copse

Spearywell Wood

SO51

28

Blackmoor Firs

Culver
Leaze

Bushy
Copse

2

Dummer
Copse

Woodland
Walk

P

Cadbury
Farm

Spearywell

Test Way

27

Mottisfont Abbey
(National Trust)

Gardens   Priory

KEEPERS LA

BENGER'S LA

Abbey
Farm

GAPLEY RD

Mottisfont

P

HATT LA

Glebe
Farm

Monarch's Way

River Test

P

River Dun

Drove Copse

Hatt Farm
Hatt Hill

1

Lockerley Endowed
CE Prim Sch

LOCKERLEY RD

Butt's
Green

The
School Farm

Dunbridge

LC

LC

Dunbridge

Test Way

River Dun

DUNBRIDGE LA

B3084

26

30   A   31   B   32   C

RUSSELL DR (
MILL RISE 2)

LOCKERLEY RD

PH

B3084

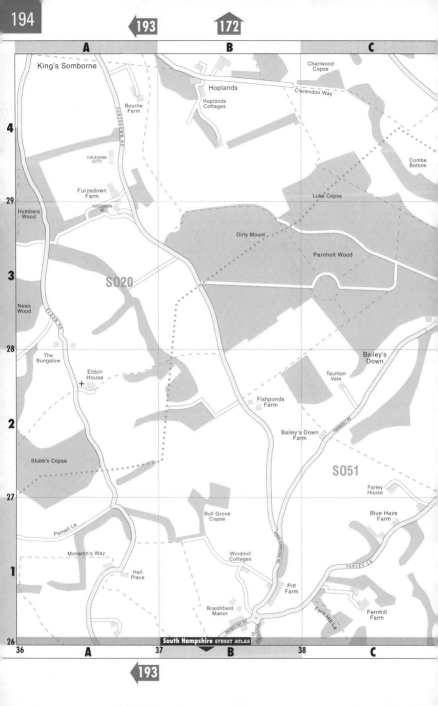

193
172

King's Somborne

Hoplands

Charlwood
Copse

Clarendon Way

Bourne
Farm

Hoplands
Cottages

4

FURZEDOWN COTTS

Combe
Bottom

29

Furzedown
Farm

Luke Copse

Humbers
Wood

PURZEDOWN RD

Dirty Mount

Parnholt Wood

3

SO20

News
Wood

ELDON RD

28

The
Bungalow

Bailey's
Down

Eldon
House

Taunton
Vale

Fishponds
Farm

2

Bailey's Down
Farm

PARNHOLT RD

SO51

Stubb's Copse

27

Farley
House

Parnell La

Bull Grove
Copse

Blue Haze
Farm

Monarch's Way

Windmill
Cottages

FARLEY LA

1

Hall
Place

Pitt
Farm

Braishfield
Manor

Fern Hill La

Fernhill
Farm

KINGS SOMBORNE RD

PAYNES HAY RD

26

36   **A**   37   **B**   38   **C**

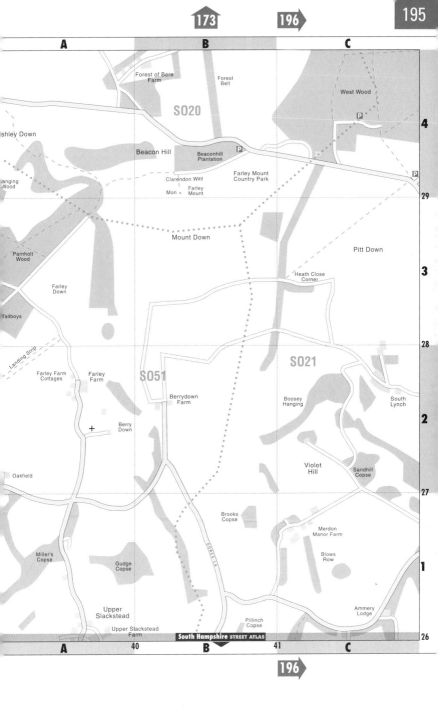

| A | B | C |

173 **196** **195**

Forest of Bere Farm

Forest Belt

SO20

West Wood

shley Down

P

4

Beacon Hill

Beaconhill Plantation

P

Farley Mount Country Park

anging Wood

Clarendon Way

Farley Mount

Mon

29

Parnholt Wood

Mount Down

Pitt Down

3

Heath Close Corner

Farley Down

Tallboys

28

Landing Strip

SO51

SO021

Farley Farm Cottages

Farley Farm

Boosey Hanging

South Lynch

Berrydown Farm

2

Berry Down

Oakfield

Violet Hill

Sandhill Copse

27

Brooks Copse

Merdon Manor Farm

Miller's Copse

Gudge Copse

Blows Row

1

Upper Slackstead

Ammery Lodge

Pillinch Copse

Upper Slackstead Farm

Farley Mount
Nature Reserve
Burrow
Copse
Crab Wood
Nature Reserve
Ashmore
Hill
Copse
West Wood
Crabwood
Farm
House
Ma
Crabwood
House
Clarendon Way
SARUM RD
Pittdown
Plantation
Pitt Down
Enmill
House
Little
Pittdown
Plantation
Enmill
Barn
ENMILL LA
Vale Farm
Enmill
Farm
Pitt View
SO22
SO21
White House
Pages
Copse
Grovelands
Copse
Yew Tree
HUNSEY MOUNT RD
SPARSHOLT RD
Stopham's
Copse
Pitt
Copse
MILLERS LA
Larkfarm
Plantation
Southlynch
Plantation
Standon
Farm
Nan Trodd's
Hill
Standon
Juniper
Bank
Down Farm
Butcher's
Plantation
PORT LA
Merdon
Castle

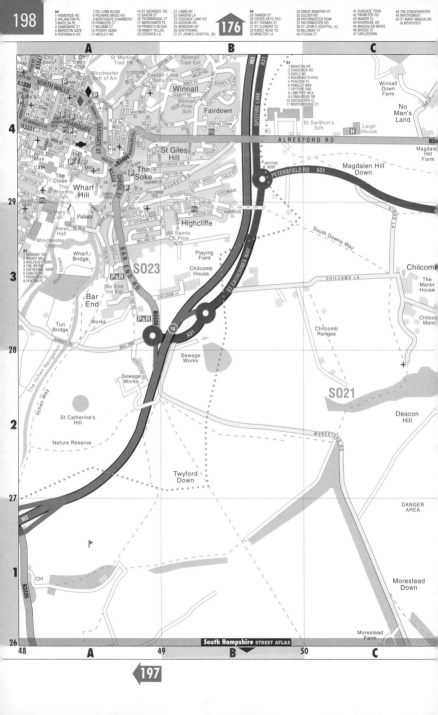

A4
1 HOMERISE HO
2 ARLINGTON PL
3 MATILDA PL
4 DANEMARK CT
5 MARSTON GATE
6 ROPEWALK HO

7 DE LUNN BLDGS
8 RICHARD MOSS HO
9 NORTHGATE CHAMBERS
10 PRINCESS CT
11 MILMAN CT
12 PRIORY GDNS
13 WESLEY HO

14 ST GEORGES' HO
15 SAXON CT
16 TROWBRIDGE CT
17 MERCHANTS PL
18 PRINCE'S BLDGS
19 HANDY VILLAS
20 COSSACK LA

21 LAWN HO
22 GARDEN LA
23 COSSACK LANE HO
24 GODSON HO
25 WINDSOR HO
26 GREYFRIARS
27 ST JOHN'S HOSPITAL (N)

A4
28 TANNER ST
29 CROSS KEYS PAS
30 ST THOMAS ST
31 ST CLEMENT ST
32 KINGS HEAD YD
33 MINSTER LA

34 GREAT MINSTER ST
35 CULVER RD
36 PATERNOSTER ROW
37 PATERNOSTER HO
38 ST JOHN'S HOSPITAL (S)
39 MIDWAY CT
40 ITCHEN CT

41 DURGATE TERR
42 PARMITER HO
43 MANOR CL
44 RIVERSIDE HO
45 MAGDALEN MEWS
46 BRIDGE ST
47 EARLSDOWN

48 THE CONSERVATORY
49 WATERSMEET
50 ST MARY MAGDALEN ALMSHOUSES

B4
1 BRAXTON HO
2 CRADDOCK HO
3 EARLE HO
4 ROUNDHUTS RISE
5 PEACOCK PL
6 RINGLET WAY
7 SPITFIRE END
8 LIMETREE WLK
9 LONGHOUSE GN
10 GATEKEEPER CL
11 NORTHBROOKE CT

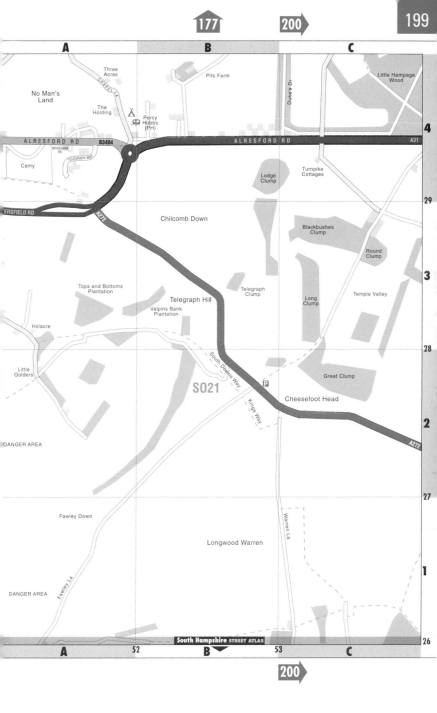

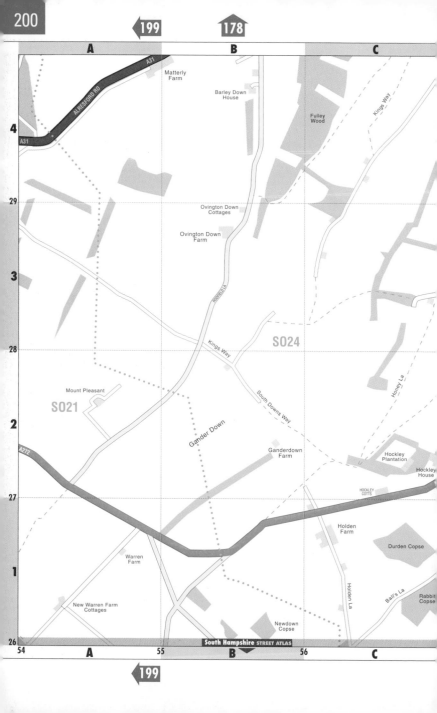

179 202

A B C

B3046

Prite La

Wayfarer's Walk

Broad La

Sevington
Farm

Cheriton Mill

Hinton La

4

Cowdown
Copse

Bramdean La

CHERITON
LA

River Itchen

Itchen Way

North End

Middle
Farm

29

NORTH END
FARM COTTS

North End
Farm

Broad La

THE PASTURES

Cheriton
Prim Sch

Upper Lamborough La

Itchen Way

3

Hill Houses

HILL HOUSES LA

Cheriton

Cheriton La

THE
GOODINGS

PARK LA

LOWER LAMBOROUGH LA

Lamborough La

Primrose
Cottages

The
Flowerpots
(PH)

Malthouse
Farm

MANOR LA

Marriners
Farm

A272

28

Westfield
Farm

SO24

B3046

Jolly Farmer
(PH)

Hinton
Marsh

Hinton
Ampner

Godwin
Farm

HINTON HILL

PETERSFIELD RD

New
Cheriton

GREYS FARM CL

The Park

Hinton Ampner
House

Manor
Farm

2

Harnham
Hill

Source of
The River
Itchen

KILMESTON RD

Durden
Copse

Durden
Lodge

Shorley
Copse

27

BARR'S LA

Powells Grove
Copse

Shorley Wood
House

KILMESTON RD

Wayfarer's Walk

Shorley
Farm

Shorley

1

Hacks
Cottage

Kilmeston

St Andrew's
House

Beauworth

WESTFIELD DRO

Manor
Farm

West
Wood

Manor
Farm

WESTWOOD
VIEW

26

A 58 B 59 C

202

A B C

4

29

3

28

2

27

1

26

CHERITON LA
Tenant Woods

Bullbeck
Copse

Cheriton Wood

Common
Farm

Old Park
Wood

Breach Plain
Cottages

Wood Farm
Cottages

Wood
Farm

Alresford Lane

Marriners
Farm

WOOD LA

Cheriton Lane

Kalamunnda
Farm

Lacey's
Farm

New
Cottages

West End
Farm

Kelsey
Farm

Woodlane
Farm

WOODLANE CL

SO24

A272

Bramdean
Manor

Manor
Farm

Bramdean

WOODCOTE
COTTS

Woodcote Manor
House

Hinton
Ampner

Manor Farm

The Malthouse

Bramdean
Farm

TICHBORNE LA

Godwin's
Plantation

Humpty's Down

A.

New Pond
Cottages

Joan's Acre

Broom
Wood

Joan's Acre
Wood

Brockwood
Park

Brockwood
Park Farm

DELL
COTTS

GU32

BROCKWOOD
BOTTOM

60 A 61 B 62 C 26

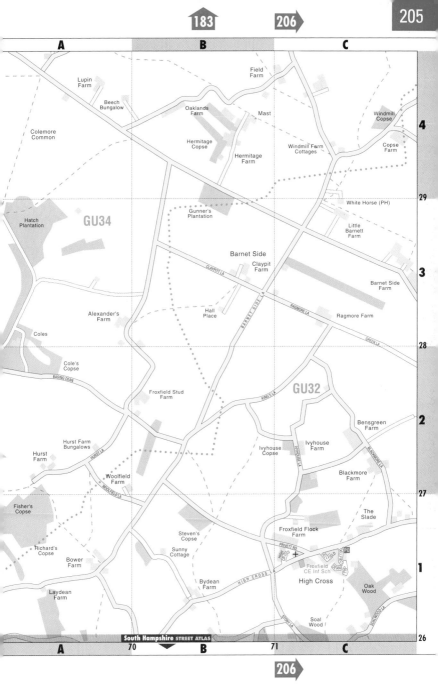

A

B

C

Lupin
Farm

Beech
Bungalow

Oaklands
Farm

Field
Farm

Mast

Windmill
Copse

Colemore
Common

Hermitage
Copse

Hermitage
Farm

Windmill Farm
Cottages

Copse
Farm

4

Hatch
Plantation

GU34

Gunner's
Plantation

White Horse (PH)

29

Barnet Side

Little
Barnett
Farm

CLAYPIT LA

Claypit
Farm

Barnet Side
Farm

3

Alexander's
Farm

BARNET SIDE LA

RAGMORE LA

Coles

Hall
Place

Ragmore Farm

GREEN LA

28

Cole's
Copse

BASING DEAN

Froxfield Stud
Farm

KING'S LA

GU32

Bensgreen
Farm

2

Hurst Farm
Bungalows

HURST LA

Ivyhouse
Copse

Ivyhouse
Farm

IVYHOUSE LA

BLACKMORE LA

Hurst
Farm

Woolfield
Farm

WOOLFIELD LA

Blackmore
Farm

27

Fisher's
Copse

Steven's
Copse

The
Slade

Richard's
Copse

Sunny
Cottage

Froxfield Flock
Farm

PRIVETT RD

Bower
Farm

Bydean
Farm

HIGH CROSS

Froxfield
CE Inf Sch

High Cross

Oak
Wood

1

Laydean
Farm

STUD LA

Soal
Wood

SHERWOOD LA

A

B

C

A B C

Church Farm

GU34

Lowergreen Farm

Lower Green

Manor House

Hawkley Hanger

Champlers Farm

4

Five Ash Farm

Hawkley

29

UPPER GN

PH

POCOCKS LA

Warren Farm

Tubb's Farm

CHEESECOMBE FARM LA

Cheesecombe Farm

3

The Warren

Reston Hanger

Oakshott Farm

Oakshott Stream

Moore's Copse

GU33

Warren Corner

WARREN LA

Shaw Wood

Roundhills Hanger

Windmill Cottage

28

Parsons

Happersnapper Hanger

GREEN LA

GU32

Oakshott

Lower Oakshott Farmhouse

Hill Farm

HONEYCRITCH LA

2

TROOPER BOTTOM

Oakshott Hanger

Hangers Way

COTTAGE LA

PH

WOODFIELD COTTS

Wheatham Hill

Ringsgreen Copse

OLD LITTEN LA

Old Litten Lane

Rings Green

Ringsgreen Lane

Woodfield Copse

27

Shoulder of Mutton Hill

Southcean Farm

Ashford Hill

COCKSHOTT LA

HIGH CROSS LA

Ashford Farm

WHITELA

1

Week Green Farm

Lutcombe Bottom

ASHFORD CHACE

SDALWOOD LA

Wyke Green Farm

Bushy Hill

Pipers Farm

Wyke Green Cottage

STONER HILL RD

Little Langleys

26

A   B   C

4

29

3

28

2

27

1

26

Mabbotts   Adam's Wood

Uplands

Lowerbarn Copse   Park Lands Farm

Scotland Farm   Primmers

Hurst Farm

Ham Barn Farm

B3006

River Rother

A3

Goleigh Farm House

Moor Park Farm

Greatham Bridge

Farewells

Manor Barn

Prouts Farm

Hurst Cottages   HAWKLEY RD

Barefoots Farm   Lyss Place Farm

Oakshott Stream

Lyss Place

Old Berry Grove Farm

CHURCH ST

Burgates

ELM TERR

HOMEFIELD COTTS

Upper Green

The Blue Bell (PH)

The Grange

Kippences

West Liss

THE ARCADE

KILN FIELD

HAWK'S MEAD

THE TREES

WOLSELEY GDNS

Mainline Bsns Ctr

P

GU33

Brows Farm

CHILMARK CT

FRENHAM RD

Batt's Brook

Wheatham Farm

Glascombe Hanger

Coldhayes Wood

Coldhayes

Woolshers Cottage

Flexcombe

Sewage Works

River Rother

C2
1 MEADOW WLK
2 SPRINGFIELD
3 SCHOOL LA
4 COLLARD WAY
5 PORTLAND SQ
6 TEACHERS TERR

STATION RD

Liss

LC

BRIDGE MDWS

LONGMEAD

RIOTHER HO

P

HILL BROW RD

B3006

Nursery Field

Andlers Ash Farm

27

Prince's Marsh

Prince's Bridge

LC

Little Stodham House

The Brickyards Ind Est

Steep Marsh

GU32

NINE ACRES

Steep Marsh Farm

The Moors

Gardner's Farm

Bowyer's Common

The Lodge

A3

Pruetts

STODHAM LA

STODHAM

PRIESTLA

GU31

Stodham Park

A   B   C

GU30

4

Longmoor
Inclosure

Little Dean
Bottom

The
Wylds

Langley

Warren
Hill

The Lake

Wylds
Farm

WARREN RD

29

SHERWOOD PL

PINE BLK

Langley Bridge
Farm

The Temple
Inn (PH)

Liss
Forest

The
Mint

TEMPLE RD

Mangers

REEDS LA

Brewells
Farm

Little
Langley
Farm

ROTHERBANK
FARM LA

MINT RD

Home
Farm

Whangerei Nursery
Palmers Farm

Reeds

3

FOREST RISE

FOREST RD

Palmers

LC

DUDLEY
TERS

WYLD GREEN LA

Ciddy
Hall

ST PATRICK'S LA

Newlands

Rake CE
Prim Sch

28

Wyld Green
Farm

MILLBROOK

SILVER BIRCH

WOODBOURNE CL

ROCKPIT
COTTS

GU33

St Patrick's
Copse

Rake
Bsns Pk

B2070

East Liss

OAK TREE DR

Liss

MEADOW
WLK

PADDOCK

RAKE RD

PENBROOK

The Flying Bull
(PH)

Coldharbour Park
Farm

FIR TREE
COTTS

HIGHFIELD RD

HATCH LA

High Firs
House

PEBBLE LA

Rake

WILLOW
RD

MOSS CL

THE
CHASE

VINSON RD

THE
RIDINGS

Highfield
Farm

2

East
Hill

Liss
Inf & Jun
Schs

CAROLINE
CL

DENNIS MEAD

LARKINS LEASE

INWOOD RD

HUNTSBOTTOM LA

Highfield
Wood

SAND LA

Sussex Border Path

Pot
Well

CAROUSE LA

Hill
Side

Black
Pond

27

HILL BROW RD

BYDOWN LA

EDGEWOOD
CT

MALTING RD

B3006

Rake
Common

Hill Brow

Rake
Hanger

GU31

1

B3006

LONDON RD

B2070

HILL BROW RD

MILL RD

Hambledon
Piece

Farther
Commons

PH

Clayton
Court

Combe
Hill

Hartin
Comb

26

West Sussex STREET ATLAS

78   A   79   B   80   C

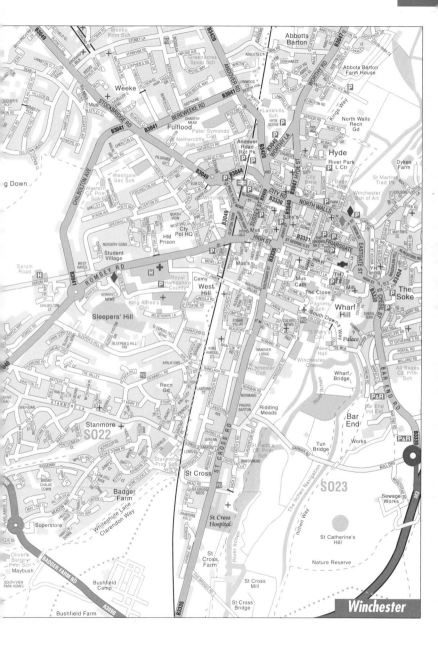

Winchester

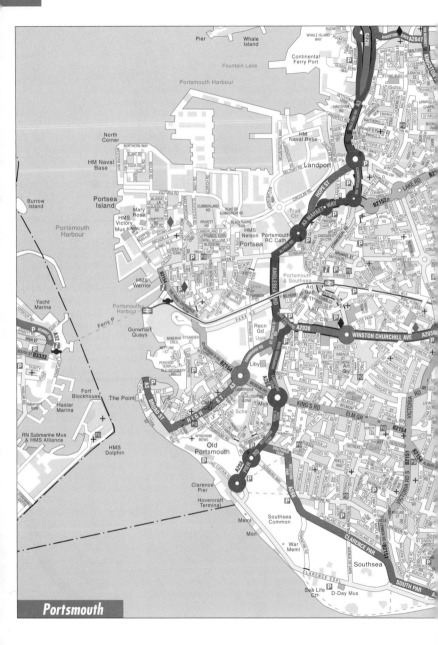

Portsmouth

Southampton

Index

Church Rd **6** Beckenham BR2..........**53** C6

Place name	Location number	Locality, town or village	Postcode district	Page and grid square
May be abbreviated on the map	Present when a number indicates the place's position in a crowded area of mapping	Shown when more than one place has the same name	District for the indexed place	Page number and grid reference for the standard mapping

Public and commercial buildings are highlighted in magenta. Places of interest are highlighted in blue with a star★

Abbreviations used in the index

Acad	Academy	Comm	Common	Gd	Ground	L	Leisure	Prom	Prom
App	Approach	Cott	Cottage	Gdn	Garden	La	Lane	Rd	Road
Arc	Arcade	Cres	Crescent	Gn	Green	Liby	Library	Recn	Recreation
Ave	Avenue	Cswy	Causeway	Gr	Grove	Mdw	Meadow	Ret	Retail
Bglw	Bungalow	Ct	Court	H	Hall	Meml	Memorial	Sh	Shopping
Bldg	Building	Ctr	Centre	Ho	House	Mkt	Market	Sq	Square
Bsns, Bus	Business	Ctry	Country	Hospl	Hospital	Mus	Museum	St	Street
Bvd	Boulevard	Cty	County	HQ	Headquarters	Orch	Orchard	Sta	Station
Cath	Cathedral	Dr	Drive	Hts	Heights	Pal	Palace	Terr	Terrace
Cir	Circus	Dro	Drove	Ind	Industrial	Par	Parade	TH	Town Hall
Cl	Close	Ed	Education	Inst	Institute	Pas	Passage	Univ	University
Cnr	Corner	Emb	Embankment	Int	International	Pk	Park	Wk, Wlk	Walk
Coll	College	Est	Estate	Intc	Interchange	Pl	Place	Wr	Water
Com	Community	Ex	Exhibition	Junc	Junction	Prec	Precinct	Yd	Yard

Index of localities, towns and villages

Abbotts Ann	105 A2	Churt	144 B1	Hawley	35 B2	Monk Sherborne	47 A3	Smannell	83 C3
Aldermaston	9 C4	Chute Forest	58 B2	Headley	165 A3	Monkwood	182 A1	South Tidworth	78 C2
Aldershot	76 A1	Cliddesden	92 A4	Headley, Nr Greenham	7 B1	Monxton	104 B3	South Warnborough	105 C3
Alton	139 C2	Cole Henley	63 B2	Heckfield	31 A3	Mortimer	11 C3	South Wonston	153 B3
Amport	104 A3	Colemore	183 B1	Herriard	93 A1	Mottisfont	192 C1	Sparsholt	174 B2
Andover	106 B4	Combe	19 B4	High Cross	205 C1	Mytchett	56 B2	St Mary Bourne	62 A1
Appleshaw	81 A3	Crawley	152 A1	Highclere	21 C3	Nether Wallop	148 A3	Standon	196 A1
Arborfield	15 A4	Crondall	97 B4	Hill Brow	208 A1	New Alresford	179 B3	Steep Marsh	207 A3
Ash	77 C2	Crookham Village	74 B3	Hindhead	167 C3	Newbury	1 B2	Sterenton	89 A2
Ashford Hill	8 B1	Deane	66 A1	Hook	51 A1	Newnham	50 B1	Stockbridge	149 C2
Ashley	172 C2	Dogmersfield	74 A3	Houghton	171 A3	Newton Toney	123 A3	Stoke	61 B2
Ashmansworth	40 C4	Dummer	90 B1	Hurstbourne Priors	85 B1	Newton Valence	184 A3	Stratfield Mortimer	12 A3
Ashmore Green	2 C4	East Dean	191 A1	Hurstbourne Tarrant	60 A4	Newtown	5 C2	Stratfield Saye	29 C4
Axford	114 B2	East Stratton	134 A2	Ibworth	45 C1	North Tidworth	79 A4	Stratfield Turgis	30 A2
Ball Hill	4 A2	East Tisted	183 B3	Idmiston	145 A3	North Waltham	89 C1	Sutton Scotney	131 B2
Barton Stacey	130 B3	East Tytherley	191 C4	Isington	119 C1	North Warnborough	72 B2	Swallowfield	14 A3
Basingstoke	68 C3	East Woodhay	20 B4	Itchen Abbas	177 C3	Northington	156 C4	Tadley	27 A4
Baughurst	26 B4	East Worldham	162 C4	Itchen Stoke	178 B3	Oakhanger	163 B2	Tangley	58 C3
Beacon Hill	167 A4	Ecchinswell	23 B2	Kilmeston	201 B1	Oakley	67 B1	Thatcham	2 C1
Beauworth	201 A1	Ellisfield	115 B4	Kimpton	80 A2	Odiham	72 C1	Three Ashes	28 A4
Beech Hill	13 A3	Enborne	4 B4	King's Somborne	172 A1	Old Alresford	157 B1	Thruxton	103 C4
Bentley	120 A3	Enham Alamein	83 B4	Kings Worthy	176 B3	Old Basing	70 B3	Tichborne	179 A1
Bentworth	138 A3	Eversley	15 C1	Kingsclere	188 A2	Old Burghclere	40 B2	Tilford	122 C2
Bramley	28 C2	Ewshot	98 A4	Kingsley	142 A1	Over Wallop	125 A1	Tongham	100 C3
Bramshill	31 C4	Faccombe	19 C1	Kintbury	3 A4	Overton	88 A4	Upper Bullington	131 B4
Bramshott	188 A3	Fair Oak Green	29 A3	Knights Enham	83 A3	Ovington	178 C2	Upper Chute	57 C4
Brimpton	8 C3	Farleigh Wallop	91 C1	Lasham	116 B1	Oxenwood	17 A2	Upper Clatford	105 C2
Broughton	170 B4	Farley Castle	15 A4	Latchmere Green	28 A3	Padworth	10 B2	Upper Farringdon	161 C2
Brown Candover	135 A2	Farley Hill	15 A3	Laverstoke	87 B3	Pamber End	27 B1	Upper Froyle	119 A1
Burghclere	22 B4	Farnborough	55 C1	Leckford	150 B4	Pamber Heath	10 B1	Upper Wield	136 C1
Buttermere	18 A4	Farnham	98 C2	Linchmere	188 C1	Penton Grafton	81 C2	Upper Wootton	46 A1
Camberley	36 B4	Finchampstead	16 B1	Lindford	164 C3	Picket Piece	84 A1	Upton	39 A2
Charlton	82 C2	Fleet	54 A1	Liphook	188 A2	Popham	112 C2	Upton Grey	94 A3
Charter Alley	46 C4	Fosbury	17 C1	Liss	208 A2	Preston Candover	136 B4	Vernham Dean	38 A3
Chawton	161 B4	Four Marks	160 B1	Litchfield	63 B4	Quarley	103 A2	West Dean	190 B2
Cheriton	201 B3	Frensham	144 A4	Little Somborne	172 C3	Quidhampton	65 A1	West End Green	29 A4
Chilbolton	129 A2	Fyfield	80 C1	Littleton	175 A3	Rake	208 C2	West Tisted	203 B4
Chilcomb	198 C3	Golden Pot	117 B2	Lockerley	191 C1	Ramsdell	46 B4	West Tytherley	169 A1
Chineham	48 C2	Goodworth Clatford	105 C1	Long Sutton	95 C2	Red Rice	127 B4	West Woodhay	3 A2
Cholderton	101 B1	Grateley	125 A4	Longmoor Camp	186 B1	Riseley	14 A2	Weyhill	81 B1
Church End	49 B3	Grayshott	166 C2	Longparish	108 B3	Ropley	181 B2	Wherwell	128 C3
		Greatham	185 C1	Longstock	149 C3	Rotherwick	50 C3	Whitchurch	86 B3
		Greenham	6 A4	Lower Froyle	119 B3	Sandhurst	35 A4	Wildhern	59 C1
		Greywell	71 C2	Ludgershall	57 A1	Seale	100 C2	Winchester	197 B3
		Hamstead Marshall	3 C4	Maplederwell	70 C2	Selborne	184 C4	Winchfield	52 B1
		Hannington	44 C2	Mattingley	51 B4	Shalden	139 A4	Winterbourne	1 B4
		Hartley Wespall	30 A1	Medstead	159 C4	Sherborne St John	47 C2	Wonston	131 C2
		Hartley Witney	52 C3	Micheldever	133 A2	Sherfield on Loddon	29 C1	Woodcott	41 B1
		Haslemere	189 C4	Michelmersh	193 B1	Shinfield	13 C4	Woolton Hill	21 B4
		Hatherden	59 B1	Middle Wallop	147 C4	Shipton Bellinger	101 B4	Wootton St Lawrence	67 C4
		Hawkley	206 C4	Middle Winterslow	168 A4	Silchester	10 C1	Yateley	34 A3

A

Abbatt Cl SP11 57 A1
Abberbury Cl (Almshouses) RG14 1 B3
Abbetts La GU15 35 C2
Abbey Bsns Pk GU9 122 B4
Abbey Cl RG14 5 C4
Abbey Ct
4 Andover SP10 105 C4
Basingstoke RG24 48 A1
Camberley GU15 36 A3
4 Farnham GU9 99 A1
Abbey Hill Cl SO23 176 A1
Abbey Hill Rd SO23 175 C1
Abbey Pas SO23 198 A4
Abbey Rd Alton GU34 160 B4
Basingstoke RG24 69 A4
Medstead GU34 160 B4
Abbey Sch The GU9 99 A1
Abbey St GU9 99 A1
Abbey Way GU14 56 A2
Abbot's Ride GU9 99 B1
Abbots Cl Fleet GU51 54 A1
North Tidworth SP9 78 C4
Abbots Ct GU47 34 B4
Abbots Rd Newbury RG14 1 C1
North Tidworth SP9 78 C4
Abbots Row 6 SO22 197 C4
Abbots Wood Forest Wlk* GU10 143 A3
Abbotstone Rd SO24 179 B4
Abbotswood Cl RG26 26 C4
Abbott Cl RG22 68 B1
Abbott's Ann CE Prim Sch SP11 104 C2
Abbott's Ann Rd SP11 104 B3
Abbotts Ann SP11 105 A2
Abbotts Ann Rd SO22 175 B2
Abbotts Cl
Abbotts Ann SP11 105 A2
Winchester SO23 176 A1
Abbotts Cotts GU10 143 B3
Abbotts Ct SO22 175 C1
Abbotts Hill SP11 105 A2
Abbotts Rd SO23 176 A1
Abex Rd RG14 2 A2
Abingdon Rd GU47 35 A4
Above Town SP11 105 C2
Acadamey Gate GU15 35 C3
Academy Cl GU15 36 B4
Accentors Cl GU34 139 C3
Acheulian Cl GU9 122 A4
Achilles Cl RG24 48 C2
Ackender Rd GU34 139 C2
Acorn Cl RG21 69 C3
Acorn Keep GU9 99 A4
Acorn Mews GU14 55 C4
Acorn Rd GU17 34 C3
Acre Almshouses 7 SP10 106 A4
Acre Ct SP10 106 A4
Acre Path SP10 106 A4
Acton Ho RG22 68 C2
Adam Cl RG26 9 B1
Adampur Rd SP9 78 B2
Adams Cl
North Tidworth SP11 79 B3
North Warnborough RG29 72 A2
Adams Dr GU51 54 B1
Adams Ho GU34 140 A2
Adams Park Rd GU9 99 A2
Adams Way GU34 140 A2
Addison Cl SO22 197 B3
Addison Gdns RG29 72 C2
Addison Rd GU16 56 B4
Adelaide Rd SP10 106 A4
Adlington Pl GU14 56 B1
Admers Cres GU30 188 A1
Admirals Way SP10 83 B1
Admiralty Way GU15 35 B2
Adrian Cl RG27 52 B3
Aerospace Bvd GU11 76 C4
Aghemund Cl RG24 48 C2
Agra Rd SP9 78 B2
Agricola Wlk SP10 83 A2
Ainger Cl GU12 77 A2
Aintree Cl RG14 2 A1
Airborne Forces Mus* GU11 76 C3
Aircraft Espl GU14 56 A1
Aird Cl RG20 21 B4
Airlie Cnr SO22 197 C3
Airlie Rd SO22 197 C3
Ajax Cl RG24 48 C2
Alamein Rd
Aldershot GU11 76 C1
Enham Alamein SP11 83 A4
Alanbrooke Cl RG27 52 B3
Alanbrooke Rd GU11 77 A3
Albany Cl GU51 75 A4
Albany Ct Camberley GU16 36 A1
Fleet GU51 54 A1
Albany Mews SP10 105 C4
Albany Park Ind Est GU16 36 A1
Albany Pk GU16 36 A1
Albany Rd Andover SP10 105 C4
Fleet GU51 75 A4
Albert Rd Aldershot GU11 76 C1
Alton GU34 139 C1
Camberley GU15 36 A3
Farnborough GU14 56 A1
Newbury RG14 1 C2
Albert St GU51 54 A1
Albert Yd 8 RG21 69 A2
Albion Pl RG27 52 B3
Albion Rd GU47 34 C4
Alder Cl Alton GU34 139 C3
Ash GU12 77 C4
Newbury RG14 2 A2
Alder Gr GU46 34 A3
Alder Rd GU35 165 C3
Aldermaston CE Prim Sch RG7 9 B4
Aldermaston Rd
Basingstoke RG24 68 C4
Pamber End RG26 27 A2
Sherborne St John RG24, RG26 47 B3
Aldermaston Rd S RG21 68 C4
Alderney Ave RG22 91 A4
Alders Ct SO24 179 B3
Alders The GU9 99 C3
Aldershot Military Mus* GU11 77 A3
Aldershot Rd Ash GU12 77 B1
Fleet GU51 75 A4
Fleet, Church Crookham GU52 75 B3
Aldershot Sta GU11 76 C1
Alderwood RG24 48 C2
Alderwood Dr RG27 51 A1
Aldrin Cl SP10 82 C2
Aldrin Pl GU14 55 A2
Aldwick Cl GU14 55 C3
Aldworth Cres RG22 68 C2
Aldwych Cotts RG14 1 B3
Alencon Link RG21 69 A3
Alexander Cl SO20 171 A3
Alexander Ho 6 SP9 78 C4
Alexander Rd RG25 88 A4
Alexander Terr RG29 72 B2
Alexandra Ave GU15 35 C3
Alexandra Ct
Bordon GU35 164 C2
9 Farnborough GU14 56 A1
Alexandra Rd
Aldershot GU11 76 B1
Alton GU34 139 C3
Andover SP10 105 C4
Ash GU12 77 B1
Basingstoke RG21 68 C3
Farnborough GU14 56 A1
Alexandra Terr
1 Aldershot GU11 76 C1
Winchester SO23 197 C4
Alexandria Rd SO21 131 B3
Alfonso Cl GU12 100 A4
Alfred Rd GU9 99 A1
Alfred St GU11 76 C1
Alice Holt Cotts GU10 120 C1
Alice Holt Forest Visitor Ctr* GU10 143 A4
Alice Rd GU11, GU12 76 C1
Alison Cl GU14 55 B2
Alison Dr GU15 36 B3
Alison Way
Aldershot GU11 76 B1
10 Winchester SO22 197 C4
Alison's Rd GU11 76 C2
All Hallows RC Sch GU9 99 B4
All Saints CE Jun Sch GU51 74 B4
All Saints CE Prim Sch SO23 198 A3
All Saints Cres GU14 35 B1
Allden Ave GU12 100 A4
Allden Gdns GU12 100 A4
Allee Dr GU30 187 C3
Allen Cl Alton GU34 140 A3
Basingstoke RG21 68 C2
Allen Gallery & Curtis Mus* GU34 139 C2
Allenby Rd GU15 35 C3
Alliston Way
Basingstoke RG22 68 A2
Whitchurch RG28 86 B2
Allnutt Ave RG21 69 B3
Alma Cl GU12 77 A1
Alma La GU9 99 A4
Alma Rd Bordon GU35 164 C2
Headley GU35 166 A3
Alma Sq GU14 77 A4
Alma Way GU9 99 A4
Almhouses SO24 183 B3
Almond Ave RG14 1 C3
Almond Cl
2 Farnborough GU14 55 C4
Old Basing RG24 70 A3
Almond Ct GU52 75 A3
Almondale Ct GU14 55 C3
Almshouses 2 RG21 69 A2
Almswood Rd RG26 9 C1
Aloes The GU51 75 A4
Alpha Rd GU12 77 A1
Alphington Ave GU16 36 B1
Alphington Gn GU16 36 B1
Alpine Cl GU14 55 A2
Alpine Ct RG22 68 A2
Alpine Rd GU35 164 B1
Alresford Dro SO21 153 C3
Alresford Rd
Chilcomb SO21, SO23 199 B4
Ovington SO24 178 C1
Winchester SO21, SO23 198 B4
Alresford Sta* SO24 179 B3
Alsace Wlk GU15 35 C1
Alswitha Terr 27 SO23 176 A1
Alton Bsns Ctr GU34 140 A2
Alton Coll GU34 139 C3
Alton Com Hospl GU34 139 B1
Alton Convent Sch GU34 140 A3
Alton Ct 12 SO23 176 A1
Alton Inf Sch GU34 140 A2
Alton La GU34 160 B1
Alton Rd Farnham GU10 121 A4
Fleet GU51 75 B4
Odiham RG29 95 A3
Alton Ride GU47 35 A4
Alton Road Cotts RG29 94 C2
Alton Sta GU34 140 A2
Altona Gdns SP10 82 C2
Alverstoke Gdns GU11 76 B1
Alwin Pl GU9 99 A4
Amazon Cl RG21 68 C2
Amber Cl GU35 164 C1
Amber Ct 2 GU12 77 A1
Amber Gdns SP10 105 B4
Amber Hill GU15 36 C2
Amberley Cl RG14 1 B2
Amberley Grange GU11 99 B4
Amberwood Dr GU15 36 B4
Ambleside Cl
Farnborough GU14 55 B2
Mytchett GU16 56 C1
Ambleside Cres GU9 98 C3
Ambrose Rd RG26 26 C4
Amery Hill GU34 139 C2
Amery Hill Sch GU34 139 C2
Amery St GU34 139 C2
Amesbury Ho 3 SP9 79 A3
Amesbury Rd
Cholderton SP4 101 A1
Newton Toney SP4 123 A3
Penton Grafton SP11 81 A1
Amesbury Sch GU26 167 B1
Amherst Rd GU35 164 B3
Ampere Rd RG14 1 C2
Amport CE Prim Sch SP11 104 A3
Amport Cl
Old Basing RG24 70 A4
Winchester SO22 175 B2
Amport Firs SP11 104 A3
Amport Park Mews SP11 103 C3
Ancells Ct GU51 54 B3
Ancells Rd GU51 54 B2
Anchor Mdw GU14 55 B2
Anchor Rd RG20 24 B1
Anchor Yd 1 RG21 69 A2
Andeferas Rd SP10 82 C2
Anders Rd SO21 153 C2
Anderson Ho GU9 99 A1
Andlers Ash Rd GU33 207 C2
Andover CE Prim Sch SP10 106 A4
Andover Com Hospl SP10 82 C1
Andover Dr 1 GU51 53 B2
Andover Dro RG20 4 C2
Andover La SP11 80 A4
Andover Rd
Blackwater GU17 35 A3
Fyfield SP11 80 C3
Micheldever SO21 111 A1
Monxton SP11 104 B3
Newbury RG14 5 A3
Oakley RG23,RG25 66 B1
Winchester SO21, SO22, SO23 175 C1
Andover Rd N SO22 175 C2
Andover Road Ret Pk SO23 175 C1
Andover Sta SP10 105 C4
Andover Way GU11 99 C4
Andrew Cl RG29 72 A2
Andrew Ct GU14 55 B4
Andrew's La
Long Sutton RG29 95 C2
Ropley SO24 181 C3
Andrewartha Rd GU14 56 B1
Andrews Cl GU52 75 A3
Andrews Endowed CE Prim Sch GU34 140 B3
Andrews Rd GU14 55 B3
Andwell La
Mapledurwell RG24 71 A3
Newnham RG27 71 A3
Angel Ct RG14 1 C2
Angel Mdws RG29 72 C2
Angelsey Rd GU12 77 A1
Anglesey Ave GU14 55 B4
Anglesey Cl
Andover SP10 106 A3
Basingstoke RG24 48 B1
Angora Way GU51 54 A2
Annandale Dr GU10 122 A3
Anne Armstrong Cl GU11 77 A3
Annes Way GU52 75 A3
Annettes Croft 4 GU52 74 C2
Ansell Rd GU16 36 B1
Anson Cl GU11 76 B2
Anstey Cl RG21 69 A1
Anstey Jun Sch GU34 139 C2
Anstey La GU34 139 C4
Anstey Mill Cl GU34 140 A3
Anstey Mill La GU34 140 A3
Anstey Rd GU34 140 A3
Antar Cl RG21 68 C2
Anton Cl RG23 67 A1
Anton Inf Sch SP10 106 A3
Anton Jun Sch SP10 106 A3
Anton La SP11 83 A3
Anton Mill Rd SP10 106 A4
Anton Rd SP10 106 A3
Anton Trad Est SP10 106 A4
Antrim Cl RG22 68 A2
Anvil Way RG26 28 C2
Anzio Cl GU11 76 C1
Apex Dr GU16 36 A1
Apollo Dr GU35 164 C1
Apollo Ho RG7 9 B1
Apollo Rise GU14 55 A2
Apple Tree Cl RG14 5 B4
Apple Tree Gr SP10 82 B1
Apple Way RG24 70 A3
Appledore Mews GU14 55 C4
Appledown Cl SO24 179 B2
Appledown La SO24 179 C2
Applegarth Cl RG21 69 B2
Applelands Cl GU10 121 C2
Appleshaw CE Inf & Jun Sch SP11 81 A4
Appleshaw Cl
12 Tadley RG26 26 C4
Winchester SO22 175 B2
Appleshaw Dene SP11 81 A3
Appleshaw Way SP11 79 B3
Appleton Cl SO20 125 B1
Appleton Mews SP10 106 A3
Appleton View SO24 183 B3
Appletree Mead RG27 51 B1
Appley Ct GU15 35 C3
Appley Dr GU15 35 C3
Approach Rd GU9 99 A1
April Cl GU15 36 A1
Apsley Cl SP10 105 C3
Arboretum The RG25 94 A3
Arbour Ct 34 SO22 197 C4
Arcade The
11 Aldershot GU11 76 C1
Liss GU33 207 C3
12 Newbury RG14 1 C2
Archaeological Trail* SO24 155 C3
Archery Fields RG29 72 C2
Archery La SO22 197 C4
Archery Rise GU34 139 C1
Arcot Rd SP9 78 C2
Ardglen Rd RG28 86 B3
Ardrossan Ave GU15 36 C3
Arena L Ctr GU15 36 A3
Arena La GU11 76 B3
Arford Comm GU35 165 B3
Arford Rd GU35 165 B3
Argent Terr GU47 35 B4
Argente Cl GU51 54 A2
Argyle Cl GU35 164 B1
Argyle Rd RG14 1 B1
Arkle Ave RG19 2 B2
Arkwright Cl RG20 21 B3
Arkwright Gate SP10 82 A1
Arle Cl SO24 179 B3
Arle Gdns SO24 179 B3
Arlebury Pk SO24 179 B3
Arlington Pl 2 SO23 198 A4
Arlington Terr GU11 76 B1
Arlott Dr RG21 69 A4
Armitage Dr GU16 36 B1
Armstrong Cl SO21 153 C2
Armstrong Mall GU14 55 A2
Armstrong Rd RG24 69 C4
Armstrong Rise SP10 82 C2
Arne Cl RG22 91 B4
Arnett Ave RG40 16 B4
Arnewood Ave RG26 10 A1
Arnhem Cl GU11 76 C1
Arnhem Rd RG14 1 C2
Arran Cl RG23 67 A1
Arrow Ind Est GU14 55 B1
Arrow La RG27 52 A4
Arrow Rd GU14 55 B1
Arthur Cl GU9 98 C1
Arthur Ct 22 RG21 69 A3
Arthur Rd Farnham GU9 99 A1
Newbury RG14 1 B1
Winchester SO23 176 A1
Arthur St GU11 76 C1
Arthur's La SP11 20 A1
Artillery Rd
Aldershot GU11 76 C1
Farnborough GU11 77 A4
Artists Way SP10 83 A1
Arun Ct RG21 69 B3
Arundel Cl Fleet GU51 75 A4
Liphook GU30 187 A4
New Alresford SO24 179 B2
Arundel Gdns RG23 68 B4
Arundell Pl 8 GU9 98 C1
Ascension Cl RG24 48 B1
Ascot Cl Alton GU34 140 A1
Newbury RG14 6 A4
Ascot Ct GU11 76 C1
Ash Church Rd GU12 77 C1
Ash Cl Ash GU12 77 C2
Blackwater GU17 35 A3
North Tidworth SP9 79 A4
Ash Ct 6 RG14 1 C2
Ash Gr Kingsclere RG20 24 B1
Liphook GU30 188 A2
Old Basing RG24 70 B3
Ash Grange Cty Prim Sch GU12 77 C1
Ash Green La W GU10 100 B4
Ash Hill Rd GU12 77 C2
Ash La Baughurst RG26 9 B1
Latchmere Green RG26 28 A3
Ash Lodge Cl GU12 77 C1
Ash Lodge Dr GU12 77 C1
Ash Manor Sch GU12 100 B4
Ash Park Cotts RG25 89 A4
Ash Path SO20 126 A2
Ash Rd Aldershot GU12 100 A4
Bishop's Green RG20 6 B2
Ash St GU12 77 C1
Ash Sta GU12 77 C1
Ash Terr RG18 2 C4
Ash Tree Cl GU14 55 A2
Ash Tree Gr RG20 3 C4
Ash Tree Rd SP10 105 B4
Ash Vale Sta GU12 77 C4
Ash Wlk SO24 179 B3
Ashbarn Cres SO22 197 C3
Ashbourne Way RG19 2 C2
Ashburton Cl SO24 179 B3
Ashburton Rd SO24 179 B3
Ashbury Dr GU17 35 C1
Ashbury Rd GU35 164 B1
Ashdell Rd GU34 140 A2
Ashdene Cres GU12 77 C2
Ashdene Rd GU12 77 C1
Ashdown Ave GU14 56 B1
Ashdown Terr SP9 78 C3
Ashfield RG24 48 C2
Ashfield Gn GU17 34 B3
Ashfield Rd SP10 105 B4
Ashfields SO21 130 B3
Ashford Chace GU32 206 C1
Ashford Hill Prim Sch RG19 8 B1
Ashford Hill Rd RG19 7 B1
Ashlawn Gdns SP10 106 A3
Ashlea RG27 51 A1
Ashley Cl Camberley GU16 56 C3
Crondall GU10 97 B4
Winchester SO22 175 B2
Ashley Ct GU34 140 A2
Ashley Dr GU17 35 A2
Ashley Dro SN8 17 C3
Ashley Ho 4 GU35 164 B1
Ashley Lodge 16 RG21 69 A2
Ashley Rd
Bentworth GU34 138 A3
Farnborough GU14 56 A2
Ashmead GU35 164 B2
Ashmoor La RG24 70 C4
Ashmore Green Rd RG18 2 C4
Ashmore La SP5 190 B1
Ashmore Rd SO22 175 B1
Ashridge GU14 55 B4
Ashridge Ct 2 RG14 1 C1
Ashton Rd RG14 1 C1
Ashtree Cnr RG20 4 A4
Ashtrees The GU12 77 C1
Ashurst Cl Tadley RG26 26 C4
Winchester SO22 175 B2
Ashurst Rd GU12 77 B2
Ashwell Ave GU15 36 B3
Ashwood Dr RG14 2 A2
Ashwood Way RG23 68 B4
Ashwood Way Rdbt RG23 68 B4
Aspen Cl GU35 164 B1
Aspen Gdns RG27 51 A1
Aspen Ho GU11 100 A4
Aspin Way GU17 34 C3
Aster Ct SP10 105 B3
Aster Rd RG22 91 A4
Atbara Rd GU52 75 A2
Athlone Cl SP11 83 A4
Atholl Ct SP10 83 A2
Atholl Rd GU35 164 B1
Attenborough Cl GU51 54 A2
Attfield Cl GU12 77 B1
Attlee Gdns GU52 74 C2
Attwood Cl RG21 68 C2
Attwoods Dro SO21 197 B1
Auchinleck Ho 3 SP9 78 C4
Auchinleck Way GU11 76 B1
Audley Cl RG14 2 A3
Audley Ho GU9 122 A4
Augustine Cl SP10 82 B2
Augustus Dr RG23 68 B4
Augustus Wlk SP10 83 A2
Aukland Cl SP9 79 A3
Auklet Cl RG22 90 C4
Austen Ave SO22 197 B2
Austen Cl SO23 176 A1
Austen Gdns RG14 5 C4
Austen Gr RG22 68 C1
Austen Rd GU14 55 C3
Austin's Cotts GU9 98 C1
Avalan Ct SO23 197 C3
Aveley La GU9 122 A4
Avenue Cl Andover SP10 105 C4
Liphook GU30 187 C2
Avenue Rd
Farnborough GU14 56 A2
Fleet GU51 53 C1
Grayshott GU26 167 A2
Lasham GU34 116 B2
Winchester SO22 197 C4
Avenue Sucy GU15 35 C2
Avenue The
Aldershot GU12 100 A4
Andover SP10 105 C4
Barton Stacey SO21,SP11 108 B2
Camberley GU15 35 C3
Farleigh Wallop RG22 91 B1
Farnham GU10 121 B2
Fleet GU51 53 C1
Grayshott GU26 167 A2
Haslemere GU27 189 B4
Hatherden SP11 59 C1
Liphook GU30 187 C2
Mortimer RG7 11 C3
New Alresford SO24 179 B3
South Tidworth SP9 78 C2
Avery Cl RG40 16 B3
Avery Ct 18 GU11 76 C1
Aviary Ct RG24 69 C4
Aviemore Dr RG23 67 A1
Avington Pk* SO21 177 C3
Avocet Cres GU47 35 B4

Avon Cl Ash GU12 .....77 B1
Farnborough GU14 .....55 B4
Avon Ct 5 Andover SP10 .83 B1
Farnham GU9 .....99 A1
Avon Rd Farnham GU9 .....99 A1
Oakley RG23 .....67 A1
South Tidworth SP9 .....78 C3
Avon Way RG14 .....2 A2
Avon Wlk 10 RG21 .....69 B3
Avondale GU12 .....77 B4
Avondale Rd
Aldershot GU11 .....99 C4
Fleet GU51 .....54 A1
Award Rd GU52 .....74 C3
Axford La RG25 .....115 A2
Ayesgarth GU52 .....75 A3
Ayjay Cl GU11 .....99 C4
Aylesfield Farm GU34 .117 C2
Aylesham Way GU46 .....33 C3
Ayliffe Ho RG22 .....68 B2
Ayling Cl GU9 .....99 B4
Ayling Hill GU11 .....76 B1
Ayling La GU11 .....99 B4
Aylings Cl RG23 .....68 A2
Aylward's Dr GU34 .....161 B2
Aylwards Way SO20 .....147 C3
Aylwin Cl RG21 .....69 A1
Ayres La RG20 .....22 C4
Ayrshire Gdns GU51 .....54 A2
Azalea Ave GU35 .....165 A3
Azalea Cl SP10 .....105 B3
Azalea Dr GU27 .....189 B4
Azalea Gdns GU52 .....75 A3
Azalea Way GU15 .....36 C3

B

Babbs Mead GU9 .....98 C1
Babs Fields GU10 .....120 A3
Bacchus Ho 7 RG7 .....9 B1
Bach Cl RG22 .....91 A4
Back La Appleshaw SP11 .81 B3
Binsted GU10 .....142 C4
Brimpton RG7 .....9 A3
Mottisfont SO51 .....192 C3
Shinfield RG7 .....13 C4
Silchester RG7 .....11 A2
Southrope RG25 .....116 B3
Vernham Dean SP11 .....38 B3
Back St SO23 .....197 C2
Bacon Cl GU47 .....35 A3
Bacon La GU10 .....144 A2
Badajos Rd GU11 .....76 B2
Baden Powell Rd GU33 .186 B1
Bader Cl GU34 .....160 B2
Badger Ct GU10 .....121 C3
Badger Farm Rd SO22, SO23 .....197 B2
Badger Ridge RG20 .....1 B2
Badger Way GU10 .....98 A4
Badger's Bank RG24 .....69 C4
Badgers Cl GU52 .....74 C4
Badgers Copse GU15 .....36 B2
Badgers Croft RG7 .....11 C3
Badgers Holt GU46 .....33 B4
Badgerwood Dr GU16 .....36 A1
Badshear La SO24 .....201 C4
Badshot Lea Rd GU9 .....99 C3
Badshot Lea Village Inf Sch GU9 .....99 C3
Badshot Pk GU9 .....99 C3
Bagmore La RG25 .....115 C3
Bagnels Way RG14 .....1 B1
Bagwell La RG29,RG27 .....73 B3
Baigent Cl GU33 .....198 B4
Bailey Cl Camberley GU15 .56 A4
Winchester SO23 .....197 B3
Bailey Ho SO24 .....179 B3
Baileys Cl GU17 .....64 C3
Baily Ave RG18 .....2 C2
Bain Ave GU15 .....35 C1
Baird Ave GU52 .....68 C1
Baird Rd Arborfield RG2 ..15 B4
Farnborough GU14 .....56 A3
Bakers Field GU33 .....185 C1
Baldreys GU9 .....121 C4
Balfour Cres RG14 .....5 A3
Balfour Dr GU33 .....207 C2
Balfour Red Cross Mus* SO22 .....197 C1
Balintore Ct GU47 .....35 A4
Balksbury Hill* SP11 .....105 C3
Balksbury Hill Ind Est SP11 .....105 C3
Balksbury Jun Sch SP10 .....105 B4
Balksbury Rd SP11 .....105 C3
Ball & Wicket La GU9 ...99 A4
Ballantyne Rd GU14 .....55 C3
Ballard Cl RG22 .....68 B2
Ballard Ct GU15 .....36 C4
Ballard Rd GU15 .....36 C4
Balmoral Cl GU34 .....139 B2
Balmoral Cres GU9 .....98 C3
Balmoral Ct RG22 .....68 B2
Balmoral Dr GU16 .....56 B4
Balmoral Ho GU12 .....77 B3
Balmoral Rd
Andover SP10 .....106 A4
Ash GU12 .....77 C2
Balmoral Way RG25 .....91 A4
Balsan Cl GU34 .....68 B4

Bamber La GU34 .....119 A2
Banbury Cl GU16 .....56 C4
Band Hall Pl RG27 .....51 A1
Bank Rd GU11 .....77 A3
Bank Side RG40 .....16 B3
Bankside GU9 .....99 B4
Bankside Ho 4 SO22 .....197 C4
Bannister Gdns
Eversley GU46 .....33 B4
Yateley GU46 .....34 B3
Bannister Pl RG7 .....83 B3
Baptist Hill SP11 .....61 C1
Bar End Ind Est SO23 .198 A3
Bar End Rd SO23 .....198 A3
Barbara Cl GU52 .....75 A3
Barbel Ave RG21 .....69 C3
Barberry Cl GU52 .....75 A3
Barberry Way GU17 .....35 B1
Barbour Cl RG29 .....95 B4
Barcelona Cl SP10 .....83 A1
Bardsley Dr GU9 .....121 C4
Bardwell Cl RG22 .....68 B2
Baredown The RG27 .....71 B4
Barfield Cl SO23 .....198 A3
Barfield Rd RG18 .....2 C2
Barfield Sch GU10 .....99 C2
Barford Cl GU51 .....54 A1
Barge Cl GU11 .....77 B3
Barge La RG7 .....13 B2
Baring Cl
East Stratton SO21 .....134 A2
Itchen Abbas SO21 .....178 A4
Baring Rd SO23 .....198 A4
Barker Cl RG2 .....15 B4
Barkham Ride RG40 .....16 B4
Barley Down Dr SO22 .197 B2
Barley Mow Cl RG27 .....73 C4
Barley Mow Hill GU35 ..165 C3
Barley View RG25 .....89 C1
Barley Ways GU51 .....54 A3
Barlows La SP10 .....105 C3
Barlows Rd RG26 .....24 C4
Barn Cl GU15 .....36 B3
Barn Close La RG20 .....40 C4
Barn Cres RG14 .....5 A4
Barn La Four Marks GU34 159 C1
Oakley RG23 .....90 A3
Barn Meadow Cl GU52 ..74 C2
Barn The 14 GU34 .....139 C2
Barnard Cl GU16 .....56 B4
Barnard Way RG18 .....76 B2
Barncroft Appleshaw SP11 .81 A3
Farnham GU9 .....99 A1
Barnes Cl
Farnborough GU14 .....56 A2
Winchester SO23 .....197 C3
Barnes Rd GU9 .....99 A1
Barnes Terr 3 RG14 .....1 B1
Barnet Side La GU32 ....205 B3
Barnetts Wood La SO24 .181 A4
Barnfield GU46 .....34 A3
Barnfield Cl GU34 .....119 A2
Barnfield Cotts GU34 ....184 A3
Barnfield Rise SP10 .....105 C3
Barns The RG25 .....113 B4
Barnside Way GU33 ....207 C2
Barnsley Cl GU12 .....56 C1
Baroda Rd SP9 .....78 B2
Barossa Rd GU15 .....36 C4
Barra Cl RG23 .....67 A1
Barrack Rd GU11 .....76 C1
Barrett Ct RG21 .....69 B1
Barrie Rd GU9 .....98 C4
Barron Pl RG24 .....68 B4
Barrow Hill SO20 .....127 C4
Barry Way RG22 .....91 B4
Bartholomew St RG14 ...1 B1
Bartholomew Cl 2 SO23 .....176 A1
Bartholomew Ct 10 RG14 .1 B1
Bartlemy Cl RG14 .....1 B1
Bartlemy Rd RG14 .....1 B1
Bartlett Cl RG26 .....29 A1
Bartley Way RG27 .....72 B4
Bartley Wood Bsns Pk RG27 .....72 B4
Bartok Cl RG22 .....68 C1
Barton Cl Aldershot GU11 ..1 B4
Charlton SP10 .....82 B2
Barton Ct 2 GU14 .....56 A1
Barton End 2 GU34 .....139 C2
Barton Stacey CE Prim Sch SO21 .....129 C1
Barton's Ct RG29 .....72 B2
Bartons La RG24 .....70 A4
Bartons Way GU14 .....55 A4
Basing Dean GU34 .....204 C2
Basing Ct GU21 .....99 C4
Basing Ho* RG24 .....70 A3
Basing Rd RG24 .....69 C3
Basing View RG21 .....70 A3
Basingbourne Cl GU52 ..75 A3
Basingbourne Rd GU52 .75 A3
Basingfield Ct RG24 .....70 B2
Basingstoke Bsns Ctr RG22 .....68 C1
Basingstoke Canal Ctr* GU16 .....56 C2
Basingstoke Coll of Tech
Basingstoke RG21 .....68 C3
Basingstoke RG21 .....69 A3
Basingstoke Rd
Aldermaston RG7 .....9 B4
Alton GU34 .....139 A3
Kings Worthy SO23 .176 B4
Kingsclere RG20 .....24 C1
Ramsdell RG26 .....44 C3
Stratfield Turgis RG27 ...30 C3

Basingstoke Rd continued
Swallowfield RG7 .....14 A3
Basingstoke Sta RG21 ...69 A3
Bassenthwaite Gdns SO30 .....164 B3
Bassett Cl GU16 .....56 B4
Bat & Ball La GU10 .....121 C3
Batchelor Dr RG26 .....70 B3
Batchelors Barn Rd SP10 .....106 B4
Bateman Gr GU12 .....100 B4
Bath Rd Camberley GU15 ...36 A3
Newbury RG14 .....1 A2
Thatcham RG18, RG19 .....2 C2
Batsford SP11 .....61 C1
Batt's Cnr GU10 .....143 A4
Battens Ave RG25 .....88 A4
Battery End RG14 .....5 A3
Battery Hill SO22 .....197 B3
Battle Cl RG14 .....1 A2
Battle Rd RG14 .....5 A3
Baughurst Rd
Baughurst RG26 .....26 B3
Ramsdell RG26 .....46 B4
Baveno Ho GU14 .....56 A1
Baverstocks GU34 .....140 A3
Bawlings The GU15 .....36 A3
Baxendales The RG14 .....2 A1
Bayfield Ave GU16 .....36 B1
Bayford Cl GU17 .....35 C1
Baynard Cl RG21 .....69 B4
Bays Cl RG26 .....9 A1
Baytree Yd SO24 .....179 B3
Baywood Cl GU14 .....55 A3
Bazaar Rd SP9 .....78 B4
Beach Piece Way RG22 .91 A4
Beach's Cres RG26 .....27 C2
Beacon Cl GU12 .....121 C3
Beacon Hill Com Sch GU26 .....167 A3
Beacon Hill Rd
Beacon Hill GU26 .....167 A3
Fleet GU10,GU52 .....75 B2
Beacon Pass RG22 .....42 A4
Beacon View Ho GU26 ..167 A2
Beaconsfield Rd RG21 ...69 B1
Beal's Pightle RG26 .....46 C4
Beale's Cl SP10 .....106 A4
Beale's Ct SP5 .....169 A1
Beales La RG21 .....121 B4
Bealeswood La GU10 ....143 B3
Beam Hollow GU9 .....99 A4
Bear Ct RG24 .....69 C4
Bear Hill RG20 .....24 B1
Bear La Farnham GU9 .....99 A2
Bearwood Cotts GU10 ..121 B4
Bearwood Gdns 11 GU51 .54 A3
Beatty Ct SP10 .....106 B4
Beauclerk Gn RG27 .....52 B1
Beaufort Rd
Aldershot GU11 .....164 B3
Farnborough GU12 .....77 B3
Farnham GU9 .....99 A2
Fleet GU52 .....75 A3
Winchester SO23 .....197 C3
Beaufront Cl GU15 .....36 C4
Beaufront Rd GU15 .....36 C4
Beaulieu Ct SO22 .....175 B2
Beaulieu Ct
22 Andover SP10 .....83 B1
8 Basingstoke RG21 .....69 B3
Blackwater GU17 .....34 C3
Beaulieu Gdns GU17 .....35 A3
Beaumaris Cl SP10 .....105 C3
Beaumaris Par GU16 .....56 B4
Beaumont Gn GU11 .....76 B1
Beaumont Jun Sch GU11 ..76 B1
Beaurepaire Cl RG26 .....28 B2
Beaver Ind Est GU30 .....188 A2
Beaver La GU46 .....34 A3
Beavers Cl Alton GU34 ...139 C2
Beavers Hill GU9 .....98 B1
Beavers Mews GU15 ....164 C2
Beavers Rd GU9 .....99 A2
Bechin Cl GU52 .....74 B2
Beck Gdns GU9 .....98 C3
Beck Ind Est The GU12 .100 A4
Becket Ct RG23 .....68 A2
Becket Ho 7 RG14 .....1 B1
Beckett Cl RG23 .....68 A3
Beckett Rd SP10 .....105 C4
Beddington Ce RG24 .....70 A4
Bede Dr SP10 .....82 B2
Bedfield Ho SO23 .....176 A1
Bedfield La SO23 .....176 A3
Bedford Ave GU16 .....56 B3
Bedford Cl
6 Bordon GU35 .....164 B1
Newbury RG14 .....5 A3
Bedford Cres GU16 .....56 B4
Bedford La GU16 .....56 B4
Bedford Wlk 6 RG21 .....69 A1
Bedser Sq SP10 .....83 A2
Beech Ave
Camberley GU15 .....36 A2
Farnham GU10 .....122 A3
Beech Cl Bramley RG26 ...29 A1
Middle Wallop SO20 .....126 A2
Penton Grafton SP11 .....82 A1
Thruxton SP11 .....103 C4
Winchester SO22 .....197 A2
Beech Copse SO22 .....175 A1

Beech Cl Crondall GU10 ...97 C1
8 Newbury RG14 .....1 C2
Whitchurch RG28 .....86 B3
Beech Down Prim Sch RG22 .....91 B4
Beech Dr GU17 .....35 A2
Beech Gr GU11 .....128 C4
Beech Grange Ave SP4 ..101 B1
Beech Hanger End GU26 .....166 C2
Beech Hanger Rd GU26 .166 C2
Beech Hill RG35 .....165 C3
Beech Hill Rd
Headley GU35 .....165 C3
North Tidworth SP9 .....79 A4
Shinfield RG7 .....13 B4
Beech Ho RG24 .....48 C4
Beech La GU10 .....166 C2
Beech Rd
Bishop's Green RG20 .....6 C1
Camberley GU16 .....56 B3
Farnborough GU14 .....55 C4
New Alresford SO24 .....179 B3
Beech Ride Fleet GU51 ...74 C4
Sandhurst GU47 .....34 C4
Beech The GU47 .....35 A3
Beech Tree Cl RG23 .....90 A4
Beech Tree Dr GU9 .....99 C3
Beech Wlk SO30 .....170 B2
Beech Way RG23 .....68 B4
Beech Wlk SP10 .....105 B4
Beech Way RG22 .....91 B4
Beechbrook Ave GU46 ...34 B3
Beechcrest View RG27 ...51 A1
Beechcroft Cl
Andover SP10 .....83 A1
Aldershot GU11 .....100 A4
Beechcroft Cotts SO20 .170 A3
Beechdown Ho GU11 .....68 B1
Beeches The
Andover SP10 .....105 C4
Ash GU12 .....56 B1
Basingstoke RG22 .....91 B3
Sutton Scotney SO21 .....131 B2
Tadley RG26 .....26 C4
Beechfield SP4 .....123 A3
Beeching Cl GU12 .....77 C2
Beechlands Rd GU34 ....160 A2
Beechnut Dr GU17 .....34 C3
Beechnut Ind Est GU11 .....76 C1
Beechnut Rd GU12 .....76 C1
Beechwood GU24 .....48 C2
Beechwood Cl
Basingstoke RG21 .....91 B3
Fleet GU51 .....74 C3
Beechwood Ct GU34 .....139 B1
Beechwood Rd GU34 ....139 B1
Beehive La GU34 .....139 B1
Beethoven Rd RG22 .....91 C4
Beeton's Ave GU12 .....77 C2
Beggar's La SO23 .....198 A4
Beggarwood La RG22 .....91 A3
Begonia Cl RG22 .....91 A4
Belaga Cl SP20 .....126 A3
Beldham Rd GU9 .....121 B4
Belfry Sq RG22 .....91 A3
Belgrave Ct GU17 .....35 A2
Belgrave Mews RG27 .....52 B1
Bell Cl GU14 .....56 A3
Bell Hill RG14 .....4 C2
Bell Holt RG14 .....4 C2
Bell La Blackwater GU17 ...35 A3
Elisfield RG25 .....115 B4
Bell Meadow Rd RG27 ...51 A1
Bell Rd Andover SP10 ....106 B4
Basingstoke RG24 .....69 C4
Lyneham GU27 .....189 C2
Bell St Ludgershall GU11 ...1 B4
Whitchurch RG28 .....86 B3
Bell Vale La GU27 .....189 C2
Belland Dr GU11 .....76 B1
Belle Vue Ct GU12 .....77 A1
Belle Vue Ent Ctr GU12 ..77 A1
Belle Vue Inf Sch GU12 ..77 A1
Belle Vue Rd
Aldershot GU12 .....77 A1
Andover SP10 .....106 A3
Old Basing RG24 .....70 B3
Belleisle Rd GU16 .....56 B3
Bellevue RG26 .....86 B3
Bellew Rd GU16 .....56 C3
Bellhanger Ents GU34 ...138 A3
Belmont Cl
Andover SP10 .....106 A3
Farnborough GU14 .....55 B4
Belstone Mews GU14 ....55 C4
Belton Rd GU15 .....53 B1
Belvedere Cl GU17 .....35 A2
Belvedere Ct GU14 .....164 B1
Belvedere Dr RG14 .....5 C4
Belvedere Gdns RG24 ...49 A2
Belvedere Rd GU14 .....56 A3
Belvoir Cl GU16 .....56 B1
Bembridge Ct 6 GU47 ...35 A4
Benbow Ct SP10 .....106 B4
Benenden Gn SO24 .....179 B2
Benett Gdns RG14 .....1 B1
Benford Ct RG27 .....72 C1
Benger's La RG18, RG19 ...2 B2
Benham RG18,RG19 ...2 B2

Benham La RG7 .....14 A2
Benhams La GU33 .....186 A2
Benin Rd SP11 .....79 B3
Bennet Cl Alton GU34 ...139 C2
Basingstoke RG21 .....69 B4
Bennett Ct GU15 .....36 A3
Bennetts Rise GU11 .....100 A4
Bent St SO20 .....147 C4
Benta Cl SO20 .....126 A3
Bentley Bsns Pk GU10 ..120 A3
Bentley CE Prim Sch GU10 .....120 A3
Bentley Cl SO23 .....176 A3
Bentley Copse GU15 .....36 C2
Bentley Dr 2 GU51 .....53 B2
Bentley Ind Ctr GU10 ...120 A2
Bentley Sta GU10 .....53 B2
Bentley Sta GU10 .....120 B2
Bentley Way SP5 .....168 A3
Benwell Cl RG29 .....95 B4
Bercote Cl SO22 .....175 B1
Bere Cl SO22 .....175 B1
Bere Hill RG28 .....86 B3
Bere Hill Cl RG28 .....86 B3
Bere Hill Cres SP10 .....106 B4
Berewick GU34 .....139 C1
Beresford Cl
Andover SP10 .....106 A3
Camberley GU16 .....56 B3
Beresford Ctr RG24 .....69 C4
Beresford Rd GU11 .....83 C1
Bereweeke Ave SO22 ...175 C1
Bereweeke Cl SO22 .....175 C1
Bereweeke Rd SO22 .....175 C1
Bereweeke Way SO22 ..175 C1
Berewyk Cl RG22 .....91 A4
Berkeley Cl GU51 .....54 A1
Berkeley Cres GU16 .....56 C4
Berkeley Dr RG22 .....91 C4
Berkeley Rd RG14 .....1 B1
Berkshire Rd GU15 .....36 B4
Bermuda Cl RG24 .....48 B1
Bernard Ave GU34 .....160 A1
Bernard Ct GU15 .....35 C2
Bernstein Rd RG22 .....91 B4
Berry Ct RG24 .....72 A4
Berry Hill SO24 .....181 A3
Berry Way SP10 .....105 B4
Berrybank GU47 .....35 B3
Berrydown La
Axford RG25 .....114 C2
Overton RG25 .....90 B1
Berrylands GU33 .....208 A4
Berrywood La SO24 .....137 A3
Berwyn Cl RG22 .....68 A2
Bessemer Rd RG21 .....68 C1
Beta Rd GU14 .....56 B1
Bethel Cl GU9 .....99 A3
Bethel La GU9 .....99 A3
Betjeman Wlk GU46 .....33 C2
Beveren Cl GU17 .....54 A2
Beverley Cl Ash GU12 ....77 B1
Basingstoke RG22 .....91 A4
Beverley Cres GU14 .....55 B1
Bevers The RG7 .....11 C3
Bexmoor RG24 .....70 A3
Bexmoor Way RG24 .....70 A3
Beyne Rd SO22 .....197 A2
Bible Fields RG25 .....113 B4
Bicester Cl RG28 .....86 B3
Bicknell Rd GU16 .....36 B1
Bidden Rd RG25 .....94 C4
Biddesden La SP11 .....57 B1
Bideford Cl GU14 .....55 C1
Bietigheim Way GU15 ...36 A3
Bigg's Hill Cotts RG20 ...4 B2
Biggs La RG40,RG42 .....16 C4
Bighton Dean La SO24 .181 A4
Bighton Hill SO24 .....181 A3
Bighton La SO24 .....180 B3
Bighton Rd GU34 .....159 B3
Bilbao Ct SP10 .....83 B1
Bilberry Ct 8 SO22 .....197 C4
Billing Ave RG40 .....16 C3
Bilton Rd RG24 .....48 C1
Binfields GU9 .....99 A2
Binfields Cl RG24 .....48 C1
Binfields Rdbt RG24 .....48 C1
Bingley Cl Alton GU34 ...139 C2
Basingstoke RG24 .....48 C1
Binley Bottom SP11 .....61 C3
Binley Ct RG26 .....27 A4
Binsted CE Prim Sch GU34 .....141 C4
Binsted Dr GU17 .....35 A3
Binswood View Bsns Ctr GU35 .....163 B3
Binton La GU10 .....100 B2
Birch Ave Fleet GU51 .....53 C1
Middle Wallop SO20 .....126 A2
Birch Cl Bordon GU35 ...164 C1
Camberley GU15 .....36 B4
Farnham GU10 .....121 C2
Liss GU33 .....208 A2
Birch Ct 8 SO22 .....197 B3
Birch Dr GU17 .....35 A3
Birch Gr Bordon GU35 ...164 B1
Chilbolton SO20 .....129 B1
Hook RG27 .....51 A1
Birch Ho 8 GU14 .....55 A1
Birch La RG7 .....11 B3
Birch Mdw GU9 .....99 A3
Birch Rd Baughurst RG26 ...9 B1
Finchampstead RG40 .....16 C3
Headley GU35 .....165 C3
Birch Tree Cl GU47 .....189 A2
Birch Way GU12 .....77 C4

Birches The
Blackwater GU17 ...34 C3
Farnborough GU14 ...55 A2
Birchett Rd
Aldershot GU11 ...76 C1
Farnborough GU14 ...55 B3
Birchfields GU15 ...36 A2
Birchland Cl RG7 ...11 B3
Bircholt Rd GU30 ...187 A2
Birchview GU46 ...34 A2
Birchwood RG12 ...48 C2
Birchwood Rd RG14 ...2 A2
Birdhaven GU10 ...121 C3
Birdwood Rd GU15 ...35 B4
Birdworld & Underwater World* GU10 ...121 A2
Birinus Rd SO23 ...176 A1
Birkenholme Cl GU35 ...166 A2
Bisbearne Gdns GU33 ...207 C3
Bishop Challoner RC Sec Sch RG22 ...68 B2
Bishop Sumner Dr GU9 ...99 A3
Bishop's Mead GU9 ...98 C1
Bishop's View GU34 ...159 C1
Bishop's Way GU17 ...105 C4
Bishops Cl
4 Baughurst RG26 ...9 C1
Fleet GU52 ...75 A3
South Tidworth SP9 ...78 C2
Bishops Dr SP10 ...105 C4
Bishops Rd GU9 ...98 C3
Bishopscroft Ct RG26 ...9 B1
Bishopswood Jun Sch RG26 ...26 C4
Bishopswood La RG26 ...26 B4
Bishopswood Rd RG26 ...9 B1
Bishopwood Inf Sch RG26 ...26 C4
Bittern Cl Aldershot GU11 ...99 C4
Basingstoke RG22 ...90 C4
Sandhurst GU47 ...35 A4
Black Dam Rdbt RG21 ...69 C2
Black Dam Way RG21 ...69 C2
Black Pond La GU10 ...122 A3
Black Swan Bldgs 20 SO22 ...197 C4
Black Swan Yd 19 GU1 ...106 A4
Blackberry Cl GU34 ...160 B2
Blackberry La GU34 ...160 B1
Blackberry Wlk RG24 ...69 C4
Blackbird Cl
Basingstoke RG22 ...90 C4
Sandhurst GU47 ...35 A4
Blackbird Ct SP10 ...83 A1
Blackbird Rd RG26 ...6 C2
Blackbushe Bsns Ctr GU46 ...34 A2
Blackbushes Rd RG27 ...53 B4
Blackcap Pl GU47 ...35 B4
Blackdown Cl RG22 ...68 A2
Blackdown Rd GU16 ...86 A3
Blackman Gdns GU11 ...99 C4
Blackmoor Ho GU33 ...185 C3
Blackmoor La GU33 ...186 A3
Blackmore La RG22 ...205 C2
Blacknest Ind Pk GU34 ...142 B4
Blacknest Rd GU34 ...120 B1
Blackstocks La Mapledurwell RG27 ...71 A3
Newnham RG27 ...71 A3
Blackstone Cl GU14 ...55 A3
Blackthorn Cl SO21 ...153 B2
Blackthorn Cres GU14 ...55 B4
Blackthorn Way RG23 ...68 B3
Blackthorne Cl Ash GU12 ...77 C1
Blackwater Cl RG14 ...2 A2
Blackwater Pk GU12 ...77 B1
Blackwater Sta GU17 ...35 B2
Blackwater Way RG40 ...16 C1
Blackwater Way GU12 ...100 A4
Blackwell Rd SO21 ...153 B2
Blagdon Cl RG19 ...6 A4
Blair Rd 17 RG21 ...69 A2
Blaire Pk GU46 ...33 C4
Blaise Cl GU14 ...96 A2
Blake Cl RG29 ...95 B4
Blake Ct RG21 ...69 A2
Blake's La Baughurst RG26 ...10 A1
Blake's Ride GU46 ...33 C3
Blakes Cotts RG29 ...72 C1
Blanket St GU34 ...162 C4
Bleach's Yard Ind Est GU30 ...188 A1
Bledlow Cl RG14 ...5 A3
Blendon Dr SP10 ...82 B1
Blenheim Cl Alton GU34 ...140 A2
Four Marks GU34 ...160 A2
Tongham GU10 ...100 B4
Blenheim Cotts RG18 ...2 C4
Blenheim Cres GU9 ...98 C2
Blenheim Ct GU14 ...56 A1
Blenheim Pk GU34 ...77 A4
Blenheim Rd
Farnborough GU11 ...76 C4
Newbury RG14 ...1 C2
Old Basing RG24 ...70 B3
Blighton La GU10 ...100 B2
Bliss Cl RG22 ...68 C1
Blissmore La SP11 ...81 B1
Bloomfieldhatch Rd RG7 ...12 C4
Bloomsbury Way GU17 ...35 A2
Bloswood Dr RG28 ...86 A3
Bloswood La RG28 ...86 A3
Blue Ball Hill SO23 ...198 A4
Blue Hayes Cl SP10 ...106 A4

Blue Pryor Ct 12 GU52 ...74 C2
Blue Timbers Cl 8 GU35 ...164 B1
Bluebell All GU51 ...53 C1
Bluebell Wlk 1 GU51 ...53 C1
Bluehaven Wlk RG27 ...50 C1
Bluethroat Cl GU47 ...35 B4
Bluff Cove GU11 ...77 A2
Blunden Cl RG21 ...69 A1
Blunden Rd GU14 ...55 B3
Blythwood Dr GU16 ...36 A1
Boames La RG20 ...4 B3
Boar's Bridge RG26 ...27 C2
Boathe Gdns RG14 ...5 C4
Bodmin Cl RG22 ...68 A2
Bogmoor Cl GU34 ...160 A1
Bohunt Manor Gdn* GU35 ...187 C1
Bohunt Sch GU30 ...187 C2
Bole Rd GU34 ...139 B1
Bolley Ave GU35 ...164 A3
Bolton Cres RG22 ...68 C2
Bond Cl Basingstoke RG24 ...69 C4
Baughurst RG26 ...9 C1
Bone La RG14 ...2 A2
Bonemill La RG14,RG20 ...1 A1
Bonhams Cl GU34 ...140 C4
Bonner Cotts SP5 ...191 C4
Bonners Field GU10 ...120 A3
Boon Way RG21 ...67 A1
Borden Gates SP10 ...106 A4
Border End GU27 ...189 A3
Border Rd GU27 ...189 A3
Borderside GU46 ...33 C3
Bordon Cl 7 RG26 ...26 C4
Bordon Jun & Inf Schs GU35 ...164 B2
Bordon Trad Est GU35 ...164 A3
Boreen The GU35 ...165 C3
Borelli Mews 8 GU9 ...99 A1
Borelli Yd 8 GU9 ...99 A1
Borkum Cl SP10 ...82 C2
Borman Way SO21 ...153 C2
Borodin Cl RG22 ...91 C4
Borough Court Rd RG27 ...51 C3
Borough The
Crondall GU10 ...97 B3
Farnham GU9 ...98 C1
Borovere Cl GU34 ...139 C1
Borovere Gdns GU34 ...139 C1
Borovere La GU34 ...139 C1
Boscobel Rd SO22 ...175 C1
Boscowen Ct SP10 ...106 B4
Bostock Cl SP10 ...174 B2
Botany Hill GU10 ...100 A3
Botisdon Cl SP11 ...38 B3
Bottle La RG27 ...51 A4
Boulters Rd GU12 ...76 C1
Boundary Rd
Farnham GU34 ...56 A1
Farnham GU10 ...121 B1
Grayshott GU26 ...167 A2
Newbury RG14 ...1 C2
Boundstone Cl GU10 ...121 C3
Boundstone Rd GU10 ...121 C2
Bounty Rd RG21 ...69 A2
Bounty Rise RG21 ...69 A2
Bourley Rd GU9,GU10, GU11,GU52 ...75 B2
Bourne Com Sch The GU10 ...122 A3
Bourne Ct Aldershot GU11 ...99 C4
2 Andover SP10 ...83 B1
3 Basingstoke RG21 ...69 B3
Bourne Dene GU10 ...121 C3
Bourne Fields GU10 ...47 C2
Bourne Firs GU10 ...122 A3
Bourne Gr GU10 ...122 B4
Bourne Grove Cl GU10 ...122 B4
Bourne Grove Dr GU10 ...122 B4
Bourne Hts GU9 ...122 A4
Bourne La SP9 ...101 C4
Bourne Mdw SP11 ...62 A1
Bourne Mill Ind Est GU9 ...99 B2
Bourne Rd
North Tidworth SP9 ...78 C3
Thatcham RG19 ...2 C1
Bourne The GU35 ...78 A3
Bourne View SP9 ...78 C4
Bournemouth Rd SP11 ...122 C3
Bournewood Pk GU10 ...122 B4
Bourton Cl RG27 ...29 B1
Bow Field RG27 ...51 B1
Bow Gdns RG27 ...49 B4
Bow Gr RG27 ...29 B1
Bow St GU34 ...139 C1
Bowcott Hill GU35 ...165 B3
Bowdown Cr RG14 ...1 B1
Bowenhurst Gdns GU51 ...74 B2
Bowenhurst La GU51 ...74 B2
Bower Rd GU10 ...121 C3
Bowers Grove La SO24 ...181 B4
Bowers La SP11 ...38 A4
Bowling Green Cl GU16 ...58 B4
Bowling Green Rd RG27 ...50 C1
Bowling Green Rd RG18 ...2 C3
Bowman Rd RG24 ...49 A2
Bowmonts Rd RG26 ...27 A4
Bowyer Cl 12 RG21 ...69 A1
Boxall's Gr GU11 ...99 C4
Boxall's La GU11 ...99 C4
Boyce Cl RG21 ...91 B4
Boyne Mead Rd SO23 ...176 B4
Boyne Rise SO23 ...176 A4
Boynescourt Cl GU34 ...160 B2
Boyneswood La GU34 ...160 B2

Boyneswood Rd GU34 ...160 B2
Brabon Rd GU14 ...55 B3
Bracebridge GU15 ...35 C3
Bracken Cl SP10 ...106 A4
Bracken Bank RG24 ...69 C4
Bracken La Bordon GU35 ...186 A4
Yateley GU46 ...33 C3
Brackenbury SO20 ...82 B1
Brackendale Cl GU15 ...36 B2
Brackendale Rd GU15 ...36 A2
Brackens The RG22 ...91 B3
Brackenmoor Dr RG26 ...9 C1
Brackenwood Pl GU51 ...53 C1
Bracklesham Cl GU14 ...55 C4
Brackley Ave RG27 ...52 B3
Brackley Way RG22 ...68 B1
Bracknell La RG27 ...52 B4
Bradbury Cl RG28 ...86 A3
Bradley Cotts SO21 ...112 A1
Bradley Peak SO22 ...175 B1
Bradley Rd RG27 ...175 B2
Bradman Sq SP10 ...83 A2
Bradwell Cl RG21 ...82 B2
Braemar Cl GU16 ...56 B4
Braemar Dr RG23 ...67 A1
Braeside Cl
Haslemere GU27 ...189 B4
Winchester SO22 ...197 A2
Brahms Rd RG22 ...91 C4
Braine L'Alleud Rd 17 RG21 ...69 A3
Braishfield Rd SO51 ...194 B1
Bramble Bank SO51 ...56 C3
Bramble Hill RG24 ...179 B3
Bramble Way RG24 ...70 B2
Brambles Cl Ash GU12 ...77 C1
Four Marks GU34 ...160 A1
Brambles The RG14 ...5 B4
Brambleton Ave GU9 ...121 C4
Bramblewood Pl GU51 ...53 C1
Brambling Cl RG22 ...90 C4
Bramblys Cl RG21 ...69 A2
Bramblys Dr RG21 ...69 A2
Bramdean Cl RG26 ...26 C4
Bramdown Hts RG22 ...91 A4
Bramley CE Prim Sch RG26 ...28 C2
Bramley Cl GU34 ...140 A2
Bramley Green Rd RG26 ...29 A1
Bramley La
Blackwater GU17 ...34 C3
Bramley RG26 ...28 C2
Bramley Rd
Camberley GU15 ...35 C1
Pamber End RG26 ...27 B1
Sherborne St John RG24 ...27 C4
Three Ashes RG7 ...28 A4
Bramley Sta RG26 ...28 C2
Bramley Wlk GU35 ...164 A1
Braming Ave GU46 ...33 C3
Bramoak RG26 ...28 B2
Brampton Gdns RG22 ...91 B3
Bramshaw Cl SO22 ...175 B2
Bramshill Cl RG21 ...15 B4
Bramshill Council Hos RG27 ...31 C4
Bramshill Ho (Police Coll) RG27 ...32 A2
Bramshot Dr GU51 ...54 A1
Bramshott Dr RG27 ...51 A1
Brancaster Ave SP10 ...82 B2
Brandon Cl GU34 ...139 C2
Brandon Rd GU52 ...74 C2
Brandy Bottom GU46 ...34 B2
Brandy Mount SO24 ...179 B3
Branksome Ave SO20 ...129 A2
Branksome Cl
Camberley GU15 ...35 B3
Chilbolton SO20 ...129 A2
Winchester SO22 ...197 A3
Branksome Hill Rd GU47 ...35 B4
Branksome Park Rd GU15 ...35 B3
Bransbury Rd GU51 ...53 C1
Bransgore Cl GU52 ...74 C2
Branton Cl RG22 ...68 B2
Brassey Rd SO22 ...175 C1
Braunfels Wlk RG14 ...1 B1
Braxton Ho 1 SO23 ...198 A4
Breach Farm Cotts RG25 ...113 B2
Breach La
Sherfield on Loddon RG27 ...49 C4
Upper Chute SP11 ...58 A4
Breachfield RG20 ...22 B4
Breadels Field RG22 ...91 A3
Brecon Cl GU14 ...55 A4
Bremen Gdns SP10 ...82 C2
Brendon Rd GU14 ...55 B3
Bret Harte Rd GU16 ...36 B1
Brew House La RG27 ...52 B3
Brewer Cl RG21 ...208 C2
Brewer Ct RG21 ...68 B2
Brewers Cl SO24 ...204 B4
Brewery Comm RG7 ...11 C4
Brewhouse Yd SO24 ...179 B3
Briar La GU34 ...160 A1
Briar Way RG26 ...27 A4
Briar Wood SO23 ...208 A4
Briarlea Rd RG7 ...11 B3
Briars Cl GU14 ...77 A4
Briars Cl SO23 ...208 B4
Briars The Ash GU12 ...77 C1
Fleet GU52 ...75 C1
Briarwood RG40 ...16 B3
Brick Kiln La Alton GU34 ...139 B2

Brick Kiln La continued
West Tisted SO24 ...204 A4
Brick La GU51 ...54 A1
Brickersbury Ho GU14 ...55 B4
Brickfields Ct RG22 ...70 A4
Brickiln La GU34 ...160 C3
Bricksbury Hill GU9 ...99 A4
Brickyards Ind Est The GU22 ...207 A1
Bridge Ct RG26 ...27 A4
Bridge Mdws GU33 ...207 C2
Bridge Mews GU34 ...100 B4
Bridge Rd Aldershot GU11 ...99 C4
Camberley GU15 ...35 C2
Farnborough GU14 ...55 B2
New Alresford SO24 ...179 A3
Bridge Sq GU9 ...99 A1
Bridge St Andover SP10 ...106 A4
1 Newbury RG14 ...1 C2
Overton RG25 ...88 A4
48 Winchester SO23 ...198 A4
Bridge Wlk GU46 ...34 A4
Bridge Works GU15 ...35 C2
Bridgefield GU9 ...99 A1
Bridgemead GU16 ...56 A4
Bridges The RG27 ...11 A3
Bridgetts La SO21 ...155 A1
Bridle Cl
East Tisted SO24 ...183 B3
Grayshott GU26 ...166 C2
Bridle Ct 7 GU11 ...76 B1
Brighton Hill Com Sch RG22 ...68 B1
Brighton Hill Ctr RG22 ...91 B4
Brighton Hill Rdbt RG22 ...68 B1
Brighton Hill Ret Pk RG22 ...68 C1
Brighton Rd GU14 ...100 A4
Brighton Way RG22 ...91 B4
Brightstone La GU34 ...160 A2
Brightwells Rd GU9 ...99 A1
Brimley Hill Ct RG20 ...24 B1
Brimpton CE Prim Sch RG7 ...8 B3
Brimpton La RG7 ...8 C2
Brimpton Rd
Baughurst RG26 ...9 A1
Brimpton RG7 ...8 B4
Brindle La GU11 ...99 C4
Brinksway GU51 ...74 A4
Brinn's La GU17 ...35 A3
Brinns Cotts GU17 ...35 A3
Brislands La GU34 ...181 C4
Bristow Cres GU15 ...36 A2
Bristow Inf Sch GU15 ...35 C1
Bristow Rd GU15 ...35 C1
Britannia Cl GU15 ...164 C2
Brittain Ct GU47 ...35 A4
Britten Cl GU12 ...77 C1
Britten Rd RG22 ...91 C4
Broad Chalke Down SO22 ...197 B2
Broad Ha'penny GU10 ...121 C3
Broad Leaze RG27 ...51 A1
Broad Oak La RG29 ...73 A2
Broad St GU34 ...104 B2
Broad St SO24 ...179 B3
Broad View La SO22 ...197 A2
Broad Wlk GU16 ...86 A3
Broadacres GU51 ...53 C1
Broadfellowpenny La RG26 ...10 A1
Broadhurst GU11 ...55 A2
Broadhurst Gr RG24 ...49 A1
Broadlands
Camberley GU15 ...56 B4
Farnborough GU14 ...56 B1
Broadlands Cl GU10 ...120 A3
Broadmead GU10 ...120 A3
Broadoak RG26 ...27 A4
Broadview Cl GU14 ...141 C4
Broadway RG28 ...86 B2
Broadway The
Andover SP10 ...106 A4
Newbury RG14 ...1 C2
Sandhurst GU47 ...34 C4
Winchester SO23 ...198 A4
Brockdown Rd GU11 ...99 C4
Brockenhurst Dr GU34 ...34 A3
Brockham Hill La GU34 ...118 A1
Brockhurst Lodge GU34 ...121 C4
Brocklands GU46 ...33 C2
Brockwood Bottom SO24 ...202 C1
Broken Way RG20 ...5 C1
Brokle Cl GU52 ...74 C2
Bromelia Cl RG26 ...28 B2
Bronte Rise RG14 ...5 C4
Bronze Cl RG22 ...91 A2
Brook Ave GU9 ...99 B4
Brook Cl SO23 ...77 C2
Fleet GU51 ...53 C1
Brook Cotts
King's Somborne SO51 ...193 B3
Medstead GU34 ...160 B1
Brook Gn RG26 ...27 A4
Brook Ho Farnham GU9 ...99 A3
Newbury RG14 ...1 C2
Brook St RG26 ...9 B2
Brook The SO24 ...179 B4
Brook Trad Est The GU12 ...77 B1
Brooke Cl GU16 ...99 C4
Brooke Cl SO23 ...176 A4
Brookfield Cl GU51 ...54 A1
Brookfield Rd GU34 ...77 B2

Brookham Prep Sch GU30 ...188 B1
Brookhouse Rd GU14 ...55 B2
Brooklands GU34 ...76 B1
Brooklands Rd RG22 ...68 A2
Brooklands Rd GU9 ...99 B4
Brooklands Way GU9 ...99 B4
Brookley Cl GU10 ...100 A2
Brookly Gdns GU51 ...54 A1
Brookmead Ct 18 GU9 ...98 C1
Brookside RG26 ...86 B2
Brooks Sh Ctr The SO23 ...198 A4
Brooksby Cl GU17 ...34 C3
Brookside Farnham GU9 ...99 A3
Sandhurst GU47 ...35 A4
Brookside Bsns Ctr RG7 ...14 A3
Brookside Cotts SO20 ...147 C3
Brookside Rd RG21 ...69 A3
Brookvale Cl RG21 ...69 A3
Brookway Newbury RG14 ...2 B1
Upper Clatford SP11 ...105 B2
Brookwood Rd GU14 ...56 A2
Broom Acres Fleet GU52 ...74 C3
Sandhurst GU47 ...34 C4
Broom Cl GU17 ...34 C3
Broom Squires GU26 ...167 B2
Broome Cl GU46 ...34 A4
Broomfield La GU10 ...121 C1
Broomfield Rd GU35 ...164 A1
Broomhill GU10 ...99 A4
Broomhill Rd GU14 ...55 A3
Broomleaf Cnr GU9 ...99 A1
Broomleaf Rd GU9 ...99 A1
Broomrigg Rd GU51 ...53 C1
Broomwood Way GU10 ...122 A3
Brougham Pl GU9 ...98 C4
Broughton Mews GU16 ...36 B1
Broughton Prim Sch SO20 ...170 A4
Broughton Rd SO20 ...148 C1
Brown Crest RG22 ...90 C4
Browning Dr SO22 ...197 B4
Browning Rd GU52 ...74 C2
Browning Rd RG26 ...28 B2
Brownsover Rd GU14 ...55 A2
Broxhead Farm Rd GU35 ...164 C4
Broxhead Trad Est GU35 ...164 C3
Bruan Rd RG14 ...5 B4
Brummell Rd RG14 ...1 B3
Brunel Cl SO21 ...111 A1
Brunel Gate SP10 ...82 A1
Brunel Rd GU14 ...68 C3
Brunelle Cl GU14 ...56 A2
Bryanstone Cl GU52 ...75 A3
Bryce Gdns GU11 ...100 A4
Bryce La SO20 ...135 A2
Bryn Rd GU10 ...121 B4
Buchan The GU15 ...56 B4
Buchanan Dr RG40 ...16 B4
Buckby La 7 RG21 ...69 B3
Buckfast Cl RG24 ...48 A1
Buckholt Rd SO20 ...170 A3
Buckhurst Rd GU16 ...56 B3
Buckingham Cl GU34 ...139 B2
Buckingham Ct RG22 ...91 A4
Buckingham Par GU52 ...68 A1
Buckingham Rd RG14 ...1 B1
Buckland Ave GU22 ...76 C4
Buckland Cl GU14 ...56 A4
Buckland Par RG22 ...68 B1
Buckskin La RG22 ...68 A1
Budd's Cl RG21 ...69 A2
Buddlesgate SO21 ...131 B2
Budds La GU35 ...164 B2
Buffbeards La GU27 ...189 B4
Buffins RG29 ...72 B1
Buffins Rd RG29 ...72 B1
Bulbery SP11 ...104 C2
Bulford Rd
Shipton Bellinger SP9 ...101 C4
South Tidworth SP9 ...78 B2
Bull Dro SO23 ...198 A3
Bull Hill GU34 ...208 C2
Bull La GU34 ...56 A1
Buller Ct 7 GU11 ...56 A1
Buller Rd GU11 ...76 C2
Bullers Rd GU9 ...99 B3
Bullfinch Cl GU47 ...35 B4
Bullington La
Barton Stacey SO21 ...130 C4
Upper Bullington SO21 ...131 B3
Bulls Dro SP5 ...191 A3
Bullsdown Cl RG27 ...28 B3
Bulpitt Hill SP11 ...38 B1
Bunch La GU27 ...189 C4
Bunch Way GU27 ...189 C4
Bungler's Hill RG14 ...14 C3
Bunkers Hill RG21 ...5 A3
Bunnian Pl RG21 ...91 A4
Bunting Mews RG22 ...91 A4
Buntings GU34 ...139 C3
Buntings The GU16 ...121 B4
Burbery Shops GU35 ...164 A1
Burbury Woods GU15 ...36 B3
Burchell Rd RG14 ...1 C3
Burchett Coppice RG40 ...16 B4
Burdock Cl SO24 ...127 C4
Burfield RG20 ...21 B3
Burford Ho GU15 ...35 C2
Burford Rd GU16 ...56 B3
Burgess La GU34 ...139 B1
Burgess La RG20 ...2 A3

Burgess Rd RG21 . . . . .69 A3
Burgh Hill Rd GU30 . . . . .187 C4
Burghclere Prim Sch
  RG20 . . . . .22 C3
Burghead Cl GU47 . . . . .35 A4
Burgoyne Rd GU15 . . . . .36 C3
Buriton Rd SO22 . . . . .175 B2
Burkal Dr SP10 . . . . .83 A2
Burleigh Rd GU16 . . . . .56 A4
Burles Bridge Cotts
  GU10 . . . . .98 A1
Burley La RG25 . . . . .88 C3
Burley Rd SO22 . . . . .175 B2
Burley Way GU17 . . . . .35 A3
Burlington Ct
  6 Aldershot GU11 . . . . . . .76 C1
  Blackwater GU17 . . . . .35 A2
Burnaby Cl RG22 . . . . .68 B2
Burnaby Rd SO22 . . . . . . .175 B1
Burne-Jones Dr GU47 . . . .35 A3
Burnett Cl SO22 . . . . .175 B1
Burney Bit RG26 . . . . .9 B1
Burnham Copse Jun & Inf
  Sch RG26 . . . . .9 B1
Burnham Manor GU15 . . . .36 C4
Burnham Rd RG26 . . . . .9 B1
Burnhams Cl SP10 . . . . .83 A2
Burnley Rd RG26 . . . . .26 C4
Burnmoor Mdw RG40 . . . . .16 B1
Burns Ave GU52 . . . . .75 A1
Burns Cl Basingstoke RG24 .69 B4
  Farnborough GU14 . . . . . . .55 B3
  South Wonston SO21 . . . .153 C2
Burnsall Cl SO22 . . . . .55 C3
Burnside GU51 . . . . .54 A1
Burnt Hill Rd GU10 . . . . . .121 C3
Burnt Hill Way GU10 . . . . .121 C3
Burnt Oak RG40 . . . . .16 B4
Burntwood Cotts SO21 . .154 C1
Burrell Rd GU16 . . . . .56 A4
Burrow Hill Sch GU16 . . . . .36 B1
Burrowfields RG22 . . . . . . .91 A3
Burrows The RG26 . . . . .9 C1
Burrwood Gdns GU52 . . . . .77 C2
Bursdon Cotts SP9 . . . . . .101 C4
Burton's Gdns RG24 . . . . . .70 A4
Bury Court Cotts GU10 . .120 A4
Bury Hill Cl SP11 . . . . .105 B2
Bury Rd RG23 . . . . .68 B3
Bury's Bank Rd RG19 . . . . . .6 B4
Burydown Mead RG25 . . . .89 C1
Buryfields RG22 . . . . .72 C1
Buryfields Inf Sch RG29 . . .72 C1
Buryhill Close Flats
  SP11 . . . . .105 B2
Bushnells Dr RG20 . . . . .24 B2
Bushywarren La RG22 . . . .92 C1
Busk Cres GU14 . . . . .55 B2
Busket La SO23 . . . . .198 A4
Butcher Cnr SO20 . . . . . . .147 C3
Butler Cl RG22 . . . . .68 B2
Butler Lodge RG25 . . . . .88 A4
Butlers Cl SO51 . . . . .191 C1
Butson Cl RG14 . . . . .1 B2
Buttenshaw Ave RG2 . . . . .15 A4
Buttenshaw Cl RG2 . . . . . . .15 C4
Buttercup Cl GU35 . . . . . .165 A3
Butterfield Cl GU35 . . . . . . .35 C2
Buttermer Cl GU10 . . . . . .121 B4
Buttermere Cl
  Bordon GU35 . . . . .164 B3
  Farnborough GU14 . . . . . . .55 B2
Buttermere Ct GU12 . . . . . .77 B2
Buttermere Dr RG22 . . . . . .91 A3
Buttermere Gdns SO24 . .179 B2
Buttery The GU34 . . . . . . .139 C2
Butts Hill SP11 . . . . .72 C4
Butts Mdw RG27 . . . . .51 A1
Butts Mews SO24 . . . . . . .139 C1
Butts Prim Sch The
  GU34 . . . . .139 C1
Butts Rd Alton GU34 . . . .139 C1
  Winchester SO22 . . . . . . .175 B1
Butts The RG7 . . . . .27 C4
Butty The 8 RG21 . . . . .69 B3
By Pass Rd SO21 . . . . .131 A2
Byes La Silchester RG7 . . . . .2 C4
  Three Ashes RG7,RG26 . . .28 A4
Byeways RG20 . . . . .21 B3
Byfields Rd RG20 . . . . .24 B1
Byfleet Ave RG24 . . . . .70 A3
Byfrons The GU14 . . . . .56 A1
Byrd Gdns RG22 . . . . .91 B4
Byron Ave
  Camberley GU15 . . . . .36 C2
  Winchester SO22 . . . . . . .197 B4
Byron Cl Basingstoke RG24 .69 B4
  Fleet GU51 . . . . .75 A4
  Newbury RG14 . . . . .1 A4
  Yateley GU46 . . . . .33 C2
Byways GU46 . . . . .33 C3
Byworth Cl GU9 . . . . .98 B1
Byworth Rd GU9 . . . . .98 B1

C

Cabrol Rd GU14 . . . . .55 C3
Cabul Rd SP9 . . . . .78 B2
Cadet Way GU12 . . . . .75 A2
Cadnam Cl
  Aldershot GU11 . . . . .100 A3
  Oakley RG23 . . . . .67 A1
Cadogan Rd GU11 . . . . . . .100 A3
Caerleon Cl GU26 . . . . . . .167 A3

Caerleon Dr SP10 . . . . .83 A2
Caernarvon GU16 . . . . .56 B4
Caernarvon Cl RG23 . . . . . .68 B3
Caesar Ct 10 RG21 . . . . .76 B1
Caesar Rd SP10 . . . . .83 A2
Caesar's Camp Rd GU15 . .36 C4
Caesar's Cl GU15 . . . . .36 C4
Caesar's Way RG28 . . . . . . .86 A3
Caesars Ct
  Camberley GU15 . . . . .36 C4
  Farnham GU9 . . . . .99 A4
Cairn Cl GU15 . . . . .36 C4
Cairngorm Cl RG22 . . . . . . .68 A2
Cairngorm Pl GU14 . . . . . . .55 B4
Caithness Cl GU30 . . . . . .187 C4
Caker Stream Rd GU34 . . .140 A2
Caker's La GU34 . . . . .140 B1
Calard Dr RG18 . . . . .2 C2
Calard Rd RG18 . . . . .2 C2
Calcott Rd GU46 . . . . .34 A3
Calder Ct 84 SP10 . . . . .83 B1
Calender Cl GU34 . . . . . . .139 C1
California City Pk*
  RG40 . . . . .16 A4
Calleva Cl RG22 . . . . .91 A4
Calleva Mus* RG7 . . . . .10 C1
Calleva Pk RG7 . . . . .9 B4
Calleva Roman Town*
  RG7 . . . . .11 A1
Calne Ho 8 SP9 . . . . .78 C3
Calshot Way GU16 . . . . .56 C4
Calthorpe Hos RG27 . . . . . .52 C4
Calthorpe Park Sch
  GU51 . . . . .74 B4
Calthorpe Rd GU46 . . . . . . .34 A3
Calthorpe Sq 17 GU51 . . . .53 C1
Calton Gdns GU11 . . . . . . .100 A4
Calvecroft GU30 . . . . .188 B2
Calvert Cl GU12 . . . . .77 A1
Calvert Ctr The SO21 . . . .112 B1
Calvin Cl GU15 . . . . .36 C2
Cam Wlk 21 RG21 . . . . .69 B1
Camberley Heath Golf Course
  GU15 . . . . .36 C2
Camberley Inf Sch GU15 . .36 A4
Camberley Sta GU15 . . . . . .36 A3
Camberley Twrs GU15 . . . . .36 A3
Camberry Cl RG21 . . . . .69 B1
Cambrian Cl GU15 . . . . .35 C3
Cambrian Rd GU14 . . . . . . .55 A4
Cambrian Way
  Basingstoke RG22 . . . . . . .68 A2
  Finchampstead RG40 . . . . .16 C4
Cambridge Cl 9 GU14 . . . . .56 A1
Cambridge Pl GU9 . . . . .99 A1
Cambridge Rd GU11 . . . . . .76 B1
Cambridge Rd E GU14 . . . .56 A1
Cambridge Rd W GU14 . . . .56 A1
Cambridge Sp GU35 . . . . . .36 A3
Cambridge Wlk GU15 . . . . .36 A3
Camden Wlk GU11 . . . . .54 B1
Camelot Cl SP10 . . . . .83 A1
Camelsdale Rd GU27 . . . .189 B3
Camelsdale Sch GU27 . . .189 B3
Cameron Rd GU11 . . . . .77 A4
Camfield Cl RG21 . . . . .69 B2
Camford Cl RG22 . . . . .91 A2
Camlea Cl RG21 . . . . .69 B1
Camoys Mead GU34 . . . . .140 B2
Camp Farm Rd GU11 . . . . . .77 A3
Camp Field SO20 . . . . .172 A2
Camp Hill GU10 . . . . .100 A1
Camp Rd Bordon GU35 . . .164 B2
  Farnborough GU14 . . . . . . .77 A4
  Padworth RG7 . . . . .11 A4
Campana Int Coll GU10 . . .99 C1
Campbell Cl
  Aldershot GU11 . . . . .100 A4
  Fleet GU51 . . . . .53 C1
  Grateley SP11 . . . . .124 C4
  Yateley GU46 . . . . .34 B3
Campbell Ct RG26 . . . . .29 A1
Campbell Pl GU16 . . . . .36 B2
Campbell Rd
  Aldershot GU11 . . . . .76 C2
  Bramley RG26 . . . . .29 A1
Campbell's Gn RG27 . . . . . .11 C3
Campion Cl
  Blackwater GU17 . . . . .35 B2
  Lindford GU35 . . . . .165 A2
Campion Ho RG14 . . . . .1 B2
Campion Way
  Hartley Wintney RG27 . . . .52 B4
  Kings Worthy SO23 . . . . .176 B4
Campsie Ct RG22 . . . . .68 A2
Camrose Way RG21 . . . . . . .69 B2
Camus Cl GU52 . . . . .74 B3
Camwood Cl RG21 . . . . .69 B2
Canada Cotts SO21 . . . . . .111 A1
Canada Way
  Bordon GU35 . . . . .164 B2
  Liphook GU30 . . . . .188 A2
Canal Cl
  Farnborough GU11 . . . . . . .77 A3
  North Warnborough RG29 .72 B2
Canal Cotts GU12 . . . . .77 C2
Canal View Rd RG14 . . . . . . .2 A2
Candleford Gate GU30 . . .187 C2
Candover Ct 14 RG26 . . . . .26 C4
Canes La GU35 . . . . .164 C3
Canhouse La GU33 . . . . . .208 C2
Canning Rd GU12 . . . . .77 A1
Cannon Cl Ellisfield RG25 .115 A3
  Sandhurst GU47 . . . . .35 B4
Canon St SO23 . . . . .197 B4
Canons Cl SP9 . . . . .78 C2
Canons Ct RG20 . . . . .24 B1
Cansfield End RG14 . . . . .1 B2

Canterbury Cl RG22 . . . . . . .91 A4
Canterbury Rd Ash GU12 . .77 C2
  Farnborough GU14 . . . . . . .56 A1
Canute Rd 6 SO23 . . . . . . .198 A3
Capital Ho 11 SO22 . . . . . .197 C4
Capper Rd GU15 . . . . .35 C4
Carbonel Cl RG23 . . . . .68 A3
Cardew Rd GU33 . . . . .208 A2
Cardinal Mews 6 SP10 . . .105 C4
Cardinals The GU10 . . . . .100 B4
Carfax Ave GU10 . . . . .100 B4
Carfax Est GU10 . . . . .100 B4
Cargate Ave GU11 . . . . .76 C1
Cargate Gr GU11 . . . . .76 C1
Cargate Hill GU11 . . . . .76 B1
Cargate Terr GU11 . . . . .76 B1
Carisbrooke GU16 . . . . .56 B4
Carisbrooke Cl
  Basingstoke RG23 . . . . . . .68 B3
  New Alresford SO24 . . . . .179 B2
Carleton Cl RG27 . . . . .50 C1
Carlina Gdns GU10 . . . . . .100 B4
Carlinwark Dr GU15 . . . . . .36 B4
Carlisle Cl RG23 . . . . .68 B3
Carlisle Rd GU10 . . . . .144 C4
Carlton Cl GU15 . . . . .36 C2
Carlton Cres GU52 . . . . .75 A3
Carlton Rd GU35 . . . . .166 A3
Carlyon Cl
  Farnborough GU14 . . . . . . .56 A2
  Mytchett GU16 . . . . .56 B2
Carmarthen Cl GU14 . . . . . .55 C4
Carmichael Way RG22 . . . .91 B4
Carnegie Rd RG14 . . . . .1 C1
Carnival Sq 18 GU51 . . . . . .53 C1
Carolina Pl RG40 . . . . .16 B4
Caroline Way GU16 . . . . . . .36 B1
Carpenter's Down RG24 . .48 B1
Carpenters SO24 . . . . .179 B3
Carpenters Ct
  Alton GU34 . . . . .140 B3
  Sherfield on Loddon RG27 .29 B1
Carpenters Ct RG22 . . . . . .68 B1
Carrick La GU46 . . . . .34 B3
Carrington Cres RG26 . . . . .26 C4
Carrington La GU12 . . . . . . .77 C4
Carshalton Rd GU15 . . . . . .36 C3
Carstairs Bsns Ctr RG24 . .69 C4
Carter's Mdw SP10 . . . . . . .82 C1
Carters Wlk GU9 . . . . .99 A4
Carthagena SO21 . . . . .131 B2
Carthona Dr GU52 . . . . .74 C4
Carwarden House Com Sch
  GU15 . . . . .36 C3
Cary Cl RG14 . . . . .5 A3
Cassino SO21 . . . . .131 B1
Casterbridge La SP11 . . . .81 B1
Castle Ave SO23 . . . . .197 C4
Castle Bridge Cotts RG29 .72 B2
Castle Cl GU15 . . . . .36 C4
Castle Ct GU35 . . . . .98 C2
Castle Field GU14 . . . . .1 B3
Castle Gr RG14 . . . . .1 B3
Castle Hill
  Farley Castle RG7,RG2 . . .15 A4
  Farnham GU9 . . . . .98 C2
  Winchester SO22 . . . . . . .197 C4
Castle Hill Schs SO23 . . . .68 B3
Castle La GU34 . . . . .1 B3
Castle of Mey Ho GU27 . .189 B3
Castle Rd Aldershot GU11 . .76 B2
  Basingstoke RG23 . . . . . . .69 A2
Castle Rise
  Kings Worthy SO23 . . . . .154 B1
  North Warnborough RG29 .72 B2
Castle Sch The RG14 . . . . . .1 B3
Castle Sq RG21 . . . . .69 B1
Castle St Farnham GU9 . . . .98 C2
  Fleet GU51 . . . . .74 C4
  Medstead GU34 . . . . .159 C4
Castlecraig Ct GU47 . . . . . .35 A4
Caston's Yd RG21 . . . . .69 A2
Castor Ct Fleet GU52 . . . . . .75 A3
  Yateley GU46 . . . . .33 C4
Caswall Ride GU46 . . . . .34 B3
Caswell Cl GU14 . . . . .55 B3
Catesby Gdns GU46 . . . . . .33 C3
Cathedral View 5 SO23 . .198 A3
Catherine Ct 2 GU11 . . . . .56 A1
Catherine Rd RG14 . . . . .1 C1
Catherine Villas GU27 . . .189 C3
Catherines Wlk SP11 . . . .104 C2
Catkin Cl RG24 . . . . .48 C3
Cattle La SP11 . . . . .104 C3
Caunter Rd RG27 . . . . .31 A4
Causeway Gn RG27 . . . . . . .52 B3
Causeway The
  Heckfield RG27 . . . . .31 A4
  Middle Winterslow SP5 . .168 A4
  Nether Wallop SO20 . . . .147 C3
Cavalier Ct Newbury RG14 . .2 A3
  Old Basing RG24 . . . . .70 B3
Cavalier Way GU34 . . . . . .139 B1
Cavalry Ct 8 GU11 . . . . . . .76 B1
Cavan's Rd GU11 . . . . .76 C2
Cavell Ct RG24 . . . . .70 A4
Cavendish Cl
  Blackwater GU17 . . . . .35 A2
  Newbury RG14 . . . . .2 B3
Cavendish Gdns GU52 . . . .74 C2
Cavendish Gr SO23 . . . . . .176 A2
Cavendish Mews GU14 . . . .55 C2
Cavendish Pk GU47 . . . . . . .35 B3
Cavendish Rd
  Aldershot GU11 . . . . .76 C1
  Fleet GU52 . . . . .75 A2

Caves Farm Cl GU47 . . . . . .34 C4
Caxton Cl SP10 . . . . .82 B1
Cayman Cl RG24 . . . . .48 B1
Cedar Ave GU17 . . . . .35 A3
Cedar Cl Aldershot GU12 .100 B4
  Kings Worthy SO23 . . . . .176 A4
Cedar Cr GU52 . . . . .74 B3
Cedar Ct GU27 . . . . .189 C3
Cedar Dr Fleet GU51 . . . . . .54 B1
  Kingsclere RG20 . . . . .24 B1
Cedar La GU14 . . . . .56 A4
Cedar Mount RG14 . . . . .5 A3
Cedar Rd GU14 . . . . .56 A2
Cedar Terr RG27 . . . . .52 A3
Cedar Tree Cl RG23 . . . . . . .90 A4
Cedar Way RG23 . . . . .68 B3
Cedar Wlk Andover SP10 . . . .105 C4
  82 Winchester SO22 . . . .197 C4
Cedars Cl GU47 . . . . .34 B4
Cedars Sch The RG7 . . . . . . .9 C4
Cedars The GU51 . . . . .75 A4
Cedarwood
  Chineham RG24 . . . . .48 C2
  Kings Worthy SO23 . . . . .176 B4
Celandine Ct GU46 . . . . . . .33 C4
Celtic Dr SP10 . . . . .105 C3
Cemetery Hill RG29 . . . . . . .72 C1
Cemetery La RG25 . . . . .94 A3
Cemetery Rd GU35 . . . . . .164 B3
Central Rd GU35 . . . . .164 B3
Central Way SP10 . . . . .83 C1
Centre Dr RG24 . . . . .48 C1
Centurion Cl GU47 . . . . . . .35 A4
Centurion Way RG22 . . . . . .91 A4
Century Cl RG22 . . . . .92 A4
Century Farm Ind Units
  RG22 . . . . .99 B3
Chaffers Cl RG20 . . . . .24 B1
Chaffinch Cl
  Basingstoke RG22 . . . . . . .91 A4
  Sandhurst GU47 . . . . .35 A4
Chalcraft Cl GU30 . . . . . . .187 C2
Chalcrafts GU34 . . . . .140 B3
Chalet Cl GU35 . . . . .164 B2
Chalet Hill GU35 . . . . .164 B2
Chalfont Dr GU14 . . . . .56 A1
Chalford Rd RG14 . . . . .1 B3
Chalk Cl GU34 . . . . .160 A1
Chalk Hill SO23 . . . . .172 C3
Chalk Ridge SO23 . . . . . . .198 B4
Chalk Ridge Prim Sch
  RG22 . . . . .68 C1
Chalk Vale
  King's Somborne SO20 . .172 C2
  Old Basing RG24 . . . . .70 B3
Chalkcroft La SP11 . . . . . . .81 C2
Chalky Copse RG27 . . . . . . .51 A1
Chalky Hill GU34 . . . . .159 A3
Chalky La RG27 . . . . .51 A1
Challenor Cl RG40 . . . . .16 B4
Challis Cl RG22 . . . . .68 B1
Challis Ct SP11 . . . . .57 A1
Challoner Cl RG22 . . . . .68 B2
Chamber La GU10 . . . . . . .121 A4
Chamberhouse Mill Rd
  RG19 . . . . .7 B4
Chamberlains Mdw RG27 .31 A3
Chambers Rd GU12 . . . . . . .77 C3
Chamomile Gdns SO43 . . .51 A3
Champion Way GU52 . . . . . .75 A3
Champney Cl GU35 . . . . . .164 A1
Chandler Rd RG21 . . . . .69 A1
Chandlers La GU46 . . . . . . .34 A4
Chandlers Rd GU12 . . . . . . .77 C2
Chandos Rd RG14 . . . . .5 B4
Chandos Terr SO21 . . . . . .177 C3
Chant Cl SP11 . . . . .128 C3
Chantreys GU51 . . . . .54 A1
Chantry Cl RG27 . . . . .72 A4
Chantry Ct GU16 . . . . .36 A1
Chantry Ctr The SP10 . . . .106 A4
Chantry Mead SO22 . . . . .175 C1
Chantry Mews RG21 . . . . . .76 A1
Chantry Sp SP10 . . . . .106 A4
Chantrys Ct GU9 . . . . .98 C1
Chantrys The GU9 . . . . .98 C1
Chapel Cl Amport SP11 . . .104 A3
  Dummer RG25 . . . . .90 B1
  Houghton SO20 . . . . .171 B2
  Old Basing RG24 . . . . .70 A4
Chapel Cotts SP11 . . . . .61 C1
Chapel Ct
  Broughton SO20 . . . . .170 A4
  Wherwell SP11 . . . . .128 C3
Chapel Field SO21 . . . . . . .177 A2
Chapel Gdns SO24 . . . . . .164 C3
Chapel Hill RG21 . . . . .69 A3
Chapel La
  Aldermaston RG7 . . . . .10 B3
  Ashford Hill RG19 . . . . .8 B1
  Baughurst RG26 . . . . .25 C2
  Broughton SO20 . . . . .170 A4
  Enham Alamein SP11 . . . .83 A3
  Farnborough GU14 . . . . . . .55 A3
  Grateley SP11 . . . . .125 A4
  Itchen Abbas SO21 . . . . .177 A2
  Riseley RG7 . . . . .14 A2
  Stoke SP11 . . . . .61 B2
Chapel Lodge RG40 . . . . . .16 B3
Chapel Mead GU34 . . . . . .159 A3
Chapel Pond Dr RG29 . . . . .72 B2
Chapel Rd
  Camberley GU15 . . . . .35 C3
  Farnham GU10 . . . . .121 B2
  Silchester RG7 . . . . .11 A3
Chapel River Cl SP10 . . . .105 C4

Chapel Row RG27 . . . . .52 B4
Chapel Sq GU15 . . . . .35 B3
Chapel St
  Farnborough GU14 . . . . . . .56 A3
  North Waltham RG25 . . . . .89 C1
Chapman Wlk RG18 . . . . . . .2 C2
Chappell Cl GU30 . . . . .188 A2
Chapter Ct 13 GU34 . . . . .139 C2
Chapter Terr RG27 . . . . .52 B3
Charfield Cl SO22 . . . . . . .197 C3
Charlcot Cl RG28 . . . . .86 B2
Charldon Gn RG24 . . . . .70 A4
Charlecote Cl GU14 . . . . . . .55 B4
Charlecote Mews 18
  SO22 . . . . .197 C4
Charledown Cl RG25 . . . . . .88 A4
Charledown Rd RG25 . . . . .88 A4
Charles Cl Hook RG27 . . . . .51 A1
  Winchester SO23 . . . . . . .176 A1
Charles Dalton Ct SP10 . .106 A4
Charles Kingsley CE Prim Sch
  RG27 . . . . .33 A4
Charles Richards Cl
  RG21 . . . . .69 A2
Charles St
  Basingstoke RG22 . . . . . . .68 C2
  Newbury RG14 . . . . .5 A3
Charlotte Cl
  Andover SP10 . . . . .106 B4
  Farnham GU9 . . . . .99 A4
Charlton Cl RG40 . . . . .16 B4
Charlton Down SP11 . . . . . .59 C1
Charlton La RG7 . . . . .14 A3
Charlton Pl RG14 . . . . .2 A3
Charlton Rd SP10 . . . . .82 C1
Charlton Sports & L Ctr
  SP10 . . . . .82 B1
Charnwood La SO24 . . . . .182 B2
Charnwood CI RG14 . . . . . . .1 B3
Charnwood Cl
  Andover SP10 . . . . .106 A3
  Basingstoke RG22 . . . . . . .68 A2
Chart House Rd GU12 . . . . .77 C4
Charter Rd RG14 . . . . .5 B4
Charters Ct GU12 . . . . .100 A4
Chartwell Camberley GU15 .56 B3
  Farnham GU10 . . . . .121 B3
Chartwell Gdns GU11 . . . . .77 A4
Chase Cl GU33 . . . . .208 A2
Chase Com Hospl GU35 .164 B1
Chase Ct GU35 . . . . .164 C3
Chase Field GU34 . . . . . . .161 B1
Chase Plain GU26 . . . . . . .167 A1
Chase Rd Lindford GU35 . .164 C3
  Liss GU33 . . . . .208 A2
Chase The
  Farnborough GU14 . . . . . . .56 A3
  Newbury RG14 . . . . .1 B4
Chasewater Ct 7 GU11 . . .76 C1
Chatfield Cl GU14 . . . . .56 A1
Chatham Rd SO22 . . . . . .197 B3
Chatsworth Dr RG21 . . . . . .69 C1
Chatsworth Gn RG22 . . . . .91 B3
Chatsworth Gr GU9 . . . . . .98 C3
Chatsworth Hts GU15 . . . .36 C4
Chatsworth Rd RG21 . . . . . .69 C1
Chatter Alley RG27 . . . . .74 A4
Chatters The RG7 . . . . .15 A4
Chatts Hill Stables
  SO20 . . . . .148 C2
Chaucer Ave SP10 . . . . .82 B1
Chaucer Cl
  Basingstoke RG24 . . . . . . .48 B1
  South Wonston SO21 . . . .153 C3
Chaucer Cres RG14 . . . . .1 B3
Chaucer Gr GU15 . . . . .36 A3
Chaucer Ind Est SO23 . . .176 B1
Chaucer Rd GU15 . . . . .55 B3
Chaundler Rd SO23 . . . . . .176 B1
Chaundlers Croft GU10 . . .97 B3
Chauntsingers Cotts 12
  GU34 . . . . .139 C2
Chauntsingers Rd GU34 . .139 C2
Chawton CE Prim Sch
  GU34 . . . . .161 B4
Chawton Cl Fleet GU51 . . . .53 B1
  Winchester SO22 . . . . . . .175 B2
Chawton End Cl GU34 . . . .160 B2
Chawton Park Rd GU34 . .159 A2
Cheam Hawtreys Sch
  GU34 . . . . .24 A4
Cheap St RG14 . . . . .1 C1
Cheavley Cl SP10 . . . . .105 B4
Cheesecombe Farm La
  GU33 . . . . .206 C3
Chelmer Ct 4 RG21 . . . . . . .69 A1
Chelsea Ho 8 RG21 . . . . . .69 A3
Chequer La RG7 . . . . .13 B1
Chequers La GU46 . . . . .33 B4
Chequers Rd RG21 . . . . .69 B3
Cherberry Cl GU51 . . . . .54 A2
Cheriton Cl
  12 Tadley RG26 . . . . .26 C4
  Winchester SO22 . . . . . . .175 B1
  Yateley GU34 . . . . .180 A1
Cheriton Prim Sch
  SO24 . . . . .201 B3
Cheriton Rd SO22 . . . . . . .197 C4
Cheriton Way GU17 . . . . . . .35 A3
Cherrimans Orch GU27 . .189 B3
Cherry Cl Hook RG27 . . . . . .51 A1
  Newbury RG14 . . . . .1 B2
  South Wonston SO21 . . . .153 B2
Cherry Tree Ave
  Haslemere GU27 . . . . . . .189 B4
  North Tidworth SP9 . . . . . .79 A4
Cherry Tree Cl
  Farnborough GU14 . . . . . . .55 A3

Cherry Tree Cl continued
Farnham GU9 ....99 A2
Cherry Tree Rd
Andover SP10 ....82 C1
Farnham GU10 ....121 B2
Cherry Tree Wlk GU10 ..121 B2
Cherryway GU14 ....139 C3
Cherrywood RG24 ....48 C2
Cherrywood Rd GU14 ..55 C4
Chesil St SO23 ....198 A4
Chesil Terr SO23 ....198 A4
Chesil Wood SO23 ....198 B4
Chesilton Cres GU52 ..75 A3
Chester Cl Ash GU12 ..77 C1
  Newbury RG14 ....2 A1
Chester Pl RG21 ....69 A2
Chester Rd Ash GU12 ..77 C1
  Winchester SO23 ....198 A4
Chester Way GU10 ....100 B4
Chesterfield Rd RG21 ..69 B2
Chesters Rd GU15 ....36 C3
Chestnut Ave
  Aldershot GU12 ....100 B4
  Andover SP10 ....105 C3
  Camberley GU15 ....36 C3
  Farnham GU9 ....121 C4
  Littleton SO22 ....175 A2
  North Tidworth SP9 ..79 A4
Chestnut Bank RG24 ..70 A4
Chestnut Cl Alton GU34 .139 C3
  Blackwater GU17 ....35 B2
  Fleet GU51 ....54 B2
  Grayshott GU26 ....167 A2
  Odiham RG29 ....188 A2
Chestnut Cres
  Middle Wallop SO20 ..126 A2
  Newbury RG14 ....1 C2
Chestnut Ct
  Aldershot GU12 ....77 A1
  Bordon GU35 ....164 C1
  [7] Newbury RG14 ....1 C2
Chestnut End GU35 ....165 C2
Chestnut Gr GU51 ....54 A1
Chestnut Rd GU14 ....55 C3
Chestnut Wlk SO24 ....179 B3
Cheswell Gdns GU51 ..74 C3
Chetwode Pl GU12 ....100 A4
Chetwode Terr GU11 ..76 B1
Cheviot Cl
  Basingstoke RG22 ....68 A2
  Farnborough GU14 ....55 B4
  Fleet GU51 ....54 A2
  Newbury RG14 ....5 A3
Cheyne Way GU14 ....55 B4
Chichester Cl SP10 ....105 B4
Chichester Pl RG22 ..68 C1
Chichester Rd GU14 ..77 C2
Chilbolton Ave SO22 ..197 B4
Chilbolton Ct SO22 ..197 B4
Chilcomb La
  Chilcomb SO21 ....198 C3
  Winchester SO23 ....198 B3
Chilcombe Hts SO23 ..198 A4
Chilcroft La GU27 ....189 C1
Chilcroft Rd GU27 ....189 B4
Chilcrofts Rd GU27 ..189 C1
Childerstone Cl GU30 .187 C2
Chilham Cl GU16 ....56 B4
Chilland La SO21 ....177 B3
Chilldenham La SO21 .155 B1
Chillingham Way GU15 .36 A2
Chilmark Ct GU33 ....207 C2
Chiltern Ave GU14 ....55 A2
Chiltern Cl
  Farnborough GU14 ....55 A2
  Haslemere GU27 ....189 C3
  Newbury RG14 ....5 A3
Chiltern Cl SO23 ....179 B3
Chiltern Way RG22 ..68 A2
Chiltlee Cl GU30 ....188 A2
Chiltlee Manor GU30 ..188 A2
Chiltley La GU30 ....188 A1
Chiltley Way GU30 ....188 A1
Chilton Farm Pk GU14 .55 A2
Chilton Ridge RG22 ..91 A3
Chine The GU10 ....121 B3
Chineham Bsns Pk RG24 .48 C2
Chineham Cl GU51 ....53 B2
Chineham District Ctr
  RG24 ....48 C1
Chineham La
  Basingstoke RG24 ....69 B4
  Basingstoke, Popley RG24 .48 A1
Chineham Park Ctr RG24 .69 B4
Chineham Park Prim Sch
  RG24 ....69 B4
Chingford Ave GU14 ..56 A3
Chinnock Cl GU52 ....74 C4
Chippendale Cl
  [18] Baughurst RG26 ..9 B1
  Blackwater GU17 ....35 B2
Chive Ct GU51 ....55 A2
Chivers Cl RG22 ....68 B2
Chivers Dr RG40 ....16 B4
Chobham Rd GU16 ....36 B1
Cholderton Rd
  Grateley SP11 ....124 C4
  Newton Toney SP4 ..123 A4
  Quarley SP4,SP11 ....102 B2
Chopin Rd RG22 ....91 B4
Christchurch Ave GU12 .77 A1
Chrismas Ct GU12 ....77 A1
Chrismas Pl GU12 ....77 A1
Christchurch Cl [2] GU52 .74 C2
Christchurch Dr GU17 .35 A3
Christchurch Gdns [1]
  ....197 C3

Christchurch Rd SO23 ..197 C3
Christie Hts RG14 ....5 C4
Christie Wlk GU47 ....34 A2
Christine Cl GU12 ....77 B1
Christopher Cr RG14 ..1 C1
Christy Ct RG26 ....27 A4
Christy Est GU12 ....77 B1
Chudleigh Ct [5] GU14 .55 C2
Church Ave GU14 ....56 A2
Church Bank Rd SO21 ..133 C2
Church Barns SO21 ....134 A2
Church Brook RG26 ....26 C3
Church Circ GU14 ....56 A1
Church Cl Andover SP10 .106 A4
  Enborne RG20 ....4 B3
Church Cotts
  Farnham GU9 ....99 C3
  Ropley SO24 ....181 B2
  Selborne GU33 ....185 C4
Church Ct [7] GU51 ....53 C1
Church Farm Barns RG7 .12 A3
Church Farm Cl RG25 ..89 C1
Church Fields GU35 ....165 A3
Church Gr GU51 ....53 C1
Church Hams RG40 ....16 A3
Church Hill
  Aldershot GU12 ....100 A4
  Camberley GU15 ....36 B3
  Nether Wallop SO20 ..148 A3
Church Hill Terr GU34 .97 B3
Church La Alton GU34 ..140 B4
  Ash GU12 ....77 C1
  Basingstoke RG23 ....69 A3
  Basingstoke, Worting RG23 .68 A2
  Baughurst RG26 ....25 B1
  Bentley GU10 ....120 A3
  Binsted GU10 ....121 B2
  Bishop's Sutton SO24 ..180 A2
  Bramdean SO24 ....202 B2
  Bramshott GU30 ....188 A3
  Brimpton RG7 ....8 B3
  Burghclere RG20 ....22 C4
  Buttermere SN8 ....18 B4
  Cliddesden RG22 ....92 A4
  Combe RG17 ....19 B3
  Dogmersfield RG27 ..74 A4
  Ellisfield RG25 ....115 B4
  Enborne RG20 ....4 B4
  Ewshot GU10 ....98 A4
  Farley Hill RG7 ....15 A3
  Farnborough GU14 ....55 B2
  Farnham GU10 ....121 B4
  Finchampstead RG40 ..16 B2
  Goodworth Clatford SP11 .106 A1
  Grayshott GU26 ....167 A2
  Greatham GU33 ....185 C1
  Hartley Wintney RG27 ..52 B3
  Headley GU35 ....165 B3
  Heckfield RG27 ....31 A3
  Houghton SO20 ....171 B3
  Itchen Abbas SO21 ....177 A3
  Kings Worthy SO23 ....176 B3
  Littleton SO22 ....175 A3
  Medstead GU34 ....159 C4
  Mottisfont SO51 ....192 C1
  Newbury RG14 ....1 A2
  Old Basing RG24 ....70 A3
  Ropley SO24 ....181 B2
  Silchester RG7 ....11 B1
  South Tidworth SP9 ..78 C2
  Sparsholt SO21 ....174 B2
  Upper Clatford SP11 ..105 C2
  Vernham Dean SP11 ..38 A4
  Woolton Hill RG20 ....21 A4
Church La E GU11,GU12 .99 C4
Church La W GU11 ....76 C1
Church Mdw GU34 ....96 B2
Church Mews SP9 ....101 C4
Church Mews
  Upper Clatford SP11 ..105 B2
  Yateley GU46 ....34 A4
Church Path GU9 ....99 B3
Church Path Ash GU12 ..77 C2
  Hook RG27 ....71 C4
Church Rd Aldermaston RG7 .9 C4
  Aldershot GU11 ....100 A4
  Bramshott GU30 ....188 A3
  Camberley GU15 ....36 A1
  Fleet GU51 ....53 C1
  Haslemere GU27 ....189 B3
  King's Somborne SO20 .172 A1
  Longstock SO20 ....149 B4
  Michelmarsh SO51 ....193 B1
  Nether Wallop SO20 ..148 A3
  Newbury RG14 ....1 C3
  North Waltham RG25 ..89 C1
  Overton RG25 ....88 A4
  Pamber Heath RG26 ..10 B1
  Privett GU34 ....204 B2
  Sandhurst GU15 ....35 B4
  Silchester RG7 ....11 A1
  Swallowfield RG7 ....14 B3
  Tadley RG26 ....26 C3
  Upper Farringdon GU34 .161 C2
Church Rd E GU14 ....56 A1
Church Rd W GU14 ....56 A1
Church Sq RG21 ....69 B1
Church St Aldershot GU11 .76 B1
  Alton GU34 ....139 C2
  Basingstoke RG21 ....69 A3
  Basingstoke RG21 ....69 A3
  Bentworth GU34 ....138 A3
  Crondall GU10 ....99 C2
  Hurstbourne Tarrant SP11 .60 C3
  Liss GU33 ....207 C3
  Micheldever SO21 ....133 C2
  North Warnborough RG29 .72 C1
  Ropley SO24 ....181 B2

Church St continued
  Wherwell SP11 ....129 A3
  Whitchurch RG28 ....86 B2
  Woolton Hill RG20 ....21 A4
Church View Ash GU12 ..77 C1
Church Wlk Andover RG27 .52 B3
  Hook RG27 ....51 A1
  South Warnborough SP9 .94 C2
  Upper Clatford SP11 ..105 C2
  Yateley GU46 ....34 A4
Churchdale [2] GU11 ....76 C1
Churchfield Ct GU30 ..187 C2
Churchfields GU35 ....142 A1
Churchill Ave
  Aldershot GU12 ....100 A4
  Odiham RG29 ....95 B4
Churchill Cl Alton GU34 .139 C1
  Farnborough GU14 ....55 C4
  Four Marks GU34 ....160 A1
  Hartley Wintney RG27 ..52 A4
  North Tidworth SP9 ..78 B4
  Odiham RG29 ....95 B4
  Tadley RG26 ....27 A4
Churchill Cres
  Farnborough GU14 ....55 C4
  Headley GU35 ....165 B2
  Yateley GU46 ....34 A3
Churchill Way
  Andover SP10 ....83 B1
  Basingstoke RG21 ....69 A3
Churchill Way E RG21 ..69 B3
Churchill Way W
  Andover SP10 ....82 B1
  Basingstoke RG21 ....69 A3
Churchyard Cotts SO24 .179 B3
Churt Cl RG24 ....70 A4
Churt Rd GU10,GU26 ..166 C4
Churt Wynde GU26 ....167 A4
Chute Cl RG25 ....28 C2
Cibbons Rd RG24 ....48 C2
City Bsns Ctr SO23 ....198 A4
City Rd SO23 ....197 C4
Claire Ct [1] SP10 ....105 C4
Clandon Ct GU14 ....56 B2
Clanfield Ride GU47 ..34 A2
Clappers Farm Rd RG7 ..11 C1
Clapps Gate Rd RG26 ..10 B1
Clare Ct [15] GU51 ....54 A1
Clare Mead GU10 ....121 B2
Clare Wlk RG14 ....5 A3
Claremont Ave GU15 ..36 B3
Clarence Cl GU12 ....77 A1
Clarence Ct [7] GU51 ..54 A1
Clarence Dr GU51 ....36 C4
Clarence Rd Andover SP10 .105 C3
Clarendon Cl GU17 ....35 A2
Clarendon Gdns RG14 ..1 C2
Clarendon Ho [5] GU51 ..53 C1
Clarendon Jun & Inf Schs
  SP9 ....78 C3
Clarendon Terr SP9 ....78 B2
Clarewood Dr GU15 ....36 B3
Clark Mews GU47 ....34 A2
Clarke Cres GU15 ....35 B4
Clarke's La GU11 ....58 C3
Clarks Hill GU10 ....98 A1
Clatford CE Prim Sch
  SP11 ....106 A1
Clatford Manor SP11 ..105 C2
Clatford Manor Ho
  SP11 ....105 C2
Claudius Cl SP10 ....83 A2
Claudius Dr RG23 ....68 B4
Clausentum Rd SO23 ..197 C3
Clay Hill Cotts GU10 ..121 B3
Clay Hill Cres RG24 ..2 A3
Clay's La Binsted GU34 .141 A3
  East Wordham GU34 ..140 C1
Claycart Rd
  Aldershot GU11 ....76 A2
  Aldershot GU11 ....76 B2
Claydon Gdns GU17 ..35 C1
Claypit La GU17 ....205 B3
Claythorpe Rd RG22 ..68 B2
Clayton Cr RG27 ....52 B3
Clayton Rd GU14 ....35 B1
Clem's Way GU51 ....54 B4
Clem's Way SO51 ....192 A1
Clemence Gdns RG28 ..86 B3
Clements Cl GU34 ....141 C4
Clere Gdns RG24 ....24 B1
Clere Gdns RG24 ....48 C1
Clere Sch The RG20 ..22 C4
Clerewater Pl RG19 ..2 B2
Clevedge Way RG29 ..72 B2
Clevedon Ct
  Camberley GU15 ....36 C4
  Farnborough GU14 ....55 A4
Cleveland Cl RG22 ....68 A1
Cleveland Gr RG14 ....1 B2
Cleves La RG25 ....94 A3
Clewborough Dr GU15 ..36 C3
Clewborough House Sch
  Camberley GU15 ....36 C3
  Mytchett GU16 ....56 C1
Cliddesden Ct RG21 ..69 A1
Cliddesden La RG21 ..91 B3
Cliddesden Prim Sch
  RG25 ....92 A3
Cliddesden Rd RG21 ..69 A1
Clifton Cl GU10 ....121 C2
Clifton Gdns GU16 ....56 B3
Clifton Rd SO22 ....197 C4
Clifton Lodge No 1 [31]
  SO22 ....197 C4

Clifton Lodge No 2 [32]
  SO22 ....197 C4
Clifton Rd Newbury RG14 .1 B1
  Winchester SO22 ....197 C4
Clifton Terr
  [8] Basingstoke RG21 ..69 A3
  Winchester SO23 ....197 C4
Clifton Wlk [6] RG21 ..69 A3
Clitheroe Rd GU46 ....34 B1
Clive Rd GU12 ....77 A1
Clockhouse Rd GU14 ..55 C2
Cloisters The
  Alton GU34 ....139 C2
  Basingstoke RG24 ....48 C2
Close The Camberley GU16 .56 A4
  Farnham GU9 ....99 A1
  Hatherden SP11 ....59 B1
  Liphook GU30 ....188 A1
  Monk Sherborne RG26 ..47 A2
  Sandhurst GU47 ....35 B4
  Thatcham RG18 ....2 C2
Closeworth Rd GU14 ..77 B4
Clouston Rd GU14 ....55 B3
Clovelly Dr GU26 ....167 A4
Clovelly Pk GU26 ....167 A4
Clovelly Rd GU26 ....167 A4
Clover Bank SO23 ....154 A1
Clover Cl GU35 ....165 A3
Clover Field RG24 ....69 C4
Clover La GU46 ....33 C3
Clover Leaf Way RG24 ..70 A2
Club La SP9 ....78 C2
Clubhouse Rd GU11 ..76 B3
Clumps Rd GU10 ....122 B2
Clyde Ct [8] SP10 ....83 A1
Coach Hill SP11 ....58 B2
Coach House Cl GU16 ..36 B2
Coach House Gdns GU14 .54 A2
Coach Rd The
  East Tytherley SP5 ....191 B4
  West Tytherley SP5 ....191 B4
Coachman's Ct RG14 ..1 C3
Coachmans Ct GU47 ..34 C4
Coachways SP10 ....106 A3
Coate Dr SO21 ....133 B1
Cobb Cl RG22 ....68 C1
Cob Tree Cotts RG25 ..70 C2
Cobbett Cl SO22 ....197 B3
Cobbett Gn RG22 ....68 C1
Cobbett's La GU46,GU17 .34 B3
Cobbetts Mews [4] GU9 .98 C1
Cobbetts Way GU10 ..121 B3
Cock-a-Dobby GU47 ..34 C4
Cocket's Mead SO21 ..177 A2
Cockshott La GU32 ....206 B1
Cody Cl GU12 ....77 B3
Cody Rd GU14 ....55 B2
Cody Tech Pk
  Farnborough GU14 ....54 C1
  Farnborough GU51 ....54 C1
Coe Cl GU11 ....76 C1
Cokenor Wood GU10 ..121 B3
Coker Cl SO22 ....197 C4
Colbeck GU52 ....75 A2
Colbourne Ct [6] SO23 .198 A4
Colbred Cnr GU51 ....54 B2
Cold Harbour
  GU12 ....106 A4
Cold Harbour La GU14 .55 B4
Colden La SO24 ....158 A2
Coldharbour RG25 ....89 C1
Coldrey Cotts GU34 ..119 B2
Cole Ave GU11 ....76 B2
Cole Cl SP10 ....83 A2
Colebrook Pl SO23 ....198 A4
Colebrook Rd SO23 ..198 A4
Colebrook Way SP10 ..83 A1
Coleford Bridge Rd GU14,
  GU16 ....56 B2
Coleford Cl GU16 ....56 B2
Coleford Paddocks GU16 .56 B2
Coleman Cl RG21 ....69 B4
Coleman Rd GU12 ....77 A1
Colenzo Dr SP10 ....83 B1
Coleridge Ave GU46 ..34 B3
Coleson Mill Rd GU10 ..121 B3
Coleville Rd GU14 ....54 C4
Coley La SP11 ....128 C2
Coliseum Bsns Ctr GU15 .35 C2
Collard Way [4] GU33 ..207 C2
College Cl GU15 ....36 A4
College Gdns GU47 ..35 B4
College Gdns GU9 ....98 C1
College La RG25 ....115 A3
College Piece RG25 ..11 B3
College Rd Ash GU12 ..77 C2
  Sandhurst GU47 ....35 B4
College Ride GU15 ....36 A4
College St SO23 ....198 A4
College Town Jun & Inf Schs
  GU47 ....35 B4
Collenorne Rd [1] GU35 .166 A4
Colley Cl SO23 ....176 A2
Collier Cl GU14 ....55 C4
Collingwood Coll GU15 .36 C4
Collingwood Grange Cl
  GU15 ....36 C4
Collingwood Mount
  GU15 ....36 C4
Collingwood Rise GU15 .36 C4
Collins Cl SP10 ....82 C2
Collins Ct [1] SP9 ....78 C3
Collins Gdns GU12 ....77 C1
Collyers Cres GU34 ..188 B2

Colne Way Ash GU12 ..77 C1
[2] Basingstoke RG21 ..69 B3
Colson Cl SO23 ....198 A4
Colson Rd SO23 ....198 A4
Coltsfoot Pl RG27 ....51 B1
Coltsfoot Rd GU35 ....165 A3
Columbia Ct RG40 ....16 B4
Columbine Rd RG22 ..91 A4
Columbus Dr GU14 ....55 A2
Columbus Way SP10 ..83 C1
Colwyn Cl GU46 ....34 A3
Colyer Cl RG22 ....68 A3
Combe La GU14 ....55 C3
Combe Rd GU33 ....208 A1
Combe Rise GU10 ....122 A3
Comet Cl GU12 ....77 B3
Comet Rd GU14 ....55 A3
Comfrey Cl RG42 ....9 B1
Commercial Ctr The
  SP11 ....84 A2
Commercial Rd GU12 ..100 A4
Commodore Ct GU14 ..76 C4
Common Hill GU34 ....159 B3
Common Rd RG19 ....7 B1
Common The
  Middle Wintersow SP5 .168 A3
  Ramsdell RG26 ....26 C1
Common Vale SP5 ....165 A3
Commonfield La RG40 ..15 C4
Communications Rd RG19 .6 B3
Compass Field RG27 ..51 A1
Complins GU34 ....140 B3
Compton Cl Fleet GU52 .75 A3
  Hook RG27 ....51 A1
  Winchester SO22 ....197 A2
Compton Ho [6] GU9 ..99 A1
Compton Place Bsns Ctr
  GU15 ....35 C2
Compton Rd Fleet GU52 .75 A3
  Winchester SO23 ....197 C4
Compton Sq SP10 ....83 B2
Compton Way
  Farnham GU10 ....99 C1
  Winchester SO22 ....197 A2
Concorde Rd GU14 ....55 A1
Conde Way GU35 ....164 B1
Coney Gn [4] SO23 ....176 A1
Congreve Cl RG7 ....9 C4
Conholt Ho [6] SP11,SN8 .37 C2
Conholt Rd SP10 ....106 A3
Conifer Cl Baughurst RG26 .9 B1
  Bordon GU35 ....164 B1
  Fleet GU52 ....74 C3
  Winchester SO22 ....175 C1
Conifer Crest RG14 ..5 A2
Conifer Dr GU35 ....36 C3
Coniston Cl
  Farnborough GU14 ....55 B2
  Thatcham RG19 ....2 C2
Coniston Ct Ash GU12 ..77 B2
[8] Newbury RG14 ....1 C2
Coniston Dr GU9 ....98 C3
Coniston Gr SO24 ....179 B2
Coniston Rd
  Basingstoke RG22 ....68 A1
  Bordon GU35 ....164 B3
Coniston Way GU52 ..74 C3
Connaught Cl
  Aldershot GU11 ....164 B1
  Yateley GU46 ....34 A3
Connaught Rd
  Aldershot GU12 ....77 A1
  Camberley GU15 ....36 B3
  Fleet GU51 ....54 A1
  Kings Worthy SO23 ....153 B1
  Newbury RG14 ....1 A2
Connaught Sch The
  GU11 ....100 B4
Connop Way GU16 ....36 B1
Conservatory The [48]
  SO23 ....198 A4
Constable Cl RG22 ....69 B2
Constable Ct SP10 ....83 A1
Constable Way GU47 ..35 B3
Constables Gate [28]
  SO22 ....197 C4
Constantine Way RG22 .91 A3
Constantius Ct [1] GU52 .74 C2
Conway Cl GU16 ....36 B1
Conway Dr
  Farnborough GU14 ....55 A2
  Thatcham RG18 ....2 C3
Cooks La SO51 ....191 C1
Coolarne Rise GU15 ..36 C3
Coolers Farm SO20 ....170 B3
Coombe Cl GU16 ....56 A4
Coombe Dr GU51 ....54 B1
Coombe Rd GU46 ....33 C4
Coombehurst Dr RG21 ..69 A1
Cooper Cl GU14 ....54 A2
Cooper Ho [8] GU15 ..164 B1
Cooper's Hill GU46 ..34 A3
Cooper's Terr GU9 ....99 A2
Cooperage The [3]
  ....139 C2
Coopers Cl SO51 ....153 B1
Coopers La RG26 ....28 C2
Coopers La RG26 ....28 C2
Cope Hall La RG14 ..5 A4
Copes La RG27 ....31 C4
Copland Cl RG22 ....91 A4
Copnor RG20 ....21 A4
Copnor Cl RG20 ....21 A4
Coppice Cl
  Baughurst RG26 ....26 A4

Coppice Cl continued
Farnham GU9 ....99 B3
Newbury RG14 ....5 C4
Winchester SO22 ....175 B1
Coppice Gdns GU46 ....34 A3
Coppice Gdns RG23 ....68 B3
Coppice Rd RG20 ....24 C1
Copse Ave GU9 ....99 B4
Copse Cl Camberley GU15 ..36 C3
Liss GU33 ....208 A2
Copse End
Camberley GU15 ....36 B3
Fleet GU51 ....74 B4
Copse Field RG24 ....70 A4
Copse La
Brown Candover SO24 ......134 C2
Fleet GU52 ....74 C3
Long Sutton RG29 ....95 B2
Copse Rd
Linchmere GU27 ....189 A1
Overton RG25 ....65 A1
Copse The
Farnborough GU14 ....55 A2
Farnham GU10 ....121 B2
Tadley RG26 ....26 C4
Copse View
Farnham GU10 ....121 B3
Finchampstead RG40 ....16 B4
Coram Cl 3 SO23 ....176 A1
Cordale Rd RG21 ....54 B2
Cordelia Gdns GU12 ....56 B1
Cordwalles Jun Sch
GU15 ....36 B4
Cordwalles Rd GU15 ....36 A4
Corfe Cl SO24 ....179 B2
Corfe Gdns GU16 ....36 B1
Corfe Way GU14 ....56 B1
Corfe Wlk RG23 ....68 B3
Corfield Cl RG40 ....16 B2
Coriander Cl GU14 ....55 A2
Corinthian Cl
Andover SP10 ....83 A2
Basingstoke RG22 ....91 A4
Cormorant Cl RG22 ....90 C4
Cormorant Pl GU47 ....35 A4
Cornbunting Cl GU47 ....35 A4
Cornelia Cl GU14 ....55 A2
Cornes Cl SO22 ....197 B4
Cornfields Andover SP10 ..106 B3
Yateley GU46 ....33 C2
Cornfields The RG22 ....91 A4
Cornish Cl RG22 ....68 B2
Cornwall Cl GU15 ....36 B4
Cornwall Rd GU35 ....164 B1
Coronation Cl
Burghclere RG20 ....22 B4
Odiham RG29 ....72 C2
Coronation Rd
Aldershot GU11 ....99 C4
Basingstoke RG21 ....69 B3
Langhall SP11 ....57 A1
North Tidworth SP9 ....78 C4
Yateley GU46 ....34 B4
Corporation Cotts 1
RG14 ....1 C1
Correlli Rd RG22 ....91 C4
Corringway GU52 ....75 A3
Corry Rd GU26 ....167 A3
Corunna Main SP10 ....83 A1
Cossack La 2 SO22 ....197 B4
Cossack Lane Ho 20
SO23 ....198 A4
Coster Cl RG41 ....1 A3
Cotswold Cl
Basingstoke RG22 ....68 A2
Farnborough GU14 ....55 B4
Cotswold Ct 10 GU51 ....53 C1
Cottage Gdns GU14 ....55 B4
Cottage Gn
Goodworth Clatford SP11 ...128 A4
Harley Whitney RG27 ....52 B3
Cottage La GU32 ....206 C2
Cottage Rd SO20 ....147 B4
Cottington Cl RG20 ....24 C1
Cottle Cl RG21 ....54 A2
Cotton Cl GU11 ....76 B2
Cottonworth Cotts SP11 ...128 B2
Cottrell Cl GU52 ....74 C2
Cottrell Flats GU14 ....77 A4
Couch Gn SO21 ....177 B4
Council Cotts SO24 ....157 B1
Council Hos
Farley Mill RG7 ....15 A3
Little Somborne SO20 ....173 A3
Council Hos The
Baughurst RG26 ....25 C2
Kingsclere RG20 ....21 C4
Council Houses The RG26 ...8 C1
Council Rd RG21 ....69 A2
Court Cl GU30 ....188 A2
Court Dr GU52 ....75 A4
Court Dro RG25 ....64 C1
Court Gdns GU15 ....36 A3
Court La
Little Somborne SO20 ....173 A3
Ropley GU34 ....181 B3
Court Moor Sch GU52 ....74 C3
Court Rd Aldershot GU11 ..76 A2
Kings Worthy SO23 ....176 B3
Court The GU10 ....143 A2
Courtenay Rd
Farnham GU9 ....99 B4
Winchester SO23 ....176 A2
Courtlands Rd RG14 ....1 C1

Courtmoor Ave GU52 ....75 A4
Courts Hill Rd GU27 ....189 C3
Courts Mount Rd GU27 ....189 C3
Courtyard The GU30 ....188 C1
Cove Inf Sch GU14 ....55 B3
Cove Jnr Sch GU14 ....55 B3
Cove Rd Farnborough GU14 ..55 B2
Fleet GU51 ....54 B2
Cove Sch GU14 ....55 B3
Coventry Cl RG22 ....91 A4
Coventry Ct 7 RG23 ....176 A1
Covert The GU14 ....55 B4
Coverts Copse GU9 ....99 B2
Coverts The RG26 ....26 C3
Covey Cl GU14 ....55 C4
Covey Way SO24 ....179 A2
Cow Drove Hill SO20 ....172 A2
Cow La SP11 ....80 A2
Crabb Hill RG26 ....25 B1
Crabtree Gdns GU15 ....36 B4
Crabtree La Churt GU10 ...144 C1
Headley GU35 ....165 B3
Crabtree Rd GU15 ....35 C1
Crabtree Way RG24 ....70 A4
Craddock Rd 2 SO23 ......198 B4
Cradle La GU35 ....143 A2
Crake Pl GU47 ....35 A4
Cramptons GU34 ....139 A1
Cranberry Wlk GU17 ....35 B2
Cranbourne Ct RG21 ....69 A1
Cranbourne La RG21 ....68 C1
Cranbourne Sec Sch
RG21 ....68 C2
Cranbrook Ct GU51 ....54 A2
Crane Ct GU47 ....35 A4
Cranes Rd RG24 ....47 C2
Cranesfield RG24 ....47 C2
Cranford Ave GU52 ....74 C3
Cranford Dr GU34 ....140 B3
Cranford Park Dr GU34 ....34 A3
Cranleigh Ct GU14 ....55 B2
Cranmore Cl GU12 ....77 C3
Cranmore Ct GU16 ....56 B2
Cranmore Gdns GU11 ....76 B1
Cranmore La GU11 ....76 B1
Cranmore Rd GU16 ....56 C2
Cranworth Rd SO22 ....175 C1
Craven Cl GU10 ....122 A3
Craven Ct GU15 ....35 B2
Craven Dene RG14 ....1 C2
Craven Ho 7 GU9 ....98 C1
Craven Rd RG14 ....1 B2
Crawford Gdns GU15 ....35 C3
Crawford Pl RG14 ....1 B2
Crawlboys La SP11 ....57 A2
Crawlboys Rd SP11 ....57 A2
Crawley Cotts SO21 ....152 A1
Crawley Cl GU15 ....36 B3
Crawley Hill GU15 ....36 B3
Crawley Ridge GU15 ....36 B3
Crawley Ridge Jun Sch
GU15 ....36 B4
Crawley Ridgel Inf Sch
GU15 ....36 B3
Crawley Wood Cl GU15 .....36 B3
Crawts Rd RG25 ....88 A4
Craydown La SO20 ....125 C1
Credon Cl GU11 ....55 B3
Crerar Cl GU14 ....55 A2
Crescent Cl SO22 ....197 A2
Crescent La GU12 ....77 C3
Crescent The
Andover SP10 ....105 B4
Basingstoke RG24 ....68 A4
Crookham Village GU51 ......74 B3
Farnborough GU14 ....56 A2
Farnham GU9 ....99 A2
Four Marks GU34 ....140 A2
Goodworth Clatford SP11 ...74 B3
Hurstbourne Tarrant SP11 ..60 C4
Mortimer RG7 ....11 B3
Yateley GU46 ....34 A4
Cress Gdns SP10 ....105 C3
Cresswell Rd RG14 ....2 A2
Cricket Cl
Beacon Hill GU26 ....167 A3
Crawley SO21 ....152 A1
Cricket Green La RG27 ......52 B3
Cricket Hill RG40 ....16 B1
Cricket Hill La GU17,
GU46 ....34 B2
Cricket La GU10 ....122 A3
Cricket Lea GU35 ....165 A3
Cricketers Way SP10 ....83 B1
Cricklade Coll SP10 ....106 A4
Cricklade Pl SP10 ....82 C2
Crimea Rd GU11 ....76 C1
Cripley Rd GU14 ....55 A3
Cripstead La SO23 ....197 C3
Criswick Cl SP11 ....104 C1

Critchmere Hill GU27 ....189 B4
Critchmere La GU27 ....189 B3
Critchmere Vale GU27 ......189 B3
Crockford La RG24 ....48 B1
Croft Ave SP10 ....106 A3
Croft Gdns Alton GU34 ....139 C2
Andover SP10 ....106 A3
Croft La Crondall GU10 ......97 B3
Newbury RG14 ....2 A2
Yateley GU46 ....34 A4
Croft Rd Aldershot GU11 ...99 C4
Mortimer RG7 ....11 B3
Newbury RG14 ....2 A2
Oakley RG23 ....67 A1
Croft The Fleet GU51 ....74 B4
Newton Toney SP4 ....123 A3
Crofter's Cl GU47 ....34 C4
Crofters Mdw RG24 ....69 C1
Crofton GU27 ....189 B4
Crofts The RG23 ....91 B3
Cromwell Cl RG24 ....70 A3
Cromwell Gdns GU34 ......139 C2
Cromwell Rd
Basingstoke RG21 ....69 A3
Camberley GU15 ....36 A4
Newbury RG14 ....2 A3
Winchester SO22 ....197 C3
Cromwell Terr RG14 ....1 A4
Cromwell Way GU14 ....56 A4
Crondall Cl GU15 ....35 C2
Crondall End GU46 ....34 A4
Crondall La GU9,GU10 ....98 B1
Crondall Prim Sch GU10 .....97 B3
Crondall Rd
Bentley GU10 ....120 C3
Crookham Village GU51,
GU10 ....74 B2
Crookham CE Inf Sch
GU52 ....74 C2
Crookham Jnr Sch GU52 ...75 A2
Crookham Rd GU51 ....74 C3
Crookham Reach GU52 ......74 C3
Crooksbury Rd GU10 ....100 A2
Cropmark Way RG24 ....91 A4
Crosby Gdns GU46 ....33 C4
Crosby Hill Dr GU15 ....36 B4
Crosby Way GU9 ....98 C1
Cross & Pillory La 6
GU34 ....139 C2
Cross Farm Inf Sch GU16 ..56 B3
Cross Gdns GU16 ....56 B3
Cross Keys Pas 8 SO23 ..198 A4
Cross La Andover SP10 ....105 C4
Ashmansworth RG20 ....41 A4
Beech Hill RG7 ....13 A4
Camberley GU16 ....56 B3
Cross Rd GU12 ....77 C2
Cross St Aldershot GU11 ...76 C1
Basingstoke RG21 ....69 A3
Farnborough GU14 ....77 A4
Winchester SO23 ....197 C4
Cross The SO20 ....172 A1
Crossborough Gdns
RG21 ....69 B2
Crossborough Hill RG21 ....69 B2
Crosswater La GU10 ....144 B2
Crossways Aldershot GU12 ..77 A1
Churt GU10 ....144 B1
Crookham Village GU51 ......74 B3
Whitchurch RG28 ....86 B3
Crossways The GU9 ....105 C4
Croucher's Croft SO22 ....175 B1
Crowder Terr SO22 ....197 C4
Crowfield Dr RG19 ....3 B2
Crowley Dr GU34 ....140 A2
Crown Cl Farnham GU9 ......99 B4
Crown Mews GU34 ....139 C2
Crown Cres RG24 ....70 A3
Crown Dr GU9 ....99 B4
Crown Gdns GU51 ....75 A4
Crown La Farnham GU9 ......99 B4
Newnham RG27 ....71 B4
Old Basing RG24 ....70 A3
Crown Way SP10 ....83 B1
Crownfields RG29 ....72 B1
Crows La GU34 ....122 A3
Crowthorne Rd GU47 ....34 C4
Croyde Cl GU14 ....55 A2
Croye Cl SP10 ....106 A4
Cruikshank Lea GU47 ....35 A3
Crumlins Bsns Est RG29 .....72 B2
Crundwell Ct GU9 ....99 A2
Cuckoo Cl RG25 ....89 C1
Cufaude La RG24 ....48 B2
Cuffelle Cl RG24 ....49 A2
Cufoude La RG24 ....48 C2
Cullen Cl GU46 ....34 A3
Cullens Mews 4 GU11 ......76 C1
Culley View RG24 ....179 B2
Culver Mews SO23 ....198 A4
Culver Rd
Basingstoke RG21 ....69 A2
Newbury RG14 ....4 A4
B Winchester SO23 ....198 A4
Culverlands Cres GU12 ......77 A2
Culvernell Gdns 2
SO23 ....197 C4
Cumberland Ave RG22 ....68 C1
Cumbria Cl GU14 ....56 B1
Cundell Way SO21 ....176 B4
Cunningham Ho 4 SP9 .....78 C4
Cunnington Rd GU14 ....55 B3
Curlew Cl RG22 ....90 C4
Curlew Ct GU11 ....99 C4
Curlews Way RG7 ....14 A3
Curling Way RG14 ....2 A2

Curly Bridge Cl GU14 ....55 B4
Curnock Ct RG14 ....1 B1
Curtis Cl GU35 ....165 B3
Curtis Ct GU52 ....75 A3
Curtis La GU35 ....165 B3
Curtis Rd GU34 ....140 A2
Curzon Dr GU52 ....75 A3
Cusden Dr SP10 ....105 C4
Cuthbert Rd GU12 ....77 C3
Cutts Rd GU11 ....77 A4
Cuxhaven Way SP10 ....82 C2
Cygnet Cl RG19 ....2 C2
Cygnet Ct Fleet GU51 ....54 A2
Newbury RG14 ....4 A2
Cygnets GU51 ....54 A2
Cypress Cl RG40 ....16 C4
Cypress Dr GU51 ....54 A2
Cypress Gr Andover SP10 ..105 B4
Ash GU12 ....77 C4
Cypress Hill Ct GU14 ....35 B1
Cypress Rd GU35 ....164 A1
Cypress Way
Blackwater GU17 ....34 C3
Grayshott GU26 ....167 A1
Cyprus Rd RG22 ....91 B3
Cyril Vokins Rd RG14 ....2 B1

D

Dacre Cl SP10 ....82 B2
Daffodil Cl RG22 ....91 A4
Dahlia Cl RG22 ....91 A4
Dahlia Ct SP10 ....105 B3
Dairy Ho SP11 ....57 A1
Dairy Wlk RG27 ....52 B3
Dalby Cres RG14 ....6 A4
Dale Cl Farnham GU10 ......121 B4
Littleton SO22 ....174 B2
Dale Gdns GU47 ....34 C4
Dale View GU47 ....189 C3
Dalewood RG22 ....68 A2
Dallence Ho RG25 ....35 A4
Dalley Cl GU47 ....35 A4
Dalzell 1 SO23 ....176 A1
Damsel Path 14 RG23 ....69 B3
Dancers Mdw RG22 ....47 C2
Dances Cl SP10 ....83 A1
Dances La RG19 ....2 C2
Danebury Rd RG22 ....91 A3
Danebury Ring * SO20 .....148 C4
Danebury View SO20 ....126 A2
Danebury Wlk SO20 ....56 B4
Danegeld Ct SP10 ....83 A2
Danehurst Pl SP10 ....105 B4
Danemark Ct 4 SO23 ....198 A4
Danes B RG23 ....176 A1
Danes The RG21 ....69 B3
Daneshill Dr RG24 ....69 C4
Daneshill East Ind Est
RG24 ....69 C4
Daneshill Sch RG27 ....30 B2
Daneshill West Ind Est
RG24 ....69 C4
Daniel Rd RG22 ....86 B2
Dankworth Rd RG22 ....91 B4
Danley La GU27 ....188 C2
Danvers Dr GU52 ....74 C2
Daphne Dr GU52 ....74 C2
Darby Green La GU17 ....34 C3
Darby Green Rd GU17 ....34 C3
Darcey Cl RG24 ....69 A3
Darcy Ho RG22 ....68 B1
Dare's Cnr GU10 ....74 C1
Dare's La GU10 ....74 C1
Darent Ct 22 RG22 ....91 A3
Dark La
Bishop's Sutton SO24 ....179 C1
Cheriton SO24 ....201 B3
Sherborne St John RG24 ....47 C2
Darlington Rd RG21 ....69 A4
Darracott Cl GU15 ....36 C4
Darset Ave GU51 ....54 A1
Dart Cl
Finchampstead RG40 ....16 B3
Thatcham RG18 ....3 B4
Dart Ct 36 SP10 ....83 B1
Dart Rd GU14 ....55 B3
Dartmoor Wlk RG22 ....68 B2
Dartmouth Rd RG22 ....68 B2
Dartmouth Wlk RG22 ....68 B2
Darvill Rd SO24 ....181 A3
Darvills La GU9 ....99 A1
Darwin Gr GU11 ....77 A2
Dashwood Cl GU34 ....139 B1
Dasna Rd SP9 ....78 B3
Daunch Cl SP9 ....78 B4
Dauntsey Dro SP11 ....81 A2
Dauntsey La SP11 ....81 A1
Davis Cl GU47 ....35 B4
Davis Gdns GU47 ....35 B4
Dawn Gdns SO22 ....197 B3
Dawnay Rd GU15 ....35 C3
Days Mdw RG21 ....68 A3
Days Mdw Bridge 7 SO23 ..198 A4
De Montfort Rd RG14 ....1 B3
De-lucy Ave SO24 ....179 A3
Deadbrook La GU12 ....77 B2
Deadmans La RG14,RG19 ...5 C1
Deadmoor La RG20 ....5 B1
Dean Cl SO22 ....175 B1
Dean La SO22 ....175 A1
Dean Par GU15 ....36 B4
Dean Rd West Dean SP5 ...190 A1
West Tytherley SP5 ....190 C2
Dean Rise SP11 ....60 C4
Dean Sta SP5 ....190 B2

Dean Terr SP11 ....38 B3
Deane Cl SO23 ....179 A3
Deane Down Dro SO22 ....175 A2
Deane's C RG21 ....69 B3
Deanes Cotts RG25 ....66 A1
Deans Cl SP9 ....78 C2
Deans Dell GU12 ....205 C1
Deanswood Rd RG26 ....26 C4
Decottere Cl GU42 ....74 C2
Deedman Cl GU12 ....77 C1
Deep La RG21 ....68 C3
Deep Well Dr GU15 ....36 B4
Deepdene Farnham GU10 ..122 A4
Haslemere GU27 ....189 B3
Deer Park View RG29 ....72 B2
Deer Rock Rd GU35 ....36 B4
Deerfield Cl RG26 ....29 A1
Deerleap GU35 ....166 A2
Delibes Rd RG22 ....91 C4
Delius Cl RG22 ....68 C1
Dell Cl GU27 ....189 C4
Dell Cotts SO24 ....202 C1
Dell Rd GU27 ....189 C4
Dell Rd Andover SP10 ....82 C1
Finchampstead RG40 ....16 C2
Winchester SO23 ....198 B3
Dell The Farnham GU9 ....99 A4
Grateley SP11 ....33 A3
Kingsclere RG20 ....24 B1
Old Basing RG24 ....70 B3
Vernham Dean SP11 ....38 A3
Yateley GU46 ....34 A3
Dellands RG25 ....88 A4
Dellands La RG25 ....88 A4
Dellfield RG23 ....67 B2
Delville Cl GU14 ....55 A2
Dempster Ho GU9 ....99 A4
Denby Ct B GU14 ....56 A1
Denly Dene GU12 ....77 C1
Dene Cl Bordon GU35 ....164 B1
Farnham GU10 ....122 B3
Ropley SO24 ....181 A3
Dene Ct SP10 ....102 B3
Dene La SP10 ....106 A3
Dene La W GU10 ....122 B3
Dene Path SP10 ....106 A4
Dene Rd Andover SP10 ....106 A4
Farnborough GU14 ....55 B2
Dene Sch SO24 ....181 A3
Dene The SO24 ....181 A3
Dene Way RG14 ....1 C3
Denham GU35 ....175 C1
Denham Ct SO23 ....176 A1
Denham Dr
Basingstoke RG22 ....68 B1
Yateley GU46 ....34 A3
Denham Terr SP11 ....61 C1
Denman Ct GU51 ....54 B1
Denmark La GU34 ....1 C2
Denmark Sq GU14 ....77 B3
Denmark St GU14 ....77 A3
Denmead RG26 ....26 C4
Dennet Ho SO23 ....176 B3
Denning Cl GU52 ....74 C2
Dennis Way GU33 ....208 A2
Dennistoun Cl GU15 ....36 A3
Denton Way GU16 ....36 B1
Denvale Trad Pk RG21 ....68 C3
Denvale Trade Pk RG14 ......2 A1
Denvers Cotts GU34 ....138 A2
Deptford La
Greywell RG29 ....72 A2
Odiham RG29 ....72 A2
Derby Rd
Haslemere GU27 ....189 C4
Newbury RG14 ....1 B1
Derbyfields RG29 ....72 B1
Derek Horn Ct GU15 ....35 C1
Derry Cl GU12 ....77 B3
Derry Rd GU14 ....55 B4
Derwent Ave GU17 ....34 C3
Derwent Cl Bordon GU35 ..164 B1
Farnborough GU14 ....55 B2
Farnham GU9 ....98 C3
Derwent Ct 37 SP10 ....179 B2
Derwent Rd
Basingstoke RG22 ....68 A1
Thatcham RG19 ....2 C1
Devenish Rd SO22 ....175 B1
Dever Cl SO21 ....133 A4
Dever Way RG23 ....68 A1
Devils La GU30 ....188 B4
Devizes Ho 10 SP9 ....78 C4
Devon Cl Fleet GU51 ....54 A
Sandhurst GU47 ....35 A4
Devon Rd GU35 ....164 B1
Devonshire Dr GU15 ....36 B3
Devonshire Pl
Aldershot GU11 ....76 A
B Basingstoke RG21 ....69 A
Dewpond Wlk RG44 ....69 C1
Dexter Sq SP10 ....83 B
Dexter Way GU14 ....54 B
Diamond Hill GU15 ....36 A
Diamond Ridge GU15 ....36 A
Diana Cl RG22 ....68 C
Dibley Cl RG22 ....68 C
Dickens La RG24 ....70 A
Dickens Way GU46 ....34 B
Dickens Wlk SO24 ....179 B
Dickenson Wlk SO24 ....179 A
Dicker's La GU34 ....140 A
Digby Rd RG14 ....1 B
Digby Way GU33 ....186 A
Dilly La RG27 ....52 C
Dines Cl SP11 ....60 C
Dingley Way GU11 ....76 C

Dinorben Ave GU52 ... 74 C4
Dinorben Beeches GU52 ... 74 C4
Dinorben Cl GU52 ... 74 C4
Dippenhall Rd GU10 ... 98 A1
Dippenhall St GU10 ... 97 B3
Dirty Cnr RG28 ... 85 C4
Ditchfield La RG40 ... 16 B4
Dittons The RG40 ... 16 B3
Divers Cl GU34 ... 139 C3
Dixon Rd RG27 ... 49 A4
Dixons La SO20 ... 170 A4
Dockenfield St GU10 ... 143 A3
Doctors Dro SP11 ... 60 B4
Dodsells Well RG40 ... 16 B4
Dogflud Way GU9 ... 99 A2
Dogmersfield CE Prim Sch RG27 ... 74 A4
Doiley Bottom SP11 ... 40 B1
Doiley Hill SP11 ... 40 B2
Dollis Ct GU9 ... 99 A2
Dollis Dr GU9 ... 99 A2
Dollis Gn RG26 ... 28 C2
Dolman Rd RG14 ... 1 C2
Dolomans La SP11 ... 60 C4
Dolphin Cl Aldermaston RG7 ... 9 B4
Haslemere GU27 ... 189 B3
Dolton Mews RG14 ... 1 B2
Doman Rd GU15 ... 35 C2
Dome Alley SO23 ... 198 A4
Dominica Cl RG24 ... 48 B1
Domitian Gdns RG24 ... 68 B4
Domum Rd SO23 ... 198 A3
Donnington Castle* RG14 ... 1 B4
Donnington Cl GU15 ... 35 C2
Donnington Ct 19 SO23 ... 176 A1
Donnington Hospl RG14 ... 1 B3
Donnington Lodge RG14 ... 1 B3
Donnington Pk RG14 ... 1 B3
Donnington Sq RG14 ... 1 B3
Dora's Green La GU10 ... 98 A2
Dorcas Ct GU15 ... 35 C2
Dorchester Cl RG23 ... 68 A3
Dorchester Rd RG27 ... 51 A1
Dorchester Way RG29 ... 72 A2
Doreen Cl GU14 ... 55 B4
Dores La SO21 ... 195 B1
Dorian Gr SO24 ... 179 A2
Dormer Cl RG14 ... 5 A3
Dorothy Ct RG14 ... 2 A2
Dorrel Cl RG22 ... 91 A3
Dorset Ct GU15 ... 36 B4
Dorset Rd GU12 ... 77 C3
Doswell Way RG21 ... 69 B3
Douai Cl GU14 ... 56 A2
Doublet Cl RG19 ... 2 C2
Doughty Way SP10 ... 83 C1
Douglas Gr GU10 ... 122 A3
Douglas Pl GU14 ... 55 C3
Douglas Rd SP11 ... 105 A4
Douglas Ride RG20 ... 21 B4
Douro Cl RG26 ... 9 A1
Dove Cl Andover SP10 ... 83 A1
Basingstoke RG22 ... 67 C1
Dove Ct GU34 ... 140 A3
Dove House Sch RG21 ... 69 A4
Dover Cl Basingstoke RG23 ... 68 B3
New Alresford SO24 ... 179 B2
Doveton Way RG14 ... 1 C2
Dowden Gr GU34 ... 140 A3
Down Farm La SO22, SO23 ... 175 C4
Down Gate SO24 ... 179 B2
Down La RG25 ... 71 A1
Down Rd SP11 ... 80 A2
Down St RG25 ... 90 B1
Downing St GU9 ... 98 C1
Downlands Rd SO22 ... 197 A2
Downlands Way SO21 ... 153 B2
Downs La SN8 ... 18 A4
Downs Rd SO21 ... 153 B2
Downs View GU34 ... 140 C4
Downs Way GU34 ... 139 B1
Downside GU26 ... 167 A4
Downside Cotts SP11 ... 124 C4
Downside Rd SO22 ... 175 A1
Downsland Par RG21 ... 68 C2
Downsland Rd RG21 ... 69 A2
Downsview Rd GU35 ... 166 A3
Downsview Way SP11 ... 79 B3
Downview Cl GU26 ... 167 A3
Doyle Gdns GU46 ... 34 A2
Dragonfly Dr RG24 ... 69 C4
Dragoon Ct 11 GU11 ... 76 B1
Drake Ave GU16 ... 56 C1
Drake Cl RG40 ... 16 B4
Drake Ct SP10 ... 83 B1
Drayman's Way GU34 ... 139 C2
Drayton St SO22 ... 197 B3
Draytons View RG19 ... 6 A4
Drift Rd GU33,GU35 ... 186 A4
Driftway Rd RG27 ... 51 B1
Drive The Farnham GU9 ... 121 C4
Newbury RG14 ... 5 B4
Oakley RG23 ... 67 A1
Old Alresford SO24 ... 158 B3
Drove Hill SO20 ... 129 A2
Drove La SO24 ... 179 A3
Drove Rd SP11 ... 129 A2
Drove The RG19 ... 7 C1
Drovers End GU51 ... 54 B2
Drovers Way GU9 ... 98 C3
Droxford Cres RG26 ... 26 C4
Drummond Cl
Four Marks GU34 ... 159 C1
Winchester SO22 ... 197 C3
Drury Cl SP11 ... 108 B4
Drury La Bentworth GU34 ... 138 A3
Mortimer RG7 ... 11 C3
Dryden Cl RG24 ... 48 B1
Dryden Rd GU14 ... 55 B3
Dryden Way GU30 ... 187 C3
Du Maurier Cl GU52 ... 74 C2
Duchess Cl GU34 ... 139 C2
Duck St SP11 ... 104 C2
Ducklands GU35 ... 164 C1
Duckmead La GU33 ... 208 A3
Ducks La SO20 ... 147 C3
Duddon Way RG21 ... 69 B3
Dudley Cl
Basingstoke RG23 ... 68 A3
Bordon GU35 ... 164 B1
Dudley Ct GU52 ... 75 A3
Dudley Terr GU33 ... 208 A3
Duke Cl SP10 ... 83 B1
Duke of Connaughts Rd GU11 ... 77 A3
Duke St SO21 ... 133 A2
Dukes Cl Alton GU34 ... 139 B1
Farnham GU9 ... 98 C3
Dukes Mead GU51 ... 53 B1
Dukes Pk GU11 ... 77 A3
Dukes Ride RG7 ... 27 C4
Dukes Wlk GU9 ... 98 C3
Dumas Cl GU46 ... 34 A3
Dummer Down La RG25 ... 113 B4
Dummer La SP11 ... 37 A1
Dummer Mews 24 SO23 ... 197 C4
Dunbar Rd GU16 ... 56 B4
Dunbridge La
Brown Candover SO24 ... 135 B3
Mottisfont SO51 ... 192 B1
Dunbridge Sta SO51 ... 192 B1
Duncan Ct SP10 ... 106 B4
Duncan's Cl SP11 ... 80 C1
Dundaff Cl GU15 ... 36 C3
Dunedin Cl SP9 ... 79 A3
Dungells Farm Cl GU46 ... 34 A2
Dungells La GU46 ... 34 A2
Dunhills La SP11 ... 83 B4
Dunketts La RG26 ... 26 A3
Dunkirt La SP11 ... 104 C2
Dunley Dr 3 GU51 ... 53 B2
Dunley's Hill RG29 ... 72 B2
Dunmow Hill GU51 ... 54 A1
Dunmow Rd SP10 ... 106 A3
Dunsell's Cl SO24 ... 181 B3
Dunsell's La SO24 ... 181 B3
Dunsford Cres RG23 ... 68 B4
Dunsmore Gdns GU46 ... 33 C3
Dunstall Pk GU14 ... 55 C4
Dunstan's Dro SP11 ... 39 B1
Durbidges RG19 ... 24 B4
Durham Way RG22 ... 91 A4
Durnford Cl SO20 ... 129 A2
Durngate Pl SO23 ... 198 A4
Durngate Terr 41 SO23 ... 198 A4
Durnsford Ave GU52 ... 75 A4
Dyson Dr SO23 ... 176 A1
Dysons Cl RG14 ... 1 B2

E

Eagle Cl Alton GU34 ... 139 C3
Basingstoke RG22 ... 90 C4
Eagle Ct Basingstoke RG24 ... 69 C3
12 Winchester SO23 ... 197 C4
Eagle Rd RG20 ... 6 C1
Eames La GU33 ... 206 C4
Eardley Ave SP10 ... 82 B1
Earle Ho 3 SO23 ... 198 B4
Earls Gr GU15 ... 36 B3
Earlsbourne GU52 ... 75 A2
Earlsdown 47 SO23 ... 198 A4
East Ave GU9 ... 99 A3
East Dean Rd SO51 ... 191 C1
East Gn GU17 ... 35 A2
East Hill SO23 ... 198 A3
East Hill Dr GU33 ... 208 A2
East La SO24 ... 178 C2
East Portway SP10 ... 82 B1
East Rd SO21 ... 130 C4
East Ring GU10 ... 100 C4
East St Andover SP10 ... 106 A4
Farnham GU9 ... 99 A2
New Alresford SO24 ... 179 B3
East Station Rd GU12 ... 76 C1
East Tree Cl RG23 ... 90 A4
East View RG27 ... 52 A2
East Woodhay Rd SO22 ... 175 B2
Eastacre SO22 ... 175 C1
Eastbrooke Rd GU34 ... 140 A2
Eastern Ave SP10 ... 106 A4
Eastern Rd Aldershot GU12 ... 77 B1
Bordon GU35 ... 164 B3
Eastfield Ave RG21 ... 69 B3
Eastfield Cl 9 SP10 ... 106 A4
Eastfield Ho SP10 ... 106 B4
Eastfield Lodge SP10 ... 106 A4
Eastfield Rd SP10 ... 106 A4
Eastgate St SO23 ... 198 A4
Eastlyn Rd RG26 ... 10 B1
Eastmans Field SO20 ... 129 A2
Eastmead GU14 ... 55 C2
Easton Common Hill SP5 ... 168 B3
Easton La
Itchen Abbas SO21 ... 177 A3
Winchester SO21 ... 176 C2
Easton Lane Bsns Ctr SO23 ... 198 A4
Eastrop La RG21 ... 69 B3
Eastrop Rdbt RG21 ... 69 B3
Eastrop Way RG21 ... 69 B3
Eastview Gdns GU34 ... 161 C2
Eastville SP11 ... 81 B4
Eaton Rd GU15 ... 35 C2
Ebble Cl SP9 ... 78 C4
Ebden Rd SO23 ... 198 A4
Ecchinswell & Sydmonton CE Prim Sch RG20 ... 23 C2
Ecchinswell Rd RG20 ... 24 A1
Echo Barn La GU10 ... 121 B3
Eddeys Cl GU35 ... 165 C3
Eddeys La GU35 ... 165 C3
Eddy Rd GU12 ... 77 A1
Eddystone Ct GU10 ... 144 B1
Edgar Cl SP10 ... 83 A2
Edgar Rd SO23 ... 197 C3
Edgar Villas SO23 ... 197 C3
Edgeborough Sch GU10 ... 122 A2
Edgecombe La RG14 ... 2 A3
Edgehill Cl RG22 ... 68 B2
Edgewood Ct GU33 ... 208 A1
Edinburgh Cl Ash GU12 ... 77 C3
Kings Worthy SO23 ... 154 A1
Edinburgh Ho 8 SO22 ... 197 C4
Edington Rd SO23 ... 176 A1
Edison Rd RG21 ... 68 C4
Edney Cl GU52 ... 75 A3
Edric's Gn SP4 ... 101 B1
Edrich Sq SP10 ... 83 A1
Edward Ave GU15 ... 35 C3
Edward Ct GU14 ... 55 C2
Edward Rd Alton GU34 ... 140 A3
Farnham GU9 ... 122 A4
Winchester SO23 ... 197 C3
Edward St GU11 ... 76 C1
Edward Terr SO24 ... 179 C3
Eeklo Pl RG14 ... 1 C1
Eelmoor Plain Rd GU11 ... 76 A3
Eelmoor Rd
Aldershot GU11 ... 76 A3
Farnborough GU14 ... 55 B1
Eelmoor Trad Est GU14 ... 55 B1
Egbert Rd SO23 ... 176 A1
Egbury Rd SP11 ... 62 A1
Egerton Rd GU47 ... 35 B4
Eggar's Ct 23 GU12 ... 76 C1
Eggar's Hill GU11 ... 99 C4
Eggar's Sch GU34 ... 140 A3
Eggars Cl GU34 ... 140 A2
Eggars Field GU10 ... 120 A3
Eggleton Cl GU52 ... 74 C3
Eglinton Rd GU10 ... 144 C3
Egret Gdns GU11 ... 99 C4
Eight Acres GU26 ... 167 A4
Eight Bells RG14 ... 1 B1
Eights The SP11 ... 104 A3
Eland Rd GU12 ... 77 A1
Elane Ho SP11 ... 57 A1
Elbe Way SP10 ... 82 C2
Elbow Cnr RG21 ... 69 A3
Elder Cl SO22 ... 197 B2
Elder Cres SP10 ... 105 B4
Elderberry Bank RG24 ... 69 C4
Elderberry Rd GU35 ... 165 A3
Eldergrove GU14 ... 56 B1
Eldon Cl SO20 ... 172 A1
Eldon Dr GU10 ... 122 A3
Eldon Rd SO20 ... 194 A3
Eleanor Cl GU30 ... 187 A4
Elgar Cl RG22 ... 91 C4
Elgin Rd GU46 ... 34 B1
Elgin Way GU16 ... 56 B4
Elgrath Dr RG40 ... 16 B4
Eling Cl SO22 ... 175 B2
Eliot Cl GU15 ... 36 C4
Eliot Dr GU27 ... 189 B3
Elizabeth Ave RG14 ... 5 A4
Elizabeth Cl SO23 ... 154 A1
Elizabeth Dr GU52 ... 75 A3
Elizabeth Par GU46 ... 34 A2
Elizabeth Rd RG22 ... 68 C2
Elizabethan Rise RG25 ... 89 C1
Elkington Cl RG20 ... 22 C4
Ellel Pierrepont GU10 ... 122 B1
Ellen Dr GU51 ... 54 B2
Ellen Gdns RG26 ... 28 C2
Elleray Ct GU12 ... 77 C3
Elles Cl GU14 ... 55 C2
Elles Rd GU14 ... 55 C1
Ellingham Cl SO24 ... 179 B3
Ellington Cl SP11 ... 105 A4
Ellington Dr RG22 ... 91 B4
Elliott Park Ind Est GU12 ... 77 B1
Ellison Way GU10 ... 100 B4
Elm Bank GU46 ... 34 A4
Elm Bank Rd SP10 ... 106 A3
Elm Bottom Cross RG24 ... 47 B1
Elm Cl Bordon GU35 ... 164 C2
Ludgershall SP11 ... 57 A1
Middle Wallop SO20 ... 126 A2
Thruxton SP11 ... 103 B4
Elm Cotts RG20 ... 4 B1
Elm Cres GU9 ... 99 A4
Elm Ct Andover SP10 ... 106 A4
Winchester SO22 ... 197 C4
Elm Gr Farnham GU9 ... 99 A4
Kingsclere RG20 ... 24 B1
Thatcham RG18 ... 2 C3
Elm Grove Flats RG20 ... 24 B1
Elm Grove Fm RG20 ... 24 B1
Elm Grove Rd GU14 ... 55 C2
Elm La GU10 ... 100 B4
Elm Piece Ho RG25 ... 88 A4
Elm Pl GU11 ... 100 A4
Elm Rd Farnham GU9 ... 99 A4
New Alresford SO24 ... 179 B3
Overton RG25 ... 65 A1
Sherborne St John RG24 ... 47 C1
Winchester SO22 ... 197 C4
Elm Terr GU33 ... 207 C3
Elm View GU12 ... 77 C2
Elmay Ho SP11 ... 57 A1
Elmcroft Cl GU16 ... 56 B4
Elmfield Ct GU35 ... 164 C3
Elmhurst RG26 ... 27 A4
Elmhurst Ballet Sch GU15 ... 36 A3
Elmhurst Rd RG18 ... 2 C3
Elms Rd Aldershot GU11 ... 76 C1
Fleet GU51 ... 75 B4
Hook RG27 ... 51 A1
Elms The Andover SP10 ... 105 C4
Blackwater GU17 ... 35 A2
7 Farnham GU9 ... 99 A1
Tongham GU10 ... 100 B4
Elmsleigh Rd GU14 ... 55 B2
Elmsley Ct GU14 ... 55 B2
Elmstead Cvn Pk SP11 ... 103 C4
Elmwood RG24 ... 48 C2
Elmwood Cl GU34 ... 139 B1
Elmwood Par RG23 ... 68 B4
Elmwood Way RG23 ... 68 B4
Elsenwood Cres GU15 ... 36 C3
Elsenwood Dr GU15 ... 36 C4
Elsley Cl GU16 ... 56 B3
Elstead Rd GU10 ... 100 C1
Elston Pl GU12 ... 100 A4
Elston Rd GU12 ... 100 A4
Elvetham Cl GU51 ... 54 A2
Elvetham Cres GU51 ... 53 B2
Elvetham Heath Prim Sch GU51 ... 53 B2
Elvetham Heath Way GU51 ... 53 B2
Elvetham La RG27 ... 53 A4
Elvetham Pl GU51 ... 53 C2
Elvetham Rd GU51 ... 53 C2
Ely Cl GU16 ... 56 C4
Embleton Rd GU35 ... 165 C3
Emden Rd SP10 ... 82 C2
Emery Down Dr 5 GU51 ... 53 B2
Empress Ave GU14 ... 55 C3
Enborne CE Prim Sch RG20 ... 4 B3
Enborne Gr RG14 ... 1 B1
Enborne Lodge La RG14 ... 5 A3
Enborne Lodge Sch RG14 ... 4 C3
Enborne Pl RG14 ... 1 B1
Enborne Rd RG14,RG20 ... 1 A1
Enborne St RG20 ... 4 C2
Enborne Way RG7 ... 8 B3
Enbourne Gate RG14 ... 1 A1
Enfield Rd GU12 ... 77 C3
Engineers Rd RG19 ... 6 C3
English Wood RG24 ... 68 B4
Enham Alamein Mus* SP11 ... 83 A4
Enham La SP10 ... 83 A2
Enmill La SO22 ... 196 C3
Ennerdale Cl RG22 ... 68 A1
Ennerdale Gdns SO24 ... 179 B2
Ennerdale Gr GU9 ... 98 C3
Ennerdale Rd GU35 ... 164 B3
Ennerdale Way RG19 ... 2 C2
Enterprise Ct RG24 ... 69 B4
Enterprise Est GU12 ... 77 C4
Enterprise Ho
Aldershot GU11 ... 76 C1
Basingstoke RG22 ... 68 A2
Epsom Cl GU15 ... 36 A4
Epsom Cres RG14 ... 1 C1
Epsom Down GU34 ... 139 C1
Equine Way RG14 ... 5 C4
Erasmus Pk SO23 ... 176 B1
Erica Cotts GU26 ... 167 A3
Erleigh Dene RG14 ... 1 B1
Erles Rd GU30 ... 188 A2
Ermine Wlk RG19 ... 2 C2
Ernest Cl GU10 ... 121 C3
Erskine Cl RG26 ... 10 B1
Erskine Rd SO22 ... 197 C4
Esher Cl RG22 ... 68 B1
Eskdale Ct GU12 ... 77 B2
Essex Cl Bordon GU35 ... 164 B2
Camberley GU16 ... 56 C4
Essex Rd
Basingstoke RG21 ... 69 A3
Bordon GU35 ... 164 B2
Essex St RG14 ... 5 A4
Ethelbert Ave SP10 ... 82 B2
Eton Cl RG22 ... 91 A3
Eton Pl GU9 ... 98 C4
Ettrick Ct GU14 ... 76 C4
Etwall SP11 ... 103 A2
Europa Cl RG26 ... 28 C2
Euskirchen Way RG22 ... 68 B3
Evans Cl SO20 ... 125 A1
Eveley Cl GU35 ... 164 A1
Evelyn Ave GU11 ... 99 C4
Evelyn Mews SO24 ... 179 B3
Evelyn Wood's Rd GU11 ... 77 A3
Evenlode Way GU47 ... 35 A4
Everest Rd GU15 ... 36 A4
Evergreen Rd GU16 ... 36 B1
Eversfield Cl SP10 ... 105 C4
Eversley Dr 4 GU51 ... 53 B2
Eversley Pl SO22 ... 197 B3
Eversley Rd Eversley GU46 ... 33 C4
Yateley GU47 ... 34 C4
Eversley St RG27 ... 15 C1
Evesham Wlk RG24 ... 48 A1
Evingar Gdns RG28 ... 86 B3
Evingar Rd RG28 ... 86 B3
Ewhurst Rd RG26 ... 46 A3
Ewins Cl GU12 ... 77 C1
Ewshot Hill GU10 ... 75 A1
Ewshot Hill Cross GU10 ... 98 A4
Ewshot La GU10,GU52 ... 74 C1
Exbury Way SP10 ... 105 C4
Exeter Cl RG22 ... 91 A4
Exeter Gdns GU46 ... 33 C4
Exeter Rd GU12 ... 77 C2
Exmoor Cl RG22 ... 68 A2
Express Way RG14 ... 2 B1

F

Fabers Yd 16 SO22 ... 197 C4
Fabian Cl 10 RG21 ... 69 A2
Factory Cotts GU10 ... 98 A1
Fair Close Ho 3 RG14 ... 1 C1
Fair La Chilcomb SO21 ... 198 C4
Itchen Abbas SO21 ... 177 A1
Fair Oak La RG7 ... 29 B4
Fair Piece SP11 ... 128 C3
Fair View SO24 ... 179 B2
Fairacre RG20 ... 21 B4
Fairacres GU10 ... 121 B2
Fairclose RG28 ... 86 B2
Fairclose Dr SO22 ... 175 A3
Fairclose Terr RG28 ... 86 B2
Faircrosse Cl GU47 ... 35 A4
Fairdown Cl SO23 ... 198 B4
Fairfax Cl SO22 ... 197 A3
Fairfax Ind Est GU12 ... 77 B1
Fairfax Mews GU14 ... 56 A1
Fairfax Pl RG14 ... 2 B3
Fairfax Rd GU14 ... 56 A4
Fairfield RG28 ... 86 B3
Fairfield Dr GU16 ... 36 B2
Fairfield Gn GU34 ... 160 B2
Fairfield Pk RG7 ... 11 B3
Fairfield Rd SO21 ... 175 C1
Fairfield The GU9 ... 99 A1
Fairfields Ct RG21 ... 69 A2
Fairfields Prim Sch RG21 ... 69 A2
Fairfields Rd RG21 ... 69 A2
Fairground The SP11 ... 81 B1
Fairholme Gdns GU9 ... 99 A1
Fairholme Par 3 RG27 ... 51 A1
Fairland Cl GU52 ... 75 A4
Fairlands GU35 ... 166 A3
Fairlawn Ho 27 SO22 ... 197 C4
Fairlawn Rd RG26 ... 27 A4
Fairlight Gdns GU34 ... 160 B2
Fairmead Cl GU47 ... 35 B4
Fairmead Ct GU15 ... 36 A2
Fairmile GU52 ... 74 C3
Fairoak Way RG26 ... 9 A1
Fairthorne Ho RG22 ... 68 C2
Fairthorne Rise RG24 ... 70 B3
Fairview RG14 ... 5 B4
Fairview Gdns GU9 ... 99 A3
Fairview Mdw RG23 ... 90 A4
Fairview Rd Ash GU12 ... 77 C2
Headley GU35 ... 166 A3
Penton Grafton SP11 ... 81 B1
Fairview Terr GU35 ... 165 C3
Fairway Cl GU30 ... 187 A2
Fairway The
Bordon GU35 ... 164 A1
Camberley GU15 ... 36 C2
Farnham GU9 ... 99 A4
Fleet GU14 ... 75 C4
Fairways
Beacon Hill GU26 ... 166 C3
Thruxton SP11 ... 81 A1
Faithfulls Dro SO20 ... 171 A2
Falaise Cl GU11 ... 76 C1
Falaise Rd SO20 ... 126 A2
Falcon Bsns Pk RG40 ... 15 C3
Falcon Cl
Basingstoke RG22 ... 67 C1
North Tidworth SP9 ... 78 C4
Falcon Coppice RG20 ... 21 B4
Falcon Ct Alton GU34 ... 139 C3
Camberley GU16 ... 36 A1
Falcon Fields RG26 ... 9 C1
Falcon House Gdns RG20 ... 4 B1
Falcon Rd SP9 ... 78 C4
Falcon View SO22 ... 197 B2
Falcon Way GU46 ... 33 C3
Falkland Ct GU14 ... 77 B4
Falkland Dr RG14 ... 5 B4
Falkland Garth RG14 ... 5 A4
Falkland Prim Sch RG14 ... 5 A3
Falkland Rd
Basingstoke RG24 ... 48 B1
Newbury RG14 ... 5 A3
Falkner Ho GU51 ... 54 B2
Falkner Rd GU9 ... 98 C1
Falkners Cl GU51 ... 54 B2
Fallow Field SO22 ... 197 B2
Fallowfield GU51 ... 54 B2
Falmouth Cl GU15 ... 36 C2
Fantails GU34 ... 139 C3
Faraday Cl RG2 ... 15 B4
Faraday Ct RG24 ... 69 B4
Faraday Off Pk RG24 ... 69 B4
Faraday Pk SP10 ... 82 A1
Faraday Rd
Basingstoke RG24 ... 69 B4
Farnborough GU14 ... 56 A3
Newbury RG14 ... 1 C2
Farcrosse Cl GU47 ... 35 A4
Fareham Dr GU46 ... 33 C4
Faringdon Ct 16 SO23 ... 176 A1
Farleigh La RG22 ... 91 A1
Farleigh Rd RG25 ... 92 A4
Farleigh Rise RG21 ... 69 B1
Farleigh Sch SP11 ... 127 A4
Farleigh Wallop Dr GU51 ... 53 B2
Farley Cl SO22 ... 197 A2

Farley Ct GU14 ....56 A1
Farley Hill Prim Sch RG7 .15 A3
Farley La SO51 ....194 C1
Farley Mount Nature
  Reserve* SO21 ....196 A4
Farley Mount Rd SO21 .196 A2
Farley St SO20 ....147 C3
Farm Cl GU46 ....34 A3
Farm Cotts RG24 ....68 B4
Farm Ct GU16 ....36 B1
Farm Dr GU51 ....54 A2
Farm Ground Cl RG27 ....51 B1
Farm La GU10 ....97 B3
Farm Rd
  Abbotts Ann SP11 ......105 A3
  Aldershot GU12 ....77 B2
  Camberley GU16 ....36 B1
Farm View GU46 ....34 A3
Farm View Dr RG24 ....49 A2
Farmhouse Way GU32 .....74 C3
Farnborough Bsns Ctr
  GU14 ....55 C2
Farnborough Coll of Tech
  GU14 ....56 A1
Farnborough Gate Ret Pk
  GU14 ....56 A4
Farnborough Grange Inf Sch
  GU14 ....55 C4
Farnborough Hill (Girls Sch)
  GU14 ....56 A3
Farnborough Ind Est
  GU14 ....55 C2
Farnborough North Sta
  GU14 ....56 A3
Farnborough Rd GU11 ...76 B2
Farnborough St GU14 ....56 A3
Farnborough Sta GU14 ...56 A3
Farnham Bsns Ctr GU9 ...99 A2
Farnham Bsns Pk GU9 ....98 A1
Farnham By-Pass GU9 ....99 A2
Farnham Castle* GU9 .....98 C2
Farnham Coll GU9 ....99 A1
Farnham Heath End Sch
  GU9 ....99 B3
Farnham Hospl GU9 ......99 B2
Farnham La GU27 ....189 C4
Farnham Mus* GU9 ....98 C3
Farnham Park Cl GU9 .....98 C3
Farnham Park Dr GU9 ....98 C3
Farnham Rd
  Bordon GU35 ....164 B3
  Fleet RG29 ....75 B4
  Liss GU33 ....207 C2
  Odiham RG29,RG27,GU10 .73 B1
  Farnham Sta GU9 ....99 A1
Farnham Trad Est GU9 ....99 B2
Faroe Cl RG24 ....48 B1
Farrell Cl GU15 ....36 A2
Farren Ho GU14 ....56 A1
Farrier Pl GU47 ....34 C4
Farrier's Field RG25 ....115 A4
Farriers Cl RG26 ....28 C2
Farringdon Bsns Ctr
  GU34 ....161 B2
Farringdon Way RG26 ....96 C4
Fars Ave SP10 ....106 A4
Farthing Fields GU35 ...165 B3
Farthingfield Ho GU9 ....99 A2
Faulkner's Cross RG28 ...85 B1
Fawconer Rd RG20 ....24 B1
Fawkham Cl GU34 ....204 A2
Fayrewood Chase RG22 .91 A4
Feathers La **B** RG21 ...69 A2
Feilden Ct RG20 ....24 B1
Felbridge Cl GU16 ....36 B1
Feld Way RG24 ....70 A4
Fellows Rd GU14 ....56 A1
Felmer Dr SO23 ....176 B4
Fencott Pl RG21 ....69 B3
Fenn's Yd GU9 ....98 C1
Fennel Cl Chineham RG24 .49 A2
  Farnham GU14 ....54 C2
  Newbury RG14 ....2 A3
Ferbies GU52 ....75 A3
Ferguson Cl RG21 ....69 A1
Fermor Dr GU11 ....76 B2
Fern Cl GU16 ....36 C2
Fern Ct GU12 ....77 B1
Fern Dr GU51 ....74 C3
Fernbank RG40 ....16 A3
Fernbrae Cl GU10 ....121 C2
Ferncote Rd GU35 ....164 C2
Ferndale Gdns RG27 .....51 A1
Ferndale Rd Andover SP10 .82 C1
  Fleet GU52 ....74 C3
Ferndown Ct Alton GU34 .140 A2
  Farnham GU10 ....122 A3
Ferndown Gdns GU14 ....55 B2
Ferney Cl GU34 ....161 B4
Ferney Rd SO24 ....159 A4
Fernhill Cl
  Farnborough GU17 ....35 A1
  Farnham GU9 ....98 C3
Fernhill Dr GU9 ....98 C3
Fernhill Ho GU14 ....56 A1
Fernhill La
  Farnborough GU17 ....35 B1
  Farnham GU9 ....98 C3
Fernhill Prim Sch GU14 ..55 B3
Fernhill Sch GU14 ....55 B3
Fernhill Sch GU14 ....55 A1
Fernhill Wlk GU14 ....55 B3
Ferniehurst GU15 ....36 B2
Fernlea GU35 ....164 A1
Ferns Mead GU9 ....98 C1

Ferns The GU9 ....99 A4
Ferrell Field RG27 ....50 C1
Ferrier Gr RG14 ....5 C4
Fiddlers Field GU34 ......139 A4
Field End Farnham GU9 ...99 B2
  Kings Worthy SO23 ....176 B4
Field Gate Rd RG20 ....24 B1
Field La GU16 ....36 B1
Field Path GU14 ....35 B1
Field Pl GU30 ....188 A2
Field Rd GU14 ....35 B1
Field Stores App GU11 ...77 A2
Field Way Aldershot GU12 .77 B2
  Tongham GU10 ....100 B4
Fielders Ct GU34 ....139 C2
Fielders The GU46 ....33 B4
Fieldfare Ave **B** GU46 .33 C3
Fieldgate Ctr RG20 ....24 B1
Fielding Rd GU47 ....35 B3
Fieldridge RG14 ....2 A3
Fieldway GU51 ....74 B4
Fiehead Cotts SO20 .....147 B4
Fifield La GU10 ....122 A1
Fifth Rd RG14 ....1 C1
Fifth St RG19 ....6 B3
Filmorehill La GU34 .....204 A2
Filnchfield Ct RG26 ......27 A4
Finchampstead CE Prim Sch
  RG40 ....16 B2
Finchampstead Rd RG40 .16 B3
Finches Gn GU34 ....139 C3
Finchorn Cl GU47 ....35 A4
Findings The GU14 ....55 B4
Fingle Dr SP10 ....105 C4
Finkley Down Farm Pk*
  SP11 ....83 C2
Finkley Rd Smannell SP11 .84 B4
  St Mary Bourne SP11 ...84 B4
Finns Ind Pk GU10 ....74 A1
Fintry Pl GU14 ....55 B4
Fintry Wlk GU14 ....55 B4
Fiona Cl SO23 ....198 B4
Fir Acre Rd GU12 ....77 C3
Fir Cl GU51 ....74 C4
Fir Cottage Rd GU40 ....16 B4
Fir Dr GU17 ....35 A2
Fir Gr GU35 ....164 A1
Fir Tree Alley **B** GU11 .76 C1
Fir Tree Cnr RG26 ....90 C1
Fir Tree Cnr **B** RG26 ..26 B3
Fir Tree Cotts GU33 ....208 C2
Fir Tree La RG14 ....2 B2
Fir Tree Piece RG26 ......45 A2
Fir Tree Prim Sch RG14 ...2 B2
Fir Tree Way GU52 ....75 A4
Fircrofts GU51 ....53 C1
Fire Station Rd GU11 .....76 C2
Fire Thorn Cl GU52 ....75 A3
Firecrest Rd RG22 ....90 C4
Firfield Rd GU9 ....121 C4
Firglen Dr GU46 ....34 A4
Firgrove Ct
  B Farnborough GU14 ..55 C2
  Farnham GU9 ....99 A1
Firgrove Hill GU9 ....99 A1
Firgrove Par **B** GU14 ...55 C2
Firgrove Rd
  Bordon GU35 ....164 A1
  Eversley GU46 ....33 C3
  B Farnborough GU14 ..55 C2
  Yateley RG27 ....33 C3
Firlands Ave GU15 ....36 A3
Firs Cl Farnborough GU14 ..55 B1
  Finchampstead RG40 ...16 B4
Firs Cres SO23 ....176 A4
Firs End RG7 ....11 B3
Firs La RG29 ....72 B2
Firs The Andover SP10 ...105 C4
  Liphook GU30 ....187 C1
  Thatcham RG18 ....2 C2
Firs Way RG23 ....68 A4
First Ave RG7 ....10 A1
First St RG19 ....6 C3
Firsway RG28 ....86 B3
Firth Cl RG7 ....27 C4
Firtree Cl GU47 ....34 B4
Firview GU30 ....187 C2
Firway GU26 ....166 B3
Firwood Cl GU15 ....36 A3
Firwood Dr GU15 ....36 A3
Fisher Cl SP10 ....106 B4
Fisher Ho **B** RG14 ....1 B1
Fisherman's La RG7 ......9 C4
Fishermen's Cl GU11 ....77 B3
Fiske Cl RG22 ....68 B2
Fiske Ct GU46 ....34 B3
Fitzgerald Ct RG14 ....1 A2
Fitzroy Rd GU51 ....53 B1
Five Acres Cl GU35 .....160 A2
Five Ash Rd GU34 ....160 A2
Five Bells La SO20 ......147 C3
Five Bridges Rd SO23 ..197 C2
Five Lanes SP11 ....61 C1
Five Lanes End RG25 ....71 A1
Fivefields Cl SO23 ......198 B3
Fivefields Rd SO23 ......198 B4
Fiveways
  Basingstoke RG22 ....68 A1
  Camberley GU15 ....36 B3
Flashett The SP5 ....168 A3
Flats The GU17 ....34 C1
Flaxfield Ct RG21 ....69 A3
Flaxfield Rd RG21 ....69 A3
  Fleet Bsns Pk GU52 .....75 B3
Fleet Cnr Hospl GU51 .....53 C1
Fleet Hill RG40 ....16 A1
Fleet Inf Sch GU52 ....75 B4
Fleet La RG40 ....15 C1

Fleet Pond (Nature
  Reserve)* GU51 ....54 B2
Fleet Rd Aldershot GU11 ..76 B3
Farnborough GU14 ....54 C2
  Fleet GU51 ....54 A1
  Hartley Wintney RG27 ..53 A2
Fleet Rd GU14 ....54 C3
Fleetwood Cl RG14 ....2 A1
Fleming Cl Arborfield RG2 .15 B4
  Farnborough GU14 ....56 A3
Fleming Rd RG14 ....5 A1
Flensburg Cl SP10 ....82 C2
Fletcher Cl RG21 ....68 C2
Fletchers Cl GU30 ......188 A2
Fletchers Ho GU30 .....187 C2
Flexford Cl RG20 ....21 B3
Flinders Cl SP10 ....83 C1
Flint Cl SP10 ....105 C3
Flint La Chute Forest SP11 .81 C4
  Penton Grafton SP11 ...81 C4
Floral Way SP10 ....105 B4
Floreat Gdns RG14 ....34 A3
Florence Cl GU46 ....34 A3
Florence Ct SP10 ....83 A2
Florence Portal Cl RG28 .87 A3
Florence Rd Fleet GU52 ..75 A3
Florence Way RG24 ......68 B4
Florrie Pl GU14 ....161 B2
Flowerdew Ct SP10 ......106 A3
Flowerdown Cvn Pk
  SO22 ....175 B3
Flowerdown Ho SO22 ..175 B2
Focus 303 SP10 ....83 B1
Focus Way GU14 ....83 C1
Foden Rd GU11 ....76 C1
Folly Cotts RG20 ....22 C4
Folly Hill GU9 ....98 C3
Folly Hill Inf Sch GU9 ...98 C3
Folly La RG26 ....29 A2
Folly La N GU9 ....98 C3
Folly Lane S GU9 ....98 C3
Folly The RG14 ....1 C2
Fontwell Cl GU12 ....77 A1
Fontwell Dr GU34 ....139 C1
Fontwell Rd RG14 ....1 C1
Forbes Chase GU47 ....35 A4
Forbes Rd SO23 ....176 A4
Forbury La RG20 ....3 A4
Forburys GU9 ....121 C4
Ford La Farnham GU10 ..121 C3
  Odiham RG25,RG29 .....95 A3
  South Warnborough RG29 .95 A3
  Swallowfield RG7 ....14 C1
Fordington Ave SO22 ..197 C4
Fordington Rd **B** SO22 .197 C4
Forehead The RG7 ....12 B2
Foreman Pk GU12 ....77 C1
Foreman Rd GU12 ....77 C1
Forest Cl RG26 ....99 A2
Forest Cnr GU35 ....208 A4
Forest Ct **B** SP9 ....79 B4
Forest Dean GU51 ....54 B2
Forest Dr Cheriton RG24 .48 C2
  Farnham GU10 ....122 A2
  North Tidworth SP9 ....79 A4
Forest End GU52 ....74 C3
Forest End Rd GU47 ......34 C4
Forest Glade GU10 ......121 A2
Forest Hills GU15 ....35 C2
Forest La Andover SP11 .106 C3
  Lindford GU35 ....165 A3
  Tadley RG26 ....27 C4
  Upper Clatford SP11 ....57 C4
Forest Lane Cl GU10 ....187 C2
Forest Rd Bordon GU35 ..164 B1
  Liss GU33 ....208 A3
Forest Rise GU33 ....208 A3
Forest Sh Ctr The GU35 .164 B1
Forestdale GU26 ....167 B2
Foresters Pk SO23 ......176 A2
Forge Cl Bramley RG26 ..29 A1
  Farnham GU9 ....99 A2
Forge Field SP10 ....83 A1
Forge La GU11 ....76 C3
Forge Rd Kingsley GU35 .164 A4
  Kingsley SP11 ....142 C1
Forsters Farm Ct RG7 ....9 C3
Fort Hill Com Sch RG22 .68 A4
Fort Narrien GU15 ....35 C4
Forth Cl GU14 ....55 A3
Forth St SP10 ....83 B1
Fortrose Cl GU47 ....35 A4
Fortuna Ct **B** RG27 .....9 B1
Forum Cl RG23 ....68 A4
Fossewood Dr GU15 .....36 A4
Fosters Bsns Pk RG27 ...71 C4
Foul La GU34 ....159 A2
Foundry La GU47 ....189 C3
Foundry Rd SP11 ....105 B2
Fountain Rd GU34 ......184 C4
Fountains Cl RG24 ....48 A1
Four Acre Coppice RG27 .31 B1
Four Houses Cnr RG7 ...11 B4
Four Houses Cnr Cvn Site
  RG7 ....11 B4
Four Lanes Cl RG40 ......16 A4
Four Lanes Com Jun Sch
  RG24 ....48 C2
Four Lanes End
  Chineham RG24 ....49 A2
  Odiham RG25 ....95 B2
Four Lanes Inf Sch RG24 .48 C2
Four Marks CE Prim Sch
  GU34 ....182 A4
Four Oaks RG20 ....21 B3

Four Ways GU10 ....142 C4
Fourth St RG19 ....6 B3
Fowler Rd GU14 ....55 B2
Fowler's Rd GU11 ....77 A3
Fox Dr GU46 ....34 A4
Fox Heath GU14 ....55 A2
Fox La Eversley GU46 .....33 B4
  Oakley RG23 ....67 B2
  Winchester SO22 ....197 B3
Fox Rd Farnham GU10 ..122 A4
  Haslemere GU27 ....189 B3
Fox Way GU10 ....98 B3
Fox Yd GU9 ....98 C1
Fox's La RG20 ....24 B1
Foxborough RG7 ....14 A3
Foxcote RG40 ....16 C4
Foxcote Cl SP10 ....82 B1
Foxcote Gr SP10 ....82 B2
Foxcote Rd SP10 ....82 B2
Foxcroft GU52 ....75 A3
Foxdown RG25 ....65 A1
Foxdown Cl GU15 ....36 A3
Foxglove Cl RG22 ....91 A4
Foxglove Dr GU35 ......164 C1
Foxhill Cres GU15 ....36 C4
Foxhunter Way RG19 .....2 B2
Foxhurst Rd GU12 ....77 C2
Foxley Cl GU17 ....35 A3
Foxmoor Cl RG23 ....67 B2
Foxs Furlong RG24 ......49 A2
Foxwood GU51 ....54 B2
Foye La GU52 ....75 A3
Foyle Pk RG21 ....69 A1
Foyle Rd SP11 ....80 B2
Frampton Way GU34 ...176 B4
France Hill Dr GU15 ......36 A3
France Hill Sch GU16 ....36 A1
Frances Rd RG21 ....69 A2
Francis Cl GU14 ....55 B2
Francis Gdns SO23 .....176 A2
Francis Way GU14 ....36 C2
Frankie Ave
  Hartley Wintney RG27 ..52 B4
  Tadley RG26 ....9 C1
Fraser Ct RG24 ....70 A3
Fraser Mead GU47 ....35 B3
Fraser Rd SO23 ....176 B4
Fraynes Croft GU51 ......74 C4
Frederick St GU11 ....76 C1
Freelands Dr GU52 ......74 C3
Freeman Ct RG14 ....1 B2
Freemantle Cl RG21 ......69 B4
Fremantle Rd GU11 ....74 B4
French Gdns GU17 ....35 A2
French Rd GU33 ....186 B2
Frenchmans Creek **B**
  GU52 ....74 C2
Frenchmoor La
  East Dean SP5 ....190 C1
  West Tytherley SP5 ....190 C2
Frensham Ave GU51 ......54 B1
Frensham Cl GU46 ....33 C3
Frensham Ctr GU10 .....121 C2
Frensham Ctry Pk*
  GU10 ....144 B3
Frensham Heights Rd
  GU10 ....121 C1
Frensham Heights Sch
  GU10 ....121 C1
Frensham La GU35 ......165 A3
Frensham Rd GU10 .....122 A3
Frensham Vale GU10 ...122 A3
Frere Ave GU51 ....74 C4
Frescade Cres RG21 ......69 A2
Freshwood Dr GU46 ......34 A2
Friar Field GU52 ....98 C2
Friars Ct Farnham GU9 ..99 A4
  Sandhurst GU47 ....34 B4
Friars Rd SO23 ....198 A4
Friary Wlk GU47 ....77 A1
Friesian Cl GU51 ....54 A2
Frimley Bsns Pk
  Camberley GU16 ....56 A4
  Farnborough GU14 ....56 A4
Frimley CE Sch GU16 ....56 B4
Frimley Green Rd GU16 ..56 B4
Frimley Grove Gdns
  GU16 ....36 B1
Frimley High St GU16 ....56 A4
Frimley Park Hospl GU16 .36 A1
Frimley Rd Ash GU12 ....77 C2
  Camberley GU15 ....35 C2
  Frimley Sta GU16 ....56 A4
Frinkham Rd SO23 ......198 B4
Frith End Rd GU34,GU35 .142 C3
Frith Hill Rd GU16 ....36 C3
Frithmead Cl RG21 ....69 A1
Frog La
  Latchmere Green RG7 ...27 C2
  Mapledurwell RG25 ....70 C2
  Rotherwick RG27 ....52 B2
Frome Cl
  Basingstoke RG21 ....69 B3
  Oakley RG23 ....67 B1
Fromond Rd SO22 ......175 B2
Frouds Cl RG27 ....51 C4
Froxfield CE Inf Sch
  GU32 ....205 C1

Froxfield Cl SO22 ....175 B2
Froyle La RG29 ....95 A2
Fry Sq SP10 ....83 A1
Fry's Acre GU12 ....77 C2
Fry's La GU46 ....34 B4
Fryers Cl SO23 ....176 B4
Fugelmere Rd GU51 ......74 B1
Fulbrook Way RG29 ......95 B4
Fulflood Ct **B** SO22 ...197 C4
Fulham Ho RG21 ....69 A3
Fullers La RG20 ....21 A4
Fullers Rd GU10 ....121 A2
Fullers Vale GU35 ....165 B3
Fullerton Cl GU51 ....53 B2
Fullerton Rd SP11 ......127 B4
Fullerton Way RG26 .....27 A4
Fulmar Cl RG22 ....91 C4
Furley Cl SO23 ....198 A4
Further Vell-Mead GU52 .74 C2
Furze Cl GU12 ....77 C4
Furze Dr SP11 ....79 B3
Furze Hill Rd
  Headley GU35 ....166 A2
  South Tidworth SP9 ....78 C3
Furze Rd RG26 ....9 B1
Furze Vale Rd GU35 ....166 A2
Furzedown Cotts SO20 .194 A4
Furzedown Ho SO20 ...194 A3
Furzedown La SP11 .....103 C3
Furzedown Rd SO20 ....194 A4
Furzen La RG25 ....115 A4
Fuzzy Dro RG22 ....90 C4
Fyfield Cl Appleshaw SP11 .81 A2
  Fyfield SP11 ....81 A1
Fyfield Rd Fyfield SP11 .81 A1
  Thruxton SP11 ....81 A1
Fyfield Way SP11 ....79 B3
Fylingdales Cl RG22 .....68 A2

G

Gable End **B** GU14 ......55 C2
Gables Cl GU14 ....55 C2
Gables Rd GU52 ....74 C2
Gables The
  Grayshott GU26 ....167 A2
  Whitchurch RG28 ....86 C3
Gabriel Dr GU15 ....36 C2
Gabriels The RG14 ....5 A3
Gaffney Cl GU11 ....77 A4
Gage Cl RG24 ....69 C4
Gainsborough Cl
  Camberley GU15 ....36 B4
  Farnborough GU14 ....56 A1
Gainsborough Ct
  Andover SP10 ....82 C1
  Farnborough GU14 ....77 A4
  B Fleet GU51 ....54 A1
Gainsborough Rd GU51 ..69 B1
Galahad Cl SP10 ....83 A2
Gales Cl SP10 ....106 A4
Galileo Pk SP10 ....82 B1
Gallaghers Mead SP10 .105 B4
Galleries The **B** GU11 ..76 C1
Galley La RG19 ....24 B4
Gallop The GU46 ....34 A4
Galloway Cl
  Basingstoke RG22 ....68 A2
  Fleet GU51 ....54 B2
Galloway Ctr The RG14 ...2 A2
Galwey Rd GU11 ....77 A2
Gally Hill Rd GU52 ....74 C2
Gander Dr RG24 ....68 B4
Ganders Cl GU34 ....184 C4
Gangbridge La SP11 .....61 C2
Gannet Cl RG22 ....90 C4
Gannet La SO22 ....197 C4
Garbett Rd SO23 ....198 B4
Garbetts Way GU10 ....100 B3
Garden Cl
  B Andover SP10 .....106 A4
  Ellisfield RG25 ....114 A3
  Farnborough GU14 ....55 B2
  Hook RG27 ....50 C1
  Kingsclere RG20 ....24 B2
Garden Close La RG14 ...5 A3
Garden Cl GU47 ....35 C4
Garden Ct SO21 ....131 B2
Garden La **B** SO23 ....198 A4
Gardener's Hill Rd
  GU10 ....121 C2
Gardeners Gn SP9 ....101 B4
Gardens The GU10 ......100 B4
Garfield Rd GU35 ....36 A3
Garford Cres RG14 ....5 A4
Garland Ct RG14 ....1 B1
Garnet Field GU46 ....33 C4
Garnet Rd GU35 ....164 C1
Garnier Rd SO23 ....198 A3
Garrett Cl RG20 ....24 B1
Garrett Rd RG40 ....16 B4
Garrick Way GU16 ......56 B4
Garston Mede SO20 ....129 A2
Garth Cl Bordon GU35 ..164 B3
  Farnham GU10 ....121 C2
Garth Rd GU11 ....11 C1
Garth The Alton GU34 ..140 A2
Ash GU12 ....77 B3
  Farnborough GU14 ....55 C2
Gascoigne La GU34 .....181 B1
Gaskell Cl GU34 ....140 B2
Gaskell Mews RG14 ......5 C2
Gason Hill Rd SP9 ....78 C4
Gaston La
  South Warnborough RG25,
  RG29 ....95 A3

Gaston La continued
Upper Farringdon GU34 ...161 C2
Gaston's Wood Ind Est
RG24 ...69 B4
Gasworks Bridge GU11 ...77 B2
Gatekeeper Cl 10 SO23 ...198 B4
Gates The GU51 ...54 B2
Gauvain Cl GU34 ...140 A1
Gawaine Cl SP10 ...83 A2
Gaywood Dr RG14 ...2 A2
Geale's Almshouses 11 GU34 ...139 C2
Geale's Cres GU34 ...140 A3
Geale's Ct GU34 ...140 A3
Geffery's Fields RG21 ...69 B2
General Johnson Ct 8 SO22 ...197 B3
Genoa Ct SP10 ...83 A2
Gentles La GU30,GU35 ...165 C2
George Eyston Dr SO22 ...197 B3
George Gdns GU12 ...100 A4
George St
Basingstoke RG21 ...68 C3
Kingsclere RG20 ...24 B1
George Yd SP10 ...106 A4
George Yd The SO24 ...179 B3
Georgia Cl GU10 ...105 C3
Georgia La SP11 ...103 C1
Georgian Cl GU51 ...36 B4
Georgina Cl GU51 ...54 A1
Georgina Gdns RG26 ...27 A4
Gerald Sq GU14 ...140 A3
German Rd RG26 ...29 A1
Gershwin Ct RG22 ...91 B4
Gershwin Rd RG22 ...91 B4
Gibbet La GU15 ...36 C4
Gibbons Cl GU47 ...35 A4
Gibbs Cl RG40 ...16 B3
Gibbs Way GU51 ...33 C2
Gibson La GU34 ...119 A2
Giffard Dr GU14 ...55 B3
Giffards Mdw GU9 ...99 B1
Gilbert Ct RG24 ...49 A2
Gilbert Rd GU16 ...48 B1
Gilbert St GU16 ...36 A1
Gilbert St SO24 ...181 C3
Gilbert Way RG40 ...5 A4
Gilbert White Way GU34 ...139 C3
Gilbert's Gn SP9 ...101 C4
Gilberts Mead Cl SP11 ...105 B2
Giles Cl RG14 ...1 B1
Giles Cres GU34 ...27 A4
Giles Rd RG26 ...27 A4
Gillham's La GU27 ...188 C3
Gillian Ave GU12 ...100 A4
Gillian Cl GU12 ...100 A4
Gillies Dr RG24 ...68 B4
Gillingham Cl SO23 ...176 B4
Gilmour Gdns GU34 ...140 A3
Gilroy Cl RG14 ...5 A3
Gisborne Cl SP9 ...79 A3
Glade Cl RG24 ...48 C1
Glade The Binsted GU10 ...120 C1
Farnham GU9 ...99 A4
Mytchett GU16 ...56 C2
Newbury RG14 ...5 B4
Gladiator Way GU11 ...76 C4
Gladstone St SO23 ...197 C4
Gladstone Terr SP11 ...108 A3
Glamis Cl 7 Camberley GU16 ...56 B4
Oakley RG23 ...67 A1
Glaston Hill Rd GU46 ...33 A4
Glastonbury Cl RG24 ...69 A4
Glayshers Hill GU35 ...165 C3
Glebe Cl B Bentworth GU34 ...138 A3
Dummer RG25 ...90 B1
Tadley RG26 ...27 A4
Glebe Ct GU51 ...53 C1
Glebe Fields GU34 ...138 A3
Glebe La Basingstoke RG23 ...68 A2
Hartley Wintney RG27 ...52 B3
Glebe Mdw
East Dean SP5 ...191 A1
Overton RG25 ...88 A4
Glebe Rd Crondall GU10 ...97 B3
Farnborough GU14 ...55 B3
Headley GU35 ...165 B3
Glebe The GU17 ...35 B2
Glebefields RG14 ...1 C3
Glebeland Rd GU15 ...35 B2
Glebelands SP11 ...106 A1
Glen Cl Andover SP10 ...105 C4
Beacon Hill GU26 ...167 A3
Glen Court Flats GU26 ...167 A3
Glen Rd Beacon Hill GU26 ...167 A3
Fleet GU51 ...54 C4
Grayshott GU26 ...167 A2
Glen The Farnham GU9 ...99 A3
Pamber Heath RG26 ...10 B1
Glenapp Grange RG7 ...11 B3
Glenavon Gdns GU34 ...142 A4
Glencoe Cl GU16 ...56 C4
Glendale Ave RG14 ...5 A3
Glendale Pk GU51 ...53 B1
Glendale Rd RG26 ...9 C1
Gleneagles Cl RG22 ...91 A3
Gleneagles Dr GU14 ...55 A2
Glenfield Cl SP5 ...168 A3
Glenhurst Cl GU17 ...35 B2
Glenlea GU26 ...167 B1
Glenlea Hollow GU26 ...189 B4
Glenmore Cl GU16 ...56 C1
Glenville Gdns GU26 ...167 B2
Glenwood GU9 ...99 A3
Globe Farm La GU17 ...34 C3

Glorney Mead GU9 ...99 C3
Gloster Cl GU12 ...77 B3
Gloucester Cl
Camberley GU16 ...56 B3
Four Marks GU34 ...160 A1
Gloucester Dr RG22 ...91 A4
Gloucester Rd
Aldershot GU11 ...100 A4
Newbury RG14 ...1 B1
Glovers Field GU27 ...189 B3
Glovers Ho GU27 ...189 B3
Glynswood
Camberley GU15 GU16 ...36 B2
Farnham GU10 ...121 C2
Goat La RG21 ...69 B3
Goatacre Rd GU34 ...159 B2
Goch Way SP10 ...82 C1
Goddard Sq SP10 ...83 B1
Goddards Cl RG27 ...49 B4
Goddards Firs RG23 ...90 B4
Goddards La
Camberley GU15 ...35 C2
Sherfield on Loddon RG27 ...49 B4
Goddards Mead SP10 ...105 C4
Godfrey Cl GU47 ...35 A4
Godson Ho 26 RG24 ...198 A4
Godwin Cl SO22 ...176 B4
Gold La GU11 ...77 B2
Goldcrest Cl 1 GU46 ...33 C3
Golden Fields GU30 ...188 A2
Golden Lion Rdbt RG21 ...69 A1
Goldenfields Cl GU30 ...188 A2
Goldfinch Cl GU11 ...99 C4
Goldfinch Gdns RG22 ...90 C3
Goldfinch La RG20 ...6 C2
Goldfinch Way SO21 ...153 C3

Gong Hill GU10 ...122 A2
Gong Hill Dr GU10 ...122 A2
Goodbye's La RG7 ...12 C4
Goodden Cres GU14 ...55 B2
Goodens The SO24 ...201 B3
Goodman Cl RG22 ...68 C2
Goodwin Wlk RG14 ...5 A3
Goodwood Cl
Alton GU34 ...139 C1
Camberley GU15 ...36 A4
Goodwood Pl GU14 ...56 B2
Goodwood Way RG14 ...2 A1
Goodwyns Cl SP9 ...101 B4
Goodwyns Gn GU34 ...140 A3
Goose La GU10 ...50 C1
Goose Sq RG27 ...51 A1
Gooserye Ct GU30 ...187 C2
Gordon Ave
Camberley GU15 ...36 A2
Fleet GU52 ...75 A3
Winchester SO23 ...198 B3
Gordon Cl RG21 ...69 B3
Gordon Cres GU15 ...36 A2
Gordon Palmer Cl RG7 ...12 A3
Gordon Rd Aldershot GU11 ...76 C1
Camberley GU15 ...36 A3
Farnborough GU14 ...77 A4
Newbury RG14 ...1 C1
Thatcham RG18 ...2 C4
Winchester SO23 ...198 A4
Gordon Wlk GU46 ...34 B3
Gore End Rd RG20 ...3 C2
Goring Field SO22 ...175 B1
Gorrings The SO20 ...172 A1
Gorse Cl GU10 ...121 C3
Gorse Cotts
Frensham GU10 ...145 B1
Haslemere GU27 ...189 A4
Gorse La GU10 ...64 A2
Gorse Rd GU16 ...36 B1
Gorse Ride Inf & Prim Sch RG40 ...16 B4
Gorse Ride N RG40 ...16 B4
Gorse Ride S RG40 ...16 B3
Gorsedown Cl GU35 ...164 A1
Gorselands Farnham GU9 ...99 A4
Yateley GU46 ...5 A3
Gorselands Cl Ash GU12 ...77 C3
Headley GU35 ...166 A2
Gorseway GU52 ...75 A4
Gort Cl GU11 ...77 B4
Goscombs La SO24 ...180 C4
Goslings Croft GU34 ...184 C4
Gothic Ct GU47 ...34 C4
Gough Rd GU51 ...53 C1
Gough's Mdw GU47 ...34 C4
Gouldings RG26 ...10 B1
Govenor's Rd GU15 ...35 B3
Government House Rd GU11,GU14 ...76 C4
Government Rd
Aldershot GU11 ...77 B1
Farnborough GU11 ...77 B2
Gower Cl RG21 ...69 A4
Gower Cres RG27 ...51 A1
Gower Pk GU47 ...35 A3
Grace Bennett Cl GU14 ...55 C4
Grace Reynolds Wlk GU15 ...36 A3
Grace Sq SP10 ...83 B1
Gracemere Cres RG22 ...90 C4

Gracious Rd GU34 ...184 B4
Gradwell La GU34 ...182 A4
Grafton Cl GU35 ...164 C1
Grafton Pl SP11 ...81 C2
Grafton Rd SO23 ...197 C3
Grafton Way RG22 ...68 B2
Graham Cl RG14 ...2 A2
Grammarsham La RG25 ...92 A1
Grampian Way RG22 ...68 A2
Granada Pl SP10 ...83 B1
Granary The RG14 ...1 B2
Grand Ave GU15 ...36 A3
Grand Par RG27 ...51 A1
Grand Trunk Rd SP9 ...78 B2
Grange Cl Fyfield SP11 ...80 C1
New Alresford SO24 ...179 B3
Winchester SO23 ...197 C2
Grange Com Jun Sch GU14 ...55 C4
Grange Ct RG14 ...1 C1
Grange Farm RG14 ...184 B4
Grange Farm Rd GU12 ...77 C2
Grange Gdns RG14 ...5 A3
Grange La RG27 ...52 A3
Grange Rd Ash GU12 ...77 C1
Camberley GU15 ...36 B3
Farnborough GU14 ...55 C4
Fleet GU52 ...74 C3
Fressham GU10 ...144 C4
New Alresford SO24 ...179 B3
Tongham GU10 ...100 B3
Winchester SO23 ...197 C2
Grange The
Fressham GU10 ...144 A4
Newbury RG14 ...5 A3
* Northington SO24 ...156 C3
Grantley Dr GU52 ...74 C4
Grantly Ct GU10 ...121 B3
Granville Pl SO23 ...198 A3
Grasmere Cl GU35 ...164 B3
Grasmere Rd
Farnborough GU14 ...55 B2
Farnham GU9 ...98 C3
Graspan Rd SP11 ...57 A1
Grateley Bsns Pk SP11 ...124 C4
Grateley Dro
Amport SP11 ...103 B2
Grateley SP11 ...103 A1
Grateley House Sch SP11 ...125 A4
Grateley Prim Sch SP11 ...125 A4
Grateley Rd SP4 ...101 B1
Grateley Sta SP11 ...124 C4
Gratton Cl SO21 ...153 C2
Gravel Cl GU34 ...135 B2
Gravel Hill Rd GU10 ...120 C2
Gravel La
Barton Stacey SO21 ...130 B4
Great Gap SO24 ...159 C1
Gravel Rd
Farnborough GU14 ...77 A4
Farnham GU9 ...98 C4
Gravelhill Cotts SO20 ...129 B3
Gravelly Cl Ball Hill RG26 ...3 C2
Tadley RG26 ...27 A3
Graveney Sq GU17 ...83 A1
Grayshot Dr GU17 ...35 A3
Grayshott CE Prim Sch GU26 ...166 C2
Grayshott SO22 ...175 B2
Grayshott Laurels GU26 ...165 A3
Grayshott Rd GU26,GU35 ...166 A3
Grayswood Dr GU16 ...56 C2
Great Austins GU9 ...98 B2
Great Austins Ho GU9 ...122 B4
Great Binfields Cres RG24 ...70 A4
Great Binfields Prim Sch RG24 ...49 A1
Great Binfields Rd
RG24 ...70 A4
Chineham RG24 ...49 A1
Old Basing RG24 ...70 A4
Great Gap SO24 ...159 C1
Great Ground RG24 ...70 A4
Great La RG25 ...28 B2
Great Minster St 34 SO23 ...198 A4
Great Oaks Chase RG24 ...48 C1
Great Sheldons Coppice RG27 ...51 A1
Greatfield Cl GU14 ...55 C4
Greatfield Rd GU14 ...55 C4
Greatham Prim Sch GU33 ...185 C1
Grebe Cl Aldershot GU11 ...99 C4
Alton GU34 ...139 C3
Grebe Rd RG22 ...90 C4
Green Acre GU11 ...76 B1
Green Acres
Barton Stacey SO21 ...130 B3
Camberley GU15 ...35 A1
Fleet GU52 ...74 C4
Green Cl
Kings Worthy SO23 ...176 A3
Old Alresford SO24 ...158 A3
South Wonston SO21 ...153 C2
Green Cross La GU10 ...144 B1
Green Dro SP11 ...60 A1
Green End GU46 ...33 A4
Green Glades GU52 ...74 C3
Green Jacket Cl SO23 ...197 C3
Green La
Bishop's Sutton SO24 ...180 B3
Blackwater GU17 ...64 C2
Blackwater RG45 ...45 A1
Churt GU10 ...144 C4
Ellisfield RG25 ...115 A4
Farnham GU9 ...99 B3

Green La continued
Farnham, Wrecclesham GU9 ...121 C4
Frensham GU10 ...143 B3
Hartley Wintney RG27 ...52 B3
High Cross GU33 ...205 C3
Monxton SP11 ...104 B3
Newbury RG14 ...1 B1
Pamber End RG26 ...27 B2
Rotherwick RG27 ...50 C3
Sandhurst GU47 ...35 A4
Shoe SP11 ...61 A3
West End Green RG27 ...29 B4
Green Lane Cl GU15 ...36 A4
Green Lane Cotts GU10 ...144 C1
Green Leys GU52 ...74 C2
Green Meadows La SP11 ...106 A1
Green Park Cl SO23 ...176 A1
Green Springs GU10 ...97 B4
Green St GU35 ...163 C4
Green Stile GU34 ...139 C4
Green The
Barton Stacey SO21 ...130 C4
Camberley GU15 ...56 B3
Charlton SP10 ...82 C1
Farnborough GU14 ...55 C4
Farnham, Upper Hale GU9 ...99 A3
Kimpton SP11 ...80 B1
Liss GU33 ...207 C3
Overton RG25 ...88 A4
Seale GU10 ...100 B1
Tadley RG26 ...27 A3
Whitchurch RG28 ...86 B3
Green Way GU12 ...77 B2
Green's School La GU14 ...55 C2
Greenacre
Broughton SO20 ...170 A3
Kingsclere RG20 ...24 B1
Greenacres Bordon GU35 ...164 C2
Woolton Hill RG20 ...21 B4
Greenacres Specl Sch SO22 ...175 C1
Greenaways Ho 4 RG14 ...1 B1
Greenaways The RG23 ...67 B1
Greenbank Way GU15 ...36 A1
Greenbirch Cl RG22 ...90 C4
Greenbury Cl RG23 ...68 B3
Greencroft 2 GU34 ...55 C2
Greenfield Cl GU30 ...188 A3
Greenfield Rd GU9 ...121 C4
Greenfields
Enham Alamein SP11 ...83 B4
Fleet GU52 ...208 A2
Greenfields Ave GU34 ...139 C2
Greenfields Jun Sch RG27 ...52 B3
Greenham Cl RG19 ...6 A4
Greenham Court Com Prim Sch RG14 ...5 C4
Greenham Mill RG14 ...1 C2
Greenham Rd RG14 ...5 C4
Greenhanger GU10 ...166 C4
Greenhaven GU46 ...33 C3
Greenhaven Cl SP10 ...106 B4
Greenhill Ave SO22 ...197 C4
Greenhill Cl
Winchester SO22 ...197 C4
Greenhill Rd
Farnham GU9 ...122 A4
Winchester SO22 ...197 B4
Greenhill Terr SO22 ...197 C4
Greenhill Way GU9 ...122 C4
Greenhills GU19 ...122 B4
Greenlands RG20 ...4 B1
Greenlands Rd
Camberley GU15 ...35 C1
Kingsclere RG20 ...24 B1
Newbury RG14 ...5 C4
Greenlea GU16 ...56 B1
Greenleas Cl GU46 ...34 A4
Greenridge Cl RG22 ...32 A2
Greensey SP11 ...81 A3
Greenway
Basingstoke RG22 ...68 B2
Sherfield on Loddon RG27 ...49 B4
Greenways Fleet GU52 ...74 C3
Woolton Hill RG20 ...21 B4
Greenwich Way SP10 ...83 A1
Greenwood Dr RG24 ...48 C2
Greenwood Manor GU51 ...53 C1
Greenwoods RG28 ...86 B3
Gregan Ct 15 GU11 ...76 B1
Gregory Ho 18 RG22 ...91 A1
Greig Cl RG22 ...68 C1
Grenadier Rd GU12 ...77 C2
Grenadiers Way GU14 ...55 A2
Grensell Cl GU40 ...16 B4
Grenville Cl GU30 ...188 A2
Grenville Dr GU51 ...74 C4
Grenville Gdns GU16 ...56 B4
Gresham Ct GU14 ...77 A4
Gresham Ind Est GU12 ...77 C3
Gresley Ho RG14 ...1 B2
Gresley Rd RG21,RG26 ...69 B3
Greville Ct GU12 ...77 B2
Grey House Sch The
Greyberry Copse Rd RG19 ...6 A4
Greyfriars RG SO23 ...198 A4
Greyhound Cl GU12 ...77 B1
Greyhound La SP11 ...88 A4
Greys Ct GU11 ...76 C1
Greys Farm GU34 ...139 A3
Greystead Pk GU10 ...121 B3
Greystoke Ct RG45 ...45 A4
Greywell Cl RG26 ...26 C4

Grieve Cl GU11 ...100 B4
Griffin Way N RG27 ...51 A1
Griffin Way S RG27 ...51 B1
Griffon Cl GU14 ...55 A2
Groombridge Pl RG14 ...1 B3
Grosvenor Cl RG22 ...91 A3
Grosvenor Ct GU17 ...35 A2
Grosvenor Dr SO23 ...176 A1
Grosvenor Lawn 6 RG14 ...1 B1
Grosvenor Rd
Aldershot GU11 ...76 C1
Medstead GU34 ...159 C1
Grove Cl RG21 ...69 B2
Grove Cross Rd GU16 ...36 A1
Grove End Rd GU12 ...5 C4
Grove Park Ind Est GU34 ...140 C2
Grove Prim Sch The GU16 ...36 B1
Grove Rd Alton GU34 ...139 C1
Ash GU12 ...77 C2
Basingstoke RG21 ...69 B1
Beacon Hill GU26 ...167 A3
Camberley GU15 ...36 B3
Fleet GU52 ...75 A3
Newbury RG14 ...1 B3
Grove The Aldershot GU11 ...76 C1
Camberley GU16 ...36 A1
Farnborough GU14 ...56 A4
Hartley Wintney RG27 ...52 B3
Liphook GU30 ...187 C2
Penton Grafton SP11 ...81 C2
Grovebell Ind Est GU9 ...121 B4
Grovefields Ave GU16 ...36 A1
Groveland Rd RG14 ...1 B3
Grovelands GU10 ...122 B4
Grovelands Rd SO22 ...175 A1
Groves Cl SO21 ...153 B2
Groves Lea RG7 ...11 A3
Guernsey Cl RG24 ...48 B1
Guernsey Dr GU51 ...54 A2
Guildford Rd
Aldershot GU12 ...100 A4
Camberley GU16 ...56 C3
Farnborough GU14 ...56 C3
Fleet GU51 ...54 B1
Mytchett GU16 ...56 C3
Guildford Rd E GU14 ...56 A1
Guildford Rd Ind Est GU9 ...99 B2
Guildford Road Trad Est GU9 ...99 A2
Guillemont Fields GU14 ...55 A3
Guillemont Jun Sch GU14 ...55 A3
Guinea Ct RG24 ...49 A2
Gun Hill GU11 ...76 C2
Gunners La GU34 ...135 A3
Gunns Farm GU30 ...188 A1
Gunville Hill SP5 ...168 A3
Gunville Rd SP5 ...168 A3
Gurdons GU34 ...139 B1
Gurkha Mus The* SO23 ...197 C4
Gurkha Sq GU51 ...74 C4
Gurney Cl GU29 ...72 C1
Guttridge La RG26 ...26 C4
Gwyn Cl RG14 ...5 B4

H

H Jones Cres GU11 ...77 A2
Hacks La SO21 ...152 A2
Hackups La SO51 ...193 B1
Hackwood Cl SP10 ...105 B4
Hackwood Cotts RG21 ...69 B2
Hackwood La RG25 ...92 B3
Hackwood Rd RG21 ...69 B2
Hackwood Road Rdbt RG21 ...69 B2
Hadleigh Gdns GU16 ...56 B3
Hadleigh Pl 10 RG21 ...69 A3
Hadleys GU10 ...121 B2
Hadrian Rd SP10 ...83 A2
Hadrians Way RG23 ...68 B4
Hagley Rd GU51 ...53 C1
Haig La GU52 ...75 A3
Haig Rd Aldershot GU12 ...77 A1
Andover SP10 ...105 C4
Camberley GU15 ...36 A3
Sandhurst GU15 ...35 C1
Hailstone Rd RG21 ...69 A4
Haining Gdns GU16 ...56 C1
Halcyon Dr SP11 ...103 C4
Hale Cl SO20 ...175 A2
Hale Farm Flats GU10 ...99 B3
Hale House Cl GU10 ...144 B1
Hale House La GU10 ...144 C1
Hale Pl GU9 ...99 B2
Hale Reeds GU9 ...99 B3
Hale Rd GU9 ...99 B2
Hale Way GU16 ...56 B4
Hale Way Cotts GU10 ...98 A4
Halifax Cl Andover SP10 ...82 C1
Farnborough GU14 ...55 B2
Halimote Rd GU11 ...76 C1
Hall Cl GU15 ...36 B3
Hall Farm Cres GU46 ...34 A4
Hall La
Upper Farringdon GU34 ...162 A1

Hall La *continued*
Yateley GU46 . . . . .34 A3
Hall Rd GU34 . . . . .140 A3
Hall Way The SO22 . . . . . .175 A3
Halliday Cl RG21 . . . . .69 A1
Hallmark Cl GU47 . . . . .35 B4
Halpin Ho RG7 . . . . .14 A2
Halters The RG14 . . . . .5 C4
Halton Rd SP11 . . . . .79 B4
Ham La RG26 . . . . .25 C3
Hamble Ave GU17 . . . . .35 A3
Hamble Cl RG23 . . . . .67 A1
Hamble Ct
 3 Andover SP10 . . . . .83 B1
 3 Basingstoke RG21 . . . . . . .69 B3
Hamble Dr RG26 . . . . .27 A4
Hambledon Cl SO22 . . . . .175 B2
Hambleton Cl GU16 . . . . . . .36 C2
Hambridge La RG14 . . . . . . .2 B1
Hambridge Rd RG14 . . . . . . .2 A1
Hamburg Cl SP10 . . . . .82 C2
Hamelyn Cl RG21 . . . . .69 A2
Hamelyn Rd RG21 . . . . .69 A2
Hamesmoor Rd GU16 . . . . .56 B2
Hamesmoor Way GU16 . . .56 B2
Hamilton Cl
 Basingstoke RG21 . . . . .68 C4
 Bordon GU35 . . . . .164 C2
Hamilton Ct
 Farnborough GU17 . . . . . . .35 B1
 Newbury RG14 . . . . .5 C4
 South Tidworth SP9 . . . . . .78 C3
Hamilton Gn SP9 . . . . .78 C3
Hamilton Pl GU11 . . . . .76 B1
Hamilton Rd
 Bordon GU33 . . . . .186 B1
 Fleet GU52 . . . . .75 A3
Hamlash Cotts GU10 . . . .122 A1
Hamlash La GU10 . . . . . . .122 A1
Hamlet Gdns SP11 . . . . .83 A3
Hammer Hill GU27 . . . . . .189 A2
Hammer La
 Bramshott GU27 . . . . .188 C3
 Headley GU26 . . . . .189 A2
 Linchmere GU27 . . . . .189 A3
Hammer Vale GU27 . . . . . .189 A4
Hammersley Rd GU11 . . . . .76 C4
Hammerwood Copse
GU27 . . . . .189 A3
Hammond Heath RG27 . . . . .11 C3
Hammond Rd 5 RG21 . . . . .69 A2
Hammond Sq RG21 . . . . .83 A1
Hammond's La SO24 . . . . .181 B2
Hampdens The RG14 . . . . . . .5 A3
Hampshire Cl
 Aldershot GU11 . . . . .100 A4
 Basingstoke RG22 . . . . .68 A2
Hampshire Cross SP9 . . . . .78 C3
Hampshire Ho GU30 . . . . .187 C4
Hampshire Int Bsns Pk
RG24 . . . . .48 C2
Hampshire Rd
 Bordon GU35 . . . . .164 B2
 Camberley GU15 . . . . .36 B4
Hampstead Ho RG21 . . . . . .69 A3
Hampton Cl GU52 . . . . .75 A2
Hampton Ct RG23 . . . . .68 B3
Hampton La SO22 . . . . . . .175 B1
Hampton Rd Farnham GU9 .98 C3
 Newbury RG14 . . . . .1 B1
Hampton Terr GU26 . . . . . .167 A3
Hanbury Way GU15 . . . . . . .36 A2
Handcroft Cl GU10 . . . . .97 B4
Handel Cl RG22 . . . . .68 C1
Handford La GU44 . . . . .34 A3
Hand Villas 15 SO23 . . . . .198 A4
Hanger Rd RG26 . . . . .9 B1
Hanger The GU35 . . . . .165 B4
Hangerfield Cl GU46 . . . . . .34 A3
Hanmore Rd RG24 . . . . .48 C2
Hannam's Farm GU10 . . . . .97 B3
Hanover Cl Andover SP10 .105 B3
 Camberley GU16 . . . . .36 B1
 Yateley GU46 . . . . .34 A4
Hanover Ct GU30 . . . . .187 C3
Hanover Dr GU51 . . . . .74 C4
Hanover Gdns
 Basingstoke RG21 . . . . .69 A1
 Farnborough GU14 . . . . . . .55 B3
Hanover Ho 14 SP10 . . . . .106 A4
Hanover Lodge SO23 . . . . .197 C3
Hanover Mead RG14 . . . . . . .5 A3
Hanson Cl GU15 . . . . .36 C4
Hanson Rd SP10 . . . . .82 C1
Harbour Rd RG14 . . . . .55 C4
Harbury Cl RG14 . . . . .1 C1
Harcourt Rd GU15 . . . . .35 C3
Harding's La RG27 . . . . .52 B3
Hardy Ave GU46 . . . . .34 A2
Hardy La RG21 . . . . .69 A2
Hardyfair Cl SP11 . . . . .83 A1
Hardys Field RG20 . . . . .24 B2
Hare's La RG27 . . . . .52 C4
Harebell Cl RG27 . . . . .52 B4
Harebell Gdns RG27 . . . . . .52 B4
Harestock Cl SO22 . . . . . . .175 B3
Harestock Cnr SO22 . . . . . .175 B3
Harestock Prim Sch
SO22 . . . . .175 B2
Harestock Rd SO22 . . . . . .175 B2
Harewood Forest Ind Est
SP11 . . . . .107 C2
Harfield Cl RG27 . . . . .51 A1
Harlech Cl RG23 . . . . .68 B3
Harlech Rd GU17 . . . . .35 A2

Harlington Way GU51 . . . . .53 C1
Harmes Way SP11 . . . . .77 A4
Harmsworth Rd RG26 . . . . .26 C4
Harold Gdns GU34 . . . . . . .140 A3
Harold Jackson Terr
RG21 . . . . .69 B2
Harpdon Par RG46 . . . . .34 A4
Harpton Cl GU46 . . . . .34 A4
Harriet Costello Sch
RG21 . . . . .69 B2
Harrington Cl RG14 . . . . .2 B3
Harris Cl GU30 . . . . .187 C1
Harris Hill RG22 . . . . .91 A4
Harrow Down SO21 . . . . . .197 B2
Harrow La SP11 . . . . .82 A1
 Oakley RG23 . . . . .68 B1
 Penton Grafton SP11 . . . . .82 A1
Harrow Way Com Sch
SP10 . . . . .82 B1
Harrow Way The RG22 . . . .68 C1
Harroway RG28 . . . . .85 B4
Hart Cl GU14 . . . . .55 B4
Hart Ctr 13 GU51 . . . . .53 C1
Hart The GU9 . . . . .98 C1
Hartfield Ho 6 GU51 . . . . .53 C1
Hartford Bridge Flats
RG27,GU17 . . . . .33 B1
Hartford Ct RG27 . . . . .52 B3
Hartford Rd RG27 . . . . .52 B4
Hartford Rise GU15 . . . . . . .36 A3
Hartford Terr RG27 . . . . . . .52 B3
Hartland Pl GU14 . . . . .55 C3
Hartley Cl GU17 . . . . .34 B3
Hartley Gdns 15 RG26 . . . . .26 C4
Hartley La RG27 . . . . .30 A1
Hartley Mdw RG28 . . . . . . .86 A3
Hartley Mews RG27 . . . . . . .52 B4
Hartleys RG7 . . . . .27 C4
Harts Cotts RG20 . . . . .22 B3
Harts La RG20 . . . . .22 B3
Harts Leap Cl GU47 . . . . . . .34 C4
Harts Leap Rd GU47 . . . . . .34 C4
Harts Yd GU9 . . . . .98 C1
Hartshill Rd RG26 . . . . .9 B1
Hartsleaf Cl GU51 . . . . .74 C4
Hartswood RG24 . . . . .48 C1
Hartvale Ct GU15 . . . . .36 C4
Harvest Cl
 Winchester SO22 . . . . . . .197 B2
 Yateley GU46 . . . . .33 C2
Harvest Cres GU51 . . . . . . .54 A1
Harvest Gn RG14 . . . . .1 B1
Harvest Way RG24 . . . . .69 C4
Harvey Rd GU14 . . . . .55 A3
Harvey Villas GU30 . . . . . .187 A4
Harveys Field RG25 . . . . . . .88 A4
Harwood Pl SO23 . . . . .176 B4
Harwood Rise RG20 . . . . . . .4 B1
Hasle Dr GU27 . . . . .189 C3
Haslemere Rd
 Linchmere GU27 . . . . .189 C1
 Liphook GU30 . . . . .188 A2
Haslemere Sta GU27 . . . . .189 C3
Hassocks Workshops The
RG24 . . . . .69 C4
Hastards La GU34 . . . . .184 C4
Hasted Dr SO24 . . . . .179 B2
Hastings Cl
 Basingstoke RG23 . . . . .68 A3
 Camberley GU16 . . . . .56 C4
Hatch Hill GU27 . . . . .189 C1
Hatch La Linchmere GU27 .189 C1
 Liss GU33 . . . . .208 B2
 Old Basing RG24 . . . . .69 B4
Hatch Warren Inf Sch
RG22 . . . . .91 B4
Hatch Warren Jun Sch
RG22 . . . . .91 B4
Hatch Warren La RG22 . . . .91 C4
Hatch Warren Ret Pk
RG22 . . . . .91 A3
Hatchbury La SP11 . . . . .38 B3
Hatches The
 Camberley GU16 . . . . .56 B3
 Farnham GU9 . . . . .121 B4
Hatchet La SP11 . . . . .59 A1
Hatchetts Dr GU27 . . . . . . .189 A4
Hatchwarren Cotts RG22 . .91 B4
Hatchwarren Gdns RG22 . .91 C4
Hatchwarren La RG22 . . . . .91 B4
Hatfield Cl GU15 . . . . .35 C3
Hatfield Gdns GU14 . . . . . . .56 B2
Hatfield Ho GU12 . . . . .77 B3
Hathaway Gdns RG24 . . . . .69 B4
Hatherden SP11 . . . . .59 B1
Hatherden CE Prim Sch
SP11 . . . . .59 B1
Hatherden Cl 8 SP10 . . . .106 A4
Hatherley Rd SO22 . . . . . . .175 C1
Hatherwood GU34 . . . . .34 B3
Hatt La SO51 . . . . .192 C1
Hattem Pl SP10 . . . . .82 C2
Hattingley Rd GU34 . . . . . .159 B4
Haughurst Hill RG26 . . . . . . .9 A1
Havelock Ho GU14 . . . . .77 A4
Haven Way GU9 . . . . .99 A2
Haweswater Cl GU35 . . . . .164 B3
Haweswater Ct GU12 . . . . . .77 B3
Hawk Cl RG22 . . . . .90 C4
Hawk Conservancy The*
SP11 . . . . .104 A4
Hawke Cl SP10 . . . . .83 B1
Hawker Rd GU12 . . . . .77 B4
Hawkes Cl RG27 . . . . .52 B4
Hawkfield La RG21 . . . . .69 A2
Hawkins Cl GU46 . . . . .33 C3
Hawkins Gr GU51 . . . . .74 B3

Hawkins Way GU52 . . . . . . .75 B4
Hawkley Dr RG26 . . . . .27 A4
Hawkley Rd
 Hawkley GU33 . . . . .207 B3
 Liss GU33 . . . . .207 B3
Hawks Mead GU33 . . . . . . .207 C3
Hawkshaw Cl GU30 . . . . . .188 A2
Hawkswood Ave GU16 . . . .36 B1
Hawkwell GU52 . . . . .74 C2
Hawley Cl GU14 . . . . .55 B4
Hawley Garden Cotts
GU17 . . . . .35 A2
Hawley Gn GU17 . . . . .35 B2
Hawley Gr GU17 . . . . .35 B1
Hawley Green Farm
GU17 . . . . .35 B2
Hawley La GU14 . . . . .55 C4
Hawley Lodge GU17 . . . . . .35 B1
Hawley Place Ind Sch
GU17 . . . . .35 B2
Hawley Prim Sch GU17 . . .35 B2
Hawley Rd GU17 . . . . .35 B2
Hawthorn Cl
 Micheldever SO21 . . . . . . .133 A1
 New Alresford SO24 . . . . .179 B3
 South Tidworth SP9 . . . . . .79 A4
Hawthorn Hill SO20 . . . . . .126 A2
Hawthorn La GU34 . . . . . . .182 C4
Hawthorn Rd
 Camberley GU16 . . . . .36 B1
 Newbury RG14 . . . . .1 C2
 North Tidworth SP9 . . . . . .79 A4
Hawthorn Way RG23 . . . . . .68 B4
Hawthorne Cl
 Aldershot GU12 . . . . .100 B4
 Grateley SP11 . . . . .103 A1
Hawthorns GU34 . . . . .139 C3
Hawthorns Sch RG22 . . . . .91 C3
Hawthorns The RG26 . . . . .26 B4
Hay Down La SP11 . . . . . . .103 C3
Haydn Cl SO23 . . . . .176 A4
Haydn Rd RG27 . . . . .91 B4
Haydock Cl GU14 . . . . .139 C1
Haydon Pl GU46 . . . . .34 B3
Haydown Leas SP11 . . . . . .38 B3
Hayes Cl SO20 . . . . .171 C1
Hayley La RG29 . . . . .95 B2
Haywaren Pl RG27 . . . . .52 B4
Haywood Dr GU52 . . . . .75 A4
Hazel Ave GU14 . . . . .55 B2
Hazel Cl Andover SP10 . . . .105 B3
 Oakley RG23 . . . . .67 A1
Hazel Coppice RG27 . . . . . .51 A1
Hazel Gn RG26 . . . . .9 B3
Hazel Gr Haslemere GU26 .167 A4
 Winchester SO22 . . . . . . .197 B3
Hazel Rd
 Four Marks GU34 . . . . . . .160 B2
 Mytchett GU16 . . . . .56 C1
 Pamber Heath RG26 . . . . . .10 B1
Hazelbank RG40 . . . . .16 B3
Hazelcombe RG25 . . . . .88 A4
Hazeldene GU34 . . . . .48 C1
Hazeldene Gdns SO21 . . .177 C4
Hazeldene Rd GU30 . . . . . .187 A2
Hazeley Cl RG27 . . . . .52 B4
Hazeley Dr 8 GU51 . . . . . . .53 C1
Hazeley Lea RG27 . . . . .31 C2
Hazell Rd GU9 . . . . .98 B1
Hazelwood RG24 . . . . .48 C2
Hazelwood Cl RG23 . . . . . . .68 B4
Hazelwood Dr RG21 . . . . . . .68 C3
Hazelbank CU30 . . . . .188 A2
Hazelbank Mews GU30 . . .188 A2
Headbourne Worthy Ho
SO23 . . . . .176 A3
Headington Cl RG22 . . . . . .91 B4
Headley Cl SO24 . . . . .179 B2
Headley Fields GU35 . . . . .165 B2
Headley Hill Rd GU35 . . . .165 C3
Headley La GU30 . . . . .165 B1
Headley Rd
 Grayshott GU26 . . . . .166 C2
 Lindford GU35 . . . . .165 A3
 Liphook GU35 . . . . .187 C3
Headmore La GU34 . . . . . .160 C1
Headon Ct GU9 . . . . .99 A1
Heanor Ct GU46 . . . . .34 B3
Hearn Vale GU35 . . . . .165 C4
Hearsey Gdns GU17 . . . . . .34 C3
Heath Cl
 Beacon Hill GU26 . . . . . . .167 A4
 Path Cnr GU12 . . . . .36 C2
Heath Cotts
 Beacon Hill GU26 . . . . . . .167 A3
 Frensham GU10 . . . . .122 A2
Heath Ct RG26 . . . . .9 B1
Heath End Farm RG26 . . . . .9 B1
Heath End Rd RG26 . . . . .9 B1
Heath Green La GU34 . . . .159 A4
Heath Hill GU34 . . . . .143 B1
Heath La Buttermere SN8 . .38 B3
 Crondall GU10 . . . . .97 C3
 Farnham GU9 . . . . .99 A4
Heath Rd
 Linchmere GU27 . . . . .189 A3
 Pamber Heath RG26 . . . . . .10 B1
 Reigate RG45 . . . . .16 C3
 Heath Rise GU15 . . . . .36 A3
 Heath Vale SP10 . . . . .106 A4
Heathcote Cl GU12 . . . . .77 C2
Heathcote Rd Ash GU12 . . .77 C2
 Camberley GU15 . . . . .36 A3
 Ash GU12 . . . . .77 C2
Heather Cl Aldershot GU11 .76 B1
 Bordon GU35 . . . . .164 C3

Heather Cl *continued*
 Farnham GU9 . . . . .121 B3
 Finchampstead RG40 . . . . .16 B4
Heather Cotts GU12 . . . . . .77 C4
Heather Ct
 2 Aldershot GU11 . . . . . .76 C1
 Hindhead GU26 . . . . .167 B2
Heather Dr
 Andover SP10 . . . . .105 C4
 3 Baughurst RG26 . . . . . .9 B3
 Fleet GU52 . . . . .74 C3
 Lindford GU35 . . . . .164 C3
Heather Gdns
 Farnborough GU14 . . . . . . .55 B2
 Newbury RG14 . . . . .5 B4
Heather Gr RG27 . . . . .52 B4
Heather La RG27 . . . . .71 B3
Heather Mead RG16 . . . . . .36 B1
Heather Mead Ct GU16 . . .36 B1
Heather Row La
 Mapledurwell RG27 . . . . . .71 C3
 Newnham RG27 . . . . .71 C3
Heather Way
 Basingstoke RG22 . . . . .91 A4
 Hindhead GU26 . . . . .167 B2
Heatherdale Rd GU15 . . . . .36 A2
Heatherfield Cl GU15 . . . . .35 C3
Heatherley Cl GU15 . . . . . . .35 C3
Heatherly Cl GU15 . . . . .35 C3
Heatherside Jun & Inf Sch
GU51 . . . . .75 A4
Heathfield RG7 . . . . .11 C3
Heathfield Ct GU51 . . . . . . .74 C4
Heathfield Rd RG22 . . . . . . .91 B4
Heathland St GU11 . . . . .76 C1
Heathlands
 2 Baughurst RG26 . . . . . . .9 B1
 Highclere RG20 . . . . .21 C4
Heathlands Ct GU46 . . . . . .34 B2
Heathman St SO20 . . . . . . .148 A3
Heathrow Copse RG26 . . . .26 A4
Heathside Cl GU26 . . . . . . .167 A3
Heathside Way RG27 . . . . . .52 B4
Heathvale Bridge Rd
GU12 . . . . .77 C3
Heathview RG27 . . . . .51 B1
Heathway GU15 . . . . .36 A3
Heathway Cl GU15 . . . . .36 A3
Heathwood Cl GU46 . . . . . .34 A4
Heathyfields Rd GU9 . . . . . .98 B3
Heckfield Dr 7 GU51 . . . . . .53 B2
Heddon Wlk GU14 . . . . .55 C4
Hedge Croft GU46 . . . . .33 C3
Hedge End Rd SP10 . . . . . .106 A3
Hedge Way RG14 . . . . .2 A2
Hedgehog La GU27 . . . . . . .189 C3
Hedgerows The RG24 . . . . .70 A4
Hedges Cl SP9 . . . . .101 B4
Heenan Cl GU16 . . . . .56 B4
Heights The GU15 . . . . .36 B3
Hele Cl RG21 . . . . .69 A1
Helen Ct GU14 . . . . .55 B4
Helford Cl 15 SP10 . . . . . . .83 B1
Helix Bsns Pk GU15 . . . . . . .35 C2
Helston Cl GU16 . . . . .56 C4
Hempland La GU34 . . . . . .204 B2
Hendon Rd GU35 . . . . .164 B1
Hendren Sq SP10 . . . . .83 B1
Hengest Cl SP10 . . . . .82 B2
Henley Cl GU14 . . . . .55 B4
Henley Dr GU16 . . . . .56 B4
Henley Gdns GU46 . . . . .34 A3
Henry Beaufort Sec Sch
SO22 . . . . .175 C2
Henry Randell's Almshouses
 2 . . . . .76 A1
Henry Tyndale Sch GU14 . .56 A3
Henshaw Cres RG14 . . . . . . .5 A4
Henwick Cl RG18 . . . . .2 C3
Henwick La RG18 . . . . .2 C3
Hepplewhite Cl 15 RG26 . .9 B3
Hepplewhite Dr RG22 . . . . .91 A4
Hepworth Cl SP10 . . . . .83 A1
Hepworth Croft GU47 . . . . .35 B3
Herald Ct 22 GU12 . . . . . . .76 C1
Herbert Rd GU51 . . . . .53 C1
Herbs End GU14 . . . . .55 A4
Hereford Cl RG29 . . . . .72 B1
Hereford Ho GU11 . . . . .76 C1
Hereford La GU9 . . . . .98 C4
Hereford Mead GU51 . . . . .54 A2
Hereford Rd RG23 . . . . .68 B3
Herewood Cl RG14 . . . . .2 B2
Heritage Pk RG21 . . . . .91 A3
Heritage View RG22 . . . . . . .91 A3
Hermes Cl GU51 . . . . .54 B1
Hermitage
 Alton GU34 . . . . .139 C1
Hermitage Cl
 Farnborough GU14 . . . . . . .36 B1
Heron Cl Alton GU34 . . . . .139 C3
 Fleet GU52 . . . . .74 C3
 Newbury RG14 . . . . .56 B2
Heron Ho RG14 . . . . .1 B1
Heron Pk RG24 . . . . .48 C1
Heron Way
 Basingstoke RG22 . . . . .90 C4
 Bordon GU35 . . . . .165 C4
Heron Wood Rd GU12 . . . .100 A4
Herondale GU27 . . . . .189 B3
Herons Rise SP10 . . . . .106 B3
Herrett St GU12 . . . . .100 A4
Herretts Gdns GU12 . . . . . .100 A4
Herriard Way RG26 . . . . . . .27 A4
Herridge Cl RG26 . . . . .29 A1
Herriot Ct GU46 . . . . .34 A2
Hesters View RG29 . . . . . . .95 B1
Hewshott La GU30 . . . . . . .188 B3

Hewshott La GU30 . . . . . . .188 B3
Hexagon The SP10 . . . . . . .105 B3
Hibiscus Gr GU35 . . . . .164 C1
Hickory Dr SO22 . . . . .175 B2
Hicks Cl RG26 . . . . .27 A4
Hicks La GU17 . . . . .34 C3
Hides Cl RG28 . . . . .86 B2
High Beech Gdns SP10 . . .106 B4
High Beeches GU16 . . . . . . .36 A1
High Copse GU9 . . . . .98 C3
High Crissels GU47 . . . . .35 A4
High Cross GU32 . . . . .205 C1
High Cross La GU32 . . . . . .205 B1
High Dr RG28 . . . . .68 B1
High Park Rd GU9 . . . . .99 A2
High Pitfold GU26 . . . . .167 A1
High St Aldershot GU11 . . . .76 C1
 Alton GU34 . . . . .139 C2
 Andover SP10 . . . . .106 A4
 Bordon GU35 . . . . .164 B2
 Broughton SO20 . . . . .170 A4
 Camberley GU15 . . . . .36 A3
 Farnborough GU14 . . . . . . .77 A4
 Farnham GU10 . . . . .121 B2
 Grateley SP11 . . . . .125 A4
 Hartley Wintney RG27 . . . . .52 B3
 Headley GU35 . . . . .165 B3
 Medstead GU34 . . . . .159 C4
 Nether Wallop SO20 . . . . .148 A3
 Odiham RG29 . . . . .72 C2
 Overton RG25 . . . . .88 A4
 Sandhurst GU47 . . . . .34 B4
 Selborne GU34 . . . . .184 C4
 Shipton Bellinger SP9 . . . .101 C4
 Stockbridge SO20 . . . . . . .197 C2
 Winchester SO23 . . . . . . .197 C4
 Winchester SO23 . . . . . . .198 A4
High Thicket Rd GU10 . . . .143 A3
High Trees Dr SO22 . . . . . .175 C1
High View Cl GU14 . . . . .55 C2
High View Lodge 2
GU11 . . . . .76 C1
High View Rd GU14 . . . . . . .55 C2
Highams Cl RG20 . . . . .24 C1
Highbury Cres GU15 . . . . . .36 C4
Highbury La RG21 . . . . .69 A2
Highclere Kashley Rd SP11 .105 B2
Highclere Castle* RG20
RG20 . . . . .21 C2
Highclere Park Gdns*
RG20 . . . . .21 C2
Highclere Rd GU12 . . . . . . .100 A4
Highclere St RG20 . . . . .21 C2
Highcliffe Rd SO23 . . . . . . .198 A4
Highcroft GU12 . . . . .167 A3
Highdown GU51 . . . . .54 A1
Highdowns RG22 . . . . .91 B3
Higher Mead RG24 . . . . .69 C4
Highfield RG20 . . . . .40 C2
Highfield Ave
 Aldershot GU11 . . . . .99 C4
 Newbury RG14 . . . . .1 C1
Highfield Chase RG21 . . . . .68 C3
Highfield Cl
 Aldershot GU11 . . . . .99 C4
 Farnborough GU14 . . . . . . .55 B2
 Farnham GU9 . . . . .121 C2
Highfield Cres GU26 . . . . . .167 B3
Highfield Gdns GU33 . . . . .208 A1
Highfield La GU10 . . . . .188 B3
Highfield Path GU14 . . . . . . .55 B2
Highfield Rd
 Farnborough GU14 . . . . . . .55 B2
 Newbury RG14 . . . . .1 B
Highfield Sch GU30 . . . . . .188 B3
Highfield Terr 62 SO22 . . .197 C2
Highfields RG21 . . . . .88 A
Highgate Ct GU14 . . . . .54 A
Highgate La GU14 . . . . .56 A
Highland Dr Fleet GU51 . . . .54 B
 Oakley RG23 . . . . .67 A
Highland Rd
 Aldershot GU12 . . . . .77 A
 Camberley GU15 . . . . .36 B
Highlands Cl GU12 . . . . . . .121 C
Highlands Rd
 Andover SP10 . . . . .106 B
 Basingstoke RG22 . . . . .68 A
 Farnham GU9 . . . . .99 A
Highmoors RG24 . . . . .48 C
Highmount Cl SO23 . . . . . .198 B
Highpath Way RG24 . . . . . . .68 B
Highridge GU34 . . . . .139 B
Highrove GU14 . . . . .55 C
Highwoods RG22 . . . . .91 A
Highview Bsns Ctr
GU35 . . . . .164 B
Higwood Cl
 Newbury RG14 . . . . .1 C
 Yateley GU46 . . . . .34 A
Highwood Ridge RG22 . . . . .91 A
Highworth Cotts RG26 . . . . .9 A
Hilary No 9 RG14 . . . . .1 C
Hilden Way SO22 . . . . .175 A
Hilder Gdns GU14 . . . . .56 B
Hill Brow Rd GU33 . . . . . . .208 A
Hill Cl RG14 . . . . .5 A
Hill Corner Farm Est
GU14 . . . . .55 B
Hill Crest Dr GU10 . . . . . . .121 C
Hill Ct GU27 . . . . .189 B
Hill Farm Cl GU27 . . . . . . .189 C
Hill Farm Rd GU34,SO24 . .182 B
Hill House Hill GU30 . . . . .188 A
Hill Houses La SO24 . . . . . .201 A
Hill Mdw RG25 . . . . .89 A
Hill Rd Beacon Hill GU26 . .167 A
 Farnham GU9 . . . . .99 A
 Grayshott GU26 . . . . .167 A
 Newbury RG14 . . . . .5 A
 Oakley RG23 90

Hill Sq RG24 ....49 A1
Hill Terr SO24 ....179 B3
Hill Top SO22 ....175 B3
Hill Top Ave SP9 ....78 C4
Hill View Rd
 Basingstoke RG22 ....68 C2
 Farnham GU9 ....98 B1
Hilland Rise GU35 ....165 B3
Hillary Cl GU9 ....121 C4
Hillary Rd
 Basingstoke RG21 ....69 A4
 Farnham GU9 ....121 C4
Hillbrook Rise GU9 ....98 C3
Hillbury Ave SP10 ....105 C3
Hillcrest Farnham GU9 ....99 A4
 Fleet GU51 ....54 A2
 Tadley RG26 ....9 C1
Hillcrest Cotts GU14 ....1 B4
Hillcrest Ct RG23 ....68 A3
Hillcrest Dr GU35 ....136 C4
Hillcrest Wlk RG23 ....68 B3
Hillfield GU46 ....34 B3
Hillgarth GU26 ....167 A3
Hillhouse La RG19 ....7 C1
Hilltop Way SO23 ....176 A1
Hillsborough Ct GU14 ....55 B4
Hillside Abbotts Ann SP11 ....104 C2
 Baughurst RG26 ....26 A2
 Littleton SO22 ....175 B3
 Sandhurst GU15 ....35 B4
 Upton SP11 ....38 C1
 Whitchurch RG28 ....86 C3
Hillside Cl Alton GU34 ....139 C3
 Crookham Village GU51 ....74 B3
 Headley GU35 ....165 C3
 West Dean SP5 ....190 B1
 Winchester SO22 ....175 B1
Hillside Cotts
 Farnborough GU14 ....35 B1
 Sparsholt SO21 ....174 A2
Hillside Cres GU16 ....56 C4
Hillside Ct SP10 ....105 C4
Hillside Flats GU26 ....167 A3
Hillside La GU9 ....99 A4
Hillside Rd
 Aldershot GU11 ....99 C4
 Ash GU12 ....77 C2
 Farnham GU10 ....122 A2
 Farnham, Weybourne GU9 ....99 B4
 Linchmere GU27 ....189 B3
 Winchester SO22 ....175 B1
Hillside Villas SP10 ....82 C1
Hillstead Ct RG21 ....69 A2
Hilltop Rd GU35 ....65 A1
Hilltop View GU46 ....33 C3
Hindell Cl GU14 ....55 C4
Hindhead Commons Nature
 Trail* GU26 ....167 C2
Hindhead Ho GU26 ....167 B2
Hindhead Rd GU26 ....167 B1
Hinstock Cl GU26 ....55 C2
Hinton Ampner Ho*
 SO24 ....201 C2
Hinton Cl RG26 ....26 C4
Hinton Hill SO24 ....201 C2
Hinwood Cl SO20 ....170 A4
Hirst Copse SP11 ....62 A1
Hitches La
 Crookham Village GU51 ....74 B4
 Fleet GU51 ....74 B3
Hobbs Cl SO24 ....180 B2
Hobbs Sq SP10 ....83 B1
Hockford La RG7 ....8 C2
Hockley Cotts SO20 ....200 C2
Hockley Link SO21 ....197 C1
Hoddington Cotts RG25 ....94 B2
Hogarth Cl
 Basingstoke RG22 ....69 C2
 Sandhurst GU47 ....35 B3
Hogarth Ct SP10 ....82 C1
Hoghatch La GU9 ....98 C3
Hogmoor Rd GU35 ....164 A2
Hogwood Ind Est RG40 ....15 C3
Hogwood La RG40 ....15 C3
Holbeche Cl GU46 ....33 C3
Holbein Cl RG21 ....69 B2
Holborne Cl RG14 ....5 A3
Holbrook Cl GU9 ....99 B4
Holbrook Way GU14 ....55 A4
Holbury La
 East Tytherley SO51 ....191 B2
 Lockerley SO51 ....182 A1
Holdaway Cl SO23 ....176 B4
Holder Rd GU12 ....77 B1
Hole La GU10 ....120 A3
Holland Cl GU9 ....99 B1
Holland Dr SP10 ....82 C2
Holland Gdns GU51 ....75 A4
Hollands Cl SO22 ....175 A3
Hollies The GU14 ....5 A3
Hollin's Wlk ⑨ RG21 ....69 A3
Hollington House Gdns*
 RG20 ....21 A4
Hollington La RG20 ....21 A2
Hollis Wood Dr GU10 ....121 B3
Hollow The
 Broughton SO20 ....170 B3
 Kingsclere RG20 ....21 A4
Hollowshot La RG20 ....24 B1
Holly Acre GU46 ....34 A3
Holly Ave GU16 ....36 C2
Holly Bush Cotts RG26 ....26 A1
Holly Bush La
 Farnham GU10 ....77 B3
 Hook RG27 ....71 C4
Holly Cl Aldershot GU12 ....77 A1
 Bramley RG26 ....29 A1
 Eversley RG27 ....33 A4

Holly Cl continued
 Farnborough GU14 ....55 C2
 Headley GU35 ....166 A3
Holly Cnr RG7 ....14 C4
Holly Cross RG26 ....28 C2
Holly Dr RG24 ....70 B3
Holly Hedge Cl GU16 ....36 B1
Holly Hedge Rd GU16 ....36 B1
Holly La RG7 ....27 C4
Holly Lodge Prim Sch
 GU12 ....77 B4
Holly Rd Aldershot GU12 ....77 A1
 Farnborough GU14 ....55 C2
Holly Tree Pk SO21 ....131 B2
Holly Way GU35 ....35 A2
Holly Wlk Ashford SP10 ....105 B3
 Middle Wallop SO20 ....126 A2
Hollybrook Cl GU35 ....164 C2
Hollybrook Pk GU35 ....164 C2
Hollybush Ind Pk GU11 ....77 B3
Hollybush La
 Eversley RG26 ....33 B4
 Ramsdell RG26 ....26 B1
Hollycombe Cl GU30 ....188 A1
Hollyfields Cl GU15 ....35 C3
Hollyhock Cl RG22 ....91 A4
Hollyridge GU27 ....189 C3
Hollytree Gdns GU16 ....56 A4
Hollytrees GU51 ....74 C3
Hollywater Rd
 Bordon GU35 ....164 C1
 Liphook GU30 ....187 A4
Holm Oak Cl SO22 ....175 A3
Holman Cl RG26 ....29 A1
Holmbrook Cl GU14 ....55 A2
Holmbrook Gdns GU14 ....55 A2
Holme CE Prim Sch The
 GU35 ....165 B3
Holmes Cl RG22 ....91 B3
Holmes Ct SP10 ....105 C4
Holmwood Cotts GU10 ....76 C4
Holmwood Terr RG27 ....52 B3
Hoist Cl RG22 ....91 C4
Holt Cl GU14 ....56 A4
Holt Cotts RG19 ....25 B4
Holt End La GU34 ....128 A2
Holt La Baughurst RG26 ....25 B2
 Hook RG27 ....51 B1
 Tangley SP11 ....59 A4
Holt Pound La GU10 ....121 A3
Holt Way RG27 ....51 B1
Holtwood Rd RG20 ....3 C3
Holy Barn Cl RG22 ....68 A1
Holy Cross Hospl GU27 ....189 B4
Holyrood Ct RG22 ....68 A2
Holywell Cl GU14 ....55 C4
Home Farm Cl SO24 ....180 B3
Home Farm Bsns Ctr
 SP5 ....191 C3
Home Farm La GU34 ....56 A3
Home Farm Gdns SP10 ....82 B2
Home Farm La RG7 ....9 A3
Home Farm Rd RG7 ....53 A3
Home La SO21 ....174 B2
Home Mead RG25 ....89 C1
Home Mead Cl RG14 ....5 B4
Home Park Rd GU46 ....34 A3
Homefield Cotts
 East Tisted SO24 ....183 B3
 Liss GU33 ....207 C3
Homefield Way RG24 ....47 B1
Homegreen Ho GU27 ....189 C3
Homelea Cl GU14 ....55 C4
Homeleigh Cres GU12 ....77 A1
Homepark Ho GU9 ....99 A1
Homerise Ho ❶ SO23 ....198 A4
Homestead Rd GU14 ....159 C3
Homesteads Rd RG22 ....91 A4
Home Hill GU47 ....34 C4
Honey Bsns Pk GU9 ....99 A1
Honey La GU34 ....185 A4
Honeybottom Rd RG26 ....9 C1
Honeycritch La GU32 ....206 B2
Honeysuckle Cl
 Basingstoke RG22 ....91 A4
 Winchester SO22 ....197 C2
 Yateley GU46 ....33 C3
Honeysuckle La GU35 ....165 C3
Honister Gdns GU51 ....54 B1
Hood Cl SP10 ....106 B4
Hook Common RG27 ....71 C4
Hook Inf Sch RG27 ....51 A1
Hook Jun Sch RG27 ....51 A1
Hook La Baughurst RG26 ....25 C4
 Oakley RG23 ....67 A4
 Ropley SO24 ....181 A2
 Wootton St Lawrence RG23 ....67 A4
Hook Rd
 Greywell RG27,RG29 ....72 A3
 Hook RG27 ....72 A4
 Kingsclere RG20 ....24 C1
 North Warnborough RG29 ....72 B2
 Rotherwick RG27 ....51 C4
 South Warnborough RG29 ....72 A4
Hookpit Farm La SO23 ....176 A4
Hookstile La GU9 ....99 A1
Hookwood La SP11 ....58 A4
Hoopers Way RG23 ....67 A1
Hoopersmead RG25 ....92 A4
Hop Garden Rd RG27 ....50 C1
Hop Gdn GU52 ....74 C2
Hop Kiln The GU9 ....121 C4
Hop Kilns The GU10 ....98 C4
Hope Fountain GU15 ....36 C2
Hope Grant's Rd GU11 ....76 C2
Hope La GU9 ....98 C3
Hope Way GU11 ....76 B2
Hopeman Cl GU47 ....35 A4

Hopeswood GU33 ....186 A1
Hopfield Rd RG27 ....52 B3
Hopkinson Way SP10 ....82 A1
Hopton Garth RG24 ....49 A1
Hopwood Cl RG14 ....2 A2
Horizon West Ind Est
 RG14 ....2 A2
Horn Rd GU14 ....55 B3
Hornbeam Cl
 Farnborough GU14 ....55 A3
 South Wonston SO21 ....153 C2
Hornbeam Pl RG27 ....51 A1
Hornbeams RG7 ....14 A3
Hornes Field Ct ⑥ GU52 ....74 C2
Horris Hill Sch RG20 ....5 B2
Horse La SO24 ....181 B4
Horsebridge Rd
 Broughton SO20 ....170 B2
 Houghton SO20 ....171 A2
Horseshoe Bend GU26 ....166 C2
Horseshoe Cl GU15 ....36 B4
Horseshoe Cres
 Bordon GU35 ....164 C2
 Camberley GU15 ....36 B4
Horseshoe End GU15 ....54 B4
Horseshoe La GU12 ....77 C4
 Hurstbourne Tarrant SP11 ....60 B4
Horwood Gdns RG22 ....68 C1
Hosketts La SO20 ....147 C3
Hospital Hill GU11 ....76 C2
Hospital Rd GU11 ....76 C2
Houghton Lodge Gdns*
 SO20 ....171 B4
Hound Green Cl RG27 ....31 A2
Houndmills Rd RG21 ....68 C1
Houndmills Rdbt RG21 ....68 C4
House Plat Flat ⑥ GU52 ....74 C2
Houseman Rd GU14 ....55 B3
Howard Cl GU51 ....54 B1
Howard Cole Way GU11 ....76 B1
Howard Rd GU14 ....55 C4
Howard Rd
 Basingstoke RG21 ....69 B2
 Newbury RG14 ....1 C1
Howard View RG22 ....68 B2
Howard's La GU14 ....160 A4
Howes Gdns GU51 ....74 C3
Hubbard Rd RG21 ....68 C4
Hubert Rd SO23 ....197 C2
Huddington GU46 ....33 C3
Huddle Cl RG27 ....52 B3
Hudson Cl GU30 ....188 A2
Hudson Mdw RG27 ....31 A2
Huish La RG24,RG25 ....70 A2
Hulbert Way RG22 ....68 B1
Hulfords La RG27 ....32 C1
Hullam La GU34 ....140 A4
Humber Cl RG18 ....2 C3
Humber Ct ⑫ SP10 ....83 B1
Humber La RG27 ....78 B2
Humber Way SO20 ....172 A1
Humberstone Rd GU47 ....35 A4
Humming Bird Ct RG22 ....90 C4
Humphrey Pk GU52 ....74 C2
Hundred Acre Cnr SP10 ....105 A4
Hungerford Cl GU47 ....35 A4
Hungerford La
 Enham Alamein SP11 ....82 C4
 Hatherden SP11 ....82 C4
 Tangley SP11 ....37 C1
Hungerford Rd SN8 ....18 A3
Hunnels Cl GU52 ....74 C2
Hunt's Cl SO22 ....153 C2
Hunt's Cotts RG14 ....1 B3
Hunter Rd GU14 ....55 B2
Hunters Cl RG23 ....67 B2
Hunters Mews GU11 ....76 B3
Hunters Rd GU33 ....186 B1
Hunting Gate SP10 ....105 B4
Huntingdon House Dr
 GU26 ....167 B2
Huntingford Cl GU26 ....54 C4
Hunton Down La SO21 ....132 B3
Hunton La SO21 ....132 A2
Hunts Cl RG27 ....51 B1
Hunts Cotts RG14 ....52 B4
Huntsbottom La GU33 ....208 A2
Huntsman's Mews GU14 ....56 B2
Huntsmead SO34 ....140 A2
Huntsmoor Rd RG26 ....26 B4
Hurland La GU35 ....165 B2
Hurlands Bsns Ctr GU9 ....99 B2
Hurlands Cl GU9 ....99 B2
Hurlands Pl GU9 ....99 B2
Hurne Ct ⑳ RG22 ....69 B3
Huron Dr GU30 ....188 A2
Hurst Cl RG24 ....47 B4
Hurst Com Sch The RG26 ....9 A1
Hurst La GU34 ....205 A2
Hurst Rd Aldershot GU11 ....77 A2
 Farnborough GU14 ....55 C4
Hurst The RG27 ....51 C4
Hurstbourne Tarrant CE Prim
 Sch SP11 ....60 C3
Hurstmere Cl GU26 ....167 A2
Hurstmere Ho GU26 ....167 A2
Hussar Ct ❶ GU11 ....76 B1
Hussell La GU34 ....140 A4
Hussey Cl ⑧ SO23 ....176 A1
Hussey's La GU34 ....119 B3
Hutton Cl RG14 ....1 C2
Hutton Rd GU32 ....77 C3
Hutton Rd RG22 ....68 B1
Hyacinth Ct RG22 ....91 A4
Hyde Abbey Rd SO23 ....198 A4
Hyde Church La SO23 ....176 A1
Hyde Church Path ㉔
 SO23 ....176 A1

Hyde Cl SO23 ....175 C1
Hyde End La RG7 ....8 A3
Hyde Farm Cotts RG20 ....95 C1
Hyde Gate SO23 ....176 A1
Hyde House Gdns ㉒
 SO23 ....176 A1
Hyde La Crondall GU10 ....97 B4
 Ecchinswell RG20 ....23 C4
Hyde Lodge SO22 ....175 C1
Hyde St SO23 ....176 A1
Hydes Platt RG7 ....27 C4
Hylde Cl RG26 ....27 A4
Hylton Ct RG26 ....27 A4
Hyson Cres SP11 ....57 A1
Hythe Cl RG26 ....26 C4

I

Iberian Way GU15 ....36 C3
Ibworth La RG26 ....45 B2
Icknield Ho ㉕ SP10 ....83 B1
Icknield Sch SP10 ....83 B1
Icknield Way SP10 ....83 A2
Iden Ct RG14 ....1 C2
Idlefield Cotts GU10 ....120 B3
Ilchester Ct RG14 ....1 C1
Ilex Cl Pamber Heath RG26 ....10 B1
 Yateley GU46 ....33 C3
Illingworth Cl RG26 ....29 A1
Imadene Cl GU35 ....164 C2
Imadene Cres GU35 ....164 C2
Imber Rd SO23 ....198 B4
Imjin Cl GU11 ....76 C2
Imperial Ct Andover SP10 ....83 C1
 ⑨ Newbury RG14 ....1 C1
Impstone Rd RG26 ....10 B1
Imran Ct GU21 ....100 A4
Inadown Bglws GU34 ....183 C4
Ingle Dell GU35 ....36 A2
Ingle Glen RG40 ....16 C4
Inglewood Dr RG22 ....91 A3
Inglis Cl GU34 ....139 C1
Inhams Rd GU34 ....140 B3
Inhams Row RG24 ....157 B1
Inhams Way RG7 ....27 C4
Inhurst House Sch RG26 ....9 A1
Inhurst La RG26 ....26 A4
Inhurst Way RG26 ....9 B1
Inkpen Gdns RG24 ....70 A4
Innisfail Gdns GU11 ....99 B4
Institute Rd GU12 ....77 A4
Intec Bsns Ctr RG24 ....69 C4
Inverness Way GU47 ....35 A4
Invincible Rd GU14 ....55 B3
Inwood Kilns GU34 ....141 C4
Inwood Rd GU33 ....208 A2
Ipoh Cl SO20 ....126 A3
Ipsley Lodge GU10 ....100 B3
Iris Cl RG22 ....91 A4
Irvine Dr GU14 ....55 B4
Irwell Cl RG22 ....69 B3
Isaac Newton Rd RG2 ....15 C4
Isington La GU34 ....119 C1
Isington Rd GU34 ....119 C1
Isis Way GU47 ....35 A4
Island Farm Rd RG7 ....11 B4
Itchel La GU10 ....97 A3
Itchen Abbas Prim Sch
 SO21 ....177 C3
Itchen Cl RG23 ....67 A2
Itchen Ct ⑯ Andover SP10 ....83 B1
 ⑳ Winchester SO23 ....198 A4
Itchen View SO23 ....178 B3
Ivanhoe Rd RG40 ....15 C3
Ivar Gdns RG24 ....49 A1
Ively Rd GU14 ....55 A4
Ively Rdbt GU14 ....55 B1
Ivo Cl GU46 ....33 C3
Ivy Cl SO22 ....197 C3
Ivy Down La RG23 ....66 C2
Ivy Orch GU15 ....54 C4
Ivy Rd GU12 ....77 B1
Ivyhole Hill RG27 ....53 A4
Ivyhouse La GU32 ....205 C2

J

Jacaranda Rd GU35 ....164 B1
Jack St RG14 ....1 C2
Jackdaw Cl RG22 ....90 C4
Jacklyns Cl SO24 ....179 B2
Jacklyns La SO24 ....179 B2
Jacob Rd GU15 ....35 B4
Jacob's Yd ④ RG21 ....69 A4
Jagdalik Rd SP9 ....78 C2
James Cl RG21 ....69 B4
James Rd GU15 ....35 C1
James Watt Rd RG2 ....15 B4
James Way RG22 ....69 B3
Jameson Ho GU51 ....74 C4
Jamrud Rd SP9 ....78 B3
Jan Smuts Cl GU33 ....186 B1
Jane Austen's Ho (Mus)*
 GU34 ....161 B4
Japonica Ct GU12 ....77 B1
Jardine Sq SP10 ....83 B1
Jaris Cl GU46 ....33 A4
Jasmine Ct SP10 ....105 C3
Jasmine Rd SP10 ....105 C3
Jasmine Way GU34 ....164 C1
Jays Cl RG22 ....69 A1
Jays Nest Cl GU17 ....35 A2
Jean Orr Ct GU52 ....75 A3
Jefferson Rd RG7 ....69 B4
Jellicoe Ct SP10 ....83 B1
Jenkins Pl GU14 ....77 A4

Jenner Way GU34 ....140 A3
Jennie Green La GU34 ....137 C1
Jenny's Wlk GU46 ....34 B3
Jenson Gdns SP10 ....105 C4
Jerrymoor Hill RG40 ....16 B4
Jersey Cl
 Basingstoke RG22 ....48 B1
 Fleet GU51 ....54 A2
Jervis Ct SP10 ....83 B1
Jesmond Dene RG14 ....1 B2
Jesse Cl GU46 ....34 B3
Jessett Dr GU52 ....74 C3
Jesty Rd SO24 ....179 A2
Jewry St SO23 ....198 A4
Jibbs Mdw RG26 ....28 C2
Jobson Cl RG28 ....86 B3
John Boys Ho RG14 ....5 A1
John Childs Cl RG14 ....1 C1
John Cl GU11 ....99 B4
John Eddie Ct RG22 ....68 B2
John Eggars Sq GU34 ....140 A3
John Hanson Com Sch
 SP10 ....105 C4
John Hunt of Everest Com
 Sch RG24 ....48 B1
John Kimber's Almshouses
 GU34 ....1 B2
John Morgan Cl RG27 ....51 A1
John Norgate Ho RG14 ....2 B2
John Pounds Ho ⑥
 GU35 ....164 B1
John Rankin Inf Sch RG14 ....5 A4
John Rankin Jun Sch
 RG14 ....5 A4
Johnson Dr RG40 ....16 C4
Johnson Way GU52 ....75 A3
Joices Yd ⑥ RG21 ....69 A4
Jolliffe Cl RG24 ....97 B3
Jonathan Hill RG20 ....5 C2
Jouldings La RG7 ....15 A2
Jubilee Cl Andover SP10 ....82 A1
 La Sa SO20 ....129 A2
Jubilee Cl
 Farnborough GU14 ....55 A2
 Litchfield RG28 ....42 B1
 Pamber Heath RG26 ....10 B1
Jubilee Cotts RG7 ....14 A2
Jubilee Ct RG19 ....2 C2
Jubilee Ct GU12 ....77 C3
Jubilee Hall Rd GU14 ....56 A2
Jubilee Ho GU35 ....164 C1
Jubilee La
 Farnham GU10 ....121 C3
 Grayshott GU26 ....167 A2
Jubilee Rd Aldershot GU11 ....99 C4
 Basingstoke RG21 ....69 A2
 Finchampstead RG40 ....56 C1
 Mytchett GU16 ....56 C1
 Newbury RG14 ....1 C1
Julius Cl RG24 ....68 B4
Jumps Rd GU10 ....144 C2
Junction Pl GU27 ....189 B3
Junction Rd SP10 ....106 A4
Junction Terr RG14 ....2 A1
June Dr RG23 ....68 A3
Juniper Cl Bordon GU35 ....164 A1
 Chineham RG24 ....49 A2
 Winchester SO22 ....197 B3
Juniper Ct ❶ SP9 ....79 A4
Juniper Rd GU14 ....55 A3
Jupiter Ho ④ RG21 ....9 B1
Jutland Cres SP10 ....82 C2

K

Kalis Cnr SP11 ....80 C3
Karachi Cl SP9 ....78 C4
Kashmir Ct ⑥ GU11 ....56 A1
Katherine Ct GU15 ....36 A3
Kathleen Cl RG21 ....69 A1
Kay Cres GU35 ....165 C3
Keable Rd GU10 ....122 B3
Keats Cl Basingstoke RG24 ....69 B4
 South Wonston SO21 ....153 B2
Keats Gdns GU51 ....54 A1
Keats Way GU46 ....52 C3
Keble St SO22 ....197 B3
Keeper's Hill SP11 ....104 A3
Keepers La SO51 ....192 B1
Keeps Mead RG20 ....24 B2
Keith Lucas Rd GU14 ....55 B1
Kellynch Cl GU34 ....139 C2
Kellys Wlk SP10 ....105 C4
Kelsey Ave RG40 ....16 B3
Kelsey Cl GU33 ....208 A3
Kelsey Ct GU34 ....140 A3
Kelvin Cl RG22 ....68 A1
Kelvin Hill RG22 ....68 C1
Kelvin Rd RG14 ....15 B4
Kember La RG25 ....7 C2
Kemmitt Way SP10 ....105 C4
Kempshott Gdns RG22 ....91 A4
Kempshott Ho RG22 ....68 A2
Kempshott Inf Sch RG22 ....91 A4
Kempshott Jun Sch
 RG22 ....91 A4
Kempshott La Alton GU34 ....139 C1
Kempton Ct GU14 ....55 B1
Kendal Cl GU14 ....55 B2
Kendal Gdns RG22 ....68 A1

Kendall Court Bsns Pk
GU15 . . . . .35 B2
Kendrick Rd RG14 . . . . .5 A3
Kenilworth Cl GU51 . . . . . .54 B1
Kenilworth Ct ❸ SO23 . .176 A1
Kenilworth Rd
Basingstoke RG23 . . . . .68 B3
Farnborough GU14 . . . . .55 A3
Fleet GU51 . . . . .54 A1
Kenley Rd GU35 . . . . .166 A3
Kenmore Cl
Camberley GU16 . . . . .56 A4
Fleet GU52 . . . . .75 A3
Kennedy Cl RG14 . . . . .5 A3
Kennel La
Frensham GU10 . . . . .122 A1
Littleton SO22 . . . . .175 B2
Kennels La GU14 . . . . .55 A1
Kennet Cl Ash GU12 . . . . . . .77 C1
❷ Basingstoke RG21 . . . . . .69 B3
Farnborough GU14 . . . . .55 B3
Kennet Ct
❷ Andover SP10 . . . . .83 B1
❻ Newbury RG14 . . . . .1 C2
Kennet Ctr The RG14 . . . . . . .1 C1
Kennet Pl ❿ RG14 . . . . .1 C2
Kennet Side RG14 . . . . .1 C2
Kennet Way RG23 . . . . .67 A1
Kensington Ct GU51 . . . . . .53 B2
Kensington Rd ❹ RG21 . . .69 A3
Kent Cotts RG7 . . . . .14 A2
Kent Rd Boordon SO45 . . . .164 B1
Fleet GU51 . . . . .54 A1
Kenton Cl GU16 . . . . .36 B1
Kenward Bglws RG25 . . . .114 B2
Kenwith Ave GU51 . . . . . . .54 A1
Kenyons Yd SP10 . . . . .105 C4
Keogh Cl GU12 . . . . .56 C1
Kerchers Field RG25 . . . . . .88 A4
Kerfield Way RG27 . . . . . . .51 A1
Kerrfield SO22 . . . . .197 B4
Kerrfield Mews SO22 . . . .197 B4
Kershaw Ind Est GU34 . . .140 A2
Kerry Cl GU51 . . . . .54 A3
Kersey Cres RG14 . . . . .1 B3
Kersley Cres RG29 . . . . .95 B4
Kestrel Cl Ewshot GU10 . . . .98 A4
North Tidworth SP9 . . . . .7 C4
Thatcham RG19 . . . . .2 C2
Winchester SO22 . . . . .197 B2
Kestrel Ct GU34 . . . . .139 C3
Kestrel Ho GU9 . . . . .121 C4
Kestrel Rd RG22 . . . . .67 C1
Ketchers Field GU34 . . . . .184 C3
Ketelbey Rise RG22 . . . . . .91 C4
Kevin Cl RG20 . . . . .24 C1
Kevins Dr GU46 . . . . .34 B4
Kevins Gr GU51 . . . . .54 A1
Kew Wlk SP10 . . . . .105 C4
Key The GU51 . . . . .53 B2
Keyhaven Cotts SO20 . . . .125 B1
Keynes Cl GU52 . . . . .75 A2
Kiel Dr SP10 . . . . .82 C2
Kildare Cl GU35 . . . . .164 B2
Kildare Rd GU35 . . . . .164 B2
Kilham La SO22 . . . . .197 A3
Kilmarlin Gdns GU16 . . . . .36 B1
Kilmeston Rd
Cheriton SO24 . . . . .201 B2
Kilmeston SO24 . . . . .201 B1
Kilmore Dr GU15 . . . . .36 C2
Kilmuir Cl GU47 . . . . .35 A4
Kiln Field GU51 . . . . .207 C3
Kiln Gdns RG27 . . . . .52 B3
Kiln Hill RG7 . . . . .14 C4
Kiln La Farnham GU10 . . . .122 A3
Monk Sherborne RG26 . . . . . .47 A3
Old Alresford SO24 . . . . .157 B1
Stratfield Mortimer RG7 . . . . .12 A3
Kiln Rd Newbury RG14 . . . . .1 C3
Sherborne St John RG24 . . . .47 C2
Kiln Ride RG40 . . . . .16 C4
Kiln Ride Extension
RG40 . . . . .16 C3
Kiln Way Aldershot GU11 . . .99 C4
Grayshott GU26 . . . . .166 B3
Kilns The GU34 . . . . .140 A2
Kilsby Flats SP9 . . . . .101 C4
Kimbell Rd RG22 . . . . .68 C1
Kimber Cl RG24 . . . . .48 C2
Kimber's Cl RG14 . . . . .1 B2
Kimberley GU52 . . . . .75 A2
Kimberley Cl SP10 . . . . . . .82 B1
Kimberley Rd GU33 . . . . .186 B1
Kimberly Rd RG22 . . . . .68 C1
Kimbers Dr RG14 . . . . .1 A3
Kimbers La Farnham GU9 . . .99 A2
Pamber End RG26 . . . . .27 A3
Kimpton Dr ❽ GU51 . . . . . .53 B2
Kimpton, Thruxton & Fyfield
CE Prim Sch SP11 . . . . . . .80 B1
King Alfred Pl SO23 . . . . . .176 A1
King Alfred Terr ❷❽
SO23 . . . . .176 A1
King Alfred's Coll SO22 .197 C4
King Arthur's Way SP10 . .83 A2
King George Cl GU14 . . . . .56 A1
King George Rd SP10 . . . . .83 A2
King Harold Ct SO23 . . . . .197 C3
King John Cl RG20 . . . . .24 B1
King John Rd RG26 . . . . . . .72 B2
King La SO20 . . . . .125 B2

King Lane Cotts SO20 . . . .125 B1
Kintyre Cl RG23 . . . . .67 A1
Kipling Cl GU46 . . . . .34 A2
Kipling Wlk RG22 . . . . .68 C2
Kirk Knoll GU35 . . . . .165 B3
Kirkby Ct GU16 . . . . .36 B1
Kirkee Rd SP9 . . . . .78 C3
Kitchener Rd GU33 . . . . . .186 B1
Kitchener's Rd GU11 . . . . . .77 A3
Kitcombe La GU34 . . . . . . .161 B1
Kitt's La SO24 . . . . .203 B1
Kitts La GU10 . . . . .144 B2
Kitwood La Ashford GU34 .182 B4
Kitwood Rd GU34,SO24 . . .182 A4
Knapp La RG26 . . . . .27 A3
Knight Cl
Crookham Village GU51 . . . . .74 B3
Winchester SO23 . . . . .176 A1
Knight St RG21 . . . . .68 C2
Knights Ct SP10 . . . . .83 C1
Knights Dr GU9 . . . . .83 A2
Knights Enham Schs
SP10 . . . . .83 A2
Knights La RG20 . . . . .3 C2
Knights Lea RG20 . . . . .3 C2
Knights Park Rd RG21 . . . .68 C4
Knights Rd GU9 . . . . .99 B4
Knights Way GU34 . . . . . .139 B2
Knights Yd SP11 . . . . .60 C4
Knightsbridge Dr RG19 . . . .6 C2
Knightsbridge Rd
Camberley GU15 . . . . .36 B4
Enham Alamein SP11 . . . . . . .83 B4
Knock Hundred La
GU7 . . . . .189 A4
Knockwood La SO20 . . . .147 C4
Knoll Cl GU51 . . . . .54 A1
Knoll Ct GU51 . . . . .54 A2
Knoll Rd Camberley GU15 . .36 A3
Fleet GU51 . . . . .54 A1
Knoll Wlk GU15 . . . . .36 A3
Knollys Rd Aldershot GU11 .76 B2
Pamber Heath RG26 . . . . . . .10 B1
Knook The GU47 . . . . .35 A4
Knowle Cres RG20 . . . . .24 B1
Knowles Cl GU35 . . . . . . .164 B1
Knowles Mdw GU33 . . . . .208 A1
Knowlings The RG28 . . . . . .86 B2
Knox Cl GU52 . . . . .74 B2
Knox Ct GU34 . . . . .140 A2
Kohat Cl SP9 . . . . .78 B4
Kohat Ct ❶ GU11 . . . . .76 B1
Kohat Rd SP9 . . . . .78 C3
Kohima Cl GU11 . . . . .76 C1
Krooner Rd GU15 . . . . .35 C4
Kurmool Mortar Cross Roads
GU15 . . . . .35 C3
Kyftle Court Flat RG14 . . . . .1 A4
Kynegils Rd SP11 . . . . . . .175 C1

L

Laburnam Gdns GU52 . . . .75 A3
Laburnham Dr SO23 . . . . .176 A4
Laburnum Cl GU11 . . . . . . .76 A2
Laburnum Gr RG14 . . . . . . .1 C2
Laburnum Pas ❸ GU11 . . .76 C3
Laburnum Rd
Aldershot GU11 . . . . .76 C1
Alton GU34 . . . . .139 B3
Laburnum Way RG23 . . . . .68 B4
Laburnums The GU17 . . . . .34 C3
Ladwell Cl RG14 . . . . .5 A3
Lady Gate Dr GU36 . . . . . .166 C2
Lady Godley Cl SP9 . . . . . .78 C3
Ladyplace Ct ❹ GU34 . . .139 C2
Ladysmith Pl GU35 . . . . . .164 B3
Ladywell La SO24 . . . . . . .179 B3
Ladywood Ave GU14 . . . . . .55 A2
Ladywood Ct GU10 . . . . . .121 B3
Laffan's Rd GU11 . . . . .76 A3
Laffans Rd RG26 . . . . .95 C4
Lahore Cl SP9 . . . . .78 C4
Lahore Rd SP9 . . . . .78 C3
Lake Cl RG26 . . . . .27 A4
Lake Dr GU35 . . . . .164 C2
Lake La GU10 . . . . .143 B3
Lake Rd GU16 . . . . .56 C3
Lake Side The GU17 . . . . . .35 A2
Lakeland Dr GU16 . . . . .36 B1
Lakelands RG26 . . . . .26 A4
Laker Sq SP10 . . . . .83 C1
Lakeside Bsns Pk GU47 . . . .34 A1
Lakeside Cl Ash GU12 . . . . .77 B2
Charlton SP10 . . . . .82 B3
Lakeside Ct GU51 . . . . .54 A2
Lakeside Dr RG27 . . . . .32 A2
Lakeside Gdns GU14 . . . . . .55 A4
Lakeside Rd Ash GU12 . . . . .77 B2
Farnborough GU11 . . . . .76 C4
Lakeside Sch GU16 . . . . . . .36 B1
Lama Ho GU17 . . . . .77 A1
Lamb Cl SP10 . . . . .106 B4
Lamb's Farm Bsns Pk
RG7 . . . . .13 C4
Lamb's Lane Prim Sch
RG7 . . . . .13 C4
Lambdens Wlk RG26 . . . . . .26 C4
Lambdown App SP11 . . . . .79 B4
Lambdown Terr SP11 . . . . .79 B4
Lambert Cres GU17 . . . . . . .34 C3
Lambourn Ct RG14 . . . . .1 C3
Lambourn Rd RG20 . . . . . . .1 A3
Lambourne Cl
Sparsholt SO21 . . . . .174 B2
Thruxton SP11 . . . . .103 C4
Lambourne Way
Thruxton SP11 . . . . .103 C4

Lambourne Way continued
Tongham GU10 . . . . .100 B4
Lambs Cl RG25 . . . . .88 A4
Lambs La RG7 . . . . .13 C4
Lambs Lease GU33 . . . . . .208 A2
Lambs Row RG24 . . . . .69 C4
Lambwood RG7 . . . . .11 B3
Lamerton Cl GU35 . . . . . .164 B2
Lamerton Rd GU35 . . . . . .164 B2
Lamp Acres RG14 . . . . .1 C3
Lampard La GU10 . . . . . . .144 A1
Lampards Cl RG27 . . . . .50 C3
Lampool Ho RG25 . . . . .88 A4
Lanark Cl GU16 . . . . .36 B1
Lancashire Cotts SP11 . . . .59 B1
Lancaster Ave GU9 . . . . . .122 A4
Lancaster Cl
Andover SP10 . . . . .82 C1
Farnborough GU17 . . . . .77 B3
Lancaster Dr GU15 . . . . . . .36 A3
Lancaster Rd RG21 . . . . . . .69 A3
Lancaster Way GU14 . . . . . .55 A4
Lancer Cl ❷ GU11 . . . . . . .76 B1
Landale Cl SP11 . . . . .63 A4
Lands End La GU35 . . . . . .164 C2
Landseer Cl
Basingstoke RG22 . . . . .69 B2
Sandhurst GU47 . . . . .35 B3
Landseer Ct SP10 . . . . .82 C1
Lane End Bramley RG26 . . .29 A1
West Tisted SO24 . . . . .204 B4
Lane End Bglws SO21 . . .133 A2
Lane The RG26 . . . . .27 A4
Langdale Cl GU14 . . . . .55 A3
Langdale Ct GU12 . . . . .77 B3
Langham Ct GU14 . . . . . . .122 A4
Langham Rd GU34 . . . . . .139 C2
Langley ❶ GU52 . . . . .74 C2
Langley Dr
Aldershot GU11 . . . . .99 C4
Camberley GU15 . . . . .36 A3
Langton Cl GU51 . . . . .175 C1
Langton Dr GU35 . . . . . . .165 C4
Langtons Ct SO24 . . . . . . .179 C3
Lanham La
Sparsholt SO22 . . . . .197 A4
Winchester SO22 . . . . .175 A1
Lankhills Rd SO23 . . . . . . .176 A1
Lankhills Sch SO23 . . . . . .175 C1
Lansdowne Ave
Andover SP10 . . . . .105 C3
Winchester SO23 . . . . .197 C3
Lansdowne Ct ❸ SO23 . .197 C3
Lansdowne Rd
Aldershot GU11 . . . . .76 C1
Alton GU34 . . . . .140 A3
Camberley GU16 . . . . .56 C4
Lansley Rd RG21 . . . . .69 A4
Lantern Ct SO23 . . . . .197 C3
Lapin La RG22 . . . . .91 B4
Lapwing Rise RG28 . . . . . . .86 A3
Lapwing RG22 . . . . .90 C4
Larch Cl Camberley GU15 . .36 B4
Kings Worthy SO23 . . . . . . .154 A1
Liphook GU30 . . . . .187 A3
Middle Wallop SO20 . . . . . .126 A2
Newbury RG14 . . . . .1 C2
Larch Dr Andover SP10 . . .105 B4
Kingsclere RG20 . . . . .24 B1
Larch Rd GU35 . . . . .165 C3
Larch Way GU14 . . . . .34 C3
Larches Way GU17 . . . . . . .34 C3
Larchfield Rd GU52 . . . . . . .75 A4
Larchwood GU47 . . . . .35 A2
Larchwood Glade GU15 . . .36 C4
Larg Dr SO22 . . . . .175 B2
Lark Cl Andover SP10 . . . . .83 A1
Basingstoke RG22 . . . . .90 C4
North Tidworth SP9 . . . . .79 A3
Lark Hill Rise SO22 . . . . . .197 B2
Lark Rise GU30 . . . . .187 C3
Larkfield RG14 . . . . .48 C1
Larkfield Cl GU9 . . . . .98 B1
Larkfield Rd GU9 . . . . .98 B1
Larkin Cl SP11 . . . . .57 A1
Larks Barrow Hill RG28 . .85 A3
Larkspur Cl GU11 . . . . .99 C4
Larkwhistle Farm Rd
SO21 . . . . .111 B1
Larmer Cl GU51 . . . . .54 A3
Larwood Sq SP10 . . . . .83 B1
Lasham Airfield GU34 . . . .116 B2
Lasham Rd GU51 . . . . .53 B2
Latchwood La GU10 . . . . .122 A3
Latham Ave GU16 . . . . .36 B1
Laud Cl RG14 . . . . .2 A2
Lauder Cl GU16 . . . . .36 B1
Lauderdale GU14 . . . . .55 A2
Launcelot Cl SP10 . . . . . . .83 A4
Laundry La Hackfield RG27 .31 A3
Sandhurst GU47 . . . . .35 A3
Laundry Rd RG26 . . . . .86 B3
Laurel Cl Camberley GU15 . .36 A2
Farnborough GU14 . . . . .55 B4
North Warnborough RG29 . . .72 B2
Laurel Gdns GU11 . . . . .99 C4
Laurel Gr GU10 . . . . .121 B3
Laurel Pl GU34 . . . . .126 A2
Laurels The Andover SP10 . .82 B3
Basingstoke RG21 . . . . .69 C3
Farnham GU9 . . . . .99 B4
Fleet GU51 . . . . .54 A1
Lavant Field GU34 . . . . . . .161 C4
Lavell's La RG7 . . . . .29 A4
Lavender Cr SP10 . . . . .105 C3
Lavender Gdns GU35 . . . .164 B2
Lavender La GU10 . . . . . . .121 B2
Lavender Rd RG22 . . . . .91 A4

Laverstoke La RG28 . . . . . .87 A2
Lawday Link GU9 . . . . .98 C4
Lawday Pl GU9 . . . . .98 C4
Lawday Place La GU9 . . . . .98 C4
Lawford Cres GU46 . . . . . . .34 A3
Lawn Ho ❷❶ SO23 . . . . .198 A4
Lawn Rd RG22 . . . . .175 B2
Lawn St SO23 . . . . .198 A4
Lawns The GU14 . . . . .55 B2
Lawrence Cl
Andover SP10 . . . . .82 C1
Basingstoke RG24 . . . . .48 B1
Lawrence Hos SP11 . . . . .103 A1
Lawrence La GU34 . . . . .36 A4
Lawrence Rd GU22 . . . . . . .74 C4
Lawrence Way GU15 . . . . . .35 B2
Lawrence Ct RG21 . . . . .68 C2
Laws Terr GU11 . . . . .77 A2
Lawy Field RG27 . . . . .50 C1
Le Borowe GU52 . . . . .74 C2
Le Marchant Rd
GU15 GU16 . . . . .36 B2
Lea Ct Ash GU12 . . . . .77 C1
Lea Gardens RG22 . . . .
Basingstoke RG22 . . . . .68 B3
Farnham GU9 . . . . .99 C3
Lea Ct GU9 . . . . .99 B4
Lea Rd GU15 . . . . .35 C1
Lea Springs GU51 . . . . .74 B4
Lea The
Finchampstead RG40 . . . . . .16 B4
Fleet GU51 . . . . .74 C4
Lea Way GU12 . . . . .77 B2
Lea Wood Rd GU51 . . . . . . .74 C4
Leaden Vere RG29 . . . . .95 B2
Leckford SO20 . . . . .150 B4
Leckford La SO20 . . . . . . .150 A3
Lee Ct GU11 . . . . .100 A4
Lees Hill RG29 . . . . .94 C2
Lees Mdw RG27 . . . . .51 A1
Lefroy Ave RG21 . . . . .69 B4
Lefroy Pk GU51 . . . . .53 C1
Lefroy's Field GU10 . . . . . .97 B4
Leger Cl GU52 . . . . .74 C2
Legge Cres GU11 . . . . .76 B1
Legion La SO23 . . . . .176 B4
Lehar Cl RG22 . . . . .91 B4
Leicester Pl SP10 . . . . . . .106 A4
Leicester Way SO23 . . . . .176 B1
Leigh Cl SP10 . . . . .106 B4
Leigh Field RG27 . . . . .11 B3
Leigh Gdns SP10 . . . . . . .106 B4
Leigh House Hospl
SO21 . . . . .198 C3
Leigh La GU9 . . . . .122 B4
Leigh Rd SP10 . . . . .106 B4
Leipzig Rd GU52 . . . . .75 A2
Leith Dr GU11 . . . . .76 B2
Lemon Gr GU35 . . . . .164 B1
Len Smart Ct ❷ RG21 . . . .69 B4
Lendore Rd GU16 . . . . .56 A3
Lennel Gdns GU52 . . . . . . .75 A3
Lennon Way RG22 . . . . .91 B4
Lennox Rd RG22 . . . . .68 C1
Lent Hill Ct ❸ SO22 . . . .197 B3
Lenten St GU34 . . . . .139 C2
Leonard Cl GU16 . . . . .56 A3
Leopold Ave GU14 . . . . . . .55 C3
Leslie Southern Ct ❿
RG14 . . . . .1 C1
Lestock Way GU51 . . . . . . .54 B1
Levern Dr GU51 . . . . .99 A3
Levignen Cl GU52 . . . . .74 B3
Lewendon Rd RG14 . . . . . . .1 B3
Lewis Cl ❹ RG21 . . . . .69 B4
Lewis Wlk RG14 . . . . .5 C4
Ley Rd GU14 . . . . .55 C3
Leys Gdns RG14 . . . . .1 B2
Leyton Way SP10 . . . . .105 C3
Lickfolds Rd GU10 . . . . . .121 B2
Liddell Cl RG40 . . . . .16 B2
Lightfoot Cl RG21 . . . . .69 A4
Lightsfield RG23 . . . . .67 A1
Lilac Cl Andover SP10 . . . .105 B4
Bordon GU35 . . . . .164 B1
Lilac Way RG23 . . . . .68 B4
Lilian Pl GU34 . . . . .161 B2
Lillywhite Cres SP10 . . . . .83 A2
Lily Cl RG22 . . . . .91 A4
Limbrey Hill RG25 . . . . .94 B3
Lime Ave Alton GU34 . . . .139 C3
Camberley GU15 . . . . .35 C1
Lime Cl RG14 . . . . .2 A2
Lime Cres GU12 . . . . .77 C1
Lime Dr GU51 . . . . .54 B2
Lime Gdns RG21 . . . . .69 B3
Lime Gr GU34 . . . . .139 C3
Lime Kiln Cotts The
RG20 . . . . .42 B4
Lime Rd SO24 . . . . .179 B3
Lime St GU11 . . . . .76 B1
Lime Tree Way RG24 . . . . .48 B3
Lime Wlk SP10 . . . . .105 B3
Limecroft GU46 . . . . .34 A3
Limekiln Rd SP11 . . . . .58 A4
Limes Ave RG20 . . . . .22 C4
Limes Cl Bramshott GU33 .188 A4
Liss GU33 . . . . .207 C2
Limes Rd GU14 . . . . .55 A3
Limes The Amport SP11 . .104 A4
Basingstoke RG22 . . . . .91 A4
Hartley Wintney RG27 . . . . . .32 B2
Haslemere GU27 . . . . .189 A3
Limetree Ave RG20 . . . . . . .21 C1
Limetree Wlk ❺ SO23 . . .198 A4
Limington House Sch
RG22 . . . . .68 B2
Linchmere Rd GU27 . . . . .189 A3

Lincoln Cl
Basingstoke RG22 ..... 91 A4
Camberley GU15 ..... 36 C2
Farnborough GU12 ..... 77 B3
Lincoln Ct
2 Liphook GU30 ..... 188 A2
Newbury RG14 ..... 1 B1
Lincoln Gn GU34 ..... 139 C4
Linden Ave Odiham RG29 .72 C2
Old Basing RG24 ..... 70 A3
Linden Ct Ludgershall SP11 .57 A1
Newbury RG14 ..... 1 B2
Linden Ct Camberley GU15 .36 A4
Old Basing RG24 ..... 70 A3
Linden Dr GU33 ..... 207 C2
Linden Rd
Bishop's Green RG20 ..... 6 B2
Headley SU35 ..... 166 A3
Lindens The GU9 ..... 99 A1
Lindenwood RG24 ..... 48 C2
Lindford Chase GU35 ..... 164 C3
Lindford Rd GU35 ..... 164 C3
Lindford Way GU35 ..... 164 C3
Lindum Cl 8 GU11 ..... 76 C1
Lindum Dene GU11 ..... 76 C1
Lines Rd GU11 ..... 77 A4
Lines The RG20 ..... 2 A2
Linford Rd GU35 ..... 164 C3
Ling Cres GU35 ..... 165 C3
Lingen Cl SP10 ..... 82 C2
Lingfield Cl Alton GU34 .139 C1
Old Basing RG24 ..... 70 B3
Lingfield Rd GU14 ..... 6 A4
Lingmala Gro GU52 ..... 75 A3
Link Ho 4 RG14 ..... 1 C1
Link Rd Alton GU34 ..... 140 A3
Kingsclere RG20 ..... 26 C2
Newbury RG14 ..... 1 C1
Link The Andover SP10 .105 B4
Yateley GU46 ..... 34 A4
Link View RG14 ..... 1 B4
Link Way Oakley RG23 ..... 67 A1
Thatcham RG18 ..... 2 C2
Linklater's Cotts GU17 .54 C3
Links Cotts SO24 ..... 179 B2
Links Rd SO22 ..... 175 B1
Links The GU35 ..... 164 A3
Links Way GU14 ..... 55 A2
Linkside E GU26 ..... 167 A4
Linkside N GU26 ..... 166 C4
Linkside S GU26 ..... 167 A3
Linkway Par GU52 ..... 74 C3
Linnet Cl RG22 ..... 68 A1
Linnet La RG20 ..... 6 B2
Linnets Way GU14 ..... 54 A4
Linnets Wy GU34 ..... 139 C3
Linsford Bsns Pk GU16 ..... 56 B2
Linsford La GU16 ..... 56 B2
Linsley Gdns SO24 ..... 179 B2
Linstead Rd GU14 ..... 55 B4
Linsted La GU35 ..... 166 C4
Linton Cl RG26 ..... 27 A4
Linton Dr SP10 ..... 83 A1
Lion & Lamb Way 5
GU9 ..... 98 C1
Lion & Lamb Yd 13 GU9 .98 C1
Lion Ct Haslemere GU27 .189 B4
Overton RG25 ..... 88 A4
Lion Ct RG24 ..... 69 C3
Lion Gn GU27 ..... 189 B3
Lion La GU27 ..... 189 B3
Lion Mead GU27 ..... 189 B3
Lion Way GU52 ..... 75 A3
Lions Field GU35 ..... 163 B2
Lions Hall 25 SO22 ..... 197 C4
Liphook CE Jun Sch
GU30 ..... 187 C2
Liphook Inf Sch GU30 ..... 187 C2
Liphook Rd Bordon GU35 .186 B4
Haslemere GU27 ..... 189 B3
Headley GU30,GU35 ..... 165 A4
Linchmere GU27 ..... 188 C2
Lindford GU35 ..... 164 C3
Liphook Sta GU30 ..... 188 A1
Lipscombe Cl RG14 ..... 1 B1
Lipscombe Rise GU34 .139 C3
Lisa Cl 8 RG21 ..... 69 A2
Liskeard Dr GU14 ..... 55 C3
Lisle Cl Newbury RG14 ..... 1 B3
Winchester SO22 ..... 197 A2
Lisle Ct SO22 ..... 197 C3
Lismoyne Cl GU51 ..... 53 C1
Liss Dr 8 GU51 ..... 53 B2
Liss Inf & Jun Schs
GU33 ..... 208 A2
Liss Sta GU33 ..... 207 C2
Lister Rd RG22 ..... 91 A1
Litchfield Cl SP10 ..... 82 B2
Litchfield Dr GU51 ..... 53 B2
Litchfield Ho 2 RG26 ..... 26 C4
Litchfield Rd SO22 ..... 175 B2
Litten The RG20 ..... 2 B4
Little Aldershot La RG26 .31 C1
Little Austins Rd GU9 ..... 122 A4
Little Barn Pl GU33 ..... 208 A2
Little Basing RG24 ..... 69 C4
Little Copse
Andover SP10 ..... 105 C3
Fleet GU52 ..... 74 C4
Yateley GU46 ..... 34 A4
Little Copse Chase GU14 .48 C1
Little Croft GU46 ..... 34 A3
Little Dean Ct SO20 ..... 150 A2
Little Dean Ho SO20 ..... 150 A2
Little Dean La
South Warnborough RG25 ..... 94 C3

Little Dean La continued
Upton Grey RG25 ..... 94 C3
Little Drove Rd SO20 ..... 129 A2
Little Fallow RG24 ..... 70 A4
Little Green La GU9 ..... 121 C3
Little Hatherden SP11 ..... 59 C1
Little Hayes La SO21 ..... 177 C4
Little Hoddington Cl
RG25 ..... 94 B3
Little Knowl Hill RG20 ..... 24 C2
Little London Rd RG7 ..... 27 C4
Little Minster St SO23 ..... 198 A4
Little Paddocks GU15 ..... 36 C4
Little Thurbans Cl GU9 ..... 121 C3
Little Vigo GU46 ..... 33 C2
Little Wellington St
GU11 ..... 76 C1
Little-Ann Bridge Farm
SP11 ..... 105 B3
Littlefield Cl GU12 ..... 77 C1
Littlefield Gdns GU12 ..... 77 C1
Littlefield Rd GU34 ..... 140 A2
Littlefield Sch GU30 ..... 188 A1
Littleton Cotts SP11 ..... 80 B2
Littleton La SO21 ..... 175 A3
Littleton St SO22 ..... 175 C2
Littleworth Rd GU10 ..... 100 B1
Litton Gdns RG23 ..... 67 A1
Livery Rd SP5 ..... 168 A1
Livingstone Rd
Andover SP10 ..... 83 C1
Newbury RG14 ..... 1 C1
Lock Rd GU11 ..... 77 A3
Lock Sq SP10 ..... 83 B1
Lock's La SO21 ..... 174 B2
Locke Cl SP11 ..... 105 C4
Locke Rd GU30 ..... 188 A2
Locke's Dro SP11 ..... 60 A4
Lockerley Endowed CE Prim
Sch SO51 ..... 192 A1
Lockerley Rd
Lockerley SO51 ..... 192 A1
Mottisfont SO51 ..... 192 B1
Lockram La RG7 ..... 12 A4
Locksmead 9 RG21 ..... 69 B3
Lockwood Cl GU14 ..... 55 B4
Loddon Bsns Ctr The
RG24 ..... 69 C4
Loddon Cl GU15 ..... 36 C3
Loddon Ct RG21 ..... 69 B1
Loddon Ctr RG24 ..... 69 B1
Loddon Dr RG21 ..... 69 B1
Loddon Mall 8 RG21 ..... 69 A3
Loddon Rd GU14 ..... 55 A3
Loddon Sch The RG27 ..... 49 B3
Loddon Way GU12 ..... 77 C1
Lodge Cl Aldershot GU11 ..... 100 A4
Andover SP10 ..... 105 C4
Lodge Dr SP11 ..... 81 B1
Lodge Gr GU46 ..... 34 B3
Lodge Hill Cl GU10 ..... 122 A3
Lodge Hill Rd GU10 ..... 122 A3
Lodge La SP11 ..... 58 A2
Lodge The Farnham GU9 .99 B2
Newbury RG14 ..... 1 C2
Lodsworth GU14 ..... 55 A2
Loggon Rd RG21 ..... 69 A1
Loman Rd GU16 ..... 56 C2
Lomond Cl RG23 ..... 67 A1
Londlandes GU52 ..... 74 C2
London Ct RG14 ..... 2 A2
London Rd Alton GU34 .140 B3
Andover SP10,SP11 ..... 106 C4
Basingstoke RG21 ..... 69 B2
Blackwater GU15 ..... 35 B3
Camberley GU15 ..... 36 A4
Hartley Wintney RG27 ..... 52 B3
Hill Brow GU33 ..... 208 A1
Hook RG27 ..... 51 B1
Kings Worthy SO23 ..... 176 A3
Laverstoke RG28 ..... 87 A3
Liphook GU30 ..... 188 A3
Newbury RG14 ..... 2 A2
Odiham RG29 ..... 72 C2
Odiham RG29 ..... 72 C3
Old Basing RG24,RG27 ..... 70 B3
Overton RG25 ..... 88 A4
Stockbridge SO20 ..... 150 B2
Whitchurch RG28 ..... 86 C3
London St Andover SP10 .106 A4
Basingstoke RG21 ..... 69 B3
Whitchurch RG28 ..... 86 B3
Long Beech Dr GU14 ..... 55 A2
Long Bridge GU9 ..... 99 A1
Long Cl SO23 ..... 197 C3
Long Copse Chase RG24 .48 C2
Long Copse Rd GU35 ..... 164 A3
Long Cross La RG22 ..... 91 A3
Long Garden Mews 11
GU9 ..... 98 C1
Long Gdn Way GU9 ..... 98 C1
Long Gdn Wlk GU9 ..... 98 C1
Long Gdn Wlk E GU9 ..... 98 C1
Long Gdn Wlk W GU9 ..... 98 C1
Long Gr RG26 ..... 9 A1
Long Hill GU10 ..... 100 B1
Long La Chineham RG24 .49 A1
Long Sutton RG29 ..... 96 A3
Newbury RG14 ..... 2 A4
Long Leaze SP11 ..... 61 B2
Long Rd The GU10 ..... 121 C2
Long Sutton Dr 11 GU51 .53 B2
Long Wlk SO21 ..... 176 C2
Longacre Ash GU12 ..... 77 C1

Longacre continued
Newbury RG14 ..... 5 A4
Longacre Cl GU33 ..... 208 A2
Longacre Rise RG24 ..... 48 C1
Longbarrow Cl SO21 ..... 153 C2
Longbridge Cl RG27 ..... 29 C1
Longbridge Rd RG26 ..... 28 C2
Longcroft GU10 ..... 120 A3
Longcroft 11 RG21 ..... 69 A2
Longcroft Rd RG26 ..... 24 B2
Longcroft Rd GU27 ..... 189 C3
Longdown GU52 ..... 74 C3
Longdown Cl GU10 ..... 122 A3
Longdown Lodge GU47 .34 C4
Longdown Rd GU10 ..... 122 A3
Longfellow Par RG24 ..... 69 B4
Longfield RG23 ..... 67 A2
Longfield Cl
Farnborough GU14 ..... 55 C4
North Waltham RG25 ..... 89 C1
Longfield Rd Ash GU12 ..... 77 C1
Winchester SO23 ..... 198 B4
Longford Cl GU15 ..... 36 A2
Longhope Dr GU10 ..... 121 C3
Longhouse Gn 9 SO23 .198 B4
Longleat Sq GU14 ..... 55 A2
Longley Rd GU9 ..... 99 A1
Longmead Fleet GU52 ..... 75 A3
Liss GU33 ..... 207 C2
Woolton Hill RG20 ..... 4 B1
Longmeadow GU10 ..... 120 A3
Longmoor Cl RG40 ..... 16 B3
Longmoor Ct 16 GU51 ..... 53 B2
Longmoor Dr GU30 ..... 187 A2
Longmoor La RG7 ..... 11 C4
Longmoor Rd
Basingstoke RG21 ..... 69 A2
Greatham GU33 ..... 186 A2
Liphook GU30 ..... 187 B2
Longparish CE Prim Sch
SP11 ..... 108 A2
Longparish Rd GU10 ..... 106 A4
Longparish Rd
Hurstbourne Priors RG28 ..... 85 B1
Longparish SP11 ..... 107 C1
Longs Ct RG28 ..... 86 B3
Longstock Cl
Andover SP10 ..... 105 C4
Chineham RG24 ..... 49 A2
Longstock Ct 15 SP10 ..... 106 A4
Longstock Rd SP11 ..... 128 A4
Longwater La
Eversley GU46 ..... 33 B4
Finchampstead RG40 ..... 16 B1
Longwater Rd RG40 ..... 16 B1
Lopcombe Cnr SP5 ..... 146 A2
Lord Wandsworth Coll
RG29 ..... 95 C1
Lordsfield Rd RG25 ..... 88 A4
Lordswood RG7 ..... 27 C4
Lorraine Rd GU15 ..... 36 B4
Lorraine Sch GU15 ..... 36 B4
Louisburg Rd GU35 ..... 164 B3
Louise Margaret Rd
GU11 ..... 76 C2
Loundyes Cl RG18 ..... 2 C2
Love La Andover SP10 .106 A4
Kingsclere RG20 ..... 24 B1
Newbury RG14 ..... 1 C3
Odiham RG29 ..... 72 B1
Lovedon La SO23 ..... 176 A4
Lovegroves RG24 ..... 49 A2
Lovell Cl
South Wonston SO21 ..... 153 C2
Thruxton SP11 ..... 103 B4
Lovells Wlk SO24 ..... 179 B3
Loveridge Cl
Andover SP10 ..... 83 A2
Basingstoke RG21 ..... 69 A1
Blackwater GU17 ..... 35 A3
Lovers Cl GU10 ..... 144 A4
Lovers Wood RG7 ..... 11 B3
Lovett Ho 2 GU51 ..... 53 B2
Lovett Wlk SO22 ..... 175 B2
Lovington La SO24,SO21 .178 B2
Low La RG29 ..... 99 C3
Lowa Rd SP9 ..... 78 C3
Lowden Cl SO22 ..... 197 B2
Lowe Cl GU11 ..... 76 B2
Lower Brook St
Basingstoke RG21 ..... 69 B3
Winchester SO23 ..... 198 A4
Lower Canes GU46 ..... 33 C3
Lower Charles St GU15 .36 B3
Lower Chestnut Dr RG21 .68 C2
Lower Church La 16 GU9 .98 C1
Lower Church Rd GU47 .34 B4
Lower Comm RG27 ..... 50 C3
Lower Evingar Rd RG28 .86 B3
Lower Farm Ct GU14 ..... 2 B1
Lower Farnham Rd
GU11,GU12 ..... 100 A4
Lower Hanger GU27 ..... 189 A3
Lower Lamborough La
SO24 ..... 201 B3
Lower Moor GU46 ..... 34 A3
Lower Mount St 10 GU51 .53 B2
Lower Neatham Mill La
Alton GU34 ..... 140 B3
Alton, Neatham GU34 ..... 140 C3
Lower Nelson St GU11 ..... 76 C1
Lower Newport Rd GU12 .77 A2
Lower Pool Rd GU34 .159 B2
Lower Rd GU27 ..... 32 A2
Lower Raymond Almshouses
12 RG14 ..... 1 B1
Lower Rd SO21 ..... 153 B2
Lower Sandhurst Rd
RG40 ..... 16 C1

Lower South View GU9 ..... 99 A2
Lower St GU27 ..... 189 C3
Lower Stanmore La
SO23 ..... 197 C3
Lower Turk St GU34 ..... 139 C2
Lower Way RG19 ..... 2 C2
Lower Weybourne La
GU9 ..... 99 C3
Lower Wote St RG21 ..... 69 A3
Loweswater Gdns GU35 .164 B3
Lowicks Rd GU10 ..... 144 C3
Lowlands Rd
Basingstoke RG22 ..... 68 A2
Blackwater GU17 ..... 35 A2
Lowndes Bldgs GU9 ..... 98 C2
Lowry Cl GU47 ..... 35 A3
Lowry Ct SP10 ..... 82 C1
Loyalty La RG24 ..... 70 A3
Lubeck Dr SP10 ..... 82 C2
Lucas Cl GU46 ..... 34 A3
Lucas Field GU27 ..... 189 B3
Ludgershall Castle Prim Sch
SP11 ..... 57 A1
Ludgershall Rd SP9 ..... 78 C4
Ludlow Cl
Basingstoke RG23 ..... 68 B3
Camberley GU15 ..... 56 C4
Newbury RG14 ..... 2 B2
Ludlow Gdns RG23 ..... 68 B3
Ludshott Gr GU35 ..... 165 C3
Lugg La GU34 ..... 99 B4
Luke Rd E GU11 ..... 99 B4
Lulworth Cl GU14 ..... 55 C4
Lundy Cl RG24 ..... 48 B1
Lune Cl 8 RG21 ..... 69 B3
Lune Ct 4 SP10 ..... 83 B1
Lupin Cl RG22 ..... 91 A4
Lutyens Cl
Basingstoke RG24 ..... 69 C4
Chineham RG24 ..... 48 C1
Lyall Pl GU9 ..... 98 C4
Lych Gate Cl GU47 ..... 34 B4
Lyde Cl RG23 ..... 67 A1
Lydford Cl
Camberley GU16 ..... 56 C4
Farnborough GU14 ..... 55 C4
Lye Copse Ave GU14 ..... 55 C4
Lyeway La GU34,SO24 .182 B2
Lyeway Rd SO24 ..... 182 A3
Lyford Rd RG21 ..... 69 A3
Lymbourne Ave GU46 ..... 34 A3
Lymington Barn Ind Est
GU34 ..... 160 A2
Lymington Bottom
GU34 ..... 160 A1
Lymington Bottom Rd
Four Marks GU34 ..... 160 A1
Medstead GU34 ..... 160 A2
Lymington Cl
Basingstoke RG22 ..... 91 A4
Farnborough GU14 ..... 55 C4
Lymington Rise GU34 ..... 160 A1
Lymington St 5 RG21 ..... 69 B3
Lynams GU21 ..... 74 C2
Lynch Cl SO22 ..... 175 C1
Lynch Hill RG28 ..... 86 B3
Lynch Hill Pk RG28 ..... 86 B3
Lynch Rd GU9 ..... 99 B1
Lynch The Overton RG25 .87 C4
Whitchurch RG28 ..... 86 B3
Lynchborough Rd GU30 .187 A4
Lynchford Rd
Farnborough GU14 ..... 77 A4
Farnborough GU14 ..... 77 B4
Lyndale Dr GU51 ..... 54 B1
Lyndford Terr GU52 ..... 74 C4
Lyndhurst Ave
Aldershot GU11 ..... 100 A3
Blackwater GU17 ..... 35 A3
Lyndhurst Cl SO22 ..... 175 B2
Lyndhurst Dr RG22 ..... 91 B3
Lyndhurst Rd GU15 ..... 35 C3
Lyndsey Cl GU14 ..... 54 C4
Lynford Ave SO22 ..... 175 C1
Lynford Way SO22 ..... 175 C1
Lynn Way GU14 ..... 54 B4
Lynton Cl GU9 ..... 121 C4
Lynton Ct RG14 ..... 1 C2
Lynton Mdw SO22 ..... 129 A2
Lynton Rd GU35 ..... 164 B2
Lynwood Cl GU35 ..... 165 A3
Lynwood Dr
Andover SP10 ..... 105 C4
Mytchett GU16 ..... 56 C2
Lynwood Gdns GU27 ..... 51 A1
Lyon Way GU16 ..... 56 C2
Lyons Dr GU11 ..... 76 C1
Lyons Rd GU11 ..... 76 C1
Lyons Way GU12 ..... 77 B4
Lytham Cl GU35 ..... 165 A3
Lytton Rd RG21 ..... 69 B3

M

Mabbs La RG27 ..... 52 B2
Mac Callum Rd SP11 ..... 83 A4
Macadam Way SP10 ..... 82 A1
Macdonald Rd GU9 ..... 98 C4
McDonald's Almshouses 33
GU9 ..... 98 C1
Macklin Ho 33 SO22 ..... 197 C4
Macnaghten Woods
GU15 ..... 36 B3

Macrae Rd GU46 ..... 34 A3
Maddocks Hill SO24 ..... 181 A2
Madeira Cl RG24 ..... 48 B1
Madeira Pl 5 RG14 ..... 1 C1
Madeley Rd GU52 ..... 75 A3
Madox Brown End GU47 .35 B3
Madrid Rd SP10 ..... 83 B1
Magdalen Hill SO23 ..... 198 A4
Magdalen Mews 48
SO23 ..... 198 A4
Magellan Cl SP10 ..... 83 C1
Magnolia Cl SP10 ..... 105 C4
Magnolia Rd RG24 ..... 48 A1
Magnolia Way GU52 ..... 75 A3
Magpie Cl
Basingstoke RG22 ..... 90 C4
Bordon GU35 ..... 164 C1
Ewshot GU10 ..... 98 A4
Magpie La
Thatcham RG19 ..... 2 C2
Main St RG19 ..... 3 C3
Mainline Bsns Ctr GU33 .207 C2
Maidhall Rd GU14 ..... 76 C4
Maitlands Cl GU10 ..... 100 B3
Majendie Cl RG14 ..... 1 A3
Majestic Rd RG22 ..... 91 A3
Majorca Ave SP10 ..... 83 B1
Makins Cl SO24 ..... 179 A2
Maldive Rd RG24 ..... 48 B1
Malham Gdns RG22 ..... 91 A3
Mall The Andover SP10 .106 A4
South Tidworth SP9 ..... 78 B2
Mallard Cl Andover SP10 .83 A1
Basingstoke RG22 ..... 91 A4
Basingstoke RG22 ..... 90 C4
Haslemere GU27 ..... 189 B3
New Alresford SO24 ..... 179 B3
Mallard Ct
Mallard Way 4 GU46 ..... 33 C3
Mallards GU34 ..... 139 C3
Mallards The GU16 ..... 36 B1
Mallow Cl GU35 ..... 165 A1
Malmesbury Gdns SO22 .175 B1
Malmesbury Ho 1 SP9 ..... 79 A3
Malmspey Rd GU35 ..... 164 B1
Malpass Rd SO21 ..... 153 B1
Malshanger La RG23 ..... 67 A2
Malta Cl RG24 ..... 48 A1
Maltbys GU34 ..... 160 A1
Malters End GU16 ..... 166 C2
Malthouse Bridge Cotts
GU11 ..... 74 B3
Malthouse Cl Fleet GU52 .74 C2
Itchen Abbas SO21 ..... 176 C2
Malthouse Cotts RG29 ..... 72 B2
Malthouse Ct GU30 ..... 188 A2
Malthouse La
Bighton SO24 ..... 158 B1
Smannell SP11 ..... 83 B4
Tadley RG26 ..... 27 A3
Upper Chute SP11 ..... 58 A4
Malthouse Mdws GU30 .188 A2
Malthouse Mews GU34 .140 B3
Maltings Cl GU34 ..... 139 C2
Maltings The
Bramley RG26 ..... 28 C1
Liphook GU30 ..... 188 A2
Malvern Cl RG21 ..... 68 C2
Malvern Ct RG14 ..... 1 C1
Malvern Rd
Farnborough GU14 ..... 55 A4
Hawley GU47 ..... 34 B1
Hill Brow GU33 ..... 208 A1
Malvern Ct Farnham GU9 .99 B2
Newbury RG14 ..... 2 A1
Mandora Rd GU11 ..... 76 C2
Manfield Rd GU12 ..... 77 C1
Manica Cl GU35 ..... 164 B2
Manley Bridge Rd GU10 .121 B3
Manley James Cl RG29 ..... 72 C2
Manley Rd RG29 ..... 86 B2
Manningford GU23 ..... 176 A2
Manor Bridge Ct SP9 ..... 78 C4
Manor Cl
Abbotts Ann SP11 ..... 105 A2
Alton GU34 ..... 140 A3
Basingstoke RG22 ..... 91 A3
Haslemere GU27 ..... 189 B3
Shipton Bellinger SP9 ..... 77 C4
Tongham GU10 ..... 100 B4
Winchester SO23 ..... 198 A4
Manor Copse SP10 ..... 83 A3
Manor Cotts 87 A3
Manor Cres GU27 ..... 189 B3
Manor Ct GU52 ..... 75 A2
Manor Farm Bsns Ctr
GU10 ..... 100 B3
Manor Farm Cl GU11 ..... 77 A1
Manor Farm Cotts SO21 .131 A1
Manor Farm La SO51 ..... 193 C1
Manor Field Ind Sch
RG22 ..... 91 C4
Manor Fields
Liphook GU30 ..... 188 A2
Seale GU10 ..... 100 C2
Manor Gdns GU10 ..... 122 A3
Manor Ho The
Camberley GU15 ..... 36 A3

Manor Ho The continued
Fleet GU51 . . . . .53 C1
Manor House Farm
SO24 .180 B2
Manor House Flats
GU10 .100 B3
Manor Inf & Jun Schs
GU14 . . . . .55 B3
Manor La Brimpton RG7 . . .8 A3
Old Basing RG24 . . . . .70 A3
Thatcham RG14 . . . . .2 B3
Manor Lea GU27 . . . . .189 B3
Manor Park Cotts
3 Alton GU34 . . . . .139 C2
Alton, Wilsom GU34 . . . . . . .140 A2
Manor Park Ctr, Farnborough
Coll of Tech GU11,GU12 . .76 C1
Manor Park Dr
Finchampstead RG40 . . . . . . .16 B3
Yateley GU46 . . . . .34 B3
Manor Park Ind Est GU12 .77 A1
Manor Pl RG14 . . . . .1 A3
Manor Rd Aldershot GU11 .99 C4
Alton GU34 . . . . .140 A3
Andover SP10 . . . . .82 C1
East Tytherley SP5 . . . . .191 C4
Farnborough GU14 . . . . .56 A2
Farnham GU9 . . . . .99 B2
Sherborne St John RG24 . . .47 C2
Tongham GU10,GU12 . . . . .100 B4
Manor Rise SP11 . . . . .105 C2
Manor View RG7 . . . . .8 B4
Manor Wlk GU12 . . . . .76 C1
Manse La RG26 . . . . .27 A3
Mansell Dr RG14 . . . . .5 A3
Mansfield Rd RG22 . . . . . . .68 C1
Mansion Dr RG27 . . . . .32 A2
Mansion House St 10
RG14 . . . . .1 C2
Maple Cl Alton GU34 . . . . .139 C3
Ash GU12 . . . . .77 B4
Blackwater GU17 . . . . .35 A3
Middle Wallop SO20 . . . . . .126 A2
New Alresford SO24 . . . . . .179 B2
Maple Cres
Basingstoke RG21 . . . . .69 A4
Ludgershall SP11 . . . . .57 A1
Newbury RG14 . . . . .1 C2
Maple Ct RG22 . . . . .68 A2
Maple Dr SO23 . . . . .176 A4
Maple Gdns GU46 . . . . .34 A3
Maple Gr RG26 . . . . .26 C4
Maple Leaf Cl GU14 . . . . . . .55 B2
Maple Leaf Dr GU35 . . . . .166 B2
Maple Ridge Sch RG21 . . .69 A4
Maple Terr 5 SP9 . . . . .79 A4
Maple Way GU35 . . . . .165 C3
Maple Wlk
Aldershot GU12 . . . . .100 A4
Andover SP10 . . . . .105 B3
Maplehurst Chase RG22 . .91 A3
Maplewood RG24 . . . . .48 C2
March Cl SP10 . . . . .83 A1
Marchant Cl RG10 . . . . .6 A4
Marchant Rd SP10 . . . . . . .105 C4
Marchants Hill Activity Ctr
GU26 . . . . .167 A4
Marconi Rd RG14 . . . . .1 C2
Mareth Cl GU11 . . . . .76 C1
Margaret Rd RG22 . . . . .91 A2
Marguerite Cl RG26 . . . . . . .28 C2
Marigold Cl RG22 . . . . .91 A4
Mariners Cl RG26 . . . . .27 A3
Mariners Dr GU14 . . . . .56 A3
Marine Way RG45 . . . . .15 C3
Mark La 3 RG21 . . . . .69 A2
Mark Way SO51 . . . . .191 B2
Market Pl
Basingstoke RG21 . . . . .69 A2
11 Newbury RG14 . . . . .1 C2
Market Sq 6 GU34 . . . . . . .139 C2
Market St Alton GU34 . . . .139 C2
Newbury RG14 . . . . .1 C1
Winchester SO23 . . . . .198 A4
Markham Ct GU15 . . . . .36 A3
Markson Rd SO21 . . . . .153 B2
Marl's La RG14 . . . . .48 A3
Marlborough Cl GU51 . . . .75 B4
Marlborough Gdns RG43 .67 A1
Marlborough Inf Sch
GU11 . . . . .77 A4
Marlborough Rise GU15 . .36 B3
Marlborough St SP10 . . . .106 A4
Marlborough Trad Mews
RG24 . . . . .49 B1
Marlborough View GU14 . .55 A3
Marley Combe Rd GU27 .189 B2
Marley Hanger GU27 . . . .189 C2
Marley La GU27 . . . . .189 B2
Marlowe Cl RG24 . . . . .48 B4
Marlowes The RG14 . . . . . . .5 B4
Marmel Com Inf Sch
RG24 . . . . .48 B1
Marnel Jun Sch RG24 . . . .48 B1
Marrowbrook Cl GU14 . . .55 C2
Marrowbrook La GU14 . . .55 C2
Mars Ho 10 RG22 . . . . .91 B1
Marsden Cl RG28 . . . . .97 B3
Marsh Cl GU35 . . . . .164 C2
Marsh Farm Bsns Ctr
GU10 . . . . .74 B1

Marsh La Bentley GU10 . . .120 B3
Eversley RG27 . . . . .33 B4
Newbury RG14 . . . . .1 C2
Marshal Cl GU34 . . . . .139 C1
Marshall Cl GU14 . . . . .55 B4
Marshall Gdns RG25 . . . . . .68 A4
Marshall Rd GU47 . . . . .35 A3
Marshall Sq SP10 . . . . .83 B1
Marshalls GU34 . . . . .121 C4
Marshalls Ct RG14 . . . . .1 A3
Marshcourt RG24 . . . . .69 C4
Marston Dr
Farnborough GU14 . . . . .55 C4
Newbury RG14 . . . . .2 A3
Marston Gate 5 SO23 . .198 A4
Marston Rd RG19 . . . . .98 B1
Marsum Cl SP10 . . . . .82 C2
Martin Cl
Basingstoke RG21 . . . . .69 B3
North Tidworth SP9 . . . . .79 A3
Martin Way Andover SP10 .83 A1
Camberley GU16 . . . . .36 B1
Martingale Ct 8 GU11 . . . .76 B1
Martins Cl Alton GU34 . . . .140 A3
Blackwater GU17 . . . . .35 A2
Martins Fields SO21 . . . . .177 B3
Martins La SO20 . . . . .129 B2
Martins Wood RG24 . . . . . . .48 C2
Marwell Rd GU51 . . . . .53 B2
Mary La
Newton Valence GU34 . . . .183 A4
North Waltham RG25 . . . . . . .89 C1
Mary Rose Ct RG21 . . . . . . .68 C2
Mary Rose Mews GU14 . .140 A3
Maryland RG40 . . . . .16 B4
Masdar Gdns RG40 . . . . . . .16 B3
Maskell Way GU14 . . . . .55 A2
Mason Cl RG20 . . . . .4 B1
Mason Pl GU47 . . . . .34 B4
Mason Rd GU14 . . . . .55 B3
Mason Way GU11 . . . . .99 C4
Mathew Terr GU11 . . . . .77 A1
Mathews Cl GU14 . . . . .77 B4
Mathias Wlk RG22 . . . . .91 B4
Matilda Dr RG22 . . . . .91 A4
Matilda Pl 3 SO23 . . . . . . .198 A4
Matthew Rd GU11 . . . . .99 B4
Matthews Rd GU15 . . . . . . .36 A4
Matthews Way RG23 . . . . . .67 B1
Mattingley Dr 12 GU51 . .53 B2
Mattock Way RG24 . . . . . . .48 C2
Maultway Cl GU15 . . . . .36 C4
Maultway Cres GU15 . . . . .36 C4
Maultway N GU15 . . . . .36 C4
Maultway The GU15 . . . . . .36 C4
Mavins Rd GU9 . . . . .122 A4
Maw Cl RG22 . . . . .91 A4
May Cl Headley GU35 . . . . .165 B2
Old Basing RG24 . . . . .70 B3
Sandhurst GU47 . . . . .35 A4
May Cres GU12 . . . . .77 B1
May Pl RG21 . . . . .69 A2
May St RG21 . . . . .68 B4
May Tree Cl SO22 . . . . .197 B2
May Tree Rd SP10 . . . . .82 B1
May's La RG7 . . . . .10 C4
Maybrook RG24 . . . . .48 C2
Maybury Cl GU16 . . . . .56 A4
Mayfair Cl GU51 . . . . .53 B2
Mayfair Dr RG14 . . . . .1 B1
Mayfair Ho 10 RG21 . . . . . .69 A3
Mayfield GU10 . . . . .121 B2
Mayfield Ave Ind Pk
SP11 . . . . .81 A1
Mayfield Cl Farnham GU9 .99 C2
Shipton Bellinger SP9 . . . . .101 B4
Mayfield Com Inf & Jun Schs
GU14 . . . . .55 C3
Mayfield Ct GU46 . . . . .33 A4
Mayfield Rd
Camberley GU15 . . . . .35 C1
Farnborough GU14 . . . . .55 B3
Mayfield Ridge RG22 . . . . .91 B3
Mayflower Cl RG24 . . . . . . .48 C1
Mayflower Dr GU46 . . . . . . .33 C4
Mayflower Rd GU35 . . . . .164 B1
Mayhill Jun Sch RG20 . . . .72 C1
Maynard's Wood RG24 . . . .48 C1
Mayors La RG14 . . . . .1 C1
Maywood Dr GU15 . . . . .36 B2
Mc Carthy Way RG40 . . . . .16 B4
McCartney Wlk RG22 . . . . .91 B4
McFauld Way RG28 . . . . . . .86 B2
Mckay Cl GU11 . . . . .77 A2
Mckernan Ct GU47 . . . . . . .34 B4
McNaughton Cl GU14 . . . . .55 A2
Mead Cl SP10 . . . . .105 C4
Mead Hatchgate RG27 . . . .51 A1
Mead Hedges SP10 . . . . . .105 C4
Mead Hedges Footpath
SP10 .105 C4
Mead La GU9 . . . . .98 C1
Mead Rd Andover SP10 . . .105 C4
Hindhead GU26 . . . . .167 B2
Winchester SO23 . . . . .197 C2
Mead The
Farnborough GU14 . . . . .55 C2
Liphook GU30 . . . . .187 C3
Liss GU33 . . . . .207 C2
Old Basing RG24 . . . . .70 A3
Meade Rd SP11 . . . . .57 A1
Meadham La RG26 . . . . .44 C2
Meadow Bank GU9 . . . . .98 C1
Meadow Cl Ash GU12 . . . . .56 B1
Blackwater GU17 . . . . .35 A2
Liphook GU30 . . . . .188 A2
New Alresford SO24 . . . . . .179 B3

Meadow Ct
Farnborough GU14 . . . . .55 B2
10 Fleet GU51 . . . . .53 C1
Meadow Dr SP11 . . . . .127 C4
Meadow End GU30 . . . . . .188 A3
Meadow La RG27 . . . . .52 B3
Meadow Rd
Basingstoke RG21 . . . . .69 A1
Farnborough GU14 . . . . .55 C4
Newbury RG14 . . . . .5 B4
Meadow Rise RG25 . . . . . . .89 C1
Meadow Spec Sch
GU35 .165 A2
Meadow Vale GU27 . . . . . .189 C3
Meadow View
Bordon GU35 . . . . .164 C2
Fleet GU52 . . . . .74 C3
Micheldever SO21 . . . . .133 A2
Ropley SO24 . . . . .181 B3
Whitchurch RG28 . . . . .86 A3
Meadow Way
Aldershot GU12 . . . . .77 B2
Blackwater GU17 . . . . .35 A3
Farnham GU10 . . . . .121 B2
Liphook GU30 . . . . .188 A3
Winchester SO22 . . . . .197 B2
Meadow Wlk Fleet GU51 . .74 B4
5 Liss GU33 . . . . .207 C2
Meadowbank RG20 . . . . .3 C4
Meadowland
Chineham RG24 . . . . .48 C2
Knaphill GU21,SO23 . . . . . .176 A4
Meadowridge RG22 . . . . . . .91 B3
Meadows The Ash GU12 . . .77 C1
Churt GU10 . . . . .144 B1
Sandhurst GU47 . . . . .35 B3
Sherfield on Loddon RG27 . .29 B1
Meadowview Cl SP11 . . . . .79 B3
Meads The GU27 . . . . .189 B3
Meadsview Ct 4 GU11 . . . .77 A2
Meadway Camberley GU16 .36 B1
Haslemere GU27 . . . . .189 B3
Mede Cl RG25 . . . . .88 A4
Medina Cl 4 SP10 . . . . .83 B1
Medina Gdns RG23 . . . . . . .67 A1
Medlar Dr GU17 . . . . .35 B2
Medonte Cl GU17 . . . . .35 A2
Medstead & Four Marks Sta
GU34 .160 A2
Medstead CE Prim Sch
GU34 .159 C3
Medstead Dr 6 GU51 . . . . .53 B2
Medstead Rd GU34 . . . . . .139 A1
Medway Ave RG23 . . . . .67 A1
Medway Cl RG18 . . . . .2 B2
Medway Ct
45 Andover SP10 . . . . .83 B1
5 Basingstoke RG21 . . . . . .69 A3
Medway Dr GU14 . . . . .55 B4
Meerut Rd SP9 . . . . .78 C3
Meitner Cl RG26 . . . . .28 C2
Meldrum Cl RG14 . . . . .5 A3
Melford Gdns RG22 . . . . . . .68 A1
Meliot Rise SP11 . . . . .106 A3
Melksham Ho 1 SP9 . . . . .78 C3
Mellersh Cl GU52 . . . . .74 C2
Melrose Ave GU14 . . . . .55 A2
Melrose Cl GU35 . . . . .164 B1
Melrose Wlk RG24 . . . . .69 A4
Melville Ave GU16 . . . . .36 B1
Melville Terr 1 GU9 . . . . . . .98 C1
Membury Cl GU16 . . . . .56 C4
Memorial Bglws RG25 . . . .87 A3
Memorial Rd RG27 . . . . .72 A4
Mendip Cl RG22 . . . . .68 A2
Mendip Rd GU14 . . . . .55 B4
Menin Way GU9 . . . . .99 A1
Meon Cl
Farnborough GU14 . . . . .55 A3
Tadley RG26 . . . . .11 A3
Meon Rd RG23 . . . . .67 A1
Meon Wlk RG21 . . . . .69 B3
Mercer Cl RG22 . . . . .90 C4
Merchants Pl 17 SO23 . .198 A4
Mercia Ave SP10 . . . . .82 B2
Mercury Cl GU35 . . . . .164 C2
Meriden Ct 13 SO23 . . . . .176 A1
Merivale GU51 . . . . .74 A4
Merlin Cl GU16 . . . . .36 A1
Merlin Mead RG22 . . . . .90 C3
Merlin Rd GU14 . . . . .160 A1
Merlin Way GU14 . . . . .55 B2
Merlins Cl GU9 . . . . .99 A1
Merriatt Cl RG21 . . . . .69 A1
Merrileas Gdns RG22 . . . . .91 A3
Merron Cl GU46 . . . . .34 A3
Merrydown La RG24 . . . . . .49 A4
Merryfield RG24 . . . . .48 C2
Merrywood Pk GU15 . . . . . .36 B2
Merryworth Cl GU17 . . . . . .35 A1
Mersey Ct 50 SP10 . . . . . . .83 B1
Merton Jun & Inf Schs
RG24 . . . . .69 A4
Merton Rd RG23 . . . . .67 A1
Meryon Rd SO24 . . . . .179 B2
Mesh Rd SO51 . . . . .193 A1
Methuen Rd GU33 . . . . . . .186 B2
Meudon Ave GU14 . . . . .55 A3
Mews La GU27 . . . . .189 C3
Mews The Andover SP10 .106 A3
Bramley RG26 . . . . .29 A1
Farley Castle RG7 . . . . .15 A4
6 Farnham GU9 . . . . .99 A1
Newbury RG14 . . . . .1 B1
Meyrick Dr RG14 . . . . .5 A3

Michael Ho SP11 . . . . .83 A4
Michaelmas Cl GU46 . . . . .34 A2
Michaelmas Dro SP11 . . . .81 A1
Micheldever CE Prim Sch
SO21 .133 A2
Micheldever Cl RG28 . . . . .86 B2
Micheldever Dr RG21 . . . . .69 A1
Micheldever Gdns RG28 . .86 B2
Micheldever Rd
Andover SP10,SP11 . . . . . .106 A4
Whitchurch RG28 . . . . .86 C2
Micheldever Sta SO21 . . .111 A1
Mid Hants Railway
Watercress Line*
GU34 .179 C3
Mid Hants Rly Watercress
Line* RG24 . . . . .179 C3
Midas Ho 8 RG7 . . . . .8 A3
Middle Ave GU9 . . . . .122 A4
Middle Bourne La GU10 .122 A4
Middle Brook St SO23 . . .198 A4
Middle Church La 3
GU9 . . . . .98 C1
Middle Cl Camberley GU15 .36 C3
Newbury RG14 . . . . .1 B3
Middle Gordon Rd GU15 . .36 A3
Middle Head RG27 . . . . .51 A1
Middle Hill GU11 . . . . .76 C2
Middle Mdw GU33 . . . . . . .208 A2
Middle Old Pk GU9 . . . . . . .98 B2
Middle Rd SO22 . . . . .197 C4
Middle Wallop Airfield
SO20 .126 A1
Middlefield GU19 . . . . .121 C4
Middlefield Cl GU19 . . . . .121 C4
Middlemead RG27 . . . . .51 A1
Middlemoor Rd GU16 . . . . .56 B4
Middleton Ct RG14 . . . . .2 A3
Middleton Gdns
Basingstoke RG21 . . . . .69 A4
Farnborough GU14 . . . . .55 B3
Middleton Rd
Camberley GU15 . . . . .36 A3
Middle Winterslow SP5 . . .168 A3
Middleway The SP11 . . . . .107 B3
Midhurst Rd
Haslemere GU27 . . . . .189 C3
Liphook GU30 . . . . .188 A1
Midlane Cl RG21 . . . . .69 A1
Mike Hawthorn Dr GU9 . .99 A2
Milden Cl GU16 . . . . .56 C3
Milden Ct GU16 . . . . .56 C3
Mildmay Ct Odiham RG29 .72 C2
50 Winchester SO23 . . . .198 A4
Mildmay St SO22 . . . . .197 B3
Mildmay Terr RG27 . . . . . . .52 B3
Miles Rd GU12 . . . . .77 A1
Milestones Living History
Mus* RG22 . . . . .68 C3
Milkingpen La RG24 . . . . . .70 A4
Mill Chase Com Sch
GU35 .164 C2
Mill Chase Rd GU35 . . . . .164 C2
Mill Cl Haslemere GU27 . .189 B3
Sherfield on Loddon RG27 . .29 C1
Mill Cnr GU51 . . . . .53 C4
Mill Copse Rd GU27 . . . . .189 C2
Mill Hall Sch RG19 . . . . .6 A4
Mill Hill GU47 . . . . .179 B3
Mill Hill Ave SP9 . . . . .78 C4
Mill La Alton GU34 . . . . .140 A2
Bishop's Sutton SO24 . . . . .180 A3
Ecchinswell RG20 . . . . .23 C2
Fair Oak Green RG7 RG27 . .29 A3
Frensham GU10 . . . . .143 C4
Hawkley GU33 . . . . .184 C1
Headley GU35 . . . . .165 A3
Kings Worthy SO21 . . . . . . .176 B3
Longparish SP11 . . . . .108 B3
Middle Winterslow SP5 . . .168 A4
North Warnborough SP9 . . . .72 A4
Rotherwick RG27 . . . . .50 B3
Sandhurst GU46 . . . . .34 A4
Steep Marsh GU32 . . . . . . .206 C1
Yateley GU46 . . . . .34 A4
Mill Lane Ind Est GU34 . .140 A2
Mill Rd Basingstoke RG24 .68 B4
Liss GU33 . . . . .208 A3
Mill Reef Cl RG19 . . . . .2 C2
Mill Rise SO51 . . . . .192 B1
Mill Stream GU9 . . . . .99 B3
Mill View RG29 . . . . .72 B2
Milland Rd SO23 . . . . .198 A3
Millard Cl RG21 . . . . .69 A1
Millbridge Rd GU46 . . . . . . .33 C4
Millbrook Cl GU33 . . . . . . .208 A2
Milldown Ho RG25 . . . . .88 A4
Millennium Cl RG21 . . . . . .68 C3
Millennium Ctr GU9 . . . . . .98 C1
Millers La SO22 . . . . .196 C2
Millers Rd RG26 . . . . .26 C4
Millers Yd SO21 . . . . .131 B2
Millgate Ct GU9 . . . . .99 A2
Millgreen La RG19 . . . . .7 B1
Millmere GU46 . . . . .34 A4
Mills Ho GU12 . . . . .77 A1
Millstream St SP10 . . . . . .105 C3
Millstream Ho RG14 . . . . . . .2 A2
Millstream The GU27 . . . .189 B3
Millway Cl SP10 . . . . .105 C4
Millway Rd SP10 . . . . .105 C4
Milman Ct 11 SO23 . . . . . .198 A4
Milner Pl SO22 . . . . .197 C3
Milnthorpe La GU22 . . . . .197 C4
Milsons The SO20 . . . . . . .149 C1
Milton Ave SP10 . . . . .82 B1
Milton Cl RG24 . . . . .49 A4
Milton Grange GU12 . . . . . .77 C3

Milverton Rd SO22 . . . . . .197 C4
Mimosa Cl GU35 . . . . .165 A3
Mimosa Ct SP10 . . . . .105 C3
Minchens La RG26 . . . . .28 C2
Minden Cl Charlton SP10 . .82 C2
Chineham RG24 . . . . .48 C1
Minden Way SO22 . . . . . . .197 B3
Minehurst Rd GU16 . . . . . . .56 B2
Minerva Ho 5 RG7 . . . . .9 B1
Ministry Rd RG19 . . . . .6 C3
Minley Cl GU14 . . . . .55 B2
Minley Gr GU51 . . . . .54 A2
Minley Rd
Farnborough GU17 . . . . .54 C4
Fleet GU51 . . . . .54 A2
Hawley GU17 . . . . .54 C4
Minshull Ct 6 SP10 . . . . . .105 C4
Minstead Cl Tadley RG26 . .26 C3
Winchester SO22 . . . . .175 B2
Minstead Dr GU46 . . . . .34 A3
Minster Ct
Camberley GU15 . . . . .36 A4
Camberley, York Town
GU15 . . . . .35 B2
Minster La 13 SO23 . . . . .198 A4
Mint Rd SO23 . . . . .208 A3
Minter Cl 8 RG26 . . . . .9 B1
Mistletoe Rd GU46 . . . . .34 A2
Mitchell Ave RG27 . . . . .52 B3
Mitchell Bldgs GU46 . . . . . .33 C3
Mitchell Cl SP10 . . . . .82 B1
Mitchell Gdns RG22 . . . . . .91 B4
Mitford Rd SO24 . . . . .179 B2
Moat Cl RG26 . . . . .28 C2
Moffatts Cl GU47 . . . . .34 C4
Mole Cl GU14 . . . . .55 A3
Momford Rd SO22 . . . . . . .197 A2
Monachus La RG27 . . . . . . .50 B4
Monarch Cl RG22 . . . . .91 A3
Monarch Way SO22 . . . . . .197 B3
Moneyer Rd SP10 . . . . .82 C2
Mongers Piece RG24 . . . . .49 A2
Monier Williams Rd
SO21 . . . . .108 A2
Monk Sherborne Ho
RG26 . . . . .46 C4
Monk Sherborne Rd
RG26 . . . . .46 C4
Monk's La RG14 . . . . .5 B4
Monk's Wlk GU9 . . . . .122 B4
Monkey Puzzle Rdbt
GU14 . . . . .55 B2
Monks Cl
Farnborough GU14 . . . . .56 A2
North Tidworth SP9 . . . . .78 C4
Monks Rd SO23 . . . . .176 A1
Monks Rise GU51 . . . . .53 B3
Monks' Well GU10 . . . . .99 C1
Monkshanger GU9 . . . . .99 B1
Monkswood Cl RG14 . . . . . .5 B4
Monkswood Cres RG26 . . .26 C4
Monkton La GU9 . . . . .99 B3
Monkton Pk GU9 . . . . .99 B3
Monktons La RG7 . . . . .12 A3
Monmouth Sq SO22 . . . . .197 A3
Mons Cl GU11 . . . . .77 B4
Mons The SO23 . . . . .197 C4
Montacute Cl GU14 . . . . . . .55 C3
Montague Cl GU15 . . . . .35 C3
Montague Pl 18 RG21 . . . .69 A2
Montague Terr RG14 . . . . . .5 C4
Monteagle La GU46 . . . . . . .33 C3
Montgomery Cl
Sandhurst GU47 . . . . .34 C4
Winchester SO22 . . . . .197 B3
Montgomery Ho 5 SP9 . . .78 C4
Montgomery Rd
Longparish SP11 . . . . .108 B3
Newbury RG14 . . . . .1 C3
Montreal Wlk GU30 . . . . . .188 A2
Montrose Cl
Bordon GU35 . . . . .164 C1
Camberley GU16 . . . . .36 B1
Fleet GU51 . . . . .75 A4
Montserrat Pl RG24 . . . . . .48 A1
Montserrat Rd RG24 . . . . . .48 A1
Monument Chase GU35 . .164 C1
Monument Ct RG14 . . . . .5 A4
Monxton Rd
Andover SP10,SP11 . . . . . .105 A4
Grateley SP11 . . . . .103 B1
Moody's Hill SP5 . . . . .190 B1
Moor Cl Bordon GU35 . . . .122 A1
Moor Ct RG24 . . . . .164 A2
Finchampstead RG40 . . . . . .16 B4
Moor Court La SO21 . . . . .174 A2
Moor La RG14 . . . . .1 B2
Moor Park Ho GU9 . . . . . . .99 C1
Moor Park Way GU9 . . . . . . .99 B1
Moor Place Farm RG27 . . .32 A3
Moor Rd Bordon GU33 . . .186 B1
Camberley GU15 . . . . .36 B4
Liphook GU30 . . . . .188 A1
Linchmere GU27 . . . . .205 C4
Moor View RG24 . . . . .49 A2
Moorcroft Cl SO21 . . . . . . .131 B2
Moorcroft Gdns RG22 . . . .68 A2
Moore Cl Andover SP10 . . . .83 A1
Fleet GU52 . . . . .75 A3
Tongham GU10 . . . . .100 B4
Moore Rd GU32 . . . . .75 A3
Moorfield Cl GU27 . . . . . . .189 B3
Moorhams Ave RG22 . . . . . .91 A3
Moorings The
Basingstoke RG22 . . . . .69 B3
Grayshott GU26 . . . . .167 B3
Moorlands Cl Fleet GU51 . .75 A4

Moorlands Cl continued
Hindhead GU26 ... 167 B2
Moorlands Rd GU11 ... 35 C2
Moorlands Rd GU15 ... 35 C2
Moors Ct RG40 ... 16 B4
Moors The GU10 ... 100 B4
Moorside Cl GU14 ... 35 C1
Moorside Rd SO23 ... 176 B1
Moot Cl SP10 ... 83 A2
Moray Ave GU47 ... 35 A4
More House Sch GU10 ... 122 A1
Moreland Cl GU34 ... 140 A1
Morestead Rd
  Winchester SO21 ... 198 C2
  Winchester SO23 ... 198 A2
Moreton Cl Churt GU10 ... 148 B1
  Fleet GU52 ... 74 C2
Morgaston Rd RG24,RG26 ... 47 C4
Morland Rd GU11 ... 100 A3
Morley Cl GU46 ... 33 C3
Morley Rd
  Basingstoke RG21 ... 69 A1
  Farnham GU9 ... 99 A1
Mornington Ave RG40 ... 16 B4
Mornington Cl
  Andover SP10 ... 106 A3
  Baughurst RG26 ... 9 B1
Mornington Dr SO22 ... 175 B1
Mornington Rd GU35 ... 164 A1
Morris Rd GU14 ... P77 A4
Morris St RG27 ... 71 C4
Morse Rd RG22 ... 68 C2
Mortimer Cl
  Hartley Wintney RG27 ... 52 A2
  Kings Worthy SO23 ... 176 A3
Mortimer Gdns RG26 ... 27 A4
Mortimer Hall RG7 ... 12 A3
Mortimer La
  20 Basingstoke RG21 ... 69 A3
  Stratfield Mortimer RG7 ... 12 A4
  West End Green RG7 ... 29 A4
Mortimer St John's CE Sch
  RG7 ... 11 C3
Mortimer Sta RG7 ... 12 B3
Morton Cl GU16 ... 56 B4
Morval Cl GU14 ... 54 B2
Morval Rd GU46 ... 34 B1
Moselle Cl GU14 ... 55 A3
Moss Cl GU33 ... 208 A2
Moss Rd SO23 ... 198 A4
Mothes Ho RG26 ... 27 A4
Mottisfont Abbey (NT)*
  SO51 ... 192 C1
Mottisfont Abbey Gdns*
  SO51 ... 192 C2
Moulsham Copse La
  GU46 ... 33 C4
Moulsham La GU46 ... 33 C4
Mount Carmel Rd SP11 ... 124 C3
Mount Cl Highclere RG20 ... 21 B3
  Newbury RG14 ... 1 C1
  Winchester SO22 ... 175 C2
Mount Hermon Rd
  SP11 ... 124 C3
Mount Hts SP5 ... 146 B2
Mount Pleasant
  Amport SP11 ... 104 A3
  Farnham GU9 ... 98 C1
  Hartley Wintney RG27 ... 52 B3
  Kings Worthy SO23 ... 176 B3
  Laverstoke RG28 ... 87 A3
  Tadley RG26 ... 26 C4
Mount Pleasant Dr RG26 ... 26 C4
Mount Pleasant Rd
  Aldershot GU12 ... 77 A1
  Alton GU34 ... 139 C1
  Headley GU35 ... 165 C3
Mount Rd RG20 ... 21 B4
Mount The Fleet GU51 ... 54 A1
  Headley GU35 ... 165 C3
Mount View GU11 ... 76 C1
Mount View Rd SO22 ... 197 A2
Mountbatten Cl RG14 ... 2 A3
Mountbatten Ct
  14 Aldershot GU11 ... 76 C1
  Andover SP10 ... 83 B1
Mountbatten Dr SO22 ... 175 C2
Mountbatten Pl SO23 ... 176 B4
Mounter's La GU34 ... 139 B1
Mounters La GU34 ... 139 B1
Mounts Way GU51 ... 53 B2
Mountsom's La GU34 ... 141 C2
Mourne Cl RG22 ... 68 A2
Mowatt Rd GU30 ... 167 A1
Mozart Cl RG22 ... 91 C4
Mud La RG27 ... 15 B1
Mulberries The GU9 ... 99 C4
Mulberry Cl Ash GU12 ... 77 C2
  Sandhurst GU47 ... 35 A4
Mulberry Ct GU34 ... 160 B2
Mulberry Ho 3 SP10 ... 106 A4
Mulberry Mead RG28 ... 86 B3
Mulberry Way RG24 ... 48 C2
Mulfords Hill 8 RG26 ... 26 C4
Mulgrave Rd GU16 ... 36 B1
Mull Cl RG23 ... 67 A1
Mullins Cl RG21 ... 69 A4
Mulroy Dr GU15 ... 54 B3
Munnings Cl RG21 ... 69 B2
Munnings Ct SP10 ... 82 C1
Munnings Dr GU47 ... 35 B3
Munro Way GU11 ... 77 A4
Murray Cl SP10 ... 105 C3
Murray Rd GU14 ... 55 B2
Murray's Rd GU11 ... 77 A3
Murrell Green Bsns Pk
  RG27 ... 51 C1
Murrell Rd GU12 ... 77 C2

Murrells La GU15 ... 35 C2
Mus of Army Flying
Explorers' World*
  SO20 ... 126 A2
Museum of the Iron Age*
  SP10 ... 106 A4
Musgrave Ct RG22 ... 91 B4
Musgrove Gdns GU34 ... 139 C2
Musket Copse RG24 ... 70 A3
Muss La SO20 ... 172 A2
Myland Ct RG21 ... 69 B4
Mylen Bsns Ctr SP10 ... 105 C4
Mylen Rd SP10 ... 82 C1
Myrtle Dr GU17 ... 64 B3
Mytchett Heath GU16 ... 56 C2
Mytchett Lake RG GU16 ... 56 C1
Mytchett Place Rd GU16 ... 56 B2
Mytchett Prim Sch GU16 ... 56 B2
Mytchett Rd GU16 ... 56 B2

N
Naafi Rdbt GU11 ... 76 C1
Nadder Rd SP9 ... 78 C3
Nairn Cl GU16 ... 36 B1
Napier Cl Ash GU11 ... 77 B4
  North Tidworth SP9 ... 79 A3
Napier La GU17 ... 77 C2
Napier Wlk SP10 ... 83 B1
Napoleon Ave GU14 ... 55 C3
Napoleon Dr RG23 ... 68 B4
Naseby Rise RG14 ... 2 A3
Nash Cl Basingstoke RG21 ... 69 B4
  Farnborough GU14 ... 55 B2
Nash Grove La RG40 ... 16 B4
Nash Mdws RG29 ... 95 A2
Nately Rd GU15 ... 71 C1
Nations Hill SO23 ... 176 B3
Naylors The RG7 ... 14 A3
Neath Rd RG21 ... 69 B3
Neelem Ct 5 GU14 ... 56 A1
Nelson Cl Aldershot GU12 ... 77 A1
  Farnham GU9 ... 99 A4
  Stockbridge SO20 ... 149 C1
Nelson Rd Farnham GU9 ... 99 A4
  Winchester SO23 ... 198 B3
Nelson St GU11 ... 76 C1
Nelson Way GU15 ... 35 B2
Nelson Wlk SP10 ... 83 B1
Nene Cl 7 SP10 ... 83 B1
Nepaul Rd SP9 ... 78 C4
Neptune Rd GU35 ... 164 C1
Nestor Cl SP10 ... 82 C1
Nether St 1 GU34 ... 139 C2
Nether Vell-Mead GU52 ... 74 C2
Nethercliffe Sch SO22 ... 175 C1
Netherfield Cl GU34 ... 139 C2
Netherhouse Ct GU51 ... 74 B3
Netherhouse Moor GU51 ... 74 B3
Netley St GU14 ... 77 A4
Nettlebeds La GU34 ... 158 A1
Neuvic Way RG28 ... 86 B2
Nevada Cl GU14 ... 55 A2
Neville Cl Andover SP10 ... 106 A3
  Basingstoke RG21 ... 69 A1
Neville Duke Rd GU14 ... 55 B4
New Barn Cl GU51 ... 74 B4
New Barn Cotts SO21 ... 152 C1
New Barn La Alton GU34 ... 139 C1
  Wherwell SP11 ... 128 C4
New Bldgs SP11 ... 58 B4
New Bridge La 10 RG21 ... 69 B3
New Cotts Bighton SO24 ... 158 B1
  South Warnborough RG29 ... 95 A2
  Sutton Scotney SO21 ... 131 B2
New Ct SO21 ... 131 B2
New Dawn Cl GU14 ... 55 A2
New Farm Cotts RG21 ... 95 B1
New Farm Rd
  East Stratton SO21 ... 134 A2
  West Alresford SO24 ... 179 A2
New Hall SO23 ... 198 A3
New House La SP11 ... 81 A4
New La SO20 ... 172 A2
New Mill La RG27 ... 30 C1
New Mill Rd RG40 ... 15 B2
New North Dr RG27 ... 49 C4
New Odiham Rd GU34 ... 139 B3
New Paddock Cl GU34 ... 140 B3
New Rd Basingstoke RG21 ... 69 B4
  Blackwater GU17 ... 35 B2
  Bordon GU35 ... 164 B1
  Eversley GU46 ... 33 B4
  Fleet GU52 ... 75 A3
  Hartley Wintney RG27 ... 52 B3
  Hook RG27 ... 72 A4
  Linchmere GU27 ... 189 B3
  Littleton SO22 ... 175 A3
  Micheldever SO21 ... 111 A1
  Newbury RG14,RG19 ... 6 A4
  North Warnborough RG29 ... 72 B2
  Over Wallop SO20 ... 147 B4
  Pamber End RG26 ... 27 B2
  Sandhurst GU47 ... 34 C4
  Stratfield Mortimer RG7 ... 12 A4
  Tongham GU10 ... 100 B3
New St Andover SP10 ... 83 A1
  Basingstoke RG21 ... 69 A2
  Stockbridge SO20 ... 149 C1
  Stratfield Saye RG7 ... 29 C4
New The GU12 ... 77 C1
New Villas RG20 ... 3 C2
Newall Rd SP11 ... 105 A4
Newark Rd GU47 ... 34 B1

Newbold Rd RG14 ... 1 A3
Newburgh St SO23 ... 197 C4
Newbury Coll RG14 ... 1 B2
Newbury Com Hospl RG14 ... 1 B1
Newbury Rd
  Andover SP10,SP11 ... 83 A3
  Enham Alamein SP10,SP11 ... 83 A3
  Kingsclere RG20 ... 24 A2
  Whitchurch RG28 ... 86 B4
  Newbury Ret Pk RG14 ... 5 C4
Newbury St RG28 ... 86 B3
Newbury St Nicolas CE Jun
  Sch RG14 ... 1 C1
Newbury Sta RG14 ... 1 C1
Newchurch Rd RG26 ... 9 C1
Newcomb Cl SP10 ... 106 A3
Newcombe Pl GU12 ... 100 A4
Newcome Rd GU9 ... 99 B3
Newfield Ave GU11 ... 55 B3
Newfield Rd GU12 ... 77 C3
  Liss GU33 ... 208 A3
Newlands Cl GU46 ... 34 A3
Newlands Dr GU12 ... 77 C2
Newlands Prim Sch
  GU46 ... 34 A3
Newlands Rd GU15 ... 35 C1
Newman La GU34 ... 140 A3
Newmans Ct GU9 ... 98 C4
Newnham La RG24 ... 70 C4
Newnham Pk RG27 ... 71 C4
Newnham Rd RG27 ... 71 C4
Newport Cl RG14 ... 1 C2
Newport Jun Sch GU17 ... 77 A1
Newport Rd
  Aldershot GU12 ... 77 A1
  Newbury RG14 ... 1 C2
Newton La GU34 ... 183 C4
Newton Pk SP10 ... 82 A1
Newton Rd GU14 ... 56 A3
Newton Toney CE Prim Sch
  SP4 ... 123 A3
Newton Villas SP11 ... 57 A1
Newton Way GU10 ... 100 B4
Newtown Rd
  Liphook GU30 ... 188 A2
  Newbury RG14,RG19,RG20 ... 5 C4
  Sandhurst GU47 ... 34 C4
Nexus Pk GU12 ... 77 B4
Nicholson Pl SO24 ... 179 A3
Nickel Cl SO23 ... 198 A4
Nicola Ct GU12 ... 77 A1
Nicotiana Ct 7 SP10 ... 74 C2
Night Owls RG19 ... 6 A4
Nightingale Cl
  Farnborough GU14 ... 55 A3
  Winchester SO22 ... 197 B3
Nightingale Dr GU16 ... 56 C2
Nightingale Gdns
  Hook RG27 ... 51 A1
  Sandhurst GU47 ... 34 C4
  Sherborne St John RG24 ... 68 B4
Nightingale La RG7 ... 12 A3
Nightingale Rd GU47 ... 35 B3
Nightingale Rise RG25 ... 88 A4
Nightingales The RG14 ... 5 C4
Nightjar Cl GU10 ... 98 A4
Nine Acres GU32 ... 207 A1
Nine Mile Ride RG40 ... 14 C2
Nine Mile Ride Ind RG40 ... 16 A3
Nine Mile Ride Prim Sch
  RG40 ... 16 B3
Norden Cl RG21 ... 69 A3
Norman Cl GU35 ... 164 C4
Norman Court La GU34 ... 105 C2
Norman Ct GU9 ... 99 A1
Norman Gate Sch GU11 ... 83 B1
Norman Rd SO23 ... 197 C3
Normandy Mews 10
  GU34 ... 139 C2
Normandy St GU34 ... 140 A2
Normans SO23 ... 197 C3
Normanton Rd RG21 ... 69 A4
Normay Rise RG14 ... 5 A3
Norn Hill RG21 ... 69 B4
Norn Hill Cl RG21 ... 69 B3
Norris Cl GU35 ... 164 A1
Norris Gdns SO21 ... 153 B2
Norris Hill RG27 ... 75 B4
Norris Ho RG25 ... 88 A4
North Acre GU11 ... 108 B3
North Ave GU9 ... 99 A4
North Camp Sta GU12 ... 77 B4
North Cl Aldershot GU12 ... 77 B1
  Farnborough GU14 ... 55 C4
North Dr SO22 ... 175 A3
North End SO20 ... 170 A4
North End Farm Cotts
  SO24 ... 201 B4
North Farm Rd GU14 ... 55 C4
North Farnborough Inf Sch
  GU14 ... 56 A3
North Field RG25 ... 67 A1
North Foreland Lodge Sch
  RG27 ... 49 C3
North Fryerne GU34 ... 34 A4
North Gate Rd GU14 ... 56 A1
North Hampshire Hospl The
North Hill Cl SO22 ... 175 C2
North Hill Ct SO22 ... 175 C1
North La Aldershot GU12 ... 77 A1
  West Tytherley SP5 ... 169 A1
North Lodge Ind Pk
  GU30 ... 188 A3
North Mall 18 GU51 ... 53 C1

North Par GU35 ... 164 B3
North Rd Ash GU12 ... 77 B2
  Farnborough GU11 ... 77 A4
  Kings Worthy SO23 ... 154 A1
North Row RG26 ... 28 C2
North Side GU10 ... 100 B4
North St
  Bishop's Sutton SO24 ... 180 B3
  Kingsclere RG20 ... 24 A1
  North View SO22 ... 197 C4
North View Gdns 14 RG14 ... 1 C2
North View Rd RG26 ... 27 A4
North Walls SO23 ... 198 A4
North Waltham Prim Sch
  RG25 ... 89 C1
North Warnborough St
  RG29 ... 72 A2
North Way SP10 ... 83 C1
Northanger GU34 ... 139 C2
Northbrook SO21 ... 168 C1
Northbrook Ave SO23 ... 198 B4
Northbrook Cl RG14 ... 1 C2
Northbrook Pl SO23 ... 198 B4
Northbrook Rd GU11 ... 99 C4
Northbrooke Ct 11
  SO23 ... 198 B4
Northcote Rd Ash GU12 ... 77 C4
  Farnborough GU14 ... 55 B3
Northcott Cl RG27 ... 95 A2
Northcroft La RG14 ... 1 B2
Northcroft Terr RG27 ... 52 B3
Northern Ave
  Andover SP10 ... 83 A1
  South Wonston SO21 ... 153 B2
Northfield Cl
  Aldershot GU12 ... 77 A1
  Fleet GU52 ... 75 B3
Northfield Rd Fleet GU52 ... 75 B3
  Oakley RG23 ... 29 B1
  Thatcham RG18 ... 2 C2
Northfields La GU34 ... 161 B4
Northgate Chambers 9
  SO23 ... 198 A4
Northgate La RG25 ... 67 A1
Northgate Way RG22 ... 91 A3
Northington Cnr SO21 ... 134 A2
Northington Rd SO24 ... 58 A4
Northlands Dr SO21 ... 176 A1
Northmead GU14 ... 55 C2
Northside La GU34 ... 180 C3
Northtown Trad Est
  GU12 ... 77 B4
Northumberland Rd 10
  SO23 ... 164 B1
Northway RG41 ... 1 C1
Northwick RG46 ... 33 B4
Northwood Dr RG14 ... 2 A2
Norton Cl RG14 ... 5 A3
Norton Cotts SO21 ... 131 B4
Norton Rd RG14 ... 5 A3
Norton Ridge RG24 ... 69 C4
Norwich Ave GU15 ... 36 B2
Norwich Cl RG22 ... 91 A4
Novello Cl RG22 ... 91 B4
Nuffield Rd RG22 ... 15 B4
Nugent Cl SO21 ... 176 A1
Nursery Cl
  Camberley GU16 ... 56 B4
  Chineham RG24 ... 49 A2
  Fleet GU51 ... 75 A4
  Fleet GU52 ... 51 A1
Nursery Field GU33 ... 207 C2
Nursery Gdns SO22 ... 197 B4
Nursery Rd Alton GU34 ... 140 A2
  New Alresford SO24 ... 179 B4
  Taylors Lane RG29 ... 72 B2
Nutbane Cl SP10 ... 105 C4
Nutbane La SP11 ... 81 C4
Nutbeam La RG7 ... 14 B3
Nutbourne GU9 ... 99 A4
Nutchers Dro SO20 ... 172 A2
Nutcombe La GU27 ... 189 B4
Nutfield Cl SO21 ... 36 A4
Nuthatch Cl GU10 ... 98 A4
Nutley Cl Bordon GU35 ... 164 C4
  Yateley GU46 ... 34 A3
Nutley Dr 8 GU43 ... 53 B2
Nutmeg Cl GU14 ... 55 A3
Nutshell La GU9 ... 99 A3
Nutter's La RG2 ... 34 A4

O
O'Bee Gdns RG26 ... 9 B1
O'Connor Rd GU11 ... 77 B4
O'Gorman Rd GU14 ... 55 C1
Oak Bank SP10 ... 106 A3
Oak Cl Basingstoke RG21 ... 69 B3
  Baughurst RG26 ... 26 A4
  Farnham GU9 ... 77 A4
  Middle Wallop SO20 ... 126 A2
  North Tidworth SP9 ... 79 A4
  Oakley RG23 ... 67 A1
  Overton RG25 ... 88 A4
Oak Cotts GU27 ... 189 B3
Oak Ct GU52 ... 74 C3
  Farnham GU9 ... 98 C1
Oak Dr RG14 ... 1 B1
Oak Farm Cl GU17 ... 35 A3
Oak Farm Com Sch GU14 ... 55 B3
Oak Grove Cres GU15 ... 35 B3
Oak Hanger Cl RG27 ... 51 A1
Oak Hill SO24 ... 179 B3
Oak Ho 3 GU46 ... 55 C4
Oak Lodge 2 GU35 ... 164 B1
Oak Rd GU14 ... 56 A2

Oak Ridge Cl RG14 ... 5 B4
Oak Tree Cl
  Aldershot GU12 ... 100 B4
  Ash GU12 ... 56 B1
  Chilbolton SO20 ... 129 A2
  Headley GU35 ... 56 B2
  8 Tadley RG26 ... 9 C1
Oak Tree Cotts RG25 ... 70 C3
Oak Tree Dr GU33 ... 208 A2
Oak Tree La GU27 ... 189 A3
Oak Tree View GU27 ... 96 B2
Oak Tree Way RG27 ... 51 A1
Oakdene GU34 ... 139 C3
Oaken Copse GU52 ... 75 A2
Oaken Copse Cres GU14 ... 55 C4
Oaken Gr RG14 ... 5 A4
Oakfield Rd
  Blackwater GU17 ... 35 B2
  Pamber Heath RG26 ... 10 B1
Oakfields GU15 ... 35 C3
Oakfields Cl RG20 ... 23 B2
Oakgreen Par GU34 ... 160 B2
Oakhanger Rd GU35 ... 164 A3
Oakhill Rd GU35 ... 165 C3
Oakhurst GU26 ... 167 A2
Oakland Ave GU9 ... 99 B4
Oakland Rd RG26 ... 86 B3
Oakland Terr RG27 ... 52 B3
Oaklands
  Hartley Wintney RG27 ... 52 B3
  South Wonston SO21 ... 153 B2
  Tadley RG26 ... 9 A4
Oaklands Cl SO22 ... 197 B3
Oaklands Way RG22 ... 68 B4
Oaklea GU12 ... 77 C3
Oaklea Dr RG27 ... 15 B1
Oaklea Gdns RG26 ... 29 B1
Oaklea Ho GU26 ... 167 A2
Oakley CE Jun Sch RG23 ... 67 A1
Oakley La RG23 ... 67 A1
Oakley Rd 11 Fleet GU51 ... 53 C1
  Hartley Wintney RG27 ... 52 B3
Oakley Rd Bordon GU35 ... 164 B3
  Camberley GU15 ... 35 C2
  Hannington RG26 ... 8 B2
  Mottisfont SO51 ... 192 C2
  Newbury RG14 ... 2 A2
Oakmead RG26 ... 28 C2
Oakridge Ctr RG21 ... 69 B4
Oakridge Jun & Inf Schs
  RG21 ... 69 A4
Oakridge Rd RG21 ... 69 A4
Oakridge Twrs 11 RG21 ... 69 B4
Oaks The GU11 ... 105 C4
  Blackwater GU17 ... 35 B2
  Farnborough GU14 ... 55 A3
  Fleet GU51 ... 53 B1
  Tadley RG26 ... 26 C4
  Yateley GU46 ... 34 A3
Oaktree Rd GU35 ... 164 B1
Oaktree Way GU34 ... 139 B3
  Farnham GU9 ... 98 C3
Oakway Aldershot GU12 ... 100 A4
  Bentley GU10 ... 120 A3
Oakway Dr GU16 ... 36 B1
Oakwood Chineham RG24 ... 48 C2
  Fleet GU52 ... 75 A2
Oakwood Dr GU34 ... 139 C1
Oakwood Inf Sch GU47 ... 52 B3
Oast House Cres GU9 ... 99 A3
Oast House La GU9 ... 99 C4
Oasthouse Dr GU51 ... 54 B2
Oasts The RG29 ... 95 B2
Oates Mus, Gilbert White's
  Ho* GU34 ... 184 C4
Oban Cl RG23 ... 67 A1
Obelisk Way GU15 ... 36 A3
Oberursel Way GU11 ... 76 B1
Ochil Cl RG22 ... 91 A3
Ockham Hall GU35 ... 142 A1
Octavia Hill SO22 ... 197 B3
Octavian Cl RG22 ... 91 A4
Oddfellows Rd RG14 ... 1 B1
Odette Gdns RG26 ... 10 A1
Odiham Cottage Hospl
  RG29 ... 72 C1
Odiham Rd Ewshot GU10 ... 98 B4
  Heckfield RG27 ... 14 A1
  Odiham RG29 ... 73 A4
Officers Row RG26 ... 29 A1
Oglander Rd SO23 ... 176 A1
Olaf Cl SP10 ... 83 A2
Old Acre Rd GU34 ... 139 C1
Old Barn Cl RG25 ... 89 C1
Old Barn La GU10 ... 144 C1
Old Basing Inf Sch RG24 ... 70 A3
Old Basing Mall 14 RG21 ... 69 A3
Old Bath Rd RG14 ... 1 A2
Old Beggarwood La
  RG22 ... 91 A3
Old Bisley Rd GU16 ... 36 A3
Old Brick Kiln Trad Est The
  RG26 ... 46 C4
Old Brickfield Rd GU11 ... 99 C4
Old Canal Pl RG21 ... 69 B3
Old Chapel La GU12 ... 122 A4
Old Comm Cl RG25 ... 69 B2
Old Common Way RG21 ... 69 B2
Old Compton La GU9 ... 99 A1
Old Cove Rd GU51 ... 54 A2
Old Ct RG29 ... 72 C1

Old Dairy The SO21 . . . . .177 A3
Old Dean Rd GU15 . . . . . .36 A4
Old Down Cl RG22 . . . . . .68 A1
Old Down Rd SP10 . . . . . .82 C1
Old English Dr SP10 . . . . .82 C2
Old Farm Pl GU12 . . . . . .77 B2
Old Farnham La
  Bentley GU10 . . . . .97 C1
  Farnham GU9 . . . . .122 A4
Old Forge End GU47 . . . . .34 C4
Old Forge Gdns SO20 . . .170 A4
Old Frensham Rd GU10 .122 B2
Old Fromans Farm
  SO20 . . . . .172 A2
Old Gdns SO22 . . . . . . .175 C1
Old Green La GU15 . . . . . .36 A4
Old Guildford Rd GU16 . .56 C3
Old Heath Way GU9 . . . . .99 A4
Old Hill The SP10 . . . . . .82 C3
Old Hillside Rd SO22 . . .175 B1
Old Iron Foundry The
  SO20 . . . . .171 C2
Old Kempshott La RG22 . .68 A2
Old Kennels Cl SO22 . . .197 A2
Old Kennels La SO22 . . .197 A2
Old Kiln GU9 . . . . .98 C1
Old Kiln Cl GU10 . . . . . .144 B1
Old Kiln Ctyd 13 GU9 . . .98 C1
Old Kiln La GU10 . . . . . .144 B1
Old La Aldershot GU11 . . .99 A4
  Ashford Hill RG19 . . . . . . .8 B1
  Frensham GU10 . . . . . .143 B2
  Kintbury RG20 . . . . .3 B4
Old Litten La GU34 . . . . .206 B2
Old London Rd SO20 . . .150 A2
Old Micheldever Rd
  SP11 . . . . .107 A3
Old Mill Pl GU27 . . . . . .189 B4
Old Newtown Rd RG14 . . .1 B1
Old Odiham Rd GU34 . . .139 C3
Old Orchard The GU9 . . .121 C4
Old Palace Farm SO20 . .172 A1
Old Park Cl GU9 . . . . . . .98 C3
Old Park Farm GU35 . . .142 B1
Old Park La GU9 . . . . . . .98 C2
Old Park Rd SO24 . . . . .180 C1
Old Pasture Rd GU16 . . . .36 B2
Old Pond Cl GU15 . . . . . .36 A1
Old Portsmouth Rd GU15 .36 C3
Old Potbridge Rd RG27 . .52 A1
Old Pump House Cl
  GU51 . . . . .54 A1
Old Quarry The GU27 . . .189 B2
Old Reading Rd RG21 . . . .69 B3
Old Rectory Ct GU12 . . . .77 C1
Old Rectory Gdns
  Farnborough GU14 . . . . . .56 A2
  Kings Worthy SO21 . . . .176 B3
Old Salisbury Rd SP11 . .105 A2
Old School Cl Ash GU12 . .77 C2
  Fleet GU51 . . . . .54 A1
  Hartley Wintney RG27 . . .52 B3
Old School La GU46 . . . . .34 A3
Old School Rd Hook RG27 .71 C4
  Liss GU33 . . . . .207 C2
Old School Terr 图 GU51 . .54 A1
Old Station App SO23 . .198 A4
Old Station Rd SO21 . . .177 C3
Old Station Way GU35 . .164 A3
Old Stockbridge Rd
  Middle Wallop SO20 . . . .125 B3
  Over Wallop SO20 . . . . .125 B3
Old Stoke Rd
  South Wonston SO21 . . .154 A4
  Wonston SO21 . . . . . . .154 A4
Old Town Mews 15 GU9 . .98 C1
Old Vicarage La SO20 . . .12 A2
Old Vyne La RG26 . . . . . .26 B1
Old Welmore GU46 . . . . .34 B3
Old Winton Rd SP10 . . .106 A3
Old Wolting Rd RG22 . . . .68 B2
Oldberg Gdns RG22 . . . . .91 C4
Oldbury Cl GU16 . . . . . . .56 B4
Oldcorne Hollow GU46 . . .33 C1
Olde Farm Dr GU17 . . . . .34 C3
Oldenburg Cl SP10 . . . . . .82 C2
Oldfield View RG27 . . . . .52 B3
Oldwood Chase GU14 . . . .55 A2
Oliver Rise GU34 . . . . . .139 C2
Oliver's Battery Cres
  SO22 . . . . .197 A2
Oliver's Battery Gdns
  SO22 . . . . .197 A2
Oliver's Battery Prim Sch
  SO22 . . . . .197 B2
Oliver's Battery Rd N
  SO22 . . . . .197 A3
Oliver's Battery Rd S
  SO22 . . . . .197 A2
Oliver's La RG26 . . . . . . .29 A2
Oliver's Wlk GU9 . . . . . . .69 C4
Olivia Ct RG26 . . . . .29 A3
Omega Pk GU34 . . . . . . .140 A2
Omni Bsns Ctr GU34 . . .140 A2
Onslow Ct GU14 . . . . . . .48 C1
Ontario Way GU30 . . . . .188 A2
Openfields GU35 . . . . . .165 B3
Orange Gr SP11 . . . . . . .124 C3
Orange La SO20 . . . . . . .125 B1
Orbit Cl RG40 . . . . .16 B3
Orchard Cl Ash GU12 . . . .77 C3
  Farnborough GU17 . . . . . .34 C3
  Farnham GU9 . . . . .99 C3
  Linchmere GU27 . . . . . .189 B3
  New Alresford SO24 . . . .179 B2

Orchard Cl continued

  Newbury RG14 . . . . .2 A3
  South Wonston SO21 . . .153 B2
Orchard Cotts SP11 . . . . .58 A2
Orchard Ct GU10 . . . . . . .97 B3
Orchard End GU10 . . . . .121 B2
Orchard Fields GU51 . . . .53 C1
Orchard Gate GU47 . . . . .34 C4
Orchard Gdns GU22 . . . .100 A4
Orchard Ho Alton GU34 . .140 A2
  Tongham GU10 . . . . . . .100 B4
Orchard La GU34 . . . . . .140 A2
Orchard Rd Andover SP10 .82 C1
  Basingstoke RG22 . . . . . .68 B2
  Farnborough, Cove Green
    GU14 . . . . .55 C2
  Farnham GU9 . . . . .99 C3
  Mortimer RG7 . . . . .11 C3
  South Wonston SO21 . . .153 B2
Orchard Terr GU34 . . . . .140 A2
Orchard The
  Kingsclere RG20 . . . . . . .24 B1
  Overton RG25 . . . . .88 A4
  Tadley RG26 . . . . .27 A4
Orchard Way SO22 . . . . .100 A4
Orchard Wlk SO22 . . . . .175 B1
Orchardene RG14 . . . . . . .1 C2
Orchid Ct SP10 . . . . . . .105 B3
Ordnance Rd
  Aldershot GU11 . . . . .77 A2
  North Tidworth SP9 . . . . .78 C3
Ordnance Rdbt GU11 . . . .76 C1
Oregon Wlk RG40 . . . . . .16 B4
Oriel Hill GU15 . . . . .36 A2
Orient Dr SO22 . . . . . . .175 B2
Orkney Cl RG24 . . . . .48 B1
Orpheus Ho 2 RG7 . . . . . .9 B1
Orts Rd RG1 . . . . .4 C4
Orwell Cl GU14 . . . . .55 B3
Osborn Rd GU9 . . . . .99 A2
Osborn Way RG27 . . . . . .72 A4
Osborne Cl Alton GU34 . .139 B2
  Camberley GU16 . . . . . . .56 B4
Osborne Ct GU14 . . . . . . .55 B3
Osborne Dr GU52 . . . . . . .75 A4
Osborne Rd
  Andover SP10 . . . . .106 A4
  Farnborough GU14 . . . . . .77 A4
Osbourne Cl RG21 . . . . . .69 A4
Osgood Ct GU10 . . . . . . .100 B4
Osier Ho 9 RG26 . . . . . . .26 C4
Osler Cl RG26 . . . . .28 C2
Osnaburgh Hill GU15 . . . .35 C3
Osprey Gdns GU11 . . . . . .99 C4
Osprey Rd RG22 . . . . .91 C2
Otterbourne Cres RG26 . .26 C3
Ottrebourne Rd SO21 . . .197 C1
Ouse Cl 10 SP10 . . . . . . .83 B2
Oval Rd SO51 . . . . .192 A1
Oval The Andover SP10 . . .83 B2
  Liss GU33 . . . . .207 C2
Overbridge Sq RG14 . . . . .2 B2
Overdale Pl 11 GU35 . . . .164 B1
Overdale Rise GU35 . . . .164 B1
Overdale Wlk GU35 . . . .164 B1
Overlord Cl GU10 . . . . . . .36 A4
Overton CE Prim Sch
  RG25 . . . . .65 A1
Overton Ct GU10 . . . . . .100 A3
Overton Ho RG25 . . . . . . .88 A4
Overton Mews RG25 . . . .88 A4
Overton Rd SO21 . . . . . .111 B2
Overton Sta RG25 . . . . . .65 A1
Ovington Dr 18 GU51 . . . .53 B2
Owen Rd RG14 . . . . .1 C2
Owen's Rd SO22 . . . . . . .175 C1
Owlsmoor Rd GU47 . . . . .34 B3
Ox Dro
  Picket Piece SP10,SP11 . . .84 A1
  South Wonston SO21 . . .153 C2
Ox Drove Rise SP11 . . . . .84 A2
Oxenden Ct GU10 . . . . . .100 B4
Oxenden Rd GU10 . . . . .100 B4
Oxford Rd
  Farnborough GU14 . . . . . .56 A1
  Newbury RG14 . . . . .1 B3
  Sutton Scotney SO21 . . .131 B2
Oxford St RG14 . . . . .1 B2
Oyster Cl RG22 . . . . .91 A4

P

Pack La Basingstoke RG23 .67 B1
  Oakley RG23 . . . . .67 B1
Pack Way GU9,GU10 . . . .122 B4
Packenham Rd RG21 . . . . .68 B2
Paddington Ho 7 RG21 . .69 A3
Paddock Cl
  Camberley GU15 . . . . . . .36 C3
  South Wonston SO21 . . .153 C2
Paddock Ct RG27 . . . . . . .52 B3
Paddock Field SO20 . . . .129 A3
Paddock Rd
  Basingstoke RG22 . . . . . .68 B2
  Newbury RG14 . . . . .5 B4
Paddock The
  Farnham GU10 . . . . .121 B2
  Grayshott GU26 . . . . . . .166 C2
  Hartley Wintney RG27 . . .52 B4
  Haslemere GU27 . . . . . .189 C4
  Headley GU35 . . . . .165 B3
  Kings Worthy SO23 . . . .176 B3
  Kingsclere RG20 . . . . . . .24 B1
Paddock Way
  Liphook GU30 . . . . .188 A3
  New Alresford SO24 . . . .179 B2

Paddockfields RG24 . . . . .70 A4
Padwick Cl RG21 . . . . . . .69 A2
Padworth Rd RG7 . . . . . . .11 A4
Pages Yd RG28 . . . . .86 B2
Paget Cl Camberley GU15 .36 C4
  North Tidworth SP9 . . . . .78 B4
Paice La GU34 . . . . .159 C2
Paices Hill RG7 . . . . .9 C2
Painters Field SO23 . . . .197 C2
Painters Pightle RG27 . . .50 C1
Pakenham Dr GU11 . . . . .76 B2
Palace Cl SO23 . . . . .171 C1
Palace Gate RG29 . . . . . .72 B2
Palace Gate Farm RG29 . .72 B2
Pale La RG27 . . . . .53 A1
  Hartley Wintney RG27 . . .53 B2
Palestine Rd SP11 . . . . .124 B3
Palliser Cc
  Beacon Hill GU26 . . . . . .167 A3
  Grayshott GU26 . . . . . . .167 A2
Palm Hall Cl SO23 . . . . .198 B4
Palmer Cl RG21 . . . . .69 B4
Palmer Dr SP10 . . . . . . .106 B4
Palmerston Cl GU14 . . . . .55 A2
Palmerston Ct 2 SO22,
  SO23 . . . . .197 C3
Palmerston Pl SP10 . . . .106 C4
Palmerston Rd RG26 . . . .10 B1
Pamber Dr 17 GU51 . . . . .53 B2
Pamber Heath Rd RG26 . .10 B1
Pamber Rd
  Charter Alley RG26 . . . . . .46 C4
  Silchester RG7 . . . . .10 C2
Pammers Mead GU52 . . . .74 C2
Pan's Gdns GU15 . . . . . . .36 B2
Pankridge St GU10 . . . . .97 B4
Pannells RG24 . . . . .122 A3
Pantile Dr RG27 . . . . .51 B1
Pantings La RG20 . . . . . . .21 B4
Paper Mill La GU34 . . . .140 A2
Papermakers RG25 . . . . .88 A4
Parade The Ash GU12 . . . .77 C2
  Basingstoke RG21 . . . . . .69 B3
  Tadley RG26 . . . . .9 C1
Parchment St SO23 . . . .198 A4
Pardown RG23 . . . . .90 A4
Parfitts Cl GU11 . . . . . . .98 C1
Parish Cl Ash GU12 . . . . .77 C1
  Farnham GU9 . . . . .98 C3
Parish Rd GU14 . . . . .77 A4
Park Ave Camberley GU15 .36 A2
  Old Basing RG24 . . . . . . .70 A3
  Winchester SO23 . . . . . .198 A4
Park Cl Binsted GU10 . . .120 C1
  Kingsley GU35 . . . . .142 B1
  Oakley RG23 . . . . .67 A1
  Winchester SO23 . . . . . .176 A1
Park Close Rd GU34 . . . .140 A3
Park Corner Rd RG27 . . . .52 B4
  Winchester SO23 . . . . . .176 A1
11 Winchester SO23 . . . .176 A1
Park Dro SO20 . . . . .125 C2
Park End RG14 . . . . .1 C2
Park Gate GU9 . . . . .99 C3
  Park Farm Ind Est GU10 .36 A4
Park Gdns RG21 . . . . .69 B2
Park Hill GU52 . . . . .74 C3
Park Ho SO23 . . . . .198 A4
Park House Mews SP4 . .101 C2
  Park House Sch RG14 . . . .5 B2
Park La Arborfield RG40 . .15 C3
  Camberley GU15 . . . . . . .36 A3
  Hamstead Marshall RG20 . . .3 C4
  Kings Worthy SO21 . . . .176 B3
  Lower Froyle GU34 . . . . .119 B3
  Newbury RG14 . . . . .1 C2
  Old Basing RG24 . . . . . . .70 A3
  Quarley SP11 . . . . .103 A2
  Ropley SO24 . . . . .181 A2
Park Mount SO24 . . . . . .179 B3
Park Pl GU27 . . . . .189 B4
  Park Prim Sch GU11 . . . .100 A4
Park Rd Aldershot GU11 . .100 A4
  Camberley GU15 . . . . . . .36 A2
  Farnham GU9 . . . . .77 B4
  Farnham GU9 . . . . .99 A2
  Sandhurst GU47 . . . . . . .35 A4
  South Tidworth SP9 . . . . .78 C3
Parkland Gr GU11 . . . . . .99 B4
Parkside GU9 . . . . .99 A3
Parkside CI GU35 . . . . . .175 B1
Parkside La SO24 . . . . . .181 A1
Parkside Rd RG24 . . . . . .48 B3
Parkstone Dr GU15 . . . . .36 A2
Parkstone Rd SO24 . . . .181 B1
Parkview Cl SP10 . . . . . . .82 C1
Parkway GU15 . . . . .36 B2
Parkwood Cl RG24 . . . . . .48 C2
Parliament Pl SO22 . . . .197 B2

Parmiter Ho 45 SO23 . . .198 A4
Parnell Ct SP11 . . . . .82 B1
Parnholt Rd SO51 . . . . .194 C2
Parsonage Cl GU34 . . . .161 C2
  Parsonage Farm Inf Sch
  GU14 . . . . .55 A3
Parsonage Way GU16 . . . .36 B1
Parsons Cl Arborfield RG2 .15 C4
  Fleet GU52 . . . . .74 C3
  Newbury RG14 . . . . .1 B3
Parsons Down Inf & Jun Schs
  RG19 . . . . .2 C2
Parsons Field GU47 . . . . .34 C4
Parsons La GU26 . . . . . .167 A3
Part La RG7 . . . . .14 B2
Partridge Ave GU46 . . . . .33 C3
Partridge Cl
  Barton Stacey SO21 . . . .130 B4
  Basingstoke RG22 . . . . . .90 C4
  Camberley GU16 . . . . . . .36 B1
  Ewshot GU10 . . . . .98 A4
Partridge Down SO22 . . .197 B2
Partridge Gn GU34 . . . . .139 C3
Paschal Rd GU15 . . . . . . .36 B4
Passet Mead GU52 . . . . . .74 C2
Passfield Ent Ctr GU30 . .187 A4
  Passfield Mill Bsns Pk
  GU30 . . . . .187 A3
Passfield Rd GU30 . . . . .165 B1
Pastures The
  Cheriton SO24 . . . . .201 B3
  Kings Worthy SO23 . . . .154 A1
Paternoster Ho 46 SO23 .198 A4
Paternoster Row
  SO23 . . . . .198 A4
Paterson Cl RG22 . . . . . . .91 B4
Paterson Rd GU33 . . . . .186 C3
Pathfinders The GU14 . . . .55 A2
Patrick's Cl GU33 . . . . . .208 A2
Patrick's Copse Rd
  GU33 . . . . .208 A2
Patten Ave GU46 . . . . . . .34 A3
Pattinson Cres SP11 . . .105 A4
Paul Cl GU11 . . . . .99 A4
Paul's Field GU34 . . . . . .33 A4
Paulet Pl Old Basing RG24 .70 A3
  Winchester SO22 . . . . . .197 C3
Pavilion Rd GU11 . . . . . . .76 B1
Pavilions End The GU15 . .36 A2
Paviors GU9 . . . . .99 A2
Pawley Cl GU10 . . . . . . .100 B4
Pax Hill GU34 . . . . .119 C2
Paxton Cl RG22 . . . . .91 A4
Payne's Mdw RG24 . . . . .70 A4
Paynes Cl
  Broughton SO20 . . . . . .170 A4
  Headley, Nr Greenham
    RG19 . . . . .24 B4
Paynes Hay Rd SO51 . . .194 B1
Paynes La SO20 . . . . . . .170 A4
Paynesdown Rd RG19 . . . .2 C2
Peabody Rd GU14 . . . . . .77 A4
Peach Gr SP11 . . . . .124 C3
Peach Tree Cl GU14 . . . . .55 C3
Peacock Pl 5 SO23 . . . . .198 B4
Peake Cl RG22 . . . . .69 C4
Peakfield GU10 . . . . .144 A4
Pear Tree Ave 4 GU51 . . .53 C1
Pear Tree Cl GU35 . . . . .164 C2
Pear Tree Ct GU35 . . . . . .36 C4
  Pear Tree La
  Farnham GU10 . . . . .121 B2
  Newbury RG14 . . . . .2 A3
Pearces Pl RG20 . . . . . . .24 B1
Pearl Ho SP11 . . . . .57 A1
Pearman Dr SP10 . . . . . .106 B4
Peatmoor Cl GU11 . . . . . .53 C1
Peckmoor Dr RG19 . . . . . .6 A2
Peddlars Gr GU46 . . . . . .34 B3
Peel Ave GU16 . . . . .56 C4
Peel Ct Farnborough GU14 .77 A4
  Hartley Wintney RG27 . . .52 A4
Peel Gdns RG20 . . . . .24 B1
Pegasus Ave GU12 . . . . . .77 B1
Pegasus Dr
  Linchmere GU27 . . . . . .189 A3
  Thatcham RG19 . . . . .2 C2
Pegasus Ct
  Farnborough GU14 . . . . . .56 B1
  Fleet GU51 . . . . .53 C1
  Whitchurch RG28 . . . . . .86 B3
Pegasus Rd GU14 . . . . . .55 B4
Pelham Cl
  18 Bordon GU35 . . . . . .164 B1
  Old Basing RG24 . . . . . . .70 A3
Pelham Ho RG26 . . . . . . .10 B1
Pelton Rd RG22 . . . . .68 C3
Pembroke Bwy GU15 . . . .36 B2
Pembroke Ct SP10 . . . . .106 A4
Pembroke Rd
  Basingstoke RG21 . . . . . .68 A3
  Newbury RG14 . . . . .1 B2
Pembury Pl GU12 . . . . . . .77 C2
Pemerton Rd
  Basingstoke RG21 . . . . . .69 B4
  Winchester SO22 . . . . . .175 B2
Pen Cl SP10 . . . . .106 B4
Pendennis Cl RG23 . . . . .68 A3
Pendle Gn SO51 . . . . . . .191 C1
Penfold Croft GU9 . . . . . .99 B2
Pengilly Rd GU9 . . . . .98 C1
Peninsula Rd SO22 . . . .197 C4
Peninsula Sq SO22 . . . . .197 C4
Peninsular Cl GU15 . . . . .36 C4
Penn Rd RG14 . . . . .1 A3

Pennefather's Rd GU11 . .76 B2
Pennine Cl RG22 . . . . . . .68 A2
Pennine Way
  Basingstoke RG22 . . . . . .68 A2
  Farnborough GU14 . . . . . .55 B4
Pennings Rd SP9 . . . . . . .78 C4
Penns Wood GU14 . . . . . .56 A2
Penny La SO20 . . . . .150 A1
Penny's Hatch RG20 . . . .24 C1
Penrhyn Cl GU12 . . . . . . .76 C1
Penrith Rd RG21 . . . . . . .69 A2
Penrose Cl RG14 . . . . . . .1 B3
Penrose Way GU34 . . . . .160 A1
Penryn Dr GU35 . . . . . . .166 A3
Penshurst Rise GU16 . . . .56 B4
Pentangle The RG14 . . . . .1 C2
Pentland Cl RG22 . . . . . . .68 A2
Pentland Pl GU14 . . . . . . .55 B4
Penton La SP11 . . . . .81 C3
Penton Pl 8 SO23 . . . . .198 A3
Penwith Dr GU27 . . . . . .189 B3
Penwood Hts RG20 . . . . .21 C4
Penwood Rd RG20 . . . . . .21 C4
Perham Cres SP11 . . . . . .57 A1
Perins Cl SO24 . . . . .179 A2
Perins Com Sch SO24 . .179 B3
Periwinkle Cl GU35 . . . .165 A3
Perowne St GU11 . . . . . . .76 B2
Perring Ave GU14 . . . . . . .55 B4
Perry Dr GU51 . . . . .53 B1
Perry Way Farnham GU9 . .98 C4
  Headley GU35 . . . . .165 B2
Pershore Rd RG24 . . . . . .48 A1
Perth Cl SP11 . . . . .79 B4
Peshawar Cl SP9 . . . . . . .78 B4
  Peter Symonds' Coll
  SO22 . . . . .175 C1
Petersfield RG21 . . . . . . .90 A4
Petersfield Cl RG24 . . . . .49 A2
Petersfield Gn SP9 . . . . .78 C3
  Petersfield Rd
  Cheriton SO24 . . . . .201 B2
  East Tisted GU34,SO24 . .182 B1
  Greatham GU33 . . . . . . .186 A3
  Greatham GU33 . . . . . . .185 C1
  Ropley SO24 . . . . .181 B2
Petersfield Sta SO23 . . .198 B4
Petrel Croft RG22 . . . . . . .90 C4
Petty's Brook Rd RG24 . . .48 C2
Petunia Cl RG22 . . . . .91 A4
Petworth Cl
  Basingstoke RG22 . . . . . .91 A3
  Camberley GU15 . . . . . . .56 B4
Petworth Ct GU15 . . . . . .56 C4
Pevensey Way GU16 . . . . .36 C4
Peveral Way RG22 . . . . . .68 B2
Peveral Wlk RG22 . . . . . .68 B2
Pewsey Ho 9 SP9 . . . . . . .78 C3
Pheaben's Field RG26 . . .28 C2
Pheasant Cl
  Barton Stacey SO21 . . . .130 C4
  Basingstoke RG22 . . . . . .90 C4
  North Tidworth SP9 . . . . .79 A3
Pheasant Copse GU51 . . .53 C3
Pheasant La RG20 . . . . . .6 B2
Pheasantry Dr RG27 . . . . .32 A2
Pheby Rd RG22 . . . . .68 B1
Pheonix Ct GU47 . . . . . . .52 A2
Pheonix Terr RG27 . . . . . .52 A2
Philips Ho GU26 . . . . . . .166 C2
Phillips Cl Headley GU35 .165 B3
  Tongham GU10 . . . . . . .100 B4
Phillips Cres GU35 . . . . .165 B3
Phoenix Ct
  36 Aldershot GU11 . . . . .76 C1
  Kingsclere RG20 . . . . . . .24 B1
Phoenix Park Terr RG21 . .69 A3
Phoenix Wlk GU12 . . . . . .77 C4
Pickaxe La RG29 . . . . . . .118 A3
Picket Twenty SP11 . . . . .106 C4
Picketts Hill GU35 . . . . .143 A1
Pickford St GU11 . . . . . . .76 C1
Pickwick Gdns GU15 . . . .36 C2
Picton Rd SP10 . . . . .106 B4
Pierrefondes Ave GU15 . .35 C3
Pigeon Cl RG24 . . . . .29 A1
Pigeonhouse Cotts
  SO21 . . . . .131 B2
Pigeonhouse Field
  SO21 . . . . .131 B2
Pigeons Farm Rd RG19 . . .6 A4
Pike St RG14 . . . . .2 A2
Pilcot Rd GU51,RG27 . . . .74 B3
Piley Rd SO21 . . . . .153 C1
Pilgrims Cl GU9 . . . . . . .121 C4
Pilgrims Gate SO22 . . . .175 C1
Pilgrims Sch The SO23 . .198 A4
Pilgrims Way
  Andover SP10 . . . . .82 C2
  Headley GU35 . . . . .165 B3
  Pilgrims' Way Sch The
  GU9 . . . . .121 C4
Pimpernel Way GU35 . . . .69 C4
Pinchington La RG14,RG19 .5 C4
Pindar Pl RG14 . . . . .2 A2
Pine Ave GU15 . . . . .36 A2
Pine Bank GU26 . . . . . . .167 B2
Pine Cl Ash GU12 . . . . . . .77 C3
  Middle Wallop SO20 . . . .126 A2
  Sandhurst GU15 . . . . . . .35 C2
  South Wonston SO21 . . .153 C2
  Winchester SO22 . . . . . .197 A4
Pine Cotts GU33 . . . . . . .208 A4
Pine Dr Blackwater GU17 .34 C1
  Peasemarsh GU9,RG40 . .16 C4
  Mortimer RG7 . . . . .11 B3
Pine Gr Farnham GU10 . .122 B3
  Fleet GU52 . . . . .75 A3

Pine Mount Rd GU15 . . . . . .36 A2
Pine Rd GU34 . . . . .160 B2
Pine Ridge RG14 . . . . .2 A3
Pine Ridge Dr GU10 . . . . . .122 C3
Pine View GU35 . . . . .166 A3
Pine View Cl GU7 . . . . .99 C3
Pine Wlk Andover SP10 . . . .105 B3
  Liss GU33 . . . . .208 A3
Pinehill Rd GU34 . . . . .164 B1
Pinehill Rise GU47 . . . . .35 A4
Pinehurst RG26 . . . . .26 C4
Pinehurst Ave GU14 . . . . . . .55 C1
Pinehurst La GU14 . . . . .55 C1
Pines Rd Fleet GU51 . . . . . . .3 C3
  Liphook GU30 . . . . .187 B2
Pines The Andover SP10 . . .105 C4
  Camberley GU15 . . . . .36 B4
Pinetree Ho 6 SP9 . . . . . . .79 A4
Pineview GU14 . . . . .55 C2
Pinewood RG24 . . . . .48 C2
Pinewood Cl
  Baughurst RG26 . . . . .9 A1
  Sandhurst GU47 . . . . .34 B4
Pinewood Cres GU14 . . . . . .55 A3
Pinewood Ct 1 GU51 . . . . . .54 A1
Pinewood Dr RG20 . . . . .5 C1
Pinewood Hill GU51 . . . . . . .54 A1
Pinewood Inf Sch GU14 . . . . .55 A4
Pinewood Pk GU14 . . . . .55 A4
Pinkerton Rd RG22 . . . . .68 B1
Pinks La RG26 . . . . .9 B1
Pinnell Cl RG22 . . . . .91 A3
Pintail Cl RG22 . . . . .90 C4
Pipers Croft GU52 . . . . .75 A4
Pipers Patch 1 GU14 . . . . . .35 C2
Pipit Cl RG19 . . . . .2 C2
Pippons Cl GU46 . . . . .34 A3
Pirbright Rd GU14 . . . . .56 A2
Pitcairn Cl RG24 . . . . .48 B1
Pitfield La RG2 . . . . .12 A2
Pitfold Ave GU27 . . . . .189 A3
Pitfold Cl GU27 . . . . .189 B3
Pither Rd RG29 . . . . .95 B4
Pithouse La RG19 . . . . .25 B3
Pitman Cl RG22 . . . . .68 A4
Pitt Hall Cotts RG26 . . . . . . .45 C3
Pitt La GU10 . . . . .143 C3
Pitt Rdbt SO22 . . . . .197 A3
Pitt Way GU14 . . . . .55 B3
Pittard Rd RG14 . . . . .68 C2
Pitter Cl SO22 . . . . .175 A3
Pitts La SP10 . . . . .106 C2
Pitts Rd GU11 . . . . .76 C4
Place Ct GU11 . . . . .100 A4
Plantation Rd
  Andover SP10 . . . . .105 C4
  Baughurst RG26 . . . . .9 B1
  Hill Brow GU33 . . . . .208 A1
  South Tidworth SP9 . . . . . .78 C3
Plantation Row GU15 . . . . . .35 C3
Plantation The RG27 . . . . . . .89 B4
Plantation Way GU35 . . . . .186 A4
Plassey Rd SP9 . . . . .78 C4
Pleasant Hill RG26 . . . . .26 C4
Plough Gdns SO20 . . . . . . .170 A3
Plough La RG27 . . . . .32 A3
Plough Rd GU46 . . . . .34 B4
Plough Way SO22 . . . . .197 B2
Plover Cl Andover SP10 . . . . .83 A1
  Basingstoke RG22 . . . . . . .68 A1
Plover La RG27 . . . . .15 B1
Plovers Down SO22 . . . . . . .197 A2
Plovers Way GU34 . . . . . . .140 A3
Plum Fell La GU34 . . . . . . .184 C4
Plumer Rd GU33 . . . . .186 B2
Plumpton Rd RG14 . . . . .2 A1
Plumpton Way GU34 . . . . . .139 C1
Poachers Field RG29 . . . . . .95 A2
Pococks La GU32 . . . . .206 C4
Poets Way SO22 . . . . .197 B3
Poland La RG29 . . . . .72 C3
Polden Cl GU14 . . . . .55 B4
Polecat Cnr RG20 . . . . .70 A1
Police Hos GU35 . . . . .164 B1
Polkerris Way GU52 . . . . . . .75 C2
Pollards The GU14 . . . . . . .120 A2
Pollen's Almshouses
  SP10 . . . . .106 A4
Polmaier Cl GU52 . . . . .75 B3
Pond Cl Newbury RG14 . . . . .5 A4
  Overton RG25 . . . . .88 A3
Pond Croft GU46 . . . . .34 B3
Pond La GU10 . . . . .144 A2
Pond Rd Bramley RG26 . . . . .29 A1
  Headley GU35 . . . . .165 C2
Pond View Cl GU51 . . . . . . .54 B1
Pondtail Cl GU51 . . . . .75 B4
Pondtail Gdns GU51 . . . . . . .75 B4
Pondtail Rd GU51 . . . . .75 B4
Pool Rd Aldershot GU11 . . . .100 A4
  Hartley Wintney RG27 . . . . .52 B1
Poors Farm Rd RG24 . . . . . .70 C4
Popes Hill RG20 . . . . .4 C2
Popham La RG25 . . . . .112 C4
Poplar Cl Basingstoke RG26 . .26 A4
  Mytchett GU16 . . . . .56 C2
  Sherfield on Loddon RG27 . .29 B1
Poplar Cotts GU16 . . . . .56 B3
Poplar Path RG20 . . . . .126 A2
Poplar Rd RG21 . . . . .1 C3
Poplar Wlk GU9 . . . . .99 A1
Poplars Rd GU14 . . . . .55 A3
Popley Way RG24 . . . . .49 B4
Poppy Fields RG24 . . . . .70 A4
Poppyhills Rd GU15 . . . . . . .36 B4
Porchester RG14 . . . . .1 C1
Porchester Sq 12 RG21 . . . . .69 A3
Port La SO22 . . . . .197 A1

Portacre Rise RG21 . . . . .68 C2
Portal Cl SP11 . . . . .105 A4
Portal Rd SO23 . . . . .198 A3
Portchester Cl SP10 . . . . . . .82 B2
Porter Cl RG29 . . . . .95 B4
Porter End RG14 . . . . .5 C4
Porter Rd RG24 . . . . .68 C1
Porters Cl Andover SP10 . . . .82 B1
  Dummer RG25 . . . . .90 B1
Portersbery Hill Dr GU15 . . .54 A4
Portesbery Rd GU15 . . . . . . .36 B3
Portesbery Sch GU15 . . . . . .36 A3
Portiswood Cl RG26 . . . . . . .27 A4
Portland Dr GU52 . . . . .75 A2
Portland Gr SP10 . . . . .106 A4
Portland Sq 8 GU14 . . . . . .207 C2
Portsmouth Cres RG22 . . . . .68 B1
Portsmouth Rd
  Bramshott GU26 . . . . . . .167 A1
  Camberley GU15 . . . . .55 B4
  Grayshott GU26 . . . . .167 A1
  Haslemere GU26 . . . . . . .167 A1
  Liphook GU30 . . . . .187 C1
Portsmouth Way RG22 . . . . .68 B1
Portsmouth Wlk RG22 . . . . . .68 B1
Portway Baughurst RG26 . . . . .9 B1
  Riseley RG7 . . . . .14 A1
Portway Cl SP10 . . . . .105 B4
Portway Ind Est SP10 . . . . . .82 A1
Portway Inf Sch SP10 . . . . . .82 A1
Portway Jun Sch SP10 . . . . .105 B4
Portway RG23 . . . . .68 A3
Post Horn La RG27 . . . . .50 C3
Post Office La RG25 . . . . . . .90 B1
Posting House Mews
  RG14 . . . . .1 B2
Pot La RG24 . . . . .24 B2
Potbridge Rd RG29 . . . . .72 C4
Potley Hill Prim Sch
  RG45 . . . . .34 A3
Potley Hill Rd GU46 . . . . . . .34 A3
Potter's Cross SP4 . . . . . . .101 C2
Potter's Wlk 5 RG21 . . . . . .69 A3
Potteries La GU16 . . . . .56 B2
Potteries The GU14 . . . . .55 B3
Potters Cres GU12 . . . . .77 C1
Potters Field GU33 . . . . . . .208 A2
Potters Gate GU9 . . . . .98 C1
Potters Gate CE Prim Sch
  GU9 . . . . .99 A1
Potters Ind Pk GU52 . . . . . . .75 B3
Pottery Cl RG21 . . . . .29 C2
Pottery Ct GU10 . . . . .121 B3
Pottery La GU10 . . . . .121 B3
Poultons Cl RG25 . . . . .88 A4
Poultons Rd RG25 . . . . .88 A4
Pound Cl Bramley RG26 . . . . .28 C2
  Baughurst RG26 . . . . .165 B3
  Over Wallop SO20 . . . . . .125 B1
  Upper Wield SO24 . . . . . .137 A1
  Yateley GU46 . . . . .34 B3
Pound Gate GU34 . . . . .140 A3
Pound La GU34 . . . . .179 B3
Pound La Burghclere RG20 . .46 C1
  Marnhull 1 A2
  Thatcham RG19 . . . . .2 C2
Pound Mdw
  Sherfield on Loddon RG27 . .49 B4
  Whitchurch RG28 . . . . .56 A2
Pound Rd
  8 Aldershot GU12 . . . . . . .77 A1
  Kings Worthy SO23 . . . . .176 B4
  Over Wallop SO20 . . . . . .125 B1
  Overton RG25 . . . . .88 A4
Pound St RG14 . . . . .1 B1
Pound View SP11 . . . . .83 C4
Poyngs Mead RG20 . . . . .29 B1
Poyle Rd GU10 . . . . .100 C4
Poynings Cres RG21 . . . . . . .69 B1
Poynters Cl GU14 . . . . .82 C1
Poyntz Rd RG25 . . . . .91 C4
Pragnells Cotts SP5 . . . . . . .169 A1
Prentice Cl GU14 . . . . .55 C4
Prescelly Cl RG22 . . . . .68 A3
Preston Pl RG14 . . . . .2 A2
Pretoria Cl GU33 . . . . .186 B1
Pretoria Rd SP11 . . . . .57 A1
Preymead Ind Est GU11 . . . .99 C4
Priest Down RG22 . . . . .90 B1
Priestley Way GU11 . . . . . . .76 A1
Priestly Rd RG24 . . . . .48 C4
Primrose Cl SP10 . . . . .105 B3
Primrose Dr RG27 . . . . .27 A4
Primrose Gdns
  Basingstoke RG22 . . . . . . .91 A3
  Farnborough GU14 . . . . . . .55 A4
Primrose La GU33 . . . . .208 B2
Primrose Wlk
  8 Fleet GU51 . . . . .53 C1
  Yateley GU46 . . . . .33 C3
Primula Rd GU33 . . . . .164 C2
Prince Albert Gdns 17
  SP10 . . . . .106 A4
Prince Charles Cres
  GU14 . . . . .56 A4
Prince Cl SP10 . . . . .83 B1
Prince Hold Rd RG19 . . . . . . .2 C1
Prince of Wales Wlk
  GU15 . . . . .36 A3
Prince's Ave GU11 . . . . .77 A4
Prince's Bldgs 18 SO23 . . . .198 A4
Prince's Mead Sch
  SO23 . . . . .176 C3
Princes Cl GU35 . . . . .164 B1
Princes Ct 18 SP9 . . . . .78 C4
Princes Mead GU14 . . . . . . .55 C2

Princes Pl SO22 . . . . .197 C3
Princes Rd GU11 . . . . .76 C1
Princes' Cres RG22 . . . . .68 C2
Princes Ct 10 SO23 . . . . . . .199 B2
Princes Dr GU34 . . . . .139 B2
Princess Marina Dr RG2 . . . .15 B4
Princess Way GU15 . . . . .36 A3
Prinstead Cl 7 SO23 . . . . . .198 A3
Printers Row 7 SO23 . . . . . .197 C3
Prior Croft Cl GU15 . . . . .36 C3
Prior End GU15 . . . . .36 C3
Prior Heath Inf Sch
  GU15 . . . . .36 C2
Prior Place Cross Roads
Prior Rd GU15 . . . . .36 C2
Prior's La GU17 . . . . .34 C3
Priors Barton SO23 . . . . . . .197 C2
Priors Cl
  Hook GU27 . . . . .55 C4
  Kingsclere RG20 . . . . .24 B1
Priors Ct GU12 . . . . .121 A2
Priors Dean Rd SO22 . . . . .175 B2
Priors Keep GU52 . . . . .75 A4
Priors Rd RG26 . . . . .9 C1
Priors Row RG29 . . . . .72 B2
Priors Way SO22 . . . . .197 A2
Priors Way The SO24 . . . . . .182 A3
Priors Wood SO27 . . . . .189 B3
Priory Cl GU51 . . . . .74 B4
Priory Cotts RG7 . . . . .13 A2
Priory Croft GU9 . . . . .122 A4
Priory Ct
  Old Basing RG24 . . . . .70 A4
  12 Winchester SO23 . . . . .197 C3
Priory Gdns
  Old Basing RG24 . . . . .70 A4
  12 Winchester SO23 . . . . .197 C3
Priory La Fresham GU10 . . . .144 B4
  Hartley Wintney RG27 . . . . .52 A1
  Laverstoke RG28 . . . . .87 A3
Priory Pl RG19 . . . . .5 C3
Priory Prim Sch The
  RG26 . . . . .27 A1
Priory Rd RG14 . . . . .1 C1
Priory St GU14 . . . . .56 A2
Pritchard Cl RG19 . . . . .4 A4
Privet La SP11 . . . . .80 A2
Privet Rd GU35 . . . . .165 A3
Privett Cl RG24 . . . . .26 C4
Privett Rd GU32 . . . . .205 C1
Project Workshops
  SP11 . . . . .103 A3
Prospect Ave GU14 . . . . . . .55 C3
Prospect Bsns Ctr SO24 . . .179 B2
Prospect Cott SO22 . . . . . .175 B4
Prospect Pl RG14 . . . . .1 B1
Prospect Rd Ash GU12 . . . . .77 C3
  Farnborough GU14 . . . . . . .55 C3
  Farnham GU10 . . . . .121 B2
Pruetts La GU33 . . . . .207 C1
Puckridge Hill Rd GU11 . . . .76 B3
Pudding La SO23 . . . . .176 A3
Puffers Way 1 RG14 . . . . . . .1 B1
Puffin Cl RG22 . . . . .90 C3
Pug's Hole SP5 . . . . .191 A3
Punshoh La SO24 . . . . .203 C3
Purbrook Rd GU14 . . . . .68 C1
Purcell Cl RG24 . . . . .48 B1
Purley Way GU16 . . . . .56 A4
Purmerend Cl GU14 . . . . . . .55 C3
Puttenham Rd
  Chineham RG24 . . . . .49 A2
  Seale GU10 . . . . .100 C2
Puttock Cl GU27 . . . . .189 B3
Pyestock Cres GU14 . . . . . . .55 A3
Pyotts Copse RG24 . . . . .49 A1
Pyotts Ct RG24 . . . . .49 A1
Pyotts Hill Chineham RG24 . .49 A1
  Old Basing RG24 . . . . .70 A4

Q

Quadrangle The RG27 . . . . .32 A2
Quadrant The GU12 . . . . . . .77 C2
Quantock Cl RG22 . . . . .68 A3
Quarry La GU46 . . . . .34 B3
Quarry Rd SO23 . . . . .198 B4
Quebec Cl GU30 . . . . .188 A2
Quebec Gdns GU17 . . . . . . .34 C2
Queen Anne's Wlk 2
  RG21 . . . . .69 A3
Queen Annes Gate GU9 . . . .99 A4
Queen Elizabeth Dr GU11 . .76 B1
Queen Mary Ave
  Basingstoke RG21 . . . . . . .69 A4
  Camberley GU15 . . . . .35 C3
Queen Mary Cl GU51 . . . . . .54 C4
Queen Mary's Coll RG21 . . .69 A2
Queen Victoria Cross Roads
  GU15 . . . . .35 C3
Queen Victoria Ct GU14 . . . .55 C3
Queen's Ave
  Aldershot GU11 . . . . .76 C3
  Farnborough GU14 . . . . . .76 C4
Queen's Cl GU14 . . . . .77 A4
Queen's Ct GU14 . . . . .77 A4
Queen's Gate Rd GU11,
  GU11 . . . . .76 C2
Queen's Par Rd RG29 . . . . . .69 A2
Queen's Rd Alton GU34 . . . .139 C2
  Basingstoke RG21 . . . . . . .68 C3
  Newbury RG14 . . . . .1 B1
  Winchester SO22 . . . . . . .197 B4

Queen's Rdbt GU11,GU14 . . .76 C4
Queens Ave SP10 . . . . .106 A4
Queens Cotts SP11 . . . . . . .61 C1
Queens Ct Farnham GU9 . . . .98 C4
  Newbury RG14 . . . . .1 C1
  50 Winchester SO23 . . . . .197 C3
Queens Keep GU15 . . . . . . .36 A3
Queens La GU9 . . . . .98 C4
Queens Mead SO22 . . . . . . .197 B3
Queens Rd Aldershot GU11 . .76 C1
  Bordon GU30 . . . . .187 A2
  Camberley GU15 . . . . .35 C2
  Farnborough GU14 . . . . . .77 A4
  Farnham GU9 . . . . .99 A3
  Fleet GU52 . . . . .75 B4
  Kingsclere RG20 . . . . .24 C1
  North Warnborough RG29 . .72 B2
  Whitchurch RG28 . . . . .86 B2
Queensberry Pl GU17 . . . . . .35 A2
Queensfield RG25 . . . . .90 B1
Queensmead GU14 . . . . . . .55 C2
Queensway Andover SP10 . . .83 B1
Queenswood Rd SO20 . . . . .170 A3
Queenwood Rise SO20 . . . . .170 A3
Queenwood Rd SO20 . . . . . .170 A3
Quennells Hill GU10 . . . . . .121 B3
Quetta Pk GU51 . . . . .75 A1
Quilter Rd RG22 . . . . .68 B1
Quince Tree Way RG27 . . . . .51 A1
Quincy Cl GU51 . . . . .74 B4
Quorn Rd GU33 . . . . .186 B2
Quorn Terr GU33 . . . . .186 B2

R

Race Course Rd RG14 . . . . . .1 C1
Race Course Sta RG14 . . . . .2 A1
Racedown Cotts SP11 . . . . .102 C3
Raceview Bsns Ctr RG14 . . . .1 C1
Rack & Manger Cotts
  SO21 . . . . .175 B4
Rack Cl SP10 . . . . .106 A4
Rack Close Rd GU34 . . . . . .139 C2
Rackfield GU47 . . . . .189 A4
Radcliffe Rd GU47 . . . . .35 B4
Radcliffe Cl GU16 . . . . .56 C4
Radford Cl GU9 . . . . .99 B3
Radford Gdns RG21 . . . . . . .68 C1
Radical Ride RG40 . . . . .16 A4
Raeburn Cl SO24 . . . . .203 B3
Raghill RG7 . . . . .10 A3
Raglan Cl Aldershot GU12 . . .77 A1
  Camberley GU15 . . . . .56 C4
Raglan Ct RG22 . . . . .91 B4
Ragmore La GU32 . . . . .205 C3
Railway Cotts
  Bordon GU35 . . . . .164 A3
  East Tisted GU34 . . . . . . .183 B3
  West Tisted GU34 . . . . . . .204 B3
Railway Rd Bordon GU35 . . .186 B2
  Newbury RG14 . . . . .1 C1
Railway Terr RG27 . . . . .12 B3
Rainbow Cl RG24 . . . . .70 B3
Rainham Cl RG22 . . . . .90 C4
Rake Bsns Pk GU33 . . . . . .208 C2
Rake Cl GU33 . . . . .208 C2
Rake Rd GU33 . . . . .208 A2
Rakemakers GU34 . . . . .140 B4
Raleigh Way GU15,GU16 . . .36 B2
Ralph Cl GU10 . . . . .97 B3
Ram Alley Ashford Hill RG19 . .8 A1
  Baughurst RG26 . . . . .25 A4
Ramilles Cl GU11 . . . . .77 B4
Ramillies Rd GU11 . . . . .77 B4
Ramparts The SP10 . . . . . . .105 C3
Rampton Rd RG28 . . . . .86 B2
Ramptons La RG24 . . . . .70 C3
Ramptons Mdw RG26 . . . . . .27 A4
Ramridge Ho RG27 . . . . .35 B4
Ramsay Rd SO23 . . . . .176 A1
Ramsdell Cl RG26 . . . . .26 C4
Ramsdell Rd
  Baughurst RG26 . . . . .25 C1
  Fleet GU51 . . . . .74 B4
  Pamber End RG26 . . . . . . .27 A1
Ramsey Cl GU15 . . . . .36 C4
Ramshott Cl RG25 . . . . .36 C4
Rances Way SO22 . . . . .197 C3
Randall Cl GU17 . . . . .35 A3
Randolph Dr GU14 . . . . .55 A3
Ranelagh Rd SO23 . . . . . . .197 C3
Range Rd RG40 . . . . .17 A4
Range Ride GU15 . . . . .35 B4
Range View GU47 . . . . .35 B4
Rank The Fyfield SP11 . . . . .80 C1
  Hurstbourne Tarrant SP11 . .60 C4
  Penton Grafton SP11 . . . . .81 B1
Rankine Cl GU7 . . . . .99 C3
Rankine Rd RG24 . . . . .49 B3
Rapallo Cl GU14 . . . . .56 A4
Raphael Cl RG21 . . . . .69 B2
Rapley Cl GU15 . . . . .36 A4
Ratcliffe Rd GU14 . . . . .56 A4
Ravel Cl RG22 . . . . .68 C1
Ravelin Cl GU10 . . . . .97 B3
Raven Cl
  North Tidworth SP9 . . . . . .78 C3
  5 Yateley GU46 . . . . .34 A3
Raven Rd GU27 . . . . .51 A1
Raven Sq GU34 . . . . .139 C3
Ravens Wood Dr GU15 . . . . .35 C3
Ravenscote Cl on Jun Sch
  GU15 . . . . .36 C4
Ravenscroft RG27 . . . . .51 A1
Ravensworth Rd RG21 . . . . .11 B3
Rawdon Rise GU15 . . . . .35 C3

Rawlings Rd RG27 . . . . .72 A4
Rawlinson Rd GU15 . . . . . . .35 C3
Raygnoldes GU52 . . . . .74 C2
Rayleigh Rd RG21 . . . . .69 A3
Rays Cl RG26 . . . . .27 A4
Read's Field GU34 . . . . . . .160 A1
Reading Dr N RG27 . . . . . . .32 A2
Reading Dr S RG27 . . . . . . .32 A2
Reading Rd
  Basingstoke RG24 . . . . . . .48 B1
  Chineham RG24 . . . . .48 C2
  Farley Hill RG40 . . . . .15 C2
  Farnborough GU14 . . . . . .56 A1
  Hook RG27 . . . . .51 A3
  Padworth RG7 . . . . .11 B4
  Sherfield on Loddon RG27 . .49 B4
  Swallowfield RG7 . . . . .15 B1
  Yateley GU46,GU17 . . . . . .34 B3
Reading Rd S GU51,GU52 . . .75 A1
Rebecca Cl GU52 . . . . .74 C2
Recreation Cl GU14 . . . . . . .35 B1
Recreation Rd
  Andover SP10 . . . . .106 A4
  Farnham GU10 . . . . .121 B2
  Odiham RG29 . . . . .72 B1
Rectory Cl Newbury RG14 . . .1 B1
  Sandhurst GU47 . . . . .34 B4
  Tadley RG26 . . . . .27 A3
Rectory Hill
  West Dean SP5 . . . . .190 B2
  West Tytherley SP5 . . . . . .169 A1
Rectory La Bentley GU10 . . .120 A2
  Bramshott GU30 . . . . . . .188 A4
  Broughton SO20 . . . . .170 A4
  Itchen Abbas SO21 . . . . .178 A4
  Kingsclere RG26 . . . . .45 A4
Rectory Pl SP11 . . . . .83 B4
Rectory Rd
  Farnborough GU14 . . . . . .56 A2
  Hook RG27 . . . . .72 A2
  Oakley RG23 . . . . .66 C1
  Padworth RG7 . . . . .11 B4
Rectory Row RG27 . . . . .92 A4
Reculver Way SP10 . . . . . . .82 B2
Red Hill
  Ashmansworth RG20 . . . . .41 A4
  Mattingley RG27 . . . . .31 C1
  Medstead GU34 . . . . .160 A3
Red La Aldermaston RG7 . . .10 A3
  Bradley RG25 . . . . .115 B2
  Headley GU35 . . . . .165 C4
  West Tytherley SP5 . . . . . .191 A4
Red Lion La
  Basingstoke RG21 . . . . . . .69 A2
  Farnham GU9 . . . . .99 A1
  Overton RG25 . . . . .88 A4
Red Oaks GU10 . . . . .121 A2
Red Post La SP11 . . . . .104 C4
Red Rice Rd SP10 . . . . .105 B1
Red Villas SP9 . . . . .101 C4
Redan Gdns 1 GU12 . . . . . .77 A1
Redan Hill Ind Est GU12 . . . .77 A1
Redan Rd GU12 . . . . .77 A1
Redbridge Dr SP10 . . . . . . .105 C3
Redbridge La
  Old Basing RG24 . . . . .69 C3
  Spencers Wood RG7 . . . . .182 A2
Redcrest Gdns GU15 . . . . . .36 B3
Rede Ct 4 GU14 . . . . .56 A1
Redenham Dro SP11 . . . . . . .81 A4
Redfield Cl RG24 . . . . .2 A2
Redfields La GU52,GU10 . . . .74 C1
Redfields Pk GU52 . . . . .74 C1
Redgauntlet Rd RG21 . . . . . .69 C2
Redgrave Ct GU12 . . . . .77 B1
Redhearne Fields GU10 . . . .144 B1
Redhouse Mews GU30 . . . . .188 A1
Redlands La GU10 . . . . .97 C4
Redlane Hill RG7 . . . . .10 A3
Redon Way SP10 . . . . .82 C1
Redvers Buller Rd GU11 . . . .77 A4
Redwing Rd RG22 . . . . .90 C4
Redwood La GU34 . . . . .160 A4
Redwoods Way GU52 . . . . . .75 A3
Reed Cl GU11 . . . . .77 A3
Reed Wlk RG14 . . . . .2 A2
Reeds La GU33 . . . . .208 B3
Reeds Rd The GU10 . . . . . .122 B2
Rees Rd SO21 . . . . .153 B1
Reeves Rd GU12 . . . . .77 A1
Regent Cl GU51 . . . . .75 A1
Regent Ct
  Basingstoke RG21 . . . . . . .69 B3
  Fleet GU51 . . . . .74 C4
  17 Winchester SO23 . . . . .176 A1
Regent St GU51 . . . . .36 C1
Regent Way GU16 . . . . .36 C1
Regents Cl Andover SP10 . . .83 C1
  Newbury RG14 . . . . .1 B2
Regents Pl GU47 . . . . .35 A4
Regnum Dr RG14 . . . . .1 A1
Reith Way SP10 . . . . .82 A1
Rembrandt Cl RG21 . . . . . . .69 B2
REME Mus * RG2 . . . . .15 C4
Remembrance Gdns
  RG24 . . . . .48 C1
Remembrance Rd RG14 . . . .1 B1
Renoir Cl RG21 . . . . .69 B2
Renown Way RG24 . . . . .48 C2
Restormel Cl RG23 . . . . .69 A3
Reuben's Cres RG26 . . . . . .26 C4
Revelstoke Ave RG22 . . . . . .90 A3
Rewlands Dr SO22 . . . . .175 B2
Rex Ct RG27 . . . . .189 B3

Reynards Cl RG26 .....26 C4
Reynolds Cl RG21 .....69 C2
Reynolds Ct SP10 .....82 C1
Reynolds Gn GU47 .....35 A3
Reynolds Ho RG22 .....68 B1
Reyntiens View RG29 .....72 C1
Rhine Banks GU14 .....55 A3
Rhodes Sq SP10 .....35 C2
Rhododendron Cnr RG40 .16 C2
Rhododendron Rd GU16 ..56 C4
Ribble Cl 5 SP10 .....83 B1
Ribble Pl GU14 .....55 A3
Ribble Way 7 RG21 .....69 B3
Richard Aldworth Com Sch
  The RG22 .....68 B1
Richard Cl GU51 .....74 C4
Richard Moss Ho 8
  SO23 .....198 A4
Richards Cl GU51 .....77 C3
Richborough Dr SP10 ..82 B2
Richmond Ave RG19 .....2 C2
Richmond Cl
  Bordon GU35 .....164 B1
  Camberley GU16 .....36 B1
  Farnborough GU14 .....55 A2
  Fleet GU52 .....74 C3
Richmond Ho
  Sandhurst GU47 .....35 B4
  9 Winchester SO22 ...197 C4
Richmond Rd
  Basingstoke RG21 .....69 A3
  Sandhurst GU47 .....35 B4
Riddings La RG19 .....1 A1
Rideway Cl GU15 .....35 C2
Ridge Cl RG22 .....91 B3
Ridge La Hook RG27 .....50 C1
  Newnham RG27 .....50 C2
Ridgemoor Cl GU46 .....67 B2
Ridges Cl SP11 .....83 B4
Ridges View SP11 .....83 B4
Ridgeway SO22 .....197 B3
Ridgeway Com Sch The
  GU9 .....122 A4
Ridgeway Par GU22 .....75 A3
Ridgeway The GU34 .....139 C1
Ridgway Hill Rd GU9 ...122 A4
Ridgway Rd GU9 .....122 A4
Ridings The
  Camberley GU16 .....36 C2
  Liss GU33 .....208 A2
Ridley Cl GU52 .....74 C4
Ridleys Piece RG29 .....95 A2
Rifle Way GU14 .....55 B3
Riley La RG24 .....70 A4
Rimbault Cl GU11 .....77 A4
Rimes's La RG26 .....26 B3
Ringlet Way 3 SO23 ...198 B4
Ringshall Gdns RG26 ...28 C2
Ringway Ctr The RG21 ..69 C3
Ringway E RG21 .....69 A4
Ringway N RG21 .....69 A4
Ringway S RG21 .....69 B2
Ringway W RG22 .....68 C3
Ringwood Rd
  Blackwater GU17 .....35 A3
  Farnborough GU14 .....56 A4
Ripon Rd GU46 .....34 B1
Ripplesmore Cl GU47 ..34 C4
Rise The RG40 .....15 C1
River Cl GU34 .....160 A1
River Ho 50 SP10 .....83 B1
River La GU9,GU10 .....121 B4
River Pk L Ctr SO23 ...176 A1
River Rd GU46 .....1 C2
River Rd GU46 .....33 C4
River Row Cotts GU14 ..121 B4
River View Cl SP11 ....128 C2
River View Cotts GU14 .140 A2
River Way SP10 .....83 B1
River Wlk RG14 .....1 A2
Riverdale GU10 .....121 B4
Riverhead SO24 .....180 B2
Rivermead Ho GU47 .....34 B4
Rivermede GU35 .....164 C2
Rivers Cl GU14 .....56 B1
Riverside
  Farnborough GU14 .....55 B3
  Liss GU33 .....207 C2
  Old Basing RG24 .....70 A4
  Overton RG25 .....88 A4
Riverside Cotts RG28 ...86 A1
Riverside Ct GU9 .....99 A2
Riverside Gn SO20 ....172 A2
Riverside Ho 4 SO23 ..198 A4
Riverside Ind Pk GU9 ..99 A2
Riverside Rd GU30 ....165 B1
Riverside Way GU14 ...99 A2
Riverway Ind Est GU34 .140 A2
Robert May's Sch RG29 .72 B2
Robert Mays Rd RG29 ..72 B1
Robert Sandilands Prim Sch
  RG14 .....1 B2
Robert Way GU16 .....56 B2
Roberts Cl SO23 .....154 A1
Roberts Rd
  Aldershot GU12 .....77 A1
  Barton Stacey SO21 ...130 C4
  Camberley GU15 .....35 C3
  Sandhurst GU15 .....35 C3
Robertsfield RG19 .....2 B2
Robertson Cl RG14 .....5 C4
Robertson Rd SO24 ...179 B2

Robertson Way GU12 ...77 B1
Robin Cl Alton GU34 ...140 A3
  Ash GU12 .....77 C3
Robin Hill GU15 .....36 C2
Robin Hood Cl GU14 ...55 C4
Robin La
  Bishop's Green RG20 ...6 B2
  Sandhurst GU47 .....34 C4
Robin Way SP10 .....83 A1
Robin's Bow GU15 .....35 C2
Robins Cl RG14 .....5 B4
Robins Grove Cres GU46 .33 C3
Robinson Way GU35 ...164 C1
Rochester Cl RG22 .....91 A4
Rochester Gr GU51 .....75 A4
Rochford Rd RG21 .....69 A3
Rock Gdns GU11 .....76 B1
Rock La GU10 .....121 C3
Rockbourne Rd SO22 ..175 B2
Rockdale Dr GU26 .....167 A2
Rockdale Ho GU26 ....167 A2
Rockery The GU14 .....55 B2
Rockfield Way GU47 ...35 A4
Rockingham Rd RG14 ...1 B1
Rockmoor La SP11 .....18 B1
Rockpit Cotts GU33 ...208 A2
Rodfield La SO24 .....200 B3
Roding Cl RG21 .....69 B3
Rodmel Ct GU14 .....56 B3
Rodney Ct SP10 .....83 B1
Roe Downs Rd GU34 ...160 A3
Roebuts Cl RG14 .....5 B4
Roedeer Copse GU27 ..189 B3
Roentgen Rd RG24 .....69 C4
Rogers Ct 1 GU34 ....139 C2
Roke La RG29 .....96 A4
Rokeby Cl RG14 .....5 C4
Rokes Pl GU46 .....33 C3
Roman Rd
  Basingstoke RG23 .....68 A3
  Stockbridge SO20 .....149 B2
Roman Way Andover SP10 .83 A2
  Barton Stacey SO21 ...130 C4
  Basingstoke RG23 .....68 A3
  Farnham GU9 .....99 B2
  Thatcham RG18 .....2 C2
Roman Way Prim Sch
  SP10 .....83 A2
Romano Ct RG14 .....1 C1
Romans Bsns Pk GU9 ..99 A2
Romans Field RG7 .....10 C1
Romans Gate RG26 .....10 B1
Romans Ind Pk GU9 ...99 A2
Romans' Rd 1 SO23 ..198 A3
Romany Cl GU14 .....55 C3
Romily^Ct GU9 .....99 A1
Romsey Cl
  Aldershot GU11 .....100 A3
  Basingstoke RG24 .....48 A1
  Blackwater GU17 .....35 A3
Romsey Rd
  Broughton SO20 .....170 A3
  King's Somborne SO20 .171 C1
  Nether Wallop SO20 ..147 C3
  Wherwell SP11 .....128 B3
  Winchester SO22,SO23 .197 B3
Ronald Barker Ct 5
  SO22 .....197 C4
Rook La SO21 .....133 A2
Rookery Cotts SP5 ....190 B2
Rookery Cl GU15 .....36 C1
Rookery La SO20 .....170 B3
Rookery The RG28 .....86 B3
Rooks Down Rd SO22 ..197 B3
Rooksbury Rd SP10 ...105 C3
Rooksdown Ave RG24 ..48 A4
Rooksdown La RG24 ....47 B1
Rooksfield RG20 .....6 C1
Rookswood GU34 .....139 C3
Rookwood La GU34 ...139 B3
Room Cotts SO20 .....129 B3
Ropewalk Ho 6 SO23 ..198 A4
Ropley CE Prim Sch
  SO24 .....181 B2
Ropley Cl RG26 .....26 C4
Ropley Rd SO24 .....183 A2
Ropley Sta* SO24 .....180 C3
Rorkes Drift GU16 .....56 C2
Rosary Gdns GU46 .....34 A3
Rosary Gdns GU46 .....91 A4
Rose Cl RG22 .....91 A4
Rose Cotts GU12 .....77 C1
Rose Est The RG27 .....72 A4
Rose Gdns GU46 .....55 B2
Rose Hodson Pl RG23 ..68 A4
Rose Wlk GU51 .....53 C1
Rosebank Cl 5 RG26 ...26 C4
Rosebay Gdns RG27 ...51 B1
Roseberry Cl RG24 .....91 A3
Rosebery Rd SO24 ....179 B3
Rosedale GU17 .....77 A1
Rosedene Gdns GU15 ..53 C1
Rosedene La GU47 .....35 A4
Rosehip Way RG24 .....69 C4
Rosemary Ave GU12 ...77 C4
Rosemary Cl GU14 .....55 B3
Rosemary Dr RG26 .....26 C3
Rosemary Gdns GU17 ..35 A3
Rosemary La
  Blackwater GU17 .....35 A3
  Farnham GU10 .....121 B2
Rosemary Terr RG14 .....1 B1
Rosetree Cotts GU34 ..160 C1
Rosewarne Ct 2 SO23 .176 A1
Rosewood Chineham RG24 .48 C2
  Mytchett GU16 .....56 C2

Rosewood Ct 4 SP9 ....79 A4
Rosewood Rd GU35 ...165 A3
Ross Cl RG21 .....69 A1
Ross Terr 15 RG14 .....1 A1
Rossini Cl RG22 .....91 C4
Rossmore Gdns GU11 ..76 B1
Rothay Ct 18 RG21 .....69 B3
Rother Cl RG21 .....35 A4
Rother Ho GU33 .....207 C2
Rother Rd GU11 .....55 B4
Rotherbank Farm La
  GU33 .....208 A3
Rotherwick Ct GU14 ....77 A4
Rotherwick Ho GU51 ..53 B2
Rotherwick La RG27 ...50 B4
Rotherwick Rd RG26 ...27 A4
Rotten Green Rd RG27 ..53 C3
Rotten Hill RG25,RG28 .87 C3
Rotunda Est The 19
  RG21 .....76 C1
Round End RG14 .....5 A3
Roundabouts The GU33 .208 A3
Roundaway La SP11 ....58 C2
Roundhuts Rise 4
  GU33 .....198 B4
Roundmead Rd RG21 ...69 A2
Roundway Ct SP10 ....105 C4
Rounton Rd GU52 .....75 A3
Row The SO21 .....177 C3
Rowan Chase GU10 ...121 C3
Rowan Cl Camberley GU15 .36 B4
  Fleet GU51 .....54 B1
  South Wonston SO21 ..153 C2
  Tadley RG26 .....27 A4
Rowan Ct 8 SP9 .....78 C4
Rowan Dale GU52 .....74 C3
Rowan Dr RG41 .....1 C3
Rowan Rd RG22 .....27 A4
Rowan Tree Cl GU33 ..208 A2
Rowans The Andover SP10 .82 C1
  Grayshott GU26 .....167 A2
Rowanside Cl GU10 ...166 A2
Rowanwood RG40 .....15 C3
Rowcroft Cl GU12 .....77 C3
Rowcroft Rd RG22 .....15 B4
Rowdell Cotts SO24 ...181 B3
Rowhill Ave GU11 .....99 B4
Rowhill Cres GU11 .....99 B4
Rowhill Nature Trail*
  GU11 .....99 A4
Rowhills GU9 .....99 A4
Rowhills Cl GU9 .....99 B4
Rowland's Cl RG27 .....11 A3
Rowledge CE Prim Sch
  GU10 .....121 B2
Rowlings Rd SO22 ....175 B2
Roxburghe Cl GU35 ...164 B1
Royal Cl RG21 .....91 A3
Royal Greenjackets Mus*
  SO23 .....197 C4
Royal Hampshire Cty Hospl
  SO22 .....197 C4
Royal Hampshire Regiment
  Mus* SO23 .....197 C4
Royal Jun Sch The
  GU26 .....167 B1
Royal Military Academy
  Hospl GU15 .....35 C4
Royal Oak Cl GU46 .....34 B3
Royal Par GU27 .....167 B2
Royale Cl GU11 .....100 A4
Royce Cl SP10 .....82 A1
Roycroft La RG40 .....16 B4
Roydon Cl SO22 .....197 C3
Royston Ctr GU12 .....77 B4
Rozeledene GU26 .....167 A2
Rozelle Cl SO22 .....175 A3
Rubens Cl RG21 .....69 B1
Rucstall Prim Sch RG21 .69 B2
Rudd Hall Rise GU15 ...36 A2
Ruffield Cl SO22 .....175 B4
Rufford Cl GU52 .....75 A3
Rune Dr SP10 .....82 C2
Runfold-St George GU10 .99 C3
Runnymede Ct 1 GU14 ..55 C4
Runwick La GU10 .....98 A1
Rupert Rd RG14 .....5 B4
Rural Life Ctr Mus*
  GU10 .....122 B2
Rushden Way GU9 .....99 A4
Rushes The 17 RG21 ...69 B3
Rushmoor Cl GU52 .....75 A4
Rushmoor Ct RG22 .....91 B3
Rushmoor Ind Est GU11 .56 A1
Ruskin Cl RG21 .....69 C2
Ruskin Rd RG21 .....69 A2
Russell Ct
  Blackwater GU17 .....35 A3
  Hindhead GU26 .....167 B2
Russell Dr SO51 .....192 B1
Russell Rd Newbury RG14 ..1 B1
  Winchester SO23 .....176 A1
Russet Cl
  New Alresford SO24 ..179 B2
  Tongham GU10 .....100 B4
Russet Gdns GU15 .....54 B2
Russet Glade GU11 .....99 B4
Russett Rd GU34 .....140 A2
Russetts Dr GU51 .....75 A4
Rustic Glen GU52 .....74 C3
Ruth Cl GU14 .....55 A3
Rutherford Rd RG24 ...69 B4
Rutland Cl GU11 .....76 C2
Ryan Mount GU47 .....34 C4
Rydal Cl Basingstoke RG22 .68 A1
  Bordon GU35 .....164 B3

Rydal continued
  Farnborough GU14 .....55 A2
Rydal Dr Fleet GU52 ...74 C3
  Thatcham RG19 .....2 A2
Ryde Cl Fleet GU51 .....77 A1
Ryde Gdns GU46 .....33 C3
Rye Cl Farnborough GU14 ..55 B4
  Fleet GU51 .....54 B3
Rye Croft 8 GU52 .....74 C2
Ryebeck Rd GU52 .....75 A3
Ryecroft Gdns GU17 ...35 B2
Ryeland Cl GU51 .....54 B3
Ryelaw Rd GU52 .....74 C3
Ryle Rd GU9 .....121 C4
Ryon Cl SP10 .....83 A2
Ryves Ave GU46 .....33 C3

S

Sabre Cl 3 GU11 .....76 B1
Saddleback Rd GU15 ..36 B4
Saddleback Way GU51 ..54 A2
Saddler Cnr GU47 .....34 C4
Saddlers Cl SO21 .....131 B2
Saddlers Cl RG14 .....1 B2
Saddlers Scarp GU26 ..166 C2
Saddlewood GU15 .....36 A2
Saffron Cl Chineham RG24 .49 A2
  Newbury RG14 .....1 B2
Saffron Ct GU14 .....55 A2
Sages La GU34 .....204 B3
Sainfoin La RG23 .....90 A4
Sainsbury Cl SP10 ....105 C3
St Albans Rdbt GU14 ...77 A4
St Andrew's Cl 5 GU9 ..99 A1
St Andrew's Inf Sch GU9 .98 C1
St Andrew's Rd RG22 ..68 B2
St Andrew's Way GU16 ..56 B4
St Andrews Rd
  Bordon GU35 .....164 A1
  North Tidworth SP9 ...78 C3
St Ann's Cl SP10 .....105 C4
St Anne's RC Prim Sch
  RG22 .....68 B2
St Annes Cl SO22 .....197 B2
St Aubins Cl GU34 ....160 A1
St Augustine's Cl GU12 ..77 A1
St Augustine's RC Prim Sch
  GU16 .....36 B1
St Austins Cl GU15 ....36 A4
St Barbara's Cl RG26 ..29 A1
St Bartholomew Sch RG14 .1 B1
St Bede CE Prim Sch
  SO23 .....198 A4
St Bede's Cl 1 SO23 ..176 A1
St Bede's RC Prim Sch
  RG24 .....48 A1
St Benedict's Convent Sch
  SP11 .....82 A2
St Benedicts Cl GU11 ..76 C1
St Bernadette RC Prim Sch
  GU14 .....99 A3
St Catherine's Hill RG7 ..11 B3
St Catherine's Rd SO23 .198 A3
St Catherine's Sch RG22 .36 A2
St Catherines Rd GU16 .56 C4
St Catherines Way
  SO23,SO21 .....198 B3
St Christopher's Gn
  GU27 .....189 C3
St Christopher's Rd
  GU27 .....189 C3
St Christophers Cl
  Aldershot GU12 .....77 A1
  Basingstoke RG22 .....68 B2
  Haslemere GU27 .....189 C3
St Christophers Pl GU14 .55 B2
St Christophers Rd GU14 .55 C2
St Clement St
  21 Winchester SO22 ..197 C4
  22 Winchester SO23 ..198 A4
St Clements Cl GU14 ...55 C4
St Cross Cl 4 SO23 ...197 C2
St Cross Hospl* SO23 .197 C2
St Cross Rd
  Camberley GU16 .....56 C4
  Crondall GU10 .....97 B3
  Farnham GU9 .....99 A2
  Winchester SO22 .....197 C2
St David's Cl
  Farnborough GU14 .....55 B4
  Farnham GU9 .....99 B4
St David's Ct GU11 .....76 C1
St David's Rd
  Basingstoke RG22 .....68 C2
  Newbury RG14 .....1 B2
St Davids Cl RG29 .....72 B1
St Donats Pl RG14 .....1 C1
St Edmunds Sch GU34 .167 A2
St Faith Cl GU34 .....160 A1
St Faith's CE Prim Sch
  SO23 .....198 A3
St Faith's Rd SO23 ....197 C3
St Gabriel's Sch RG20 ..5 C3
St George's Cl GU9 ....99 C3
St George's Cl SP9 .....78 C3
St George's Ho 16 SO23 .198 A3
St George's Rd
  Aldershot GU11 .....76 C1
  Farnham GU9 .....99 A1
St George's Rd E GU12 .77 B2
St George's Sch SO23 .198 A4
St Georges Ave RG14 ...1 A1
St Georges Ind Est GU15 .35 C2
St Georges Mews GU9 ..99 A2

St Georges Rd
  Farnham GU9,GU10 .....99 C3
  North Tidworth SP9 ...78 C3
St Giles Ct SO23 .....198 A4
St Giles Cl SO23 .....198 A4
St Giles Hill SO23 ....198 A4
St Helens Cres GU47 ..34 C4
St Hubert Rd SP10 ....105 C4
St James Cl RG26 .....29 A1
St James Ct Farnham GU9 .99 A2
  Fleet GU51 .....74 C4
St James Rd
  Finchampstead RG40 ..16 B4
  Fleet GU51 .....74 C4
St James' Ave GU9 .....99 A2
St James' La SO22,SO23 .197 C4
St James' Terr
  Farnham GU9 .....99 A2
  Winchester SO22 .....197 C4
St James's Rd SP11 .....81 B1
St John Cl RG26 .....29 A1
St John the Baptist RC Prim
  Sch SP10 .....105 B4
St John the Evangelist Inf
  Sch RG14 .....1 B1
St John's CE Prim Sch
  RG14 .....1 A1
St John's CE Prim Sch
  RG21 .....69 A2
St John's Cross SP11 ..105 A1
St John's Ct
  Farnborough GU14 .....55 A3
  Fleet GU51 .....54 A1
St John's Gdns 15 RG14 .1 C1
St John's Hospital
  (Almshouses)(N) 27
  SO23 .....198 A4
St John's Hospital
  (Almshouses)(S) 38
  SO23 .....198 A4
St John's Piece RG23 ..90 A4
St John's Rd
  Andover SP10 .....106 A4
  Farnborough GU14 .....55 B3
  Farnham GU9 .....121 C4
  Mortimer RG7 .....11 C3
  Newbury RG14 .....1 C2
  Oakley RG23 .....67 B1
  Sandhurst GU47 .....34 C4
  Winchester SO23 .....198 A4
St John's St SO23 .....198 A4
St John's Wlk 18 RG21 ..69 A3
St Johns Cl Inf Sch
  GU10 .....144 B1
St Johns Cl RG27 .....51 A1
St Johns Gr GU11 .....76 C2
St Johns Rd RG27 .....52 B3
St Joseph's Cres RG24 .48 A1
St Joseph's RC Prim Sch
  RG14 .....1 C2
St Joseph's Rd GU12 ...76 C1
St Josephs Ct RG14 .....1 C2
St Josephs RC Prim Sch
  GU11 .....99 C4
St Lawrence CE Prim Sch
  GU34 .....139 C2
St Lawrence Rd GU34 ..139 C2
St Leger Ct RG14 .....1 B2
St Leonard's Ave RG24 ..49 A2
St Leonard's Rd SO23 .198 B3
St Leonards Cl SO21 ..153 B2
St Luke's Cl GU12 .....68 B2
St Margarets SP11 .....81 C4
St Mark's CE Prim Sch
  Basingstoke RG22 .....91 A3
  Farnborough GU14 .....56 A1
St Marks Cl Bramley RG26 .28 C4
  Farnborough GU14 .....56 A1
St Marks Pl GU9 .....98 C4
St Martin Cl SO23 .....198 A4
St Martin's CE Prim Sch
  RG20 .....20 C4
St Martins Trad Pk
  SP11 .....61 C1
St Mary Magdalen
  Almshouses 35 SO23 .198 A4
St Mary St SO23 .....197 B3
St Mary's Almshouses 14
  SO23 .....198 A4
St Mary's CE Inf Sch
  GU10 .....144 A4
St Mary's CE Jun Sch
  RG24 .....70 A3
St Mary's Cl
  Kings Worthy SO21 ...176 B3
  Old Basing RG24 .....70 A3
St Mary's Coll SO23 ..198 A3
St Mary's Cotts GU10 .144 A4
St Mary's Ct
  Bramley RG26 .....29 A1
  4 Newbury RG14 .....1 C2
St Mary's Mdw SP11 ..105 A2
St Mary's Pl Farnham GU9 .99 A2
  Newbury RG14 .....1 C2
St Mary's Rd Ash GU12 ..77 C3
  Camberley GU15 .....36 A3
  Hartley Wintney RG27 ..52 B3
  Kingsclere RG20 .....20 C4
  Liss GU33 .....208 A2
  Mortimer RG7 .....11 C3
  Newbury RG14 .....1 C2
St Marys Bentworth CE Prim
  Sch GU34 .....138 A3

St Marys CE Jun Sch RG7 ....12 A3
St Marys Cl Alton GU34 ..139 C2
Sandhurst GU47 ....35 A4
St Matthew's CE Prim Sch GU33 ....186 A4
St Matthews Rd SO22 ...175 B1
St Michael's CE Inf Sch GU11 ....99 C4
St Michael's CE Jun Sch GU11 ....100 A4
St Michael's CE Prim Sch GU47 ....34 B4
St Michael's Cl RG25 ....89 C1
St Michael's Gdns 26 SO22 ....197 C4
St Michael's Hall GU11 ...99 C4
St Michael's Pas SO23 ..198 A3
St Michael's Rd
Aldershot GU12 ....76 C1
Basingstoke RG22 ....68 B2
Farnborough GU14 ....55 C3
Newbury RG14 ....1 B1
Sandhurst GU47 ....34 B4
Winchester SO22 ....197 C3
St Michaels Ave SP9 ....78 C3
St Michaels Cl GU51 ....75 A4
St Michaels Rd GU15 ....35 C3
St Michaels Sch RG20 ....21 B3
St Neot's Rd RG27 ....32 B4
St Neot's Sch RG27 ....32 B4
St Nicholas Cl Fleet GU51 .53 C1
Ludgershall SP11 ....57 A1
St Nicholas Ct RG22 ....68 B2
St Nicholas Rd RG14 ....1 B1
St Nicholas Rise SO23 ...176 A3
St Nicholas Sch GU52 ...74 C1
St Patrick's La GU33 ....208 B3
St Patrick's RC Prim Sch GU14 ....56 A2
St Patrick's Rd RG22 ....68 C2
St Patricks Ave SP9 ....78 C3
St Paul's Hill SO22 ....197 C4
St Paul's Rd RG22 ....68 C2
St Pauls Cl GU10 ....100 B4
St Pauls Pl 19 SO22 ....197 C4
St Peter St SO23 ....198 A4
St Peter's CE Jun Sch
Farnborough GU14 ....56 A2
Yateley GU46 ....34 B3
St Peter's CE Prim Sch GU10 ....121 C3
St Peter's Cl SP11 ....106 A1
St Peter's Cl RG26 ....26 C4
St Peter's Gdns
Farnham GU10 ....121 B3
Yateley GU46 ....34 A3
St Peter's RC Prim Sch SO22 ....197 A3
St Peter's Rd RG22 ....68 B2
St Peter's Way GU16 ....56 B4
St Peters Cl
Headley, Nr Greenham RG19 ..7 A1
Shipton Bellinger SP9 ....101 C4
St Peters Mead GU12 ....77 C1
St Peters Pk GU11 ....99 B4
St Philips Ct 4 GU51 ....54 A1
St Polycarp's RC Prim Sch GU9 ....99 A1
St Richards Rd RG14 ....1 C3
St Stephen's Rd SO22 ...175 B1
St Stephens Cl GU27 ....189 B3
St Swithun St SO23 ....198 A4
St Swithun's Sch SO21 ..198 B4
St Thomas Cl SP10 ....82 C2
St Thomas Mews 22 SO23 ....197 C4
St Thomas St SO22 ....197 C4
St Thomas' Cl RG21 ....69 A4
St Thomas' Inf Sch RG20 ....21 A4
Salcombe Rd RG14 ....1 B1
Salcot Rd SO23 ....176 A1
Salerno Cl GU11 ....76 C1
Sales Ct 5 GU11 ....76 C1
Salesian Coll GU14 ....56 A1
Salesian View GU14 ....77 B4
Salisbury Cl Alton GU34 ..140 A1
Odiham RG29 ....72 B1
Salisbury Gdns RG22 ....68 B2
Salisbury Gr GU16 ....56 C2
Salisbury Ho 12 SP9 ....78 C4
Salisbury La SO20 ....147 B4
Salisbury Rd
Abbotts Ann SP11 ....105 A2
Andover SP10 ....105 C3
Ash GU12 ....77 C1
Blackwater GU17 ....35 A3
Broughton SO20 ....169 C4
Farnborough GU14 ....56 A2
New Alresford SO24 ....179 B3
Over Wallop SP11 ....124 C3
Shipton Bellinger SP9 ....101 C3
Upper Clatford SP11 ....105 C3
Salisbury Terr GU16 ....56 C2
Salmon Rd GU11 ....77 A3
Salmond Rd SP11 ....105 A4
Salmons Rd RG29 ....72 B1
Salters Acres SO22 ....175 B2
Salters Heath Rd RG26 ...47 A4
Salters La SO22 ....175 A1
Saltram Rd GU14 ....56 B1
Sam Whites Hill SP11 ...105 C2
Samarkand Cl GU15 ....36 C2
Sampson Bsns Pk GU15 ..35 C2
Sampson's Almshouses 22 GU9 ....98 C1
Samuel Cody Ho GU12 ...77 C4
Samuel Cody Sch The GU14 ....76 C4
San Carlos App GU11 ....77 A1
Sand Hill GU14 ....55 C4
Sand Hill Ct GU14 ....55 C4
Sandbanks Dr RG22 ....91 A4
Sandford Cl RG20 ....24 C1
Sandford Ct GU11 ....76 B1
Sandford Ho RG20 ....24 C2
Sandford Rd
Aldershot GU11 ....76 B1
Farnham GU9 ....98 C4
Tadley RG26 ....26 C4
Sandham Meml Chapel*
Bishop's Green RG20 ....6 A1
* Burghclere RG20 ....22 B3
Sandheath Rd GU26 ....167 A4
Sandhurst La GU17 ....34 C3
Sandhurst Rd
Finchampstead RG40 ....16 C4
Yateley GU46 ....34 B4
Sandhurst Royal Military Acad GU15 ....35 C4
Sandhurst Sch GU47 ....35 A4
Sandhurst Sta GU47 ....34 C4
Sandleford Hospl RG14 ....5 C4
Sandleford Rise RG14 ....5 C4
Sandown Cl Alton GU34 ..140 A1
Blackwater GU17 ....35 A3
Sandown Cres GU11 ....99 C4
Sandown Dr GU16 ....36 A1
Sandown Way RG14 ....2 A1
Sandpiper Way RG22 ....90 C4
Sandpit Cotts GU10 ....75 A1
Sandpit Hill RG20 ....5 A2
Sandpit La RG7 ....14 C3
Sandringham Cl
Alton GU34 ....139 B2
Farnborough GU14 ....76 C4
Sandringham Ct RG22 ....68 B2
Sandringham Ho 5 SP10 ....83 A2
Sandringham Inf Sch GU16 ....56 B4
Sandringham Way GU16 ..56 B4
Sandrock Hill Rd GU10 ..121 C3
Sands Cl GU10 ....100 B1
Sands Rd GU10 ....100 A1
Sands The GU35 ....164 A1
Sandy Cross GU10 ....100 B2
Sandy Hill Rd GU9 ....98 C4
Sandy La
Bramshott GU27 ....189 A4
Camberley GU15 ....36 B3
Farnborough GU14 ....55 A4
Fleet GU52 ....75 A2
Frensham GU10 ....144 C3
Frensham GU10 ....122 A1
Hartley Wintney RG27 ....52 B3
Haslemere GU26 ....167 B1
Rake GU33 ....208 C2
Tadley RG26 ....27 A4
Sandys Cl RG22 ....68 C2
Sandys Rd RG22 ....68 C2
Sandys Road Rdbt RG22 ..68 C2
Sankey La GU51 ....54 B2
Santina Cl GU9 ....99 A4
Saor Mews 3 SP10 ....105 C4
Sapley La RG25 ....88 A4
Sarah Way GU14 ....55 C2
Sarisbury Cl RG26 ....26 C4
Sarson Cl SP11 ....104 A3
Sarson La SP11 ....104 A4
Sarum Cl
Over Wallop SO20 ....147 B4
Shipton Bellinger SP9 ....101 B4
Winchester SO22 ....197 B4
Sarum Hill RG21 ....69 A2
Sarum Rd Tadley RG26 ....9 C1
Winchester SO22 ....197 A4
Sarum Road Hospl SO22 ....197 B4
Sarum View SO22 ....197 A4
Saturn Ho 9 RG7 ....9 B1
Saunders Gdn 6 RG26 ...26 C4
Saunton Gdns GU14 ....55 C3
Savernake Ho 2 SP9 ....78 C3
Savile Cres GU35 ....164 B2
Saville Gdns GU15 ....36 C3
Savoy Cl SP10 ....106 A4
Savoy Ct GU15 ....36 A3
Savoy Gr GU17 ....35 A2
Sawyer Cl SO22 ....175 A1
Sawyers Ley RG7 ....12 A4
Saxon Croft GU9 ....99 A1
Saxon Ct 1 Andover SP10 .83 A2
Thatcham RG19 ....2 C2
Saxon Leas SP5 ....168 A3
Saxon Mews 9 GU34 ...139 C2
Saxon Rd SO23 ....176 A1
Saxon Way Charlton SP10 ..82 C2
Old Basing RG24 ....69 C4
Saxon Wood Sch RG24 ...68 A4
Saxton Ct 15 SO23 ....198 A4
Sayers Cl Camberley GU16 .56 B4
Newbury RG14 ....5 C4
Scamblers Mead SP11 ...81 C2
Scarlatti Rd RG22 ....91 C4
Scarlet Oaks GU15 ....36 B2
Scarlett's Rd GU11 ....76 C2
School Cl SP11 ....38 B3
School Fields GU35 ....142 A1
School Hill
Farnham GU10 ....121 B3
Seale GU10 ....100 C2
School La Bentley GU10 ...120 A3
Bishop's Sutton SO24 ....180 A2
Broughton SO20 ....170 A4
School La *continued*
Ewshot GU10 ....98 A4
Farnham GU10 ....122 A3
Itchen Abbas SO21 ....177 C4
Kings Worthy SO23 ....176 A3
3 Liss GU33 ....207 C2
Michelmersh SO51 ....193 B1
Middle Wallop SO20 ....147 C4
Riseley RG7 ....14 B2
Ropley SO24 ....181 B2
Silchester RG7 ....10 C1
Yateley GU46 ....33 C3
School Lane Cotts SO20 .147 C4
School Rd Bordon GU35 ..164 B2
Farnham GU10 ....121 B2
Grayshott GU26 ....166 C2
Linchmere GU27 ....189 B3
Riseley RG7 ....14 B2
Schroeder Cl RG21 ....69 A1
Schubert Rd RG22 ....91 C4
Scotland Cl GU12 ....77 C3
Scotland Farm Rd GU12 ..77 C3
Scotland Hill GU47 ....34 C4
Scotland La GU27 ....189 C3
Scotlands Cl GU27 ....189 C3
Scotlands Dr GU27 ....189 C3
Scotney Rd RG21 ....69 A4
Scott Cl Andover SP10 ....83 C1
King's Somborne SO20 ....172 A1
Scott's Ct GU14 ....55 C4
Scrubbs La SO24 ....180 A2
Scures Rd RG27 ....50 C1
Seagull Cl RG22 ....90 C4
Seal Rd
15 Basingstoke RG21 ....69 A2
Basingstoke RG21 ....69 A3
Searing Way RG26 ....9 C1
Searle Rd GU9 ....122 A4
Searle's La Hook RG27 ....51 A2
Hook RG27 ....51 B1
Searles Cl SO24 ....179 B3
Seaton Rd GU15 ....35 C3
Sebastopol Rd GU11 ....76 C1
Second Ave RG7 ....10 A1
Second St E RG19 ....6 C3
Second St W RG19 ....6 B2
Sedgefield Rd RG14 ....6 A4
Sedgemoor GU14 ....55 C4
Seebys Oak GU17 ....35 A3
Sefton Ho 12 GU11 ....76 C1
Sek Kong Cl SO20 ....126 A2
Selborne Ave GU11 ....100 A3
Selborne CE Prim Sch GU34 ....184 B4
Selborne Cl
Blackwater GU17 ....35 A3
Hook RG27 ....51 A1
Selborne Pl SO22 ....197 B3
Selborne Rd Alton GU34 ..162 B3
East Worldham GU34 ....162 B3
Selborne GU34 ....162 B3
Selborne Way GU35 ....164 A1
Selborne Wlk RG26 ....26 C4
Selbourne Gdns GU9 ....121 C4
Selbourne Rd GU34 ....139 C1
Selby Wlk RG24 ....48 A1
Seldon Cl SO22 ....197 A2
Selwyn Dr GU46 ....33 C3
Sepen Meade GU52 ....74 C2
Seremban Cl SO20 ....126 A3
Sermon Rd SO22 ....175 A1
Seton Dr RG27 ....71 C4
Sett The GU46 ....33 C3
Seventh St RG19 ....6 B3
Severals The RG24 ....47 C2
Severn Cl Sandhurst GU47 .35 A4
Thatcham RG18 ....2 C3
Severn Ct 52 SP10 ....83 B1
Severn Gdns RG23 ....67 A1
Severn Rd GU14 ....55 B3
Severn Way 29 RG21 ....69 B3
Seville Cres SP10 ....83 B1
Seymour Ct GU51 ....54 A1
Seymour Dr GU15 ....36 C4
Seymour Pl RG29 ....72 C2
Seymour Rd
Basingstoke RG22 ....68 B1
Headley GU35 ....166 A2
Shackleton Cl GU12 ....77 B3
Shackleton Sq SP10 ....83 B1
Shady Nook GU9 ....98 C3
Shafer Ct RG14 ....1 C1
Shaftesbury Ct
3 Bordon GU35 ....164 B1
Farnborough GU14 ....77 A4
Shaftesbury Mount GU17 .35 A2
Shakespeare Ave SP10 ...82 B1
Shakespeare Gdns GU14 .55 A3
Shakespeare Rd RG24 ....69 B4
Shalbourne Rise GU15 ...36 A3
Shalden La GU34 ....138 C4
Shalden Rd GU12 ....100 A4
Shamrock Cl GU16 ....56 A4
Shanklin Ct GU12 ....77 A1
Shannon Ct 33 SP10 ....83 B1
Shapley Heath RG27 ....52 A1
Shapley Hill RG27 ....52 B1
Shaw Cl SP10 ....105 B4
Shaw cum Donnington Parochial Sch RG14 ....1 B3
Shaw Farm Rd RG14 ....1 C3
Shaw Hill RG14 ....1 C3
Shaw Ho SP11 ....81 A3
Shaw La RG26 ....26 B4
Shaw Mill RG14 ....1 C3
Shaw Pightle RG27 ....50 C1
Shaw Rd RG14 ....1 C2
Shawfield La GU12 ....77 B1
Shawfield Prim Sch GU12 ....77 C2
Shawfield Rd GU12 ....77 C1
Sheddon Pl SO21 ....174 B1
Sheep Dro SO20 ....147 B2
Sheep Fair SP10 ....106 B4
Sheep Fair Cl SP10 ....106 B4
Sheephatch La GU10 ...122 C3
Sheephouse GU9 ....122 A4
Sheepwash La
Burghclere RG20 ....5 C1
Ramsdell RG26 ....46 B4
Sheerlands Rd RG2,RG40 ..15 B3
Sheffield Cl GU14 ....55 B2
Shefford Lodge 7 RG14 ...1 C1
Sheldon's La RG27 ....51 A1
Sheldon's Rd RG27 ....51 A1
Shell La SO24 ....183 A1
Shelley Cl
Basingstoke RG24 ....69 B4
Fleet GU51 ....75 A4
Itchen Abbas SO21 ....177 C3
Winchester SO22 ....197 B4
Shelley Ct GU15 ....36 A3
Shelley Rise GU14 ....55 B3
Shelleys La GU34 ....140 C1
Shenstone Cl RG40 ....16 C4
Shepherd & Flock Rdbt GU9 ....99 B2
Shepherds Cl SO22 ....197 A2
Shepherds Ct GU9 ....122 A4
Shepherds Down SO24 ..179 B2
Shepherds Rd SO23 ....198 B4
Shepherds Rise SP11 ....38 B3
Shepherds Row SP10 ...106 B4
Shepherds Spring La SP10 ....83 A1
Shepherds Spring Schs SP10 ....83 A2
Shepherds Way GU30 ...188 A2
Shepherds Wlk GU14 ....55 B4
Sheppard Almshouses SP11 ....104 A3
Sheppard Cl RG28 ....86 B2
Sheppard Rd RG21 ....69 A1
Sheppard Sq SP10 ....83 B1
Sheraton Ave RG22 ....91 A4
Sheraton Cl GU17 ....35 B2
Sherborne Rd
Basingstoke RG21 ....69 A4
Farnborough GU14 ....77 A4
Sherborne St John RG24 ...47 C1
Sherborne St John CE Prim Sch RG24 ....47 C2
Sherbrooke Cl SO23 ....176 B4
Sherfield Rd RG26 ....29 A1
Sheridan Cl
Aldershot GU11 ....99 C4
Winchester SO22 ....197 B3
Sheridan Cres RG26 ....9 B1
Sheridan Ct
Camberley GU16 ....56 A4
Newbury RG14 ....2 A2
Sheridan Rd GU16 ....56 A4
Sherlock Lea GU17, GU46 .33 B4
Sherrard Mead RG14 ....1 C3
Sherrington Way RG22 ...68 C1
Sherwin Cres GU14 ....56 A4
Sherwood Cl
Basingstoke RG22 ....91 B3
Liss GU33 ....208 A4
Sherwood Terr GU34 ....140 A2
Shetland Rd RG24 ....48 B1
Shetland Way GU51 ....54 A2
Ship Alley GU14 ....56 A4
Ship La GU14 ....56 A3
Shipley Cl GU34 ....140 A3
Shipley Ct 3 GU30 ....188 A2
Shipton Bellinger Prim Sch SP9 ....101 B4
Shipton Way RG22 ....68 B1
Shire Ave GU51 ....54 B2
Shire Ct 2 GU11 ....76 B1
Shires Way GU46 ....34 A4
Shoddesden La
Kimpton SP11 ....80 B3
Ludgershall SP11 ....57 A1
Shoe La GU11,GU14 ....76 C3
Shooters Way RG21 ....69 B3
Shop La RG14 ....1 B3
Short Dale Rd GU11 ....100 A3
Short La SP11 ....82 A1
Short St Aldershot GU11 ...76 C1
Ludgershall SP11 ....57 A1
Shortfield Rd GU10 ....122 A1
Shortheath Crest GU10 ..121 B3
Shortheath Rd GU9 ....121 C3
Shotter's La GU34 ....183 C3
Shotterfield Terr GU33 ..207 C2
Shottermill Fst Sch GU27 ....189 B4
Shottermill Jun Sch GU27 ....189 B4
Shottermill Pk GU27 ....189 B4
Shottermill Rd GU27 ....189 B3
Shrave The GU34 ....160 C2
Shrewsbury Terr RG14 ....1 B1
Shrivenham Cl GU47 ....35 A4
Shrubbery The GU14 ....55 A2
Shrubbs La GU10 ....121 B2
Shyshack La RG26 ....9 B1
Sian Cl GU52 ....75 A3
Sibelius Cl RG22 ....91 C4
Sickle Mill GU27 ....189 B3
Sickle Rd GU27 ....189 C3
Sickles Rd GU35 ....142 A1
Sidbury Circular Rd SP9 ..78 B4
Sidbury Hill Ave SP9 ....78 C4
Sidestrand Rd RG14 ....5 B4
Sidings The GU11 ....77 A2
Sidlaw Cl RG22 ....68 A2
Sidlaws Rd GU14 ....55 A3
Sidmouth Rd SP10 ....106 B4
Silchester CE Prim Sch RG7 ....10 C1
Silchester Cl SP10 ....82 C1
Silchester Dr GU51 ....53 B2
Silchester Rd
Bramley RG26 ....28 B2
Pamber End RG7,RG26 ....27 C2
Pamber Heath RG7,RG26 ...10 B1
Silk Mill La RG25 ....87 C4
Silkweavers Rd SP10 ...106 A4
Silver Birch Cl Fleet GU52 .74 C3
Liss GU33 ....208 A2
Silver Birch Rd SP10 ....82 C1
Silver Hill Sandhurst GU47 .35 B4
Winchester SO23 ....198 A4
Silver La RG7 ....10 C4
Silver Park Cl GU52 ....75 A3
Silverdale GU52 ....75 A3
Silverdale Rd RG26 ....9 C1
Silverglades GU46 ....34 A2
Silverwood Cl SO22 ....197 B3
Silverwood Dr GU15 ....36 C4
Silvester Cl RG21 ....69 B4
Silvester Way GU52 ....74 C3
Silwood Cl SO22 ....175 B1
Simmondstone La GU10 .144 A1
Simmons Wlk 27 RG21 ....69 B3
Simms Farm La RG7 ....11 B2
Simonds Ct 5 SO23 ....176 A1
Simons Cl RG24 ....48 C1
Simons Rd RG24 ....48 C1
Sims Cl RG26 ....29 A1
Sine Cl GU14 ....55 C4
Sinhurst Rd GU15 ....35 C2
Sixth Form Coll The GU14 ....55 C3
Sixth St RG19 ....6 B3
Skates La RG26 ....27 A3
Skew Rd SP11 ....103 A2
Skinners Green La RG14 ...4 C4
Skippetts La E RG21 ....69 B1
Skippetts La W RG21 ....69 A1
Skippons Cl RG14 ....5 A3
Skylark Rise RG28 ....86 A3
Skylings RG14 ....2 A2
Slade Hill Gdns RG20 ....4 B1
Sleeper's Hill Ho SO22 ..197 B3
Sleeper's Hill Rd SO22 ..197 B3
Sleepers Delle Gdns SO22 ....197 C3
Sleepers Hill Gdns SO22 ....197 B3
Sleepy Hollow (Cvn Pk) RG26 ....27 A4
Slessor Cl SP11 ....105 A4
Slim Cl GU11 ....77 B4
Slim Rd GU15 ....35 C4
Smallfield Dr RG27 ....51 B1
Smallridge RG20 ....5 A2
Smannell & Enham CE Prim Sch SP11 ....83 C4
Smannell Rd
Andover SP10,SP11 ....83 B2
Smannell SP10,SP11 ....83 B2
Smay Down La SN8 ....17 A2
Smeaton Rd SP10 ....82 A1
Smithfield La GU10, GU35 ....143 C1
Smiths Mead RG25 ....89 C1
Smithy Cl GU34 ....140 B4
Smithy La GU10 ....143 B1
Smithy The RG26 ....28 C2
Smugglers La SO24 ....182 A1
Smugglers' Way GU10 ...100 B1
Snailing La GU33 ....207 B4
Snailslynch GU9 ....99 A1
Snipe La
Bishop's Green RG20 ....6 B1
Linchmere GU27 ....189 C1
Snoddington Rd SP11 ....80 A1
Snode Hill GU34 ....139 A2
Snowdon Rd GU14 ....55 B4
Snowdrop Cl RG22 ....91 A4
Snowdrop Wlk 2 GU51 ...53 C1
Soalwood La GU32 ....205 C1
Soame's La SO24 ....181 C1
Sobers Sq SP10 ....83 B1
Society of St Pius X St Michael's Sch RG20 ....22 B3
Soke Hill SO24 ....159 C1
Soke Rd RG7 ....10 B2
Soke The SO24 ....179 B3
Solarton Rd GU14 ....55 C2
Solby's Rd 21 RG21 ....69 A3
Soldridge Rd GU34 ....159 C2
Solent Dr RG22 ....91 A4
Somborne Park Rd SO20 ....172 B4
Somers Cl SO22 ....197 B3
Somerset Ave GU35 ....164 B2
Somerset Ct 11 GU14 ....56 A1
Somerset Rd GU14 ....56 A1
Somerville Cres GU47 ....34 B3
Somerville Ct SP10 ....83 B1
Somerville Rd SO23 ....176 B4
Somme Rd SP11 ....79 B4
Sonnige Cl GU47 ....35 A4
Sonning Cl RG22 ....90 C4
Soper Gr RG21 ....69 A3
Sopwith Cl SO20 ....172 A1

Sopwith Pk SP10 ....82 A1
Sorrel Cl
  Farnborough GU14 ....55 A3
  Newbury RG14 ....2 A3
Sorrell's Cl RG24 ....48 C2
Sotherington La GU34 ...185 B3
South Atlantic Dr GU11 ..77 A2
South Ave GU9 ....99 A3
South Cl SO24 ....179 A3
South Dr Littleton SO22 .175 A2
  Sherfield on Loddon RG27 .49 B4
  South Tidworth SP9 .....78 C2
South End Rd SP10 ....106 A3
South Farnborough Inf Sch
  GU14 ....77 A4
South Farnham Com Sch
  GU9 ....99 A1
South Gr GU51 ....54 B2
South Ham Rd RG22 ....68 C2
South Hill RG25 ....94 B3
South Hurst GU35 ....164 B1
South La GU17 ....77 C1
South Mall **16** GU51 ......53 C1
South Rd Broughton SO20 .170 B3
  Kingsclere RG20 ....24 C1
  Liphook GU30 ....188 A1
  New Alresford SO24 .....179 A3
South Ridge RG29 ....72 C1
South Side GU10 ....100 B4
South St Andover SP10 ...106 A4
  Ash GU12 ....77 C2
  Farnborough GU14 ....56 B1
  Farnham GU9 ....99 A1
  Ropley SO24 ....181 B2
South Town Rd GU34 ......159 C3
South View SO22 ....197 C4
South View Cl SO21 ......131 B2
South View Cotts
  Bentley GU10 ....120 A2
  Hook RG27 ....72 A4
South View Gdns
  Andover SP10 ....106 A4
  15 Newbury RG14 ....1 C2
South View Jun & Infs Sch
  RG21 ....69 B4
South View Park Homes
  SO22 ....197 B2
South View Rd SO22 ......197 B2
South View Terr SP11 ....85 A4
South Way SP10 ....83 C1
South Wlk SP10 ....77 A1
South Weston Prim Sch
  SO21 ....153 B2
Southampton Cl GU17 ....35 A3
Southampton St GU14 ....76 C4
Southbrook Cotts SO21 ..133 A2
Southbrook Pl SO21 .....133 A2
Southby Dr GU51 ....54 A1
Southcote Dr GU15 ......36 C3
Southdown Rd
  Tadley RG26 ....26 C4
  Thatcham RG19 ....2 B2
Southdowns SO24 ....157 C1
Southend Rd RG21 ....69 A3
Southern Haye RG27 .....52 B3
Southern Rd
  Basingstoke RG21 ....69 A2
  Bordon GU35 ....164 B3
  Camberley GU15 ....36 A3
Southern Way
  Farnborough GU14 ....55 B2
  Farnham GU9 ....99 A2
Southgate St SO23 ......197 C4
Southgate Villas SO23 ..197 C4
Southington La RG25 ....67 A4
Southlands RG24 ....48 C2
Southlands Cl GU17 ....77 C1
Southlands Rd GU12 ....77 C1
Southlea RG25 ....92 A4
Southmead Rd GU11 ....99 C4
Southrope Gn RG25 .....116 B4
Southside Cotts SO20 ..149 C2
Southside Rd SP11 .....108 A3
Southview Cotts GU10 ..122 A1
Southview Rd GU35 .....165 C3
Southview Rise GU34 ...139 C3
Southwark Cl GU46 .....34 A3
Southway GU15 ....35 C2
Southwell Park Rd GU15 .36 A3
Southwick Cl SO22 .....175 B2
Southwood Cres GU14 ..55 A2
Southwood Inf Sch GU14 .98 A4
Southwood La
  Farnborough GU14 .....55 A2
  Farnborough GU51 .....54 C2
Southwood Rd
  Farnborough GU14 .....55 B2
  Hawley GU46 ....34 B1
  Shalden GU34 ....139 A4
Sovereign Ct **11** GU51 ..53 C1
Sovereign Dr GU15 .....36 C4
Sowcroft La RG29 ......118 A3
Spa Meadow Cl RG19 ...6 A4
Spain La RG25 ....115 C2
Sparkford Cl SO22 .....197 C3
Sparkford Rd SO22 .....197 C4
Sparrowhawk Cl GU10 ..98 A4
Sparsholt CE Prim Sch
  SO21 ....174 B2
Sparsholt Coll Hampshire
  SO21 ....174 A2
Sparsholt Rd SO21,SO22 .196 B2
Sparvell Way GU15 .....36 A3

Sparvells GU46 ....33 B4
Spats La GU35 ....165 B4
Speckled Wood Rd RG24 .48 A1
Speen Hill Cl RG14 .....1 B2
Speen La RG14 ....1 B2
Speen Lodge Ct RG14 ...1 B2
Speen Pl RG14 ....1 B2
Speenhamland Ct **3** RG14 .1 C2
Speenhamland Prim Sch
  RG14 ....1 B2
Spencer Cl
  Camberley GU16 ....56 B3
  Fleet GU52 ....75 B3
  Four Marks GU34 ....160 A2
  Pamber Heath RG26 ....10 B1
Spencer Ct GU35 ....164 B1
Spencer Rd RG14 ....1 A2
Spenser Cl GU34 ....140 A3
Sperrin Cl RG22 ....68 A2
Spey Ct **18** SP10 ....83 B1
Spicers GU34 ....140 A2
Spicers Cl **5** SO22 .....197 C4
Spiers Cl RG26 ....27 A4
Spiers La SO24 ....135 C2
Spindle Ho **2** SP10 ....106 A4
Spinney The
  Finchampstead RG40 ...16 B4
  Fleet GU51 ....74 B4
  Grayshott GU26 ....166 C2
  Hook RG27 ....51 A1
  Yateley GU46 ....34 A4
Spitalfields Rd GU34 ..139 C2
Spitalhatch GU34 ......140 A2
Spitfire End **7** SO23 ...198 B4
Spitfire Link SO23 ....198 B4
Spitfire Rdbt SO23 ....198 B4
Spokane Cl GU11 ....99 B4
Sprat's Hatch La RG27 .73 C4
Spray Leaze SP11 ......57 A1
Sprents La RG25 ....88 A4
Spring Cl RG24 ....47 C2
Spring Gdns
  Camberley GU15 ....36 C3
  Farnborough GU14 .....55 C4
  New Alresford SO24 ...179 B2
Spring Hill La SP11 ...61 C1
Spring La
  Aldermaston RG7 ......10 A4
  Burghclere RG20 ......22 B3
  Mortimer RG7 ....11 C3
  Swallowfield RG7 .....2 C4
Spring La W GU9 ....98 C3
Spring Mews SP10 ......83 A1
Spring Way SO24 ....179 B2
Spring Woods GU52 ....74 C4
Springcross Ave GU14 .35 A2
Springdale RG40 ......16 B4
Springfarm Rd GU27 ...189 B3
Springfield **2** Liss GU33 .207 C2
  Oakley RG23 ....67 B1
Springfield Ave RG27 ..52 B4
Springfield Cl SP10 ...106 B4
Springfield La Fleet GU51 .53 C1
  Newbury RG14 ....1 B2
Springfield Rd Ash GU12 .77 C3
  Camberley GU15 ....36 C3
  Pamber Heath RG26 ...10 B1
Springholme Cl GU9 ...99 C3
Springlakes Est GU12 .77 B4
Springmead Ct GU27 ..189 A3
Springs The RG7 ......29 A4
Springvale Ave SO23 ..176 A3
Springvale Rd SO23 ...176 A4
Springwell La RG27 ...52 C4
Spruce Ave GU15 ......164 A2
Spruce Cl Andover SP10 .105 B4
  South Wonston SO21 ..153 C2
Spruce Way GU51 .....54 B3
Spurs Ct **8** GU12 .....76 B1
Spybush La SO24 .....135 B1
Square Dr GU27 ......189 C1
Square The
  Farnham GU10 ....121 B2
  Grayshott GU26 ......167 A2
  Liphook GU30 ....187 C2
  Nether Wallop SO20 ..148 A3
  Sutton Scotney SO21 .131 B2
  Upper Froyle GU34 ...119 A1
  Winchester SO23 .....198 A4
Squarefield Gdns RG27 .51 B1
Squires Ct GU15 ....36 A2
Squirrel Cl GU47 ......34 C4
Squirrel La GU14 ......55 C3
Stable Cl RG27 ....50 C1
Stable Ct RG14 ....1 C3
Stable Rd GU35 ....164 B3
Stable View GU46 .....34 A4
Stables Rd SP9 ....78 C2
Stables The RG26 .....28 C1
Staddlestones Cotts
  SP11 ....82 A2
Staff College Rd
  Camberley GU15 .....35 C3
  Sandhurst GU15 .....35 C3
Staff Rd Aldershot GU12 .77 A1
  Michelmersh SO51 ...193 A1
Stag Hill RG22 ....68 B1
Stag Oak La RG24 ....48 C2
Stainers La SO21 ....153 B2
Stake La GU14 ....55 C2
Stamford Ave GU16 ...36 B1
Stanbury Cl SP11 ....103 C4
Stanbury Rd SP11 ....80 B1
Stancomb Broad La
  GU34 ....159 B1
Stancombe La GU34 ...159 B1
Standford Hill GU35 ..165 A1

Standford La GU35 ....165 A2
Standing Hill SP5 ....190 C4
Stanfield RG26 ....26 C4
Stanford Rd RG22 ....91 B4
Stanham Cl SO21 .....153 B1
Stanhope Rd GU15 ....35 B2
Stanley Dr GU14 .....55 B3
Stanley Rd RG14 .....1 C1
Stanmore Gdns RG7 ...11 B3
Stanmore La SO22 ....197 B3
Stanmore Prim Sch
  SO22 ....197 C3
Stanton Dr GU51 .....74 C4
Staple Gdns SO23 ....197 C4
Stapleton Cl RG14 ...5 A3
Stapley La SO24 .....181 B1
Star Hill Churt GU10 .144 A1
  Hartley Wintney RG27 .52 B1
Star Hill Dr GU10 ...144 A2
Star La RG40 ....77 B1
  Highclere RG20 .....21 B3
Star Post Rd GU15 ...36 B4
Starling Cl RG22 ....90 C4
Starting Gates RG14 .2 A1
Statham Sq SP10 ....83 B2
Station App
  Andover SP10 ....105 C4
  Ash GU12 ....77 C4
  Blackwater GU17 ....35 B2
  Grateley SP11 ......124 C4
  Haslemere GU27 .....189 C3
  Medstead GU34 .....160 B2
  New Alresford SO24 .179 B3
  Overton RG25 ....65 A1
Station Cl SO21 .....177 C3
Station Hill Farnham GU9 .99 A1
  Itchen Abbas SO21 .177 B1
  Ropley SO24 ....180 C3
  Station SO23 ....197 C4
Station Ind Est GU51 .54 A2
Station Mall **18** RG21 .69 A3
Station Rd Aldershot GU11 .76 C1
  Alton GU34 ....140 A2
  Bentley GU10 ....120 C2
  Bordon GU35 ....164 B3
  Camberley GU16 ....56 A4
  Chilbolton SO20 ...128 C2
  East Tisted GU34,SO24 .183 B3
  Farnborough GU14 ...55 C2
  Grately SP11 ......125 A4
  Hook RG27 ....72 A4
  Liphook GU30 ......188 A1
  Liss GU33 ....207 C2
  New Alresford SO24 .179 B3
  Newbury, Speen RG14 .1 A3
  Oakley RG23 ....66 C1
  Over Wallop SO20 ..125 B1
  Overton RG25 ......65 A1
  South Tidworth SP9 .78 C3
  Stratfield Mortimer RG7 .12 B3
  Whitchurch RG28 ...86 B3
  Winchfield RG27 ...52 B1
  Woolton Hill RG20 ..4 C1
Station Rd E GU12 ...77 C4
Station Rd W GU12 ...77 B4
Station View GU11 ...77 C4
Staveden Rd SO21 ....153 B2
Steele's Rd GU11 ...76 C2
Steeple Dr GU34 ....139 C2
Steepways GU26 ....166 C3
Stenbury Dr RG25 ...136 A4
Step Terr SO21 .....153 B2
Stephen Gould Ho GU14 .76 C4
Stephen's Cl RG7 ...11 B3
Stephen's Rd RG7 ...11 B3
Stephendale Rd GU9 .99 A2
Stephens Firs RG7 ...11 B3
Stephens Rd RG26 ...27 A4
Stephenson Cl SP10 ..82 B1
Stephenson Ct GU9 ..121 C4
Stephenson Rd
  Arborfield RG2 .....15 C4
  Basingstoke RG21 ...68 C3
Sterling Gdns GU47 ...35 B4
Sterling Pk SP10 ....82 B1
Stevens Dro SO20 ....171 B3
Stevens Gn SP11 .....62 A1
Stevens Hill GU46 ...34 B3
Steventon Rd RG25 ..89 C1
Stewards Rise SO20 .121 B4
Stewart Rd RG24 ....69 C4
Stile Gdns GU27 ....189 B3
Stiles Dr SP10 .....106 B4
Stillions Cl GU34 ...140 A2
Stilwell Cl GU46 ...34 B3
Stirling Cl
  Camberley GU16 ....36 B1
  Farnborough GU14 ..77 B3
  Farnborough GU14 ..55 C2
Stirling Est RG14 ...1 C1
Stirrup Cl RG14 .....5 C4
Stoatley Hollow GU27 .189 C4
Stoatley Rise GU27 ..189 C4
Stockbridge Cl RG24 .49 A2
Stockbridge Dr GU11 .100 A3
Stockbridge Prim Sch
  SO20 ....149 C2
Stockbridge Rd
  King's Somborne SO20 .172 A2
  Red Rice SP11 ......127 A3
  Sutton Scotney SO21 .131 B2
  Winchester SO21,SO22,
  SO23 ....175 B1
Stockbridge Way GU46 .34 A3
Stocker Cl RG21 .....68 B2
Stockers Ave SO22 ...175 B1

Stockton Ave GU51 ...53 C1
Stockton House Sch
  GU51 ....53 C1
Stockton Pk GU51 ...53 C1
Stockwood Rise GU15 .35 C3
Stockwood Way GU9 ..99 B4
Stodham La GU33 ....207 C1
Stoke Charity Rd SO21,
  SO23 ....154 A1
Stoke Gate SP11 ....61 B3
Stoke Hill SP11 .....61 A2
Stoke Hills GU9 ....99 A2
Stoke Ho RG26 ......26 C4
Stoke La SP11 ......61 A3
Stoke Rd Stoke SP11 .61 A1
  Winchester SO23 ...154 C1
Stokes La RG27 ....51 C4
Stokes La RG26 ....9 A1
Stone Cl Andover SP10 .105 C3
  Middle Winterslow SP5 .168 A3
Stone Copse RG14 ....2 B4
Stone St GU12 ....100 A4
Stonedene Cl GU35 ...165 C2
Stonehill Pk GU35 ...165 C2
Stonehill Rd GU35 ...166 A2
Stonehills RG25 .....89 A3
Stonehouse Gdn GU30 .188 A2
Stonehouse Rise GU16 .36 B1
Stoneleigh Cl GU16 ..35 C1
Stoner Hill Rd GU32 .206 A1
Stoney Bottom GU26 .167 A2
Stoney La GU46 .....34 A2
Stony La GU32 ......205 C1
Stonycroft **8** GU11 ..76 B1
Stoneyfields GU9 ....99 B1
Stooke Way GU46 ...33 C2
Stour Rd RG23 .....67 A1
Stourhead Cl
  Andover SP10 ....105 C4
  Farnborough GU14 ..56 A2
Stovold's Way GU11 ..99 B4
Stratfield Rd RG26 ..26 C4
Stratfield Cl RG26 ..26 C4
Stratfield Ho **16** GU51 .76 C1
Stratfield Rd RG21 ..69 A4
Stratfield Saye Ho* RG7 .30 B4
Stratfield Saye Rd RG7 .29 A3
Stratford Ct
  Farnborough GU14 ..56 A2
  Farnham GU9 ......99 A1
  9 Winchester SO23 .176 A1
Stratford Rd GU12 ..77 B4
Strathfield Rd SP10 .106 A3
Strathmore Ct GU15 .36 A3
Stratton Cl SO21 ...134 A2
Stratton La SO21 ...134 A2
Stratton Rd
  Basingstoke RG21 ...68 C1
  Basingstoke RG21 ...68 C3
Stratton Wlk GU14 ..55 B3
Strauss Rd RG22 ....91 B4
Stravinsky Rd RG22 .91 C4
Strawberry Fields RG26 .28 C2
Stream Farm Cl GU10 .122 A4
Stream Valley Rd GU10 .123 A3
Streamside GU51 ....75 A4
Street End RG27 ....53 A2
Street The Aldermaston RG7 .9 C4
  Binsted GU34 ......141 C4
  Bramley RG26 ......28 B2
  Crookham Village GU51 .74 B3
  Farnham GU10 ......121 B3
  Frensham GU10 ....144 A4
  Frensham, Dockenfield
  GU10 ....143 B3
  Greywell RG29 .....71 C2
  Long Sutton RG29 .95 B2
  North Warnborough RG29 .72 B2
  Old Basing RG24 ...70 C4
  Rotherwick RG27 ...50 C3
  Stratfield Mortimer RG7 .12 A3
  Swallowfield RG7 ...14 A3
  Tongham GU10 ......100 B3
Stroller Cl RG19 ....2 B2
Stroud Cl Chineham RG24 .48 C1
  Pamber Heath RG26 ..10 B1
Stroud La
  Crookham Village GU51 .74 B3
  Yateley GU17 ....34 C2
Stroudley Rd RG24 ...69 C4
Stuart Cl GU14 .....55 C3
Stuart Cres RG02 ....197 C3
Stuart Ct **2** SP10 ...83 A2
Stuart Rd RG14 .....5 C4
Stubbington Ave RG25 .164 B1
Stubbs Cl SP10 .....82 C1
Stubbs Folly GU47 ..44 A4
Stubbs Ind Site GU11 .77 B3
Stubbs Moor Rd GU14 .55 B2
Stubbs Rd RG21 .....69 C4
Stud Offices The SP11 .80 C4
Studland Ind Est RG20 .3 C2
Stukeley Rd RG21 ...69 A2
Sturdee Cl GU16 ....36 B1
Sturt Ave GU27 ....189 B3
Sturt Rd Camberley GU16 .56 B3
  Farnham GU9 ......98 C4
  Mytchett GU16 .....56 B3
Stymies GU51 ......164 A1
Suddern Cotts SO20 .147 B4
Suffolk Rd SP10 ....105 C4

Sullivan Cl GU14 ....55 C2
Sullivan Rd
  Basingstoke RG22 ...68 C1
  Camberley RG22 ....35 C3
Summer Down La RG23,
  RG26 ....66 C3
Summerdown Cotts
  RG23 ....109 C1
Summerfield La GU10 .121 C1
Summerfields RG24 ...56 A4
Summerstown Ct GU26 .167 A2
Summit Cl GU44 .....167 A2
Summit Ct GU14 .....44 A4
Summersfield GU33 ..207 C2
Summit Ave GU44 ....55 A2
Summit Cl RG40 .....16 B4
Sumner Cl GU9 .....99 A2
Sumner Rd GU9 .....99 A2
Sun Brow GU27 .....189 C3
Sun Cl GU34 ....179 B2
Sun Hill Inf & Jun Sch
  SO24 ....179 B3
Sun La
  New Alresford SO24 .179 B3
  Swallowfield RG7 ...13 C1
Sun Ray Est GU47 ...34 B4
Sunbury Cl GU35 ....164 C2
Sunflower Cl RG22 ...91 A4
Sunley Cl RG14 .....5 A3
Sunny Hill Rd GU11 ..76 A1
Sunny Mead RG23 ....90 A4
Sunny View Cl **5** GU12 .77 A1
Sunnybank SO21 ....104 C3
Sunnybank Mews GU12 .77 C2
Sunnybank Rd GU14 ..55 A3
Sunnydell La GU10 ..121 C3
Sunnydown Rd SO22 .197 A2
Sunnyside Fleet GU51 .53 C1
  Kingsley GU35 .....142 B1
  Newbury RG14 .....1 B3
Sunnyside Cl SP10 ..82 C1
Sunnyside Cotts RG20 .24 B1
Sunnyside Rd GU35 ..166 A2
Sunvale Ave GU27 ...189 A3
Sunvale Cl GU27 ....189 A3
Surrey Ave GU15 ....35 C2
Surrey Heath Mus GU15 .36 A3
Surrey Inst of Art & Design
  The GU9 ....99 B2
Sussex Gdns GU51 ...54 B2
Sussex St SO23 .....197 C4
Sutcliffe Sq SP10 ...83 B2
Sutherland Cl GU35 .164 B1
Sutherland St SP10 .83 A1
Sutherlands RG14 ...1 C4
Sutton Field GU35 ..164 B1
Sutton Gdns SO21 ...198 A4
Sutton Pk SO21 .....131 B2
Sutton Rd
  Basingstoke RG22 ...69 A4
  Camberley GU15 ....36 C4
  Newbury RG14 .....1 B3
Suttonwood La SO24 .180 C4
Swains Cl RG26 .....26 C4
Swains Rd RG26 ....26 C4
Swale Rd GU14 .....55 B3
Swaledale Gdns GU51 .54 A2
Swallow Cl Alton GU34 .140 A3
  Basingstoke RG22 ...90 C4
  North Tidworth SP9 ..78 C3
Swallow Ct GU35 ....164 B1
Swallowfield Pk* RG7 .14 A4
Swallowfield Rd RG7,RG2 .14 C4
Swallowfields SP10 ..83 A1
Swan Ct
  15 Andover SP10 ...106 A4
  Binsted GU34 ......34 C4
  Newbury RG14 .....1 B3
Swan Ho GU47 .....34 C4
Swan La Sandhurst GU47 .34 C4
  Winchester SO23 ...197 C4
Swan Mews RG29 ....72 B2
Swan St RG20 ......24 B1
Swan Way GU51 ....74 B4
Swanmore Cl SO22 ..175 B2
Swansdown Wlk RG19 .2 C2
Swanwick Wlk **8** RG26 .26 C4
Swedish Hos RG26 ...2 C4
Sweetzer's Piece RG7 .11 B3
Swelling Hill SO24 ..182 A3
Swift Cl Andover SP10 .83 A1
  Basingstoke RG22 ...197 B3
Swift Rd GU9 ......99 C1
Swift's Cl GU10 ....99 C1
Swindon Ho **9** SP9 ..78 C4
Swing Swang La RG24 .69 C4
Swingate Rd GU9 ...122 A4
Swiss Cl GU10 .....121 C2
Switchback La
  Farnham GU10 .....121 B2
  Farnham GU10 .....121 C2
Sycamore Cl
  Camberley GU15 ...36 B1
  North Tidworth SP9 .79 A3
  Sandhurst GU47 ...54 C4
Sycamore Cres
  Fleet GU51 ....74 C3
  Middle Wallop SO20 .126 C4
Sycamore Dr Ash GU12 .77 C4
  Camberley GU16 ...56 B1
  Farnham GU10 .....121 C3
  Kings Worthy SO23 .176 A4
Sycamore Rd GU14 ..49 A2
Sycamore Rd GU14 ..55 A2
Sycamore Rise RG24 .48 C2
Sycamore Way RG23 .68 B4
Sycamore Wlk GU27 .105 B3
Sycamores The
  Blackwater GU17 ...34 C3
  Farnborough GU14 .56 A2
Sydings The RG14 ..1 A3

Sydney Rd GU35 ....164 B2
Sydney Villas GU12 ......77 C4
Syers Cl GU33 ....207 C2
Syers Rd GU33 ....207 C2
Sylvan Way GU52 ....74 C3
Sylvaner Ct RG21 ....69 A3
Sylvester Cl RG14 ....1 B3
Sylvia Cl RG21 ....69 A2
Symonds St SO23 ....198 A4
Sympson Rd RG26 ....10 A1
Syon Pl GU14 ....56 A2

T

Tadley Cl GU51 ....53 B2
Tadley Com Prim Sch
RG26 ....27 A3
Tadley Common Rd
RG26 ....10 A1
Tadley Hill RG26 ....27 A4
Tadpole La GU10 ....75 A1
Taiping Rd SO20 ....126 A3
Talavera Inf & Jun Sch
GU11 ....76 C2
Talbot Cl Mytchett GU16 .56 C2
  Newbury RG14 ....1 B3
Talbot Rd GU14 ....121 C4
Talgarth Dr GU14 ....56 A1
Tallis Gdns RG22 ....68 C1
Talmey Cl RG24 ....48 C2
Tamar Dr RG23 ....87 A2
Tamarisk Cl RG22 ....91 B3
Tamworth Dr GU51 ......54 A2
Tangier Ct [9] GU11 .....76 B1
Tanglewood RG40 ....16 C4
Tangway RG24 ....44 B3
Tanhouse La GU34 .....139 C2
Tank Rd GU15 ....35 B3
Tanner Ct RG14 ....1 C2
Tarn Howes Cl RG19 .....2 C2
Tarn La RG14 ....5 B4
Tarn Rd GU26 ....167 B2
Tarragon Cl GU14 ....55 A2
Tarrant Gdns RG27 ......52 B2
Taskers Dr GU51 ....105 B2
Tasmania Cl RG24 ....48 B1
Tate Sq SP10 ....83 B2
Taverner Cl RG21 ....69 B4
Tavistock Gdns GU14 ....55 C4
Tavistock Inf Sch GU51 ..74 B4
Tavistock Rd GU51 ......74 B4
Tawny Gr GU14 ....160 A1
Tay Cl GU14 ....55 B3
Taylor Dr RG26 ....29 A1
Taylor Rd GU11 ....77 B4
Taylors Cl GU35 ....164 C3
Taylors Cnr SO23 ......176 A3
Taylors La GU34 ....164 C3
Teachers Terr [6] RG23 .207 C2
Teal Cres RG22 ....90 C4
Tedder Cl GU11 ....105 A4
Tees Cl GU14 ....55 B3
Teg Down Meads SO22 .175 B1
Tegg Down Rd SO24 ...180 C2
Tekels Ave GU15 ....36 B2
Tekels Ct GU15 ....36 B2
Tekels Way GU15 ....36 B2
Teleconia Cl GU35 .....166 A2
Telegraph La GU34 ....160 B1
Telegraph Way SO21 ...199 A4
Telford Gate SP10 ......82 A1
Telford Rd RG21 ....68 C4
Templar Cl GU47 ....34 C4
Temple Rd GU33 ......208 A3
Temple Twrs RG21 ......69 A2
Temple's Cl GU10 ......100 A1
Ten Acre Wlk GU10 ....121 B2
Tenby Rd GU16 ....56 C4
Tennyson Way RG22 ....68 C1
Tern Cl RG22 ....90 C4
Terra Cotta Ct GU11 ...121 B3
Terrace The
  Camberley GU15 ....35 C3
  Chawton GU34 ....161 B4
Terrys Cotts RG29 ......72 A2
Tesimond Dr GU46 ......33 C3
Test Cl [5] SP10 ....83 B1
Test Mews RG28 ....86 B2
Test Rd RG28 ....86 B2
Test Rise SO20 ....129 A2
Test Valley Sch SO20 ..149 B1
Test Way RG21 ....69 B3
Testbourne Com Sch
RG28 ....86 B2
Tewkesbury Cl RG24 ....48 A1
Texas Dr SO21 ....197 A2
Thackham's La RG27 ....52 A3
Thames Cl RG14 ....55 B3
Thames Ct
  [4] Andover SP10 ....83 B1
  [6] Basingstoke RG21 ....69 C3
Thames Rd RG18 ....2 C3
Thatcham Nature Discovery
  Ctr* RG19 ....2 C1
Theal Cl GU47 ....35 A4
Thibet Rd GU47 ....35 A4
Third St RG19 ....6 B3
Thirlestone Ct GU20 ...167 B3
Thirlmere Cl
  Bordon GU35 ....164 B3

Thirlmere Cl continued
  Farnborough GU14 ......55 B2
Thirlmere Cres GU52 ...74 C3
Thirsk Ct GU12 ....77 A1
Thirt Way SO20 ....129 B1
Thistledown Gl SP10 ...82 C1
Thomas La RG40 ....16 B4
Thomas Merriman Ct [1]
  RG14 ....1 C1
Thomas Rd GU11 ....77 B4
Thorlands GU27 ....189 C4
Thorn Ct GU10 ....121 B2
Thorn Cres GU34 ......160 A1
Thorn Dr GU34 ....160 B1
Thorn La GU34 ....160 B1
Thorn Rd GU10 ....121 C3
Thornburn Chase GU47 .35 B3
Thorneley Rd RG20 .....24 B1
Thornfield RG19 ....7 A2
Thornford Gn GU17 ....35 B2
Thornford Rd
  Greenham RG19 ....7 A3
  Headley, Nr Greenham RG19 ..7 A2
Thorngrove Prep Sch
  RG26 ....21 B4
Thornhill Cres GU11 ....77 A2
Thornhill Rd GU11 ......77 A2
Thornhill Way RG24 ....49 A2
Thornton Cl RG26 ......29 A1
Thornton End GU34 ....83 B3
Thornycroft Ind Est RG21 .68 C3
Thornycroft Rdbt RG22 .68 C3
Thornyhurst Rd GU16 ...56 C2
Thorold Rd GU9 ....99 A2
Thorpe Gdns GU34 ....139 C2
Threadgill Way SP4 ....101 B4
Threadneedle Ho [4]
  SP10 ....106 A4
Three Acre Rd RG14 ....5 B4
Three Horse Shoes La
  SO24 ....203 C1
Three Stiles Rd GU10 ...98 B1
Three Ways GU10 .....143 A3
Threshers Cnr GU51 ....54 B2
Throakmead GU34 .....120 A1
Throgmorton Rd GU46 ..33 C3
Thrush Cl RG22 ....67 C1
Thruxton Airfield Rd
  SP11 ....103 A4
Thruxton Ind Est SP11 .103 B4
Thumwood RG24 ....48 C2
Thundery Hill GU10 ...100 B2
Thurbans Rd GU9 ......121 C4
Thurmond Cres SO22 .197 B3
Thurmond Rd SO22 ...197 B3
Thurstons GU34 ....141 C4
Thyme Cl RG24 ....49 A3
Thyme Ct GU14 ....55 A3
Tibb's Mdw SP11 ....57 C4
Tiberius Cl RG23 ....68 B4
Tiberius Rd SP10 ....83 A2
Tichborne Cl GU17 .....35 A3
Tichborne Down SO24 .179 B2
Tichborne Pl GU12 ....100 A4
Tichbourne Cl GU16 ....36 B2
Tickenor Dr RG40 ......16 B4
Tidbury Cotts SP11 ....109 A1
Tidworth L Ctr SP9 .....78 C3
Tidworth Rd SP9 ....101 A4
Tigwells Field RG40 ....95 A2
Tilbury's Cl GU35 .....164 B2
Tile Barn Cl GU41 ......55 C3
Tile Barn Row RG20 .....4 B1

Tilford Rd
  Beacon Hill GU26 ......167 A3
  Farnham GU9,GU10 ....122 B3
Tilling Cotts GU34 .....141 A1
Tilney Cl GU34 ....139 C2
Timber Bank GU16 .....56 C3
Timber Cl [6] GU9 ......98 C1
Timbercroft Cl GU34 ..160 A1
Timberlake Rd RG21 ....69 A3
Timbermill Ct GU27 ...189 B3
Timor Cl RG24 ....48 B1
Timothy's Field SP11 ..104 C2
Timson Ct RG14 ....1 C2
Tindal Cl GU46 ....34 A3
Tinker's Cnr RG20 ....3 A4
Tinley Gdns RG29 ......72 C2
Tintagel Ct Andover SP10 .83 A2
  Basingstoke RG23 ....68 B3
Tintagel Dr GU34 ......160 A1
Tintagel Rd GU16 ......56 B4
Tintern Cl RG24 ....68 C4
Tippet Gdns RG22 ......91 C4
Titan Ho [6] RG27 ......9 B1
Titchfield Cl RG26 ......27 A4
Titelands La SO24 ....202 C2
Tittymouse La SP11 .....81 B1
Tiverton Rd RG23 ......68 A3
Tiverton Way GU16 .....36 B1
Toad La GU17 ....35 B2
Tobago Cl RG24 ....48 A1
Tobruk Cl GU11 ....83 A4
Tockington Ct GU46 ....34 A3
Todmore GU33 ....185 C2
Toledo Gr SP10 ....83 B1
Tollgate Cl RG23 ....68 A2
Tollgate Rd SP10 ....82 C1
Tollgate The [2] SO23 .176 A1
Tollway RG24 ....49 A2
Tolpuddle Way GU46 ...34 B3
Tomlins Ave GU16 ......56 B4
Tomlins Cl [3] RG26 ....26 C4
Tomliniscote Sch GU16 .36 C1
Tomliniscote Way GU16 .36 C1
Tomlison Dr RG40 ......16 C4

Tongham Mdws GU10 ..100 B4
Tongham Rd
  Aldershot GU12 ....100 A4
  Farnham GU10 ....100 A3
  Farnham, Runfold GU10 .100 A2
Tope Cres RG22 ....15 B4
Tope Rd RG22 ....15 B4
Topiary The
  Farnborough GU14 ......55 B2
  Old Basing RG24 ....70 A4
Toplady Pl GU9 ....99 A4
Tor Rd GU9 ....98 B1
Torriden Cl GU30 ......187 C3
Torrington Cl GU35 ...165 A3
Tothill RG20 ....22 B4
Tottland Ct GU14 ....55 C3
Tottenham Ct RG26 ....28 C2
Totters La RG27 ....51 C1
Tournai Cl GU11 ....77 B4
Tovey Ct SP10 ....83 B1
Tovey Pl SO23 ....176 B4
Tower Ct Clariton SP10 .82 B2
  Winchester SO23 ....197 C3
Tower Ct GU34 ....187 C3
Tower Hill GU34 ....55 C2
Tower Hill Com Sch
  GU14 ....55 B2
Tower Rd Hindhead GU26 .167 B2
  Liphook GU30 ....187 C2
  Winchester SO22 ....197 C4
Tower St Alton GU34 ..139 C1
  Winchester SO23 ....197 C4
Town Cl SO24 ....181 B3
Town Hall Ct RG28 .....86 B3
Town Hall La RG28 .....88 A4
Town Mills RG14 ....1 B2
Town Mills La RG14 .....1 B2
Town Sq GU15 ....36 A3
Townsend Cl RG21 .....68 C2
Townside GU15 ....36 A3
Trade St RG20 ....21 A4
Trafalgar Cl RG14 ....99 A1
Trafalgar St
  Stockbridge SO20 .....149 C2
  Winchester SO23 ....197 C4
Trafalgar Way
  Camberley GU15 ....35 B2
  Stockbridge SO23 .....149 C1
Trafford Rd GU16 ......56 A4
Trenchard Pk GU35 ...164 B2
Trenchard Rd SP11 ....103 A4
Trenchmead Gdns RG24 .68 B4
Trent Cl GU14 ....55 B3
Trent Ct SP10 ....83 B1
Trent Ct [2] SP10 ......83 B1
Trent Way RG21 ....69 B3
Trenton Cl GU16 ....36 C1
Tresham Cres GU46 ....33 C3
Triangle The RG14 ......5 C4
Trilakes Ctry Pk* GU46,
  GU47 ....34 B4
Trimmer's Almshouses [20]
  GU9 ....98 C1
Trimmers Cl GU9 ....99 A4
Trimmers Field GU9 ....99 B1
Trimmers Wood GU26 .167 B3
Trinidad Cl RG24 ....48 A1
Trinity Fields GU9 ......98 C3
Trinity Hill Farnham GU9 .98 C3
  Medstead GU34 ....139 C4
Trinity Rd GU34 ....137 C1
Trinity Rise SP11 ....81 C2
Trinity Sch RG14 ....1 C3
Trooper Bottom GU32 .206 A2
Trotsford Mdw GU17 ...35 A2
Trout Rd GU27 ....189 B3
Trout Wlk RG14 ....1 C2
Trowbridge Ct [3] SO23 .198 A4
Trowbridge Ho [9] SP9 .78 C4
Trowe's La Beech Hill RG7 .13 A2
  Swallowfield RG7 ....14 A3
Trueman Sq SP10 ......83 B2
Trunk Rd GU14 ....55 A3
Trussell Cl GU27 ......175 B2
Trussell Cres SO22 ....175 B2
Tubb's La RG27 ....72 C2
Tubb's La GU46 ....47 A4
Tubbs La RG20 ....21 B3
Tudor Cl Bramley RG26 .28 B1
  Yateley GU46 ....34 A3
Tudor Ct [1] Andover SP10 .83 A2
  Ash GU12 ....77 A1
  Basingstoke RG21 ......69 A2
Tudor Dr GU46 ....34 A2
Tudor Rd GU14 ....55 C4
Tudor Rd RG14 ....1 C1
Tudor Way Fleet GU52 ..75 A2
  Kings Worthy SO23 ....176 A4
Tulip Cl RG22 ....91 A4
Tulls La GU35 ....165 A1
Tunball Cl GU11 ....77 C1
Tunball La SN8 ....37 B4
Tunbridge Cres GU30 .187 C3

Tunbridge La
  Bramshott GU30 ....187 C3
  Liphook GU30 ....187 C2
Tunnel La RG29 ....72 A2
Tunworth Cl GU51 .....53 C2
Tunworth Ct RG26 .....27 A4
Tunworth Mews RG26 ..55 C2
Tunworth Rd RG25 .....70 C1
Turbary Gdns [7] RG26 ..9 C1
Turf Hill Rd GU15 ......36 B4
Turin Cl SP10 ....83 A2
Turk St GU34 ....139 C2
Turk's La RG27 ....11 B2
Turnberry Dr RG22 .....91 A3
Turner Cl RG21 ....69 C2
Turner Cl SP10 ....82 C1
Turner Ct GU47 ....35 A3
Turner's Green La RG27 .53 B3
Turners Ave GU15 ......53 C2
Turners Way GU51 .....53 C2
Turnpike Cotts RG25 ...88 A4
Turnpike Down SO23 ..198 B4
Turnpike Ind Est RG14 ...2 A3
Turnpike Rd RG14 ....2 B2
Turnpike Way RG23 ....67 A1
Turnstone End [4] GU46 .33 C3
Tuscam Way GU15 .....35 B2
Tweed Cl GU14 ....55 B3
Tweedsmuir Cl
  Basingstoke RG22 ......68 A2
  Farnborough GU14 ......55 A2
Twelve Acre Cres GU14 .55 B3
Tweseldown Inf Sch
  GU52 ....75 A2
Tweseldown Rd GU52 ..75 A2
Twigley Ho [1] RG27 ....9 B1
Twill La
  Laverstoke RG28 ....87 A3
  Whitchurch RG28 ......64 A1
Twisell Thorne [8] GU52 .74 C2
Two Gate La RG25 .....89 B4
Two Gate Mdw RG25 ..88 A4
Two Rivers Way RG14 ...2 B2
Twoways Ct [2] GU35 .164 B1
Twyford Ct [15] SO23 ..176 A1
Twyford La GU10 ....99 C2
Tydehams RG14 ....5 B4
Tyfield Rd RG14 ....5 A4
Tyler Dr RG22 ....47 C2
Tyler Rd RG22 ....50 B1
Tylston Mdw GU30 ...187 C3
Tyndalls Est GU26 ....167 B2
Tyne Cl GU14 ....55 B3
Tyne Ct SP10 ....83 B1
Tynley Wood GU26 ...166 B4
Tytherley Rd SP5 ......168 B3

U

Ullswater Ave GU14 ....55 B2
Ullswater Cl
  Bordon GU35 ....164 B3
  Farnham GU9 ....98 C3
  Thatcham RG19 ....2 C2
Ullswater Ct GU14 ......55 B2
Ullswater Gr SO24 ....179 B2
Underhill La GU10 ....121 C4
Underwood Ave GU17 ..77 B1
Underwood Rd GU27 ..189 B4
Unicorn Trad Est The
  GU27 ....189 C3
Union La RG20 ....24 B3
Union Rd GU9 ....99 A1
Union Rise GU33 ......186 B1
Union St Aldershot GU11 .76 C1
  Andover SP10 ....106 A4
  Farnborough GU14 .....55 C2
  Winchester SO23 ......198 A4
Union Terr GU11 ....76 C1
Up St Summer RG25 ..113 B4
  North Waltham RG25 ....89 C1
Upfallow RG27 ....70 A4
Uphill Rd GU27 ....175 B3
Upland La GU33 ....207 A4
Upland Rd GU15 ....36 A4
Uplands Cl GU47 ......34 A4
Uplands Rd GU34 .....160 A1
Uplands Prim Sch GU47 .34 C4
Uplands Rd Farnham GU9 .99 B1
  Winchester SO22 ......175 C2
Upnor Ct SP11 ....79 A4
Upper Bourne La GU10 .121 C3
Upper Bourne Vale
  GU10 ....121 C3
Upper Brook St SO23 ..198 A4
Upper Charles St GU15 .36 A3
Upper Chestnut Dr RG21 .68 C2
Upper Chobham Rd
  GU15 ....36 C2
Upper Church La [14] GU9 .98 C1
Upper College Ride
  GU15 ....36 B4
Upper Dro SP10 ....82 B1
Upper Elms Rd GU11 ...76 C1
Upper Farm Rd RG23 ...90 A4
Upper Froyle Dr GU51 ..53 B2
Upper Gn GU33 ....206 C4
Upper Gordon Rd GU15 .36 A3
Upper Grove Rd GU34 .139 C1
Upper Hale Rd GU9 ....99 A3
Upper High St SO23 ..197 C4
Upper Mount Cl GU33 ..186 C2
Upper Mount St GU33 .207 C2
Upper Mount [18] GU51 .53 B2
Upper Neatham Mill La
  GU34 ....140 B3

Upper Old Park La GU9 ..98 C3
Upper Park Rd GU15 ...36 B3
Upper Raymond Almshouses
  [12] RG14 ....1 B1
Upper School Dr GU27 .189 B3
Upper Sherborne Rd
  RG21 ....69 A4
Upper Soldridge Rd
  GU34 ....159 B1
Upper South View GU9 ..99 A2
Upper St GU51 ....53 C1
Upper St Michael's Rd
  GU11 ....99 C4
Upper Union St GU11 ..76 C1
Upper Union Terr GU11 .76 C1
Upper Verran Rd GU15 ..36 A2
Upper Way GU9 ....121 C4
Upper Weybourne La
  GU9 ....99 B4
Upron Field Cl RG22 ....91 A4
Upton Cl RG22 ....54 A2
Upton Cres RG21 ....69 A2
Upton Grey Cl SO22 ..175 B2
Upton Grey Dr GU51 ...53 C2
Upton Grey Rd RG29 ...71 C1
Urchfont Ho [1] SP9 ....79 A3

V

Vale Cl GU10 ....122 A2
Vale Ct GU12 ....77 C4
Vale Rd Ash GU12 ......77 C3
Valentine Wood Ind Est
  RG7 ....10 B2
Valley Cl The GU22 ...197 B3
Valley La GU10 ....122 A4
Valley Mead SP11 .....105 B2
Valley Rd Camberley GU16 .56 C4
  Littleton SO22 ....175 A3
  Newbury RG14 ....1 B3
Valley Rise GU11 ......105 C2
Valley Side GU33 .....187 C3
Valley The SO22 ......197 B3
Valley View GU47 ......36 A2
Valley Way RG26 ....10 B1
Valmeade Cl RG27 ......51 A1
Valon Rd RG2 ....15 B4
Valroy Cl GU15 ....36 A3
Van Dyck Cl RG21 .....69 C2
Vanburgh Gdns RG22 ...91 A4
Vanners La RG20 ....4 A3
Varna Rd GU35 ....164 C2
Varney Cl GU14 ....55 B3
Vaughans GU34 ....140 A2
Vectis Cl GU34 ....160 A1
Velmead Cl GU52 ......75 A4
Velmead Jun Sch GU52 .75 A4
Velmead Rd GU52 .....75 A4
Venice Ct SP10 ....83 B2
Venison Terr SO20 ....170 A4
Venning Rd RG2 ....15 B4
Ventnor Terr GU17 .....77 A1
Venture Rdbt RG21 ....69 B2
Verden Way SP10 ......82 C2
Verdi Cl RG22 ....91 A4
Verge Wlk GU11 ....99 C4
Verity Sq SP10 ....83 B2
Verlynch Cotts SO20 ..149 C4
Vermont Woods RG40 ..16 B4
Verne The GU27 ....75 A2
Vernes The GU33 .....165 B2
Vernham Dean Gillum's CE
  Prim Sch SP11 ....38 B3
Vernham Rd SO22 ....175 C1
Vernon Ct GU9 ....98 C2
Veronica Cl RG27 ......91 A4
Veronica Dr GU51 .....74 B3
Vesey Cl GU14 ....55 C3
Vespasian Gdns RG24 ..68 B4
Vespasian Rd SP10 .....83 A2
Vestry Ct SP10 ....103 C4
Vetch Fields RG27 .....51 B1
Viables La RG22 ....69 A1
Viables Rdbt RG21,RG22 .68 C1
Vian Pl SO23 ....176 B4
Vicarage Cl GU9 ......100 A4
Vicarage Gdns Fleet GU52 .74 C2
  Grayshott GU26 ....167 A2
Vicarage Hill Alton GU34 .139 C2
  Farnham GU9,GU10 ...122 B4
  Hartley Wintney RG27 ...52 B3
Vicarage La
  Farnham GU9 ....122 A4
  Farnham GU9 ....98 C1
  Farnham, Upper Hale GU9 .99 A4
  Haslemere GU27 ....31 A1
  Marlborough RG26 ......28 A3
  Ropley SO24 ....181 A2
  Yateley GU46 ....34 A4
Vicarage Rd Alton GU34 .139 C1
  Blackwater GU17 ....77 C4
  Yateley GU46 ....34 A4
Vickers Bsns Ctr RG24 ..68 C4
Vickers Rd GU11 ....77 B3
Victoria Ave GU15 ......35 C3
Victoria Cotts RG20 ....20 C4

Victoria Ct Andover SP10 . .105 C4
  ⑨ Fleet GU51 . . . . .53 C1
Victoria Dr GU17 . . . . .35 A2
Victoria Gdns
  ⑨ Fleet GU51 . . . . .53 C1
  Newbury RG14 . . . . .1 C2
Victoria Hill Rd GU51 . . . .53 C1
Victoria Pl
  Basingstoke RG22 . . . . .68 A2
  Hurstbourne Tarrant SP11 . .60 C4
Victoria Rd
  Aldershot GU11 . . . . .76 C1
  Alton GU34 . . . . .139 C2
  Farnborough GU14 . . . . .55 C2
  Farnham GU9 . . . . .99 A1
  Fleet GU51 . . . . .53 C1
  Mortimer RG7 . . . . .11 C3
  Winchester SO23 . . . . .175 C1
Victoria Rd E GU34 . . . . . .140 A2
Victoria St RG21 . . . . .69 A2
Victory Rdbt RG21 . . . . .69 A3
Vidlers Farm RG24 . . . . .47 C2
Vienna Ct GU14 . . . . .55 C3
Vigo Inf & Jun Schs
  SP10 . . . . .83 B1
Vigo La GU46 . . . . .34 A3
Vigo Rd SP10 . . . . .83 B1
Viking Way SP10 . . . . .83 A2
Villa PI RG7 . . . . .14 A3
Village St
  Bentworth GU34 . . . . .138 A3
  Chilbolton SO20 . . . . .129 A3
Village The
  Finchampstead RG40 . . . . . . .16 B2
  Litchfield RG28 . . . . .63 B4
Village Way GU46 . . . . .34 A4
Villiers Way RG14 . . . . .5 A3
Villiers WIk RG14 . . . . .5 A3
Vincent Dr SP10 . . . . .106 A4
Vindomis Cl GU34 . . . . .140 B4
Vine Cl Farnborough GU14 . . .76 C3
  Farnham GU10 . . . . .121 C2
Vine Ct RG14 . . . . .1 C2
Vine House Cl GU16 . . . . . . .56 C2
Vine La GU10 . . . . .121 C3
Vine St GU11 . . . . .76 C1
Vine Tree Cl RG26 . . . . .27 A4
Vine Way GU10 . . . . .121 C3
Vinns La RG25 . . . . .87 C4
Vinson Rd GU33 . . . . .208 A2
Violet Cl RG22 . . . . .91 A4
Virginia Gdns GU14 . . . . . . .56 A1
Viscount Cl GU12 . . . . .77 B3
Viscourts Cl SP10 . . . . .83 C1
Vitellius Gdns RG24 . . . . . . .68 B4
Vivaldi Cl RG22 . . . . .91 C4
Vivian Cl GU52 . . . . .75 A3
Vivian Rd RG21 . . . . .69 B4
Vixen Cl GU14 . . . . .55 C4
Vockins Cl ⑤ SP9 . . . . .78 C4
Vulcan Cl GU47 . . . . .34 C4
Vulcan Ct GU47 . . . . .34 C4
Vulcan Ho ⑤ RG7 . . . . .9 B1
Vulcan Way GU47 . . . . .34 C4
Vyne Cl GU14 . . . . .139 C2
Vyne Com Sch The RG21 . .69 A4
Vyne Mdw RG24 . . . . .47 C2
Vyne Rd Basingstoke RG21 . .69 A3
  Bramley RG24,RG26 . . . . . . .28 B1
  Sherborne St John RG24,
  RG26 . . . . .48 A3
Vyne The* RG24 . . . . .47 C4

W

Wade Rd RG24 . . . . .69 C4
Wadwick Bottom SP11 . . . .62 A3
Waggoners Way GU26 . .166 C2
Waggoners Wells Rd
  GU26 . . . . .166 C1
Wagner Cl RG22 . . . . .91 C4
Wakeford Cl RG26 . . . . .10 B1
Wakeford Ct RG26 . . . . .10 B1
Wakefords Copse GU52 . . .75 A2
Wakefords Pk GU52 . . . . .75 A2
Wakes Cotts GU34 . . . . .184 C4
Walburton Ho RG27 . . . . .52 B3
Waldegrave Pl RG14 . . . . .1 C2
Waldorf Hts GU17 . . . . .35 A2
Wales St SO23 . . . . .198 A4
Walk The RG27 . . . . .47 C4
Walker's Ridge GU15 . . . . . .36 B3
Wall La RG7 . . . . .11 A1
Wallace Way GU11 . . . . .76 B2
Walldown Rd GU35 . . . . . . .164 C1
Walled Mdw SP10 . . . . .106 A4
Waller Dr RG14 . . . . .2 B3
Wallins Copse RG24 . . . . . . .48 C1
Wallis Ct RG23 . . . . .68 B3
Wallis Dr RG26 . . . . .29 A1
Wallis Rd RG21 . . . . .69 A3
Wallop Dr RG22 . . . . .91 A3
Wallop Dro SO20 . . . . .147 B2
Wallop Prim Sch SO20 . .147 C4
Wallop PdB
  Grately SO20,SP11 . . . . . . .125 A4
  Over Wallop SO20,SP11 . . . .125 A2
Walmer Cl GU16 . . . . .56 C4
Walnut Cl Aldershot GU11 . . .99 C4
  Alton GU34 . . . . .139 C3
  Yateley GU46 . . . . .34 A2
Walnut Tree Cl SO21 . . . . .153 B2
Walnut Tree Ground
  SP11 . . . . .80 C1
Walnut Tree Rd SP10 . . . .105 C4

Walnuts The GU52 . . . . .74 C3
Walpole Gdns RG27 . . . . . . .52 B4
Walpole Ho ⑰ GU11 . . . . . . .76 C1
Walpole Rd SO22 . . . . .197 B3
Waltham Ct RG25 . . . . .88 A4
Waltham La
  North Waltham RG25 . . . . . . .88 B3
  Overton RG25 . . . . .88 A3
Waltham Rd RG25 . . . . .88 A4
Walton Cl GU51 . . . . .74 C4
Walton Pl SO22 . . . . .197 B3
Walton Way RG14 . . . . .2 A2
Walworth Ent Ctr SP10 . . .83 C1
Walworth Ind Est SP10 . . .83 C1
Walworth Rd
  Andover SP10 . . . . .83 B1
  Picket Piece SP11 . . . . .84 B2
Wandle Cl GU12 . . . . .77 C1
Wandsdyke Cl GU16 . . . . . . .56 B4
Wansey Gdns RG14 . . . . .2 A3
Wantage Rd GU47 . . . . .35 A4
Warbleton Rd RG24 . . . . .49 A2
Warblington Cl RG26 . . . . . .27 A4
Warbrook La RG27 . . . . .51 A1
Ward Cl SP10 . . . . .83 A1
Warehouse Rd RG19 . . . . .6 B3
Wargrove Dr GU47 . . . . .35 A4
Warminster Ho ⑪ SP9 . . . . .78 C4
Warner Ct Sandhurst GU47 .35 A4
  ⑧ Winchester SO23 . . . . . .176 A1
Warren Cl Bordon GU35 . . .164 A1
  Finchampstead RG40 . . . . . . .16 B3
  Fleet GU52 . . . . .75 A4
  Hartley Wintney RG27 . . . . . .52 B3
  Sandhurst GU47 . . . . .34 C4
Warren Cnr GU10 . . . . .98 A4
Warren Dr SP11 . . . . .104 C2
Warren La
  Colemore GU32 . . . . .206 A3
  Finchampstead RG40 . . . . . . .16 B3
  High Cross GU32 . . . . .206 A3
Warren Rd Bordon GU33 . . .186 B1
  Liss GU33 . . . . .208 A4
  Newbury RG14 . . . . .5 A3
  Winchester SO23 . . . . .198 B4
Warren Rise GU16 . . . . .36 B2
Warren The
  Aldershot GU11 . . . . .76 B1
  Farnham GU9 . . . . .99 B4
  North Tidworth SP11 . . . . . . .79 B3
  Tadley RG26 . . . . .26 C4
Warren Way RG22 . . . . .68 B2
Warrington Mews GU11 . . .99 B4
Warton Rd RG23 . . . . .69 B3
Warwick Cl
  Aldershot GU11 . . . . .100 A4
  Camberley GU15 . . . . .36 C2
  Whitchurch RG28 . . . . .86 B3
  ⑬ Winchester SO23 . . . . . .176 A1
Warwick Dr RG14 . . . . .1 C1
Warwick Rd Ash GU12 . . . . . .77 C4
  Basingstoke RG23 . . . . .68 B3
Wash Brook RG27 . . . . .51 A1
Wash Water RG20 . . . . .4 C2
Washbury Ho RG14 . . . . .5 B4
Washford Cl GU35 . . . . .164 C2
Washford La
  Bordon GU35 . . . . .164 C2
  Lindford GU35 . . . . .164 C2
Washington Gdns RG40 . . .16 C4
Wasing La RG7 . . . . .9 B4
Watchetts Dr GU15 . . . . .36 A2
Watchetts Jun Sch The
  GU15 . . . . .35 C1
Watchetts Lake Cl GU15 . .36 A2
Watchetts Rd GU15 . . . . .35 C1
Watchmoor Pk GU15 . . . . . .35 C2
Watchmoor Rd GU15 . . . . . .35 C2
Watchmoor Trad Ctr
  GU15 . . . . .35 C1
Water Cl SO23 . . . . .198 A4
Water End La RG24 . . . . .71 A4
Water La
  Bishop's Sutton SO24 . . . . .180 B2
  Farnborough GU14 . . . . .55 C4
  Farnham GU9 . . . . .99 B2
  Greenham RG19 . . . . .6 A4
  Upper Clatford SP11 . . . . . .105 C2
  Winchester SO23 . . . . .198 A4
Water Rede GU52 . . . . .74 C2
Water Ridges RG23 . . . . .68 A3
Water Way ⑪ RG21 . . . . .69 B3
Watercress Ct GU34 . . . . . .140 A2
Watercress Mdw SO24 . . .179 A2
Waterfront Bsns Pk
  GU51 . . . . .54 A2
Waterhouse Mead GU47 . .35 A4
Wateridge Rd RG21 . . . . .69 B4
Waterlily Cl ⑬ RG21 . . . . . . .69 B3
Waterloo Ave RG23 . . . . .68 B4
Waterloo Cl GU15 . . . . .36 C4
Waterloo Ct
  Andover SP10 . . . . .106 A4
  Whitchurch RG28 . . . . .86 B3
Waterloo Rd GU12 . . . . .77 A1
Waterloo Terr GU35 . . . . . .163 B2
Waterman Cl GU35 . . . . . . .164 C1
Watermead SO23 . . . . .197 C3
Watermeadows The
  SP10 . . . . .105 C3
Waterside GU30 . . . . .187 B4
Waterside Cl GU35 . . . . . . .164 C2
Waterside Ct Alton GU34 . .140 A2
  Fleet GU51 . . . . .54 A2

Waterside Ct *continued*
  Newbury RG14 . . . . .2 A2
Waterside Mews GU11 . . . .54 A2
Watermeet ⑳ SO23 . . . . . .198 A4
Watery La Andover SP10 . . .83 A1
  Crookham Village GU52 . . . .74 C2
  Hannington Marshall RG20 . . . .3 B3
Watkins Cl RG40 . . . . .16 B4
Watley La SO21 . . . . .174 B2
Watling End RG22 . . . . .91 A4
Watson Acre SP10 . . . . .105 C4
Watson Way RG23 . . . . .68 B3
Watt Cl SP10 . . . . .82 B1
Watts Rd GU14 . . . . .55 B3
Wavell Cl RG22 . . . . .68 C1
Wavell Rd SP9 . . . . .88 B1
Wavell Sch The GU14 . . . . .76 C4
Wavell Way SO21 . . . . .89 A4
Waverley Abbey* GU9 . . .122 C4
Waverley Ave
  Basingstoke RG21 . . . . .69 A1
  Fleet GU51 . . . . .54 A1
Waverley Cl
  Camberley GU15 . . . . .36 B2
  Farnham GU9 . . . . .99 A1
  Odiham RG29 . . . . .72 C2
Waverley Dr Ash GU12 . . . . .77 C3
  Camberley GU15 . . . . .36 B3
  South Wonston SO21 . . . . . .153 C2
Waverley Gdns GU12 . . . . . .77 C3
Waverley La GU9 . . . . .99 B1
Waverley Rd
  Farnborough GU14 . . . . .56 A2
  Finchampstead RG40 . . . . . . .16 B4
Wayman Rd GU14 . . . . .55 B4
Waynflete La GU9 . . . . .98 B1
Waynflete Pl SO23 . . . . .197 B3
Ways End GU15 . . . . .36 B2
Waysend Ho GU15 . . . . .36 B2
Wayside Cotts GU10 . . . . .144 B2
Weale Ct RG21 . . . . .69 A3
Weatherby Gdns RG27 . . . . .52 B3
Weathermore La GU34 . . .160 B1
Weaver Moss GU47 . . . . .34 C4
Weaver's Wlk RG14 . . . . .1 C2
Weavers Cl
  Andover SP10 . . . . .106 A4
  Middle Wintersiow SP5 . . . .168 A3
Weavers Gdns GU9 . . . . .121 B4
Weavers Yd ⑰ GU9 . . . . .98 C1
Webbs Farm Cl RG26 . . . . . .26 B2
Webster Rd SO22 . . . . .175 A1
Wedman's La RG27 . . . . .50 C3
Wedman's Pl RG27 . . . . .50 C3
Weeke Manor Cl SO22 . . .175 B1
Weeke Prim Sch SO22 . . .175 B1
Weir Ave GU14 . . . . .55 C2
Weir Cl GU14 . . . . .55 C2
Weir Cotts RG20 . . . . .4 C2
Weir Rd RG21 . . . . .52 A2
Weir The RG26 . . . . .86 B2
Weirs The ④ SO23 . . . . . . .198 A3
Welbeck Cl GU14 . . . . .55 B2
Welch Way SO23 . . . . .75 A1
Well Cl Camberley GU15 . . . .35 C2
  North Waltham RG25 . . . . . . .89 C1
  Wooton St Lawrence RG23 . .67 C4
Well House La
  Bramshill RG27 . . . . .14 C2
  Kings Worthy SO22 . . . . . . .175 C3
Well La GU51 . . . . .119 A4
Well Mdw RG14 . . . . .1 C3
Well Rd GU10 . . . . .97 B3
Well St RG20 . . . . .22 C3
Wella Rd RG22 . . . . .68 C1
Welburn Cl GU47 . . . . .34 C4
Weller Dr Arborfield RG40 . .15 C3
  Camberley GU15 . . . . .36 A2
Wellesley Cl GU12 . . . . .77 B4
Wellesley Gate ② GU12 . . .77 B4
Wellesley Gdn GU9 . . . . .99 A4
Wellesley Rd
  Aldershot GU11 . . . . .76 B1
  Andover SP10 . . . . .106 A3
  Frensham GU10 . . . . .144 C3
Wellhouse Rd GU34 . . . . . . .138 C1
Wellington Ave
  Aldershot GU11 . . . . .76 B1
  Bordon GU35 . . . . .164 B1
  Fleet GU51 . . . . .54 A1
Wellington Cl
  Newbury RG14 . . . . .2 A3
  Sandhurst GU47 . . . . .35 A4
Wellington Cotts RG20 . . . . .3 C1
Wellington Cres RG20 . . . . . .3 A2
Wellington Ctr The ⑥
  GU11 . . . . .76 C1
Wellington Ctry Pk*
  RG7 . . . . .14 B1
Wellington Gdns GU16 . . . .
Wellington La GU9 . . . . .99 A4
Wellington PI GU12 . . . . .77 C4
Wellington Rd
  Aldershot GU11 . . . . .76 B1
  North Tidworth SP9 . . . . . . .79 A3
  Sandhurst GU47 . . . . .35 A4
Wellington Rdbt GU11 . . . .76 C1
Wellington St GU11 . . . . .76 C1
Wellington Terr
  Basingstoke RG23 . . . . .68 A4
  Sandhurst GU47 . . . . .35 A4
Wellingtonia Cotts RG27 .31 A4
Wellmans Mdw RG20 . . . . . .24 B2

Wells Cotts GU9 . . . . .121 C4
Wells's La RG28 . . . . .86 A2
Wellspring Ho RG22 . . . . . . .68 B1
Wellum Ct SP10 . . . . .106 A4
Welsh La RG7 . . . . .13 C1
Welshman's Rd RG7 . . . . . . .10 C3
Welton Ct RG21 . . . . .69 A3
Wendan Rd RG14 . . . . .5 B4
Wensley Dr GU51 . . . . .54 A2
Wentworth Cl Ash GU12 . . . .77 C4
  Farnham GU9 . . . . .99 B3
  Yateley GU46 . . . . .34 A3
Wentworth Cres
  Ash GU12 . . . . .77 C3
  Basingstoke RG22 . . . . .91 A3
Wentworth Ct RG14 . . . . .1 C1
Wentworth Gdns GU34 . .139 C2
Wentworth Grange
  SO22 . . . . .197 C3
Wentworth Lodge ⑤ RG14 .1 B1
Wesley Ho ⑬ SO23 . . . . . . .176 B4
Wesley Rd SO23 . . . . .176 B4
Wesley WIk RG21 . . . . .69 A3
Wessex Ave RG29 . . . . .72 B1
Wessex Cl RG21 . . . . .69 A3
Wessex Cres RG29 . . . . .72 B1
Wessex Dr Odiham RG29 . . . .72 B1
  Winchester SO22 . . . . .175 C1
Wessex Gdns SP10 . . . . .105 C4
Wessex Mews SO20 . . . . . .149 C2
Wessex PI GU9 . . . . .99 A1
West Ave GU9 . . . . .99 A4
West Berkshire Mus*
  RG14 . . . . .1 C2
West Cl GU9 . . . . .99 A4
West Cotts GU26 . . . . .167 A4
West End Rd RG14 . . . . .47 B2
West End Cl SO22 . . . . .197 C4
West End Gr GU9 . . . . .98 C1
West End Ho RG14 . . . . .1 B1
West End Inf Sch GU11 . . .76 B1
West End La
  Frensham GU10 . . . . .121 C1
  Medstead GU34 . . . . .159 A2
West End Rd RG7 . . . . .11 B3
West End Terr SO22 . . . . . . .197 C4
West Field Rd SO23 . . . . . . .197 C4
West Fryerne GU46 . . . . .34 A4
West Ga GU46 . . . . .33 C4
West Green House Gdn*
  RG27 . . . . .51 C3
West Green Rd RG27 . . . . . . .51 C4
West Ham Cl RG22 . . . . .68 B2
West Ham Est RG22 . . . . . . .68 C2
West Ham La
  Basingstoke RG22 . . . . .68 B3
  Basingstoke, Worting RG22 . .68 A2
West Ham Rd RG22 . . . . .68 B2
West Hayes SO21 . . . . .197 B4
West Heath Rd GU14 . . . . . . .55 B2
West Hill Dr SO22 . . . . .197 C4
West Hill Rd RG21 . . . . .69 A1
West Hill Rd N SO21 . . . . . .153 C3
West Hill Rd S SO21 . . . . . .153 C2
West Mills RG14 . . . . .1 B2
West Mills Yd RG14 . . . . .1 B2
West Pk SP11 . . . . .81 A3
West Portway SP10 . . . . . . .82 B1
West Rd
  Barton Stacey SO21 . . . . . .130 B4
  Camberley SO21 . . . . .36 A3
  Farnborough GU14 . . . . .55 C4
  Fleet GU51 . . . . .53 C2
  West St Andover SP10 . . . .105 C4
  Burghclere RG20 . . . . .22 B2
  Farnham GU9 . . . . .98 C1
  New Alresford SO24 . . . . . .179 B3
  Odiham RG29 . . . . .72 B1
  Tadley RG26 . . . . .27 A4
West St Cl RG26 . . . . .27 A4
West Tisted Cl GU51 . . . . . . .54 A1
West Tytherley CE Prim Sch
  SP5 . . . . .191 A4
West View Andover SP10 . .106 A4
  Bordon GU34 . . . . .164 A1
West View Rd SO20 . . . . . . .129 A2
West View Rd GU35 . . . . . . .166 A2
West Way SP10 . . . . .83 B1
Westbourne Rd GU47 . . . . . .35 A4
Westbourne Terr ② RG14 .1 C2
Westbrook Cl RG22 . . . . .90 A4
Westbrook Ct RG22 . . . . .68 A2
Westbrook Rd
  GU34 . . . . .139 C2
Westbrooke ⑱ SP10 . . . . .106 A4
Westbrooke Rd GU34 . . . .139 C2
Westburn Fields GU34 . . .119 B2
Westbury Cl GU51 . . . . .75 B4
Westbury Ct GU51 . . . . .75 B4
Westbury Gdns
  Farnham GU9 . . . . .99 B2
  Fleet GU51 . . . . .75 B4
Westbury Ho ⑤ SP9 . . . . . . .78 C4
Westbury Rd GU14 . . . . .55 B4
Westdeane Ct RG21 . . . . . . .68 C2
Westerdale Dr GU16 . . . . . . .36 C3
Western Ave
  Andover SP10 . . . . .106 A4
  Newbury RG14 . . . . .1 B2
Western CE Prim Sch
  SO22 . . . . .197 B4
Western Cl RG21 . . . . .69 A1
Western Cross RG29 . . . . . . .72 B1
Western End ④ RG14 . . . . . .1 C2
Western La RG22 . . . . .72 B2
Western Rd
  Aldershot GU11 . . . . .76 B1
  Andover SP10 . . . . .106 A4

Western Rd *continued*
  Bordon GU35 . . . . .164 B3
  Liss GU33 . . . . .207 C2
  Winchester SO22 . . . . .197 C4
Western Way RG22 . . . . .68 B2
Westfield Cl RG26 . . . . .27 C4
Westfield Cres RG18 . . . . .2 C3
Westfield Ct ⑱ GU51 . . . . . .54 A1
Westfield Dro SO24 . . . . . . .201 A1
Westfield Rd
  Basingstoke RG21 . . . . .69 B2
  Camberley GU15 . . . . .35 C1
  Littleton SO22 . . . . .175 A3
  Thatcham RG18 . . . . .2 C3
Westfield Way ⑤ RG14 . . . . .1 B1
Westfields Schs GU46 . . . .33 C3
Westgate Cl RG23 . . . . .68 A3
Westgate Ct RG14 . . . . .1 A3
Westgate Mus* SO23 . . . .197 C4
Westgate Rd RG21 . . . . .69 A1
Westgate Sec Sch SO22 .175 C1
Westglade GU14 . . . . .55 B4
Westland RG18 . . . . .2 C2
Westlands Rd RG14 . . . . .5 C4
Westley Cl SO22 . . . . .175 B1
Westley Cotts SO21 . . . . . .174 A2
Westley La SO21 . . . . .174 B2
Westlyn Rd RG26 . . . . .10 B1
Westmarch Bsns Ctr
  SP10 . . . . .83 A1
Westmead
  Farnborough GU14 . . . . .55 C2
  ⑧ Farnham GU9 . . . . .98 C1
Westmead Dr RG14 . . . . .5 B4
Westminster Cl
  Basingstoke RG22 . . . . .91 A4
  Fleet GU51 . . . . .54 A1
Westminster Gate SO22 .197 A3
Westminster Ho ⑤ RG21 .69 A3
Westmorland Dr GU15 . . . .36 C2
Weston Cl RG25 . . . . .94 A3
Weston Colley SO21 . . . . . .132 B2
Weston Ct SP11 . . . . .83 A4
Weston Down Rd SO21 . . .132 C3
Weston Ho RG27 . . . . .29 B1
Weston La SP5 . . . . .168 A3
Weston Terr SP11 . . . . .128 A3
Westover Farm SP11 . . . . .128 A3
Westover Rd GU51 . . . . .54 B1
Westray Cl RG21 . . . . .69 B4
Westridge RG20 . . . . .21 B3
Westside Cl RG22 . . . . .68 B2
Westview Rd SO22 . . . . .175 A1
Westwood RG14 . . . . .2 A1
Westwood Rd RG14 . . . . .6 A4
Westwood View SO21 . . . .201 C1
Wetherby Gdns
  Charlton SP10 . . . . .82 C1
  ⑩ Farnborough GU14 . . . . . .56 A1
Wetherby Ho GU15 . . . . .36 A4
Wey Bank GU10 . . . . .120 B2
Wey Cl Ash GU12 . . . . .77 C1
  Camberley GU15 . . . . .35 C3
Wey Lodge Cl GU30 . . . . . .188 A2
Weybank Cl GU9 . . . . .99 A2
Weybourne Inf Sch GU9 . .99 A3
Weybourne Rd
  Aldershot GU9 . . . . .99 B3
  Farnham GU9 . . . . .99 A3
Weybridge Mead GU46 . . . .34 B4
Weybrook Ct RG24 . . . . .47 B2
Weydon Hill Cl GU9 . . . . . .121 C4
Weydon Hill Rd GU9 . . . . . .121 C4
Weydon La GU9 . . . . .121 B4
Weydon Mill La GU9 . . . . . . .98 C1
Weydon Sch GU9 . . . . .121 B4
Weydown Cl GU27 . . . . .189 C4
Weydown Ind Est GU27 . .189 C4
Weydown Rd GU27 . . . . . . .189 C4
Weyford Jun & Inf Schs
  GU35 . . . . .164 C2
Weyhill Cl GU27 . . . . .189 C3
Weyhill Ho GU27 . . . . .189 C3
Weyhill CE Prim Sch
  SP11 . . . . .81 A1
Weyhill Ct GU27 . . . . .189 C3
Weyhill Rd Andover SP10 . .105 B4
  Penton Grafton SP11 . . . . . . .81 C1
Weyland Cl GU30 . . . . .188 A3
Weyside GU9 . . . . .99 A1
Weysprings GU27 . . . . .189 C4
Weysprings Cl ⑤ RG21 . . . .69 B3
Weywood Cl GU9 . . . . .99 B4
Weywood La GU9 . . . . .99 B4
Wharf Hill SO23 . . . . .198 A3
Wharf Rd ⑥ SO23 . . . . .198 A3
Wharf Rd Ash GU12 . . . . .77 C2
  Camberley GU15 . . . . .56 C3
  Newbury RG14 . . . . .1 C1
Wharf St RG14 . . . . .1 C1
Wharf The Newbury RG14 . . .1 C1
  Odiham RG29 . . . . .72 C2
Wharf Way GU16 . . . . .56 C3
Wharfenden Way GU16 . . . .56 B3
Wheatland Cl SO22 . . . . . . .197 B3
Wheatlands La RG14 . . . . . . .1 C2
Wheatley La GU34,GU35 . .142 A3
Wheatley Rd GU11 . . . . .76 B2
Wheatleys Cl RG25 . . . . .29 A4
Wheatsheaf La RG14 . . . . . . .1 C2
Wheeler Ho RG27 . . . . .51 B1
Wheelers Yd SO21 . . . . .131 B2
Wheelwrights La GU26 . .166 C2
Wherwell Prim Sch
  SP11 . . . . .129 A4
Whetstone Rd GU14 . . . . . . .55 A2
When Holt GU33 . . . . .75 A3
Whinchat Cl RG27 . . . . .52 B4
Whins Cl GU15 . . . . .35 C2

Whins Dr GU15 .....35 C2
Whistler Cl RG21 .....69 B2
Whistler Gr GU47 .....35 A3
Whistlers La RG26 .....10 C1
Whitakers Cl RG18 .....2 C2
Whitby Cl GU14 .....56 B1
Whitchurch CE Prim Sch RG28 .....86 B2
Whitchurch Cl GU11 .....100 A3
Whitchurch Rd GU11 .....53 C2
Whitchurch Silk Mill* RG28 .....86 B2
Whitchurch Sta RG28 .....86 B3
White Acres Rd GU16 .....56 B2
White Ave GU33 .....186 B1
White Cottage Cl GU9 .....99 A3
White Farm La SN8 .....18 A3
White Hart Ho GU17 .....35 B2
White Hart Ind Est GU17 .....35 B3
White Hart La
Basingstoke RG21 .....69 B2
Charter Hart Par GU17 .....35 B2
White Hill
Burghclere RG20 .....22 A1
Ecchinswell RG20 .....23 B2
Kingsclere RG20 .....44 A3
Long Sutton RG29 .....96 A1
White Ho The SP9 .....78 C3
White Horse La RG40 .....16 A3
White House Cl RG22 .....68 C1
White House Gdns GU46 .....34 A4
White House Wlk GU9 .....99 A4
White La Greywell RG29 .....71 B1
Hannington RG26 .....66 B3
White Lion Way GU46 .....34 A4
White Oak Way SP11 .....105 B2
White Post La GU10 .....121 C2
White Rd GU15 .....35 B3
White Rose La GU10 .....121 C4
White Swan Ct SO21 .....131 B2
Whitebeam Gdns GU14 .....55 A2
Whitedales GU9 .....99 A1
Whitedown GU34 .....139 C1
Whitedown Cotts GU34 .....139 C2
Whitedown La GU34 .....139 B1
Whitedown Rd RG26 .....26 B4
Whitedown Sch GU34 .....139 C1
Whitehall Dr RG2 .....15 B4
Whitehall Rd SO20 .....172 C4
Whitehead Ct RG24 .....69 C4
Whitehill Cl GU15 .....36 A4
Whitehill La SO24 .....179 C2
Whitehill Pk GU35 .....186 C4
Whitehill Rd GU35 .....164 C1
Whitehouse Cl GU14 .....55 C3
Whites Cl RG27 .....50 C1
Whites Rd GU14 .....56 B1
Whiteshoot SO20 .....170 A3
Whiteshute La SO23 .....197 C3
Whitestones RG22 .....91 B3
Whitethorn Cl GU12 .....77 C1
Whitewater CE Prim Sch RG27 .....50 C3
Whitewater Rd RG29 .....72 B2
Whitewater Rise RG27 .....51 B1
Whiteways Ind GU10 .....100 A2
Whitewood Rd GU34 .....48 C2
Whitlet Cl GU9 .....98 C1
Whitley Rd GU46 .....34 A2
Whitmoor Vale Rd GU26 .....166 C3
Whitmore Cl GU47 .....35 A4
Whitmore Gn GU9 .....99 B3
Whitmore Vale GU26 .....166 B3
Whitmore Vale Rd
Grayshott GU26 .....166 C2
Headley GU26 .....166 B4
Whitney Rd RG24 .....69 C4
Whittle Cl
Farnborough GU12 .....77 B3
Finchampstead RG40 .....16 B4
Whittle Cres GU14 .....55 B4
Whittle Rd SP10 .....82 A1
Whittle Rdbt GU14 .....55 A1
Whitworth Rd RG40 .....15 A2
Whynot La SP10 .....105 C4
Whyte Ave GU12 .....100 A4
Wick Hill La RG40 .....16 C3
Wicket Hill GU10 .....121 C3
Wickham Cl Alton GU34 .....139 B1
Fleet GU52 .....74 C3
Tadley RG26 .....26 C4
Wickham Ct GU52 .....74 C3
Wickham Pl GU52 .....74 C3
Wickham Rd
Camberley GU15 .....36 B4
Fleet GU52 .....74 C3
Wicksw Cl RG22 .....68 A2
Widgeons GU34 .....139 C3
Widmore Rd RG22 .....68 B1
Wield Grange SO24 .....136 C1
Wield Industries SO24 .....137 A2
Wield Rd GU34 .....115 B4
Wights Wlk RG22 .....91 A4
Wigmore Rd RG26 .....26 A3
Wilberforce Rd [2] SO22 .....197 B3
Wild Briar RG40 .....16 B4
Wild Herons RG27 .....51 B1
Wilderness Rd GU16 .....36 B1
Widers Cl GU15 .....36 A2
Wildhern SP11 .....59 C1
Wildmoor La
Church End RG27 .....49 A4
Sherfield on Loddon RG27 .....49 C4
Wildwood Dr RG26 .....9 A1
Wildwood Gdns GU46 .....34 A4

Will Hall Cl GU34 .....139 B2
Willems Ave GU11 .....76 B1
Willems Rdbt GU11 .....76 B1
William Cobbett Jun Sch GU9 .....99 B3
William Ct GU14 .....55 C2
William Farthing Cl GU11 .....76 A1
William Hitchcock Ho [5] GU14 .....55 C4
William Ho SP11 .....83 A4
William Way GU34 .....140 A3
Williams Way GU11 .....54 B1
William Pl GU26 .....167 B3
Willington Cl GU15 .....35 C3
Willis La GU34 .....160 C1
Willis Mus The* RG21 .....69 A2
Willis Waye SO23 .....176 B3
Willoughby Cl GU34 .....139 C2
Willoughby Way RG23 .....68 B3
Willow Cl Bordon GU35 .....164 C2
Liphook GU30 .....188 A2
Mytchett GU16 .....56 B2
Newbury RG14 .....1 B1
Willow Cres GU14 .....55 C4
Willow Ct Alton GU34 .....139 B2
Ash GU12 .....77 C4
Camberley GU16 .....36 A1
Willow Gdns GU30 .....188 A2
Willow Gr SP11 .....105 C4
Willow Ho RG24 .....49 A2
Willow Mews [3] SP9 .....79 A4
Willow Pk GU12 .....77 B1
Willow Rd
Bishop's Green RG20 .....6 B1
Liss GU33 .....208 A2
Tadley RG26 .....26 C4
Willow Way
Aldershot GU12 .....100 B4
Basingstoke RG23 .....68 B4
Farnham GU9 .....99 A1
Middle Wallop SO20 .....126 A2
Sherfield on Loddon RG27 .....29 A2
Willowdale RG40 .....16 B4
Willowford GU46 .....34 A3
Willowmead Ct RG14 .....5 A3
Willows End GU47 .....34 C4
Willows The
Andover SP10 .....105 C3
Farnham GU10 .....100 A2
North Warnborough RG29 .....72 B2
Wilmot Way
Basingstoke RG23 .....68 B3
Camberley GU15 .....35 C3
Wilmot Wlk RG14 .....5 A3
Wilsom Rd GU34 .....140 A2
Wilson Cl Alton GU34 .....140 A2
Middle Wallop SO20 .....126 A2
Wilson Ho [14] SP9 .....78 C4
Wilson Rd Aldershot GU12 .....77 A1
Farnborough GU14 .....55 B4
Wilton Valkenburg Ct RG14 .....1 B2
Wilsons Rd GU15 .....165 C3
Wilton Cl GU14 .....56 A2
Wilton Pl RG21 .....68 C2
Wilton Rd GU15 .....35 C3
Wilton Terr SP9 .....101 C4
Wimborne Ho GU14 .....76 C1
Wimbushes RG40 .....16 A3
Wincanton Cl GU34 .....140 A1
Winchcombe Cl GU51 .....75 A4
Winchcombe Jun & Inf Schs RG14 .....1 C1
Winchcombe Rd
Basingstoke RG21 .....69 A2
Newbury RG14 .....1 C1
Winchester Cath* SO23 .....198 A4
Winchester Cl
Winchester SO22 .....197 C3
Winchester SO23 .....198 A3
Winchester City Mill* SO23 .....198 A4
Winchester City Mus* SO23 .....198 A4
Winchester Gdns SP10 .....106 A3
Winchester Hill SO21 .....131 B2
Winchester Rd
Andover SP10 .....106 A2
Ash GU12 .....77 C2
Basingstoke RG22 .....161 B4
Chawton GU34 .....160 B2
Four Marks GU34 .....160 B2
Frensham GU10 .....144 C4
Goodworth Clatford SP11 .....106 A2
King's Somborne SO20 .....172 A2
Kingsclere RG20 .....44 B4
Micheldever SO21 .....133 A1
New Alresford SO24 .....179 A3
Ropley SO24 .....181 B4
Upper Clatford SP10, SP11 .....106 A2
Whitchurch RG28 .....86 B2
Winchester Road Rdbt RG21 .....68 C2
Winchester Sch of Art SO23 .....198 A3
Winchester St
[1] Andover SP10 .....106 A4
[7] Basingstoke RG21 .....69 A2
Chilbolton SO20 .....129 A3
Farnborough GU14 .....77 A4
Overton RG25 .....88 A4
Whitchurch RG28 .....86 B2
Winchester Sta SO23 .....197 C4
Winchester Way GU17 .....35 A3

Winchfield Ct GU51 .....53 C2
Winchfield Ct RG27 .....53 A1
Winchfield Gdns RG26 .....27 A4
Winchfield Hurst RG27 .....52 C1
Winchfield Sta RG27 .....52 B1
Windermere Ave RG22 .....68 A1
Windermere Cl GU14 .....55 B2
Windermere Ct GU12 .....77 B2
Windermere Gdns SO24 .....179 B2
Windermere Way GU35 .....164 B3
Windermere Way
Farnham GU9 .....98 C3
Thatcham RG19 .....2 C3
Winding Wood Dr GU15 .....36 C2
Windmill Cnr RG7 .....11 C3
Windmill Ct
[4] Aldershot GU12 .....77 A1
Alton GU34 .....139 C1
Mortimer RG7 .....11 C3
Windmill Dr GU35 .....165 C3
Windmill Fields
East Worldham GU34 .....141 A1
Four Marks GU34 .....160 B2
Windmill Hill GU34 .....140 A1
Windmill La Alton GU34 .....140 A1
Hurstbourne Tarrant SP11 .....60 B4
Windmill Rd
Aldershot GU12 .....77 A1
Mortimer RG7 .....11 C3
Windmills The GU34 .....139 C2
Windrush Cl [2] RG21 .....69 B3
Windrush Hts GU47 .....34 C4
Windsor Cl GU34 .....139 B2
Windsor Cres GU9 .....98 C3
Windsor Ct
Camberley GU15 .....36 A2
[9] Fleet GU51 .....54 A1
Newbury RG14 .....1 C1
Windsor Gdns Ash GU12 .....77 A1
Basingstoke RG22 .....91 A3
Windsor Ho [2] SO23 .....198 A4
Windsor Pk GU34 .....139 C1
Windsor Rd
Andover SP10 .....105 C4
Farnborough GU14 .....56 A1
Lindford GU35 .....164 C3
Medstead GU34 .....160 A2
New Alresford SO24 .....179 B2
Windsor Ride
Finchampstead RG40 .....16 C4
Sandhurst GU15 .....35 C4
Windsor Way
Aldershot GU12 .....76 C1
Camberley GU15 .....36 A4
Windsor Wlk GU35 .....164 C3
Wingate Ct GU11 .....76 A1
Wingate La RG29 .....95 B2
Wings Cl GU9 .....98 C3
Wings Rd GU9 .....98 C3
Winkfield Ctr RG23 .....68 B3
Winkbury Inf & Jun Sch RG23 .....68 B3
Winkbury Way RG23 .....68 B3
Winkworth Ct RG7,RG26 .....10 A1
Winkworth Pl GU9 .....99 A2
Winnall Cl SO23 .....198 A4
Winnall Manor Rd SO23 .....198 B4
Winnall Prim Sch SO23 .....198 B4
Winnall Trad Est SO23 .....198 B4
Winnall Valley Rd SO23 .....198 B4
Winnipeg Cl GU30 .....188 A3
Winslade La RG25 .....115 B4
Winslade Rd SO22 .....175 B2
Winston Ave RG26 .....27 A3
Winston Cl GU16 .....55 C3
Winston Rise GU34 .....160 A2
Winston Way RG19 .....2 B2
Winston Wlk GU10 .....122 A3
Winterbourne Ho RG22 .....68 A1
Winterbourne Wlk RG26 .....56 B4
Winterdyne Mews SP10 .....105 C4
Winterthur Way RG21 .....69 A3
Winterton Dr RG14 .....1 A3
Winton Chase SP10 .....106 A3
Winton Cl
South Tidworth SP9 .....78 C2
Winchester SO22 .....175 C1
Winton Cres GU46 .....34 A3
Winton Hill SO20 .....150 A2
Winton Rd
[20] Aldershot GU11 .....76 C1
Basingstoke RG22 .....91 A3
Winton Sch SP10 .....106 B4
Winton Sq RG21 .....69 A2
Wiremead La SP11 .....103 C4
Wishanger La GU10 .....143 C1
Wishmoor Cl GU15 .....36 B4
Wishmoor Rd GU15 .....36 B4
Wisley Gdns GU14 .....55 A1
Wisley Rd SP10 .....105 C4
Wistaria Ct GU46 .....34 A3
Wistaria La GU46 .....34 A3
Wisteria Ct GU9 .....99 A1
Wisteria Dr [1] GU35 .....164 B3
Wisteria Mews GU34 .....140 B3
Witan Ct SO21 .....83 A2
Witan Ct RG28 .....86 A3
Wither Rise RG23 .....67 A4
Witherslack Ct GU35 .....166 A2
Withes The GU10 .....97 B3
Withies The
Longparish SP11 .....108 A3
Sherfield English SP5 .....169 A1
Witt Rd SP5 .....165 A1
Witcomb Terr [1] GU35 .....164 B1
Wittmead Rd GU16 .....56 B4
Witton Hill SO20 .....179 B2

Woodpecker Cl continued
Bordon GU35 .....164 B1
Ewshot GU10 .....98 A4
Woodpeckers [1] SP10 .....106 A4
Woodpeckers Dr SO22 .....175 B1
Woodridge Manor GU15 .....36 A4
Woodroffe Rd RG22 .....68 B1
Woods La RG25 .....91 C4
Woodside
Blackwater GU17 .....35 A2
Farnborough GU14 .....55 C4
Farnham GU9 .....5 A4
Sandhurst GU15 .....35 B4
Woodside Cl
Bordon GU35 .....164 B2
Finchampstead RG40 .....16 B4
Mortimer RG7 .....11 C3
Woodside Cres GU35 .....164 B2
Woodside Gdns
Chineham RG24 .....49 A2
Fleet GU51 .....54 B1
Woodside La GU34 .....161 A2
Woodside Pk GU35 .....164 B2
Woodside Rd
Farnborough GU11 .....76 B4
Farnham GU9 .....99 B4
Woodstock Mead RG22 .....91 A3
Woodstocks GU14 .....56 A3
Woodville Cl
Blackwater GU17 .....34 C3
Chineham RG24 .....48 C1
Woodville Rise GU34 .....48 C1
Woodway GU15 .....35 C3
Wood Gr SP10 .....106 B4
Wooland Ct [3] GU52 .....54 A1
Woolings Farm Vineyard* RG28 .....63 C1
Woolridge Cres RG19 .....95 B4
Woolfield La GU32,GU34 .....205 A2
Woolford Cl [1] SO22 .....197 B3
Woolford Way GU33 .....68 B3
Woollards Rd GU12 .....77 C2
Woolley Sq SP10 .....99 A2
Woolmead Rd GU9 .....99 A2
Woolmead La GU9 .....99 A2
Woolmead The GU9 .....99 A2
Woolmead Wlk GU9 .....99 A2
Woolmer Hill Rd GU27 .....189 A4
Woolmer Hill Sch GU27 .....189 A4
Woolmer La GU30 .....188 A4
Woolmer Rd GU33 .....186 A2
Woolmer Terr GU33 .....186 A2
Woolmer Trad Est GU35 .....164 B2
Woolmer View GU26 .....167 A2
Woolton Hill Jun Sch RG20 .....21 B4
Woolton Lodge Gdns RG20 .....4 B1
Wootey Inf & Jun Schs GU34 .....139 C3
Wooteys Way GU34 .....139 C3
Worcester Ave RG25 .....91 A4
Worcester Cl GU14 .....55 C4
Wordsworth Ave GU46 .....33 C2
Wordsworth Cl
Basingstoke RG24 .....69 B4
Winchester SO22 .....197 B4
Wordham Hill GU34 .....141 A1
Wormersley Rd RG19 .....2 B3
Worrell Sq SP10 .....83 B2
Worsley Rd GU16 .....56 B4
Worthy La GU33 .....175 C1
Worthy Rd SO23 .....176 A1
Worting Inf & Jun Schs RG23 .....68 A2
Worting Rd
Basingstoke RG21,RG22 .....68 C2
Basingstoke RG22,RG23 .....68 B2
Wote St RG21 .....69 A2
Wouldham Cl SP11 .....79 B4
Wrecclesham Hill GU10 .....121 B3
Wrecclesham Rd GU9 .....121 B4
Wrekin Cl RG22 .....68 B4
Wrekin The GU14 .....56 B1
Wren Cl Alton GU34 .....140 A3
Winchester SO22 .....197 B3
Yateley GU46 .....33 C3
Wren Ct GU12 .....77 C2
Wren Way GU14 .....55 B4
Wrights Cl SO21 .....153 B2
Wrights Way SO21 .....153 B2
Wuthering Hts SO22 .....197 C3
Wychwood Cl GU12 .....77 B1
Wychwood Pl GU15 .....36 C4
Wyck La Binsted GU34 .....141 C3
Binsted, Wyck GU34 .....141 A2
Wye Ct [15] SP10 .....83 B1
Wykeham Cl RG29 .....95 B4
Wykeham Dr RG23 .....68 A2
Wykeham Ho GU14 .....55 B4
Wykeham Ind Est The SO23 .....176 B2
Wykeham Pk SO21 .....199 A4
Wykeham Pl SO22 .....197 B3
Wykeham Rd GU11 .....99 A2
Wykwood GU30 .....188 A2
Wyld Green La GU33 .....208 A3
Wylye Rd SP9 .....78 C4
Wymering Ct GU14 .....56 A2
Wyndham Cl GU46 .....34 A3
Wyndham Ct
Andover SP10 .....105 C3
Newbury RG14 .....2 A3
Wyndham St GU12 .....77 A1

Wivelrod Rd GU32 .....138 B1
Woburn Ave GU14 .....56 A2
Woburn Cl GU16 .....36 C1
Woburn Gdns RG22 .....68 B2
Wokefield Row RG7 .....12 A4
Wolds The RG22 .....68 A2
Wolf's La GU34 .....161 C4
Wolfe Cl SO22 .....197 B3
Wolfe Rd GU12 .....77 A1
Wolseley Cl GU33 .....186 A1
Wolseley Rd GU11 .....76 C1
Wolverdene Specl Sch SP10 .....106 A4
Wolversdene Cl SP10 .....106 B4
Wolversdene Gdns SP10 .....106 B4
Wolversdene Rd SP10 .....106 B4
Wolverton La RG26 .....25 B1
Wolverton Rd
Ashford Hill RG26 .....25 C3
Baughurst RG26 .....25 C3
Wolverton Towns End RG26 .....25 C1
Wolvesey Castle (Old Bishop's Palace)* SO23 .....198 A3
Wolvesey Terr [3] SO23 .....198 A3
Wonston Cl SO21 .....131 B2
Wonston La SO21 .....131 B1
Wood Cl RG21, RG22 .....91 A3
Wood End GU32 .....138 C4
Wood Hill La RG29 .....95 B2
Wood La Beech Hill RG7 .....13 B3
Bramdean SO24 .....202 C3
Farnborough GU14 .....55 C2
Fleet GU51 .....54 B1
Hook RG27 .....71 B3
Seale GU10 .....100 C3
Wood Moor RG40 .....16 B1
Wood Rd
Beacon Hill GU26 .....167 A3
Camberley GU15 .....35 C1
Farnham GU9 .....99 A4
Wood Ridge RG14 .....5 B4
Wood St GU12 .....77 C3
Woodbarn The GU9 .....99 A1
Woodbine Cl GU47 .....35 A4
Woodbine La RG20 .....6 A3
Woodbourne GU9 .....99 B4
Woodbourne Cl
Liss GU33 .....208 A2
Farnborough GU14 .....34 A3
Woodbridge Dr GU15 .....36 A4
Woodbridge Rd GU15 .....36 A4
Woodbury Rd RG22 .....91 A3
Woodcock Ct SP9 .....78 C3
Woodcote Gdns GU51 .....74 B4
Woodcote Cotts SO24 .....202 B2
Woodcote Rd SN8 .....18 A4
Woodcote Ho [1] RG26 .....26 C4
Woodcott Terr GU12 .....100 A4
Woodcut Rd GU10 .....121 B3
Woodend Camberley GU15 .....36 C4
Farnborough GU14 .....55 B2
Woodfield GU35 .....142 A1
Woodfield Cotts GU12 .....100 A4
Woodfield Dr SO22 .....197 A3
Woodgarston Dr RG23 .....91 A3
Woodgate SO22 .....54 B2
Woodgreen Rd SO22 .....175 B2
Woodland Cres La RG7,RG19 .....8 B1
Woodland Cres GU14 .....56 A3
Woodland Dr
Bramley RG26 .....29 A1
Farnham GU10 .....121 C3
Woodland Rise GU32 .....138 C4
Woodland Wlk* SO51 .....192 B2
Woodlands
Andover SP10 .....106 B4
Chineham RG24 .....49 A2
Farnham GU10 .....100 A2
Fleet GU51 .....74 B4
Highclere RG20 .....21 C4
Overton RG25 .....88 A4
Yateley GU46 .....34 A2
Woodlands Ave GU34 .....139 C1
Woodlands Bsns Village RG21 .....69 B3
Woodlands Cl Ash GU12 .....77 B1
Farnborough GU17 .....35 B1
Woodlands Cl
Alton GU34 .....139 B1
[3] Winchester SO23 .....176 A1
Woodlands La
Haslemere GU27 .....189 B4
Liss GU33 .....208 A2
Woodlands Rd
Baughurst RG26 .....9 A1
Camberley GU15 .....25 C3
Farnborough GU34 .....55 A3
Woodlands The
Bordon GU35 .....186 B4
Kings Worthy SO23 .....176 B3
Woodlands Way SP10 .....106 B4
Woodlands Wlk GU17 .....35 A3
Woodlea Cl SO22 .....202 B3
Woodlea GU22 .....175 C1
Woodlea Prim Sch GU35 .....164 B1
Woodleigh GU51 .....75 A4
Woodleys RG20 .....44 B3
Woodman La SO21 .....174 B1
Woodmanfield RG25 .....116 A4
Woodmere Croft RG22 .....90 C4
Woodpecker Cl
Basingstoke RG22 .....90 C4

Wynfields GU16 ....**56** B2
Wynne Gdns GU52 ....**75** A3
Wyvern Cl GU12 ....**77** B3

Y

Yarnhams Cl GU34 ......**160** A1
Yateley Common (Ctry Pk)*
  GU46 ....**34** B2
Yateley Inds GU46 ....**34** A4
Yateley Inf Sch GU46 ...**34** A3
Yateley Manor Prep Sch
  GU46 ....**34** A3
Yateley Rd GU47 ....**34** B4
Yateley Sch GU46 ....**34** A3

Yates Copse RG14 ....**2** B3
Yatesbury Cl GU9 ....**121** B4
Yellowhammer Rd
  RG22 ....**90** C3
Yellowhammers
  GU34 ....**139** C3
Yeomans GU46 ....**33** B4
Yeomans Cl
  Farnborough GU14 ......**55** C3
  Tongham GU10 ....**100** B4
Yeomans La
  Burghclere RG20 ....**5** C1
  Liphook GU30 ....**187** C2
Yeomans Pl GU35 ....**165** B3
Yeomans Way GU15 .....**36** B3
Yeosfield RG7 ....**14** A2
Yeovil Cl GU14 ....**56** A1
Yeovil Rd GU14 ....**56** B1
Yetminster Rd GU14 ....**56** A1

Yew Cl RG20 ....**24** C1
Yew Gate RG14 ....**1** B3
Yew Tree Cl
  Bramley RG26 ....**29** A1
  Farnborough GU14 ......**55** A2
  Goodworth Clatford SP11 .**106** A1
  Oakley RG23 ....**90** A4
Yew Tree La
  North Waltham RG25 .....**89** C1
  West Tytherley SP5 ......**169** A2
Yew Tree Pl GU33 ......**208** A2
Yew Tree Wlk GU16 ....**36** B1
Yolland Cl GU9 ....**99** A4
York Cl
  Basingstoke RG22 ....**91** A4
  Bordon GU35 ....**164** B1
  Newbury RG14 ....**1** C1
York Cres GU11 ....**76** B1
York Ct **4** SP10 ....**83** A2

York Ho
  17 Aldershot GU11 ....**76** B1
  Basingstoke RG22 ....**68** C2
  32 Winchester SO23 ....**176** A1
York La RG27 ....**52** B3
York Mews GU34 ....**140** A2
York Pl GU15 ....**36** A4
York Rd Aldershot GU11 ..**76** B1
  Ash GU12 ....**77** C2
  Farnborough GU14 ......**56** A1
  Farnham GU9 ....**99** A1
  Newbury RG14 ....**1** C1
York Terrace La GU15 ...**35** C3
  York Town Ind Est GU15 ..**35** C2
York Way GU47 ....**34** C4
Yorktown Rd GU47 ......**35** B4
Yorkwood GU33 ....**207** C2
Youlden Cl GU15 ....**36** C3
Youlden Dr GU15 ....**36** C3

Young Cres RG19 ....**6** A4
Young's Ind Est RG7 ......**9** B2
Youngs Dr GU12 ....**77** B1
Youngs Paddock SP5 ...**168** A3
Youngs Rd GU34 ....**139** C2

Z

Zephyr Ho **11** RG7 ....**9** B1
Zinnia Cl RG22 ....**91** A4
Zion Rd SP11 ....**124** B3
Zodiac Ho **7** RG7 ....**9** B1
Zouch Ave **5** SP9 ....**78** C4
Zouch Cl SP9 ....**78** C4
Zouch Farm Rd SP9 .....**78** C4
Zouch Mkt SP9 ....**78** C4
Zouch Prim Sch SP9 .....**78** B4

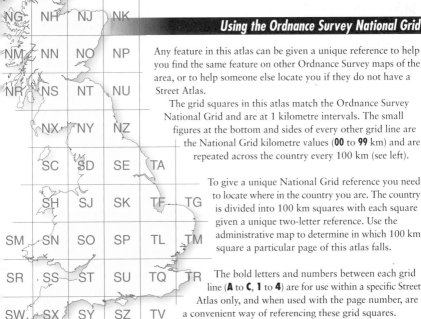

Any feature in this atlas can be given a unique reference to help you find the same feature on other Ordnance Survey maps of the area, or to help someone else locate you if they do not have a Street Atlas.

The grid squares in this atlas match the Ordnance Survey National Grid and are at 1 kilometre intervals. The small figures at the bottom and sides of every other grid line are the National Grid kilometre values (**00** to **99** km) and are repeated across the country every 100 km (see left).

To give a unique National Grid reference you need to locate where in the country you are. The country is divided into 100 km squares with each square given a unique two-letter reference. Use the administrative map to determine in which 100 km square a particular page of this atlas falls.

The bold letters and numbers between each grid line (**A** to **C**, **1** to **4**) are for use within a specific Street Atlas only, and when used with the page number, are a convenient way of referencing these grid squares.

Example The railway bridge over DARLEY GREEN RD in grid square A1

Step 1: Identify the two-letter reference, in this example the page is in **SP**

Step 2: Identify the 1 km square in which the railway bridge falls. Use the figures in the southwest corner of this square: Eastings **17**, Northings **74**. This gives a unique reference: **SP 17 74**, accurate to 1 km.

Step 3: To give a more precise reference accurate to 100 m you need to estimate how many tenths along and how many tenths up this 1 km square the feature is. This makes the bridge about **8** tenths along and about **1** tenth up from the southwest corner.

This gives a unique reference: **SP 178 741**, accurate to 100 m.

Eastings (read from left to right along the bottom) come before Northings (read from bottom to top). If you have trouble remembering say to yourself "Along the hall, THEN up the stairs"!

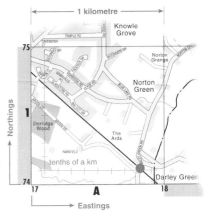

Addresses

Name and Address	Telephone	Page	Grid reference

Street Atlases from Philip's

Philip's publish an extensive range of regional and local street atlases which are ideal for motoring, business and leisure use. They are widely used by the emergency services and local authorities throughout Britain.

Key features include:

◆ Superb county-wide mapping at an extra-large scale of 3½ inches to 1 mile, or 2½ inches to 1 mile in pocket edition

◆ Complete urban and rural coverage, detailing every named street in town and country

◆ Each atlas available in two handy sizes – standard spiral and pocket paperback

'The mapping is very clear... great in scope and value'
★★★★ BEST BUY   AUTO EXPRESS

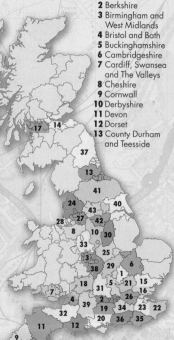

1 Bedfordshire
2 Berkshire
3 Birmingham and West Midlands
4 Bristol and Bath
5 Buckinghamshire
6 Cambridgeshire
7 Cardiff, Swansea and The Valleys
8 Cheshire
9 Cornwall
10 Derbyshire
11 Devon
12 Dorset
13 County Durham and Teesside
14 Edinburgh and East Central Scotland
15 North Essex
16 South Essex
17 Glasgow and West Central Scotland
18 Gloucestershire
19 North Hampshire
20 South Hampshire
21 Hertfordshire
22 East Kent
23 West Kent
24 Lancashire
25 Leicestershire and Rutland
26 London
27 Greater Manchester
28 Merseyside
29 Northamptonshire
30 Nottinghamshire
31 Oxfordshire
32 Somerset
33 Staffordshire
34 Surrey
35 East Sussex
36 West Sussex
37 Tyne and Wear and Northumberland
38 Warwickshire
39 Wiltshire and Swindon
40 East Yorkshire and Northern Lincolnshire
41 North Yorkshire
42 South Yorkshire
43 West Yorkshire

How to order

The Philip's range of street atlases is available from good retailers or directly from the publisher by phoning 01903 828503